'This book is a timely and contemporary contribution to the highly dynamic and disputed area of drugs policing. It provides a much-needed examination of the conceptualizations and application of "harm reduction policing" as a distinct and alternative policing model. The contributions are an excellent collection of approaches, views, and theories to think about the current state and potential future of policing of drug use and markets'.

Alissa Greer, Assistant Professor in Criminology, Simon Fraser University

'Everyone wants to minimize the harms of drugs and policing. But how? This book gives us answers. It is an outstanding contribution at the intersection of addiction research, drug studies, criminology, and criminal justice. It will appeal to people on the left, the right, and between'.

Scott Jacques, Professor of Criminal Justice and Criminology, Georgia State University

'This extraordinary edited volume provides the most extensive collection of research on harm reduction policing to date. The book is well-written and leads the reader on a journey through some of the most important research on the topic. This book should be on the shelf of all academics, researchers, and practitioners interested in drugs policing, and is well suited for undergraduate and graduate coursework'.

Aili Malm, Professor of Criminology and Criminal Justice, California State University

'This timely book makes a vital contribution to the drug policy literature by giving a comprehensive and detailed account of a burgeoning area of study: police-led changes to drug policy and practice. In the UK, the 2011 Police Reform and Social Responsibility Act, which created offices of Police and Crime Commissioners (PCCs), has afforded variation in local drug policing practice and enabled force areas to develop policing priorities shaped by local needs and priorities. A key development has been the increasing use of diversionary methods by the police to channel drug users away from the criminal justice system and into forms of support. Although becoming more widespread, there is a limited evidence base as to how these strategies were formulated, how they have been implemented and the ways in which they have been evaluated. This book addresses this gap. In doing so, it expertly brings together key thinkers and doers in the field. It advances knowledge by the array of contributors nationally and internationally as well as those working across research, policy and practice. It is edited by two important voices in the field, both of whom make telling contributions to the work. It will be of interest for researchers and practitioners in criminal justice, public health drug policy and beyond'.

Mark Monaghan, Reader in Criminology and Social Policy, University of Loughborough

'Where drugs policing debates are filled with cliches from both libertarians and warriors, this invaluable collection brings light rather than heat to the field. Anyone with an interest in how the harms associated with drugs, with policy, and with law enforcement can be reduced and managed will benefit from reading the diverse and important analyses contained here. Cutting across disciplines and academic/practitioner divides, and with an international outlook, this book is required reading'.

Karim Murji, Professor of Social Policy and Criminology, University of West London

'"Harm reduction policing" may sound to some like an oxymoron. This precious volume demonstrates – with fascinating case studies, provocative insights and creative theoretical formulations – not just the negative consequences of punitive drugs policing but also the ways in which "harm reduction" makes just as much sense for policing as it does for drug use'.

Ethan Nadelmann, Founder and Former Executive Director (2000–2017) of the Drug Policy Alliance

'This book provides a comprehensive overview of what we have learned with harm reduction and a valuable guide to continue walking down the path created by the reforms to drug policies and policing in several countries around the world'.

Eduardo Paes Machado, Professor of Sociology, Federal University of Bahia

'Drugs present a uniquely troubling challenge for the police. At one extreme, in the Philippines the police have carried out thousands of extra-legal executions of drug dealers and users. At the other extreme, there are police forces in Western Europe and North America that see their primary role as helping persuade drug users to enter treatment. This entirely original collection of essays is the first effort to survey the many drug policing reform efforts that incorporate the insights of harm reduction that have been so influential in other areas of drug policy. It will inform both policymakers and researchers'.

Peter Reuter, Professor of Public Policy and Criminology, University of Maryland

'This outstanding edited collection brings together a rich array of material on drugs policing. Absent hysterical hyperbole, chapter authors summarise research and practice experience and consider how drugs policing could be reformed. The multidisciplinary and global contributions provide a comprehensive one-stop-shop for understanding the relationships between policy, police practices directed towards illicit drugs, and harm reduction. I can highly recommend this important volume to students, scholars, practitioners, and anyone interested in reconfiguring drugs policing to reduce harms'.

Alison Ritter AO, Professor and Director of the Drug Policy Modelling Program, University of New South Wales

'Bacon and Spicer have assembled an outstanding collection. The role of policing in drug control and in the enforcement of drug laws is surprisingly under-researched, despite its centrality to drug policy. By curating a set of contributions that are international in scope, empirically-oriented and theoretically-engaged, Bacon and Spicer have produced a book that will undoubtedly prove influential, both intellectually and in terms of policy reform, for many years to come'.

Toby Seddon, Professor of Social Science, UCL

'This collection is welcome for many reasons but not least are that it really understands the potential of a harm reduction perspective, it reminds us that "policing" should be flexible and enabling rather than discriminating and disabling, it contextualises drugs policing locally and globally – from the legacy of colonialism to the implications of digital markets, it provides evidence that policing the public should also be about the good health of the public, and finally, it's highly original and long overdue!'

Nigel South, Professor of Sociology, University of Essex

'Harm reduction policing is an idea whose time has come. In this fascinating book, Bacon and Spicer have brought together an impressive range of international contributors – with both research and practical expertise – to inform us of the latest thinking and evidence from the field. This theoretically robust and empirically informed collection offers new ways to reduce the harms done by both drugs and policing'.

Alex Stevens, Professor in Criminal Justice, University of Kent

DRUG LAW ENFORCEMENT, POLICING AND HARM REDUCTION

The policing of drugs is an intriguing, complex, and contentious domain that brings into sharp focus the multifaceted nature of the police role and has far-reaching consequences for health, crime, and justice. While research on drugs policing has historically been surprisingly sparse, fragmented, and underdeveloped, the field has recently become a burgeoning area of academic study, influenced by contemporary trends in policing practices, changes in drug policy, and wider social movements. This book makes a much-needed interdisciplinary and international contribution that engages with established and emerging areas of scholarship, advances cutting-edge debates, and sets an agenda for future directions in drugs policing.

Drug Law Enforcement, Policing and Harm Reduction is the first edited collection to devote its attention exclusively to drugs policing. It brings together a range of leading scholars to provide a deep and thorough account of the current state of knowledge. In addition to academic analysis, authors also include serving police officers and policymakers, who have influenced how drugs policing is framed and carried out. Together, the contributors draw on a diverse set of empirical studies and theoretical perspectives, with the thread running throughout the book being the concept of harm reduction policing. With accounts from various countries, localities, and contexts, topics covered include the (in)effectiveness and (un)intended consequences of the 'war on drugs', attempts to reform drugs policing, and the role of partnerships and policy networks. The broader theme of inequality lies at the heart of this collection.

An accessible and compelling read, this book will be of interest to academics and students of criminology, public health, and social policy, especially those researching policing, drug policy, and harm reduction. It also offers valuable insights and practical guidance for professionals working in the drugs field.

Matthew Bacon is a Senior Lecturer in Criminology at the University of Sheffield.

Jack Spicer is a Lecturer in Criminology at the University of Bath.

Routledge Studies in Policing and Society

Series Editors

Jenny Fleming, University of Southampton, UK

Jennifer Wood, Temple University, USA

Routledge Studies in Policing and Society aims to establish an inter-disciplinary, international intellectual space of original contributions to either classic or emerging debates about the nature and effects of policing in society. The works in this series will advance our theoretical, methodological and/or empirical knowledge of policing in various societies across the world. It is the hope of the series editors that the works in this series will help fill gaps in our global understanding of policing and society.

Criminal Futures
Predictive Policing and Everyday Police Work
Simon Egbert and Matthias Leese

Women Police in Contemporary China
Gender and Policing
Anqi Shen

Electric-Shock Weapons, Tasers and Policing
Myths and Realities
Abi Dymond

Police, Organization, and Wellbeing
An Ethnography
Jamie Ferrill

Policing in a Changing Vietnam
Towards a Global Account of Policing
Melissa Jardine

Drug Law Enforcement, Policing and Harm Reduction
Ending the Stalemate
Edited by Matthew Bacon and Jack Spicer

DRUG LAW ENFORCEMENT, POLICING AND HARM REDUCTION

Ending the Stalemate

Edited by Matthew Bacon and Jack Spicer

Routledge
Taylor & Francis Group
LONDON AND NEW YORK

Designed cover image: Anastasiia_Guseva / Getty images

First published 2023
by Routledge
4 Park Square, Milton Park, Abingdon, Oxon OX14 4RN

and by Routledge
605 Third Avenue, New York, NY 10158

Routledge is an imprint of the Taylor & Francis Group, an informa business

British Library Cataloguing-in-Publication Data
A catalogue record for this book is available from the British Library

ISBN: 978-0-367-72269-2 (hbk)
ISBN: 978-0-367-72270-8 (pbk)
ISBN: 978-1-003-15413-6 (ebk)

DOI: 10.4324/9781003154136

Typeset in Bembo
by Deanta Global Publishing Services, Chennai, India

CONTENTS

FIGURES

CONTRIBUTORS

Evan Anderson is a senior lecturer at the University of Pennsylvania, where he teaches in multiple schools and programmes. Dr Anderson is a public health law researcher. With doctoral training in law and public health, his research blends doctrinal legal analysis and epidemiologic methods. His most recent work explores pre-booking diversion programmes, 'drug courts', and other specialised court programmes, and drug consumption rooms. Dr Anderson was formerly the senior fellow at the Public Health Law Research programme, a national programme office of the Robert Wood Johnson Foundation, which supports empirical research on the health effects of laws and legal processes.

Elizabeth Aston is the director of the Scottish Institute for Policing Research (SIPR) and a professor of criminology at Edinburgh Napier University. Liz has a strong record of collaborative research on policing in both Scotland and mainland Europe, and is experienced in knowledge exchange and building strong researcher–practitioner relationships. Her research interests centre on local policing and intersections with health, and she is currently involved in projects on drug checking and police carriage of naloxone. Liz has conducted research on the relationship between substance use and offending, community policing, stop and search, and youth diversionary projects. She is a member of Police Scotland's Drug Strategy Board and the Naloxone Delivery Steering Group.

Matthew Bacon is a senior lecturer in criminology at the University of Sheffield. Before joining Sheffield, he worked as a research associate at the University of Manchester on a project examining the contractual governance of drug users in treatment. Matthew's research broadly focuses on policing and drug policy. He is the author of *Taking Care of Business* (OUP, 2016), an ethnography of police detectives, drug law enforcement, and proactive investigation. His current research is concerned with innovation and reform in drugs policing, especially alternatives to criminalisation and other harm reduction measures. Matthew is institutional co-lead of the N8 Policing Research Partnership and a founding member of the Sheffield University Policing Research Group. These roles involve promoting evidence-based practice and collaborations in knowledge exchange, enhanced training, and research co-production.

Katherine Beckett is S. Frank Miyamoto professor of sociology and professor and chair of the Department of Law, Societies, and Justice at the University of Washington. Her recent research projects have explored the consequences of penal expansion for social inequality, the role of race in drug law enforcement, and the transformation of urban social control practices in the United States. She is the author of numerous articles and four books on these topics, including, most recently, *Ending Mass Incarceration: Why it Persists and How to Achieve Meaningful Reform*, published in 2021 by Oxford University Press.

Monica Bell is a professor of law at Yale Law School and an associate professor of sociology at Yale University. Her areas of expertise include criminal justice, welfare law, housing, race, qualitative research methods, and law and sociology. She previously served as a Liman fellow at the Legal Aid Society of the District of Columbia, and earned her PhD in sociology and social policy from Harvard University in 2018.

Matthew Louis Bishop is senior lecturer in international politics at the University of Sheffield and was previously based at the University of the West Indies (UWI) in Trinidad between 2009 and 2016. His work broadly focuses on the political economy of development, with a particular focus on the Caribbean, and his recent work has examined processes of cannabis legalisation in the Americas, drugs and weapons trafficking, the gendered drivers of gang violence, and participatory development in post-conflict Colombia.

Ross Coomber is a professor of criminology and sociology with more than 30 years research experience in the drug and alcohol field. He has written extensively and broadly in this area – particularly on the machinations of illicit drug markets, nationally and internationally, and across different cultural and environmental spaces. His research is strongly inter/multidisciplinary and boasts ongoing collaborations with forensic chemists/scientists, medics, public health practitioners, and researchers, as well as, perhaps more predictably, disciplines across the humanities and social sciences.

Benson Egwuonwu is a solicitor and member of StopWatch. He has conducted research on international human rights law for The Law Society of England and Wales, and has also written about human rights and policing for the award-winning digital charity EachOther. Benson has a BA in law (jurisprudence) from the University of Oxford, and an LLM in professional legal practice from BPP University.

Maria Fotopoulou is a senior lecturer in criminology at the University of Stirling. Her research interests revolve around drug policy and its intersection with criminal justice systems; human trafficking where this intersects with drugs use/trade; and gender and drug use. Maria has worked in the field of policy and service evaluation of the health and social care of people who use drugs and more broadly marginalised and minority groups in the United Kingdom and Greece.

Esben Houborg is associate professor at the Centre for Alcohol and Drug Research, Aarhus University. His main areas of research are drug policy in a historical and contemporary perspective, criminological research particularly concerning law enforcement, sociological research in the areas of drug treatment and harm reduction, and urban studies of drug-related issues.

Meg Jones is director of new business and services at the social justice charity, Cranstoun. Meg leads on identifying, developing, and delivering innovative, evidence-informed solutions that rebuild lives. Meg is currently a selected expert supporting the United Nations Office on Drugs and Crime for the Vienna and New York Committee on Drugs. Prior to this, Meg was head of policy for the West Midlands police and crime commissioner, with responsibility for delivering the PCC's police and crime plan. Meg has a strong academic background with an MSc public management distinction, an MA international relations distinction, and a BA in history and international relations, combined with practical experience in both the public and private sectors. Throughout her career, Meg has been known to develop and deliver collaborative policies, improving systems in the criminal system as well as in drug policy. As regional policy officer, working for four police and crime commissioners in the West Midlands, the first role of its kind in the country, Meg worked at regional and national level to create and develop innovative changes to collaborative policing.

Habib Kadiri is research and policy manager for StopWatch, a charity that works for fair and accountable policing. He also has public health policy experience from a previous appointment, as well as an interest in digital rights issues. Habib has a BA in modern history with economics and an MA in political economy from the University of Manchester.

Tobias Kammersgaard is a research associate at the University of York working at the ESRC Vulnerability and Policing Futures Research Centre. His research revolves around policing, drug policy and marginalisation. In his PhD dissertation, he investigated private and public policing of marginalised drug users in two cities in Denmark.

Dylan Kerrigan is a peace and development officer with the United Nations Development Program (UNDP) in Trinidad. Previously he was a lecturer in criminology at the University of Leicester, UK, working with a multidisciplinary research team on the definition, extent, experience, and treatment of mental, neurological, and substance use (MNS) disorders in Guyana's jails. From 2010 to 2019 he was a lecturer at the University of the West Indies (UWI), St Augustine Campus, and was a visiting lecturer with the UWI until 2021, supervising graduate students in cultural and political sociology. His publications include research on the militarisation of policing, state violence and anti-black racism, and the relationship between masculinities and community violence.

Jason Kew is a former detective chief inspector with Thames Valley Police and lead for drugs, exploitation, and harm reduction. Jason began his career in the Royal Navy and has since had a 26-year career serving in the police. During his career, Jason developed a deep understanding and compassion for people who use drugs and their families or friends facing all aspects of addiction. He is industrious to carefully and thoughtfully deliver policies and plans to reduce stigma and marginalisation with professional experience working with governments in numerous countries, the Home Office, academics, various cross-sector charities, and, most importantly, people with lived experience. Jason continues his vocation and passion for social justice with the Centre for Justice Innovation.

Charlie Lloyd is a professor of social policy and criminal justice at the University of York. Charlie has a background in criminology, undertaking research at the University of Cambridge and then the Home Office, where he undertook research on prisons and probation and managed a programme of research on drugs prevention. He then moved to the Joseph Rowntree Foundation, where he managed research programmes on young people, drugs, and alcohol. At the University of York he has undertaken research on police responses to substance use, stigmatisation of people who use drugs, and drug use in prison and on release. He currently co-directs the ESRC Vulnerability and Policing Futures Research Centre.

Monique Mann is a senior lecturer in criminology and a member of the Alfred Deakin Institute for Citizenship and Globalisation at Deakin University. Dr Mann is an adjunct researcher with the Law, Science, Technology and Society Research Centre at Vrije Universiteit Brussel. Mann's research expertise concerns three main interrelated lines of inquiry: (1) new technology for policing and surveillance, (2) human rights and social justice, and (3) governance and regulation.

James Martin is a senior lecturer in criminology at the School of Humanities and Social Sciences at Deakin University. James is a leading authority on cryptomarkets and the dark web drugs trade, and has published two books as well as numerous quantitative and qualitative journal articles on this topic.

Leah Moyle is a senior lecturer in criminology and sociology at Royal Holloway, University of London. Leah's research interests focus principally on illicit drug supply. She has published widely in this area with recent work spanning the policing of street-level drug markets, the sentencing and punishment of low-level 'drug dealers', and the use of social media in drug markets. Leah's work is internationally recognised and her findings have informed policy reports by the Global Commission on Drug Policy, the UK government, and the Advisory Council for Misuse of Drugs (ACMD).

Sidsel Schrøder is an educational anthropologist and part of the administrative staff at the Centre for Alcohol and Drug Research, Aarhus University. She works across different drug research areas, including young people, marginalised drug users, and treatment.

Ruth Shefner is a doctoral student in sociomedical sciences at Columbia University's Mailman School of Public Health, and a pre-doctoral fellow in Columbia's NIDA T32 training programme on HIV and Substance Use in the Criminal Justice System. A practicing social worker, Ruth formerly directed a re-entry programme, which provides therapeutic case management services along a continuity-of-care model to individuals transitioning out of Philadelphia's county jail system. She received her master's degrees in public health and social work from the University of Pennsylvania, where her research examined connections between criminal justice contact and fatal overdose, pre-booking diversion programmes, and criminal justice–public health collaborations.

Michael Shiner is an associate professor in the Department of Social Policy at the London School of Economics and Political Science, and a member of StopWatch. He has conducted extensive research on drug policy and policing, with particular reference to stop and search and 'race', and has a longstanding interest in police reform and organisational change.

Thomas Friis Søgaard is associate professor at the Centre for Alcohol and Drug Research, Aarhus University. Thomas is a qualitative researcher and his research interests include drug markets, policing, drug policy, and the night-time economy.

Jack Spicer is a lecturer in criminology at the University of Bath. Following his doctoral studies, he has written extensively on the emergence of the 'County Lines' drug supply model and the responses to it. This reflects his wider research interests into the functioning of illicit drug markets, the enforcement of drug laws, and drug policy reform. Dr Spicer has published articles in leading journals and presented papers at a range of international conferences. In 2019, he was awarded 'Best Early Career Researcher' by the International Society for the Study of Drug Policy. In 2021 he was the recipient of the prestigious Radzinowicz Prize. As a member of a number of domestic and international networks, he regularly contributes to practitioner events, public engagement initiatives, and media engagements. He is the co-editor of Routledge's Drugs, Crime and Society book series and sits on the editorial board for the *Journal of Qualitative Criminal Justice and Criminology*. His first book entitled *Policing County Lines: Responses to Evolving Provincial Drug Markets* was published in 2021.

Wojciech Spyt is a serving detective chief inspector with Thames Valley Police (TVP). Wojciech has previously worked in the Policing Strategy Unit, during which time he worked together with DCI Jason Kew over a period of two years in designing, implementing, and providing analysis of two separate drug diversion schemes currently operating in TVP. During his time with the police, he has completed a doctorate in criminal justice studies at the University of Portsmouth focused on how officers evidence electronic material that is stored in cloud computing networks.

Forrest Stuart is a professor of sociology at Stanford University, where he is also the director of the Stanford Ethnography Lab. As an urban ethnographer, he uses fieldwork, archival, and other qualitative methods to investigate the causes, contours, and consequences of urban poverty in spaces ranging from Los Angeles' Skid Row to Chicago. A 2020 MacArthur fellow, he is the author of *Down, Out, and Under Arrest: Policing and Everyday Life in Skid Row* and *Ballad of the Bullet: Gangs, Drill Music, and the Power of Online Infamy*.

Ben Twomey is director of policy and communications for a leading children's rights charity, NYAS (National Youth Advocacy Service), where he supports and empowers care-experienced children and young people. Having previously worked for three police and crime commissioners, Ben led on drug policy in both the West Midlands and County Durham. Ben's policies have been praised by government ministers, cross-party parliamentary groups, national treatment agencies, and senior police officers. Nationally, Ben sits on the Labour Campaign for Drug Policy Reform's Expert Working Group, as well as co-chairing the Alliance for Children in Care and Care Leavers. He has an LLM with distinction from the University of Warwick, and a first-class history and politics BA from the University of York. When he was 22 years old, Ben also became the youngest candidate ever in the country to stand in a police and crime commissioner election, where he emphasised treating addiction as a health issue rather than a criminal justice one.

Ian Warren is a senior lecturer in criminology at Deakin University. He has written widely on comparative legal and criminological developments, focusing primarily on US processes of extraterritorial law enforcement. He is involved in ongoing research examining the laws of extradition and evidence exchange, with specific reference to new developments in information communications technology and their impacts on transnational police cooperation.

DRUG LAW ENFORCEMENT, POLICING AND HARM REDUCTION

An introduction

Matthew Bacon and Jack Spicer

The seeds of this book were planted when we embarked on our respective doctoral projects. Empirically, both theses, and the monographs that followed (Bacon 2016; Spicer 2021), reported on our time spent in the field observing drugs policing 'in action'. As budding ethnographers, experiencing the realities of this intriguing, hidden world at first hand deepened our understanding, honed our sense of purpose, and was perhaps the most 'fun' part of the research process. But, as part of these projects, we also immersed ourselves in the existing literature and read what others had to say on the matter. Among other things, reviewing this body of work led us to two broad observations, each revolving around a paradoxical core. The first was that, while undoubtedly some 'classic' texts have been published in decades past – or at least publications that have been hugely influential on our own academic journeys, such as Peter Manning's (2004) *The Narcs' Game*, Nicholas Dorn and Nigel South's (1990) article 'Drug markets and law enforcement', Mike Collison's (1995) *Police, Drugs and Community*, and Lisa Maher and David Dixon's (1999) work on 'Policing and public health' – scholarship with drugs policing as its dedicated, primary focus is surprisingly light. This is especially so given the centrality of policing in drug policy debates; the fact that drug law enforcement receives the largest share of government spending on drugs; the considerable amount of time taken up by drug problems in the working lives of many police officers; and its wider cultural standing. The second observation was that, while a number of insightful concepts and theories have been put forward to help make sense of the complex, contradictory, and controversial nature of drugs policing, attempts at theoretical development and advancement through empirical exploration have been rather sporadic and

DOI: 10.4324/9781003154136-1

disjointed. As a result, the area remains underdeveloped. This book seeks to remedy this situation. In doing so, we have endeavoured to produce a text that we wish had been available to us when we were attempting to assimilate all that had been written on the subject a few years ago.

Aims and approach

This edited collection is the first of its kind on this important and now burgeoning field of study. Demonstrating the status of drugs policing as a growth area of scholarly interest, recent years have seen the publication of two special issues of journals that broadly focus on the subjects of policing and drug policy. In 2016, Eduardo Paes-Machado and Christopher Birkbeck brought together a range of international perspectives on the policing of drug markets for *Police Practice and Research*. The articles examine the tensions, conflicts, and prospects of change in various countries and regions of the world (see Paes-Machado and Birkbeck 2016). The following year, Alison Ritter and Alex Stevens guest edited a special issue of the *International Journal of Drug Policy*, with the aim of improving knowledge on law enforcement in drug policy through a mixture of original articles and commentaries (see Ritter and Stevens 2017). Our goal with this book is to continue this momentum. It brings together a range of leading scholars, some of whom contributed to the above-mentioned special issues. Importantly, it also boasts valuable insights from experienced practitioners, including serving police officers and those who have sat around the policy table. Combined, the academic and 'pracademic' contributions that comprise this book make a much-needed interdisciplinary and international contribution that engages with established and emerging areas of scholarship, advances cutting-edge debates, and sets an agenda for future directions in drugs policing.

As we will go on to outline in more detail below, the individual chapters that comprise the content of this book are diverse and eclectic. Utilising a variety of methodological approaches, analysing various data, and adopting a number of theoretical standpoints, the authors focus on a range of issues and contexts specifically relevant to drugs policing. This includes responses to specific drug market issues, such as 'county lines' supply, drug trafficking in transit countries, and the 'dark web'; situating drugs policing within wider social contexts, such as calls for defunding the police; and the (in)formal ways and means in which drugs policing operates, including various attempts at diversion. The central thread that connects the chapters is the concept of 'harm reduction policing'. Despite being well established in the drugs field more broadly, ideas surrounding 'harm reduction' are relatively new to drugs policing and are receiving increasing attention in the drug policy and policing literature (Bacon 2016, 2022; Beckett 2016; Caulkins and Reuter 2009; Kammersgaard 2019; Perrone et al. 2022; Shiner 2016; Spicer 2021; Stevens 2013). At its core, harm reduction policing involves the adoption of evidence-based policies and practices which aim to reduce the adverse health, social, and economic consequences associated with drug use, drug markets, and efforts to control them through the criminal justice system. It sits in opposition to 'drug war'-style forms of policing that follow the logic of prohibition in pursuing blunt, punitive interventions that can be not only ineffective in their stated aims of reducing production, supply, and use, but often counterproductive in their wider outcomes. The harmful impact of criminalisation on violence, security, civil liberties, human rights, police legitimacy, public health, and social inequality has been extensively documented throughout the world (Rolles et al. 2016). Yet, harm reduction policing is not dogmatic or necessarily demanding of root and branch reform. As a perspective, or model, it allows for pragmatism and highlights the potential for positive change and progressive development to be achieved within the confines of the current policy context. In other words, harm reduction policing provides a way to end the stalemate and bring about meaningful reform.

From the outset, we think it is necessary to address a common issue with terminology and distinguish between 'drugs policing' and 'drug law enforcement' – hence the title of the book. Drugs policing is sometimes treated as if it were synonymous with drug law enforcement. This is inaccurate and problematic as it overlooks and undervalues the wider purpose of drugs policing. While there is a lack of consensus on how to define 'policing' and the question of the police mission is recurring and contested, it is generally accepted in the field of police studies that policing is much broader than the exercise of legal powers (Bowling et al. 2019; Loader 2020). Enforcement is certainly a core element of the police mandate. Policing, however, encompasses a host of social service functions and activities that are aimed at the promotion of order and assurances of safety. For us, drug law enforcement should be viewed as a means to an end rather than an end in itself. Drug laws are resources that can be enforced in order to achieve the goals of harm reduction policing.

Contemporary issues

With this in mind, there has arguably never been a more important time for harm reduction policing to come to the fore as a theoretically robust and practically feasible model for organising how drugs policing is structured and undertaken. Across the world, we find ourselves in a precarious position where drug-related harms are at risk of intensifying beyond their already damaging levels. The *World Drug Report* (UNODC 2021) predicts that the number of people using drugs could rise by 11 per cent over the next decade, with as much as 40 per cent in Africa alone. It also highlights that more people are suffering from drug use disorders and losing their lives, with, for example, roughly 50,000 people dying from opioid overdoses in the United States in 2019, more than double the 2010 figure. The fallout from COVID-19, including increased unemployment and inequality, could well generate more problematic drug use and engagement with illicit markets. As the *European Drug Report* (EMCDDA 2021) also documents, despite some minor disruption, restrictions associated with the pandemic have not had any significant impact on production or supply, with the market rapidly adapting to changing environments and circumstances. In fact, there continues to be surges in the supply of many drugs, such as cocaine, with uncertainty around others. What impact the Taliban rule in Afghanistan will have on global heroin markets, for example, remains to be seen (Felbab-Brown 2021).

Combined with other major trends, such as digital developments, globalisation, demographic shifts, migration, and climate change, it is unsurprising that the *European Drug Report* (EMCDDA 2021, p. 7) concludes that 'both the drug market and patterns of drug use are becoming ever more dynamic, complex and globally connected'. Of course, simultaneously, policy responses are also being formulated to this context. A 'quiet revolution' (Eastwood et al. 2016) of progressive drug policy reform is visible in many countries, with decriminalisation becoming more popular and attempts at legalisation no longer only residing in the dreams of drug policy activists. Policing typically remains a central component of drug strategies throughout the world. But there are signs that the focus and nature of drugs policing are changing. The United Nations Office on Drugs and Crime (UNODC 2021) stress that tackling drug trafficking requires international cooperation and the transfer of best law enforcement practices. The increased number of people with drug use disorders, however, requires a multifactorial approach. Importantly, UNODC (2021, p. 48) state that '[p]rotecting the human rights of people who use drugs by treating them with dignity, removing stigma and providing equal access to health and social services need to be the underlying principles of all interventions relating to drug use'. Similarly, the European Monitoring Centre for Drugs and Drug Addiction (EMCDDA 2021) draws attention to the new EU drug strategy, which makes explicit that the response to drugs should be evidence based and judged on its impact on the health, safety, and well-being of citizens. In the United Kingdom, part of the government's response to Dame Carol Black's (2020) commissioned report into the state of the domestic drug market was to promote tough enforcement activities targeted at all levels of the supply chain and 'meaningful consequences' for people who use drugs (HM Government 2021). The second part of Black's (2021) independent review focuses on prevention, treatment, and recovery. One of the many recommendations that has found its way into the government's strategic approach is the promise to divert more drug-related offenders to treatment instead of prison. What plays out in practice will be the focus of much attention for years to come.

Chapter synopsis

Harm reduction policing should be central to national and international debates about the future of drugs policing and the wider dynamics of drug policy reform playing out across the globe. Lessons can be learnt and evidence can be drawn upon to try to ensure that drugs policing actually reduces rather than exacerbates drug harms. In various ways, the contributions in this book all seek to promote this goal.

Key concepts, issues, and themes

Chapter 1 sets the scene for the rest of the book by examining the origins, development, and current standing of harm reduction policing. We synthesise the existing literature on the topic and offer a detailed overview of developing trends and specific examples from around the world. Our aim is to bring together this growing body of work for the first time, conceptualise harm reduction policing as a distinct policing model, and provide a framework for future research. Key points of discussion include enforcement-led prohibition and its shortcomings, the emergence, evolution, and application of the notion of 'harm reduction' in drug policy and practice, and the meaning and types of 'harm'. Drawing on the concepts of the 'risk environment' (Rhodes 2002) and 'responsive regulation' (Braithwaite 2011), the chapter also considers theoretical tools that can be employed to inform harm reduction policing. To date, the application of harm reduction principles to drugs policing has only been realised to a limited extent in responses to drug use and markets. The chapter therefore concludes by considering the prospects of harm reduction policing, including the barriers and facilitators to its expansion.

Harm reduction and harmful drugs policing

The following section examines established drug law enforcement practices and considers the extent to which they reduce or result in harm.

In Chapter 2, Charlie Lloyd presents the first international literature review on the policing of drug possession. It focuses on three broad themes: (1) policy change, including the 'Lambeth Experiment', cannabis reclassification, diversion, and order maintenance policing in New York; (2) the impacts of policing – both positive and negative, including consequences for police legitimacy, patterns of drug use, and other social issues; and (3) variation in enforcement and the use of police discretion – the differences between laws and policies 'in the books' and 'in action' on the streets. The chapter concludes that policing drug possession is doing more harm than good and highlights the need for new thinking and approaches. For Lloyd, by far the largest weight on the negative side of the scale is the gross over-representation of young black men among those stopped and searched on suspicion of possession.

In Chapter 3, Benson Egwuonwu, Habib Kadiri, and Michael Shiner examine the role of drug law enforcement in the over-policing of black and minority ethnic communities in the United States and England and Wales. They demonstrate that drugs policing is a key driver of the problems underpinning recent calls to 'defund' the police on both sides of the Atlantic, most notably racial discrimination, disparities, and disadvantages. This leads the authors to conclude that the defunding agenda should be taken more seriously in the United Kingdom. In light of the failure of repeated reform efforts, however, as well as the likelihood that the police will adapt to budget cuts in ways that perpetuate existing practices, which is demonstrated through an analysis of policing under austerity, they argue for a broader focus on structural racism and institutional transformation. Drug reform, in particular the decriminalisation of drug possession, should be at the forefront of this process, alongside community investment, therapeutic interventions, employment programmes, and public health approaches to policing.

Chapter 4 considers the nature and consequences of symbolic forms of drugs policing. Building on the framework originally presented in Coomber et al. (2019), Ross Coomber, Matthew Bacon, Jack Spicer, and Leah Moyle start by discussing further concepts that can advance theoretical perspectives on symbolic policing, including Goffman's (1959) concept of 'performances', Manning's (1997) dramaturgical analysis of policing, and Loader's (1997) work on 'symbolic power'. The authors then draw on their respective empirical studies to illustrate how symbolic drugs policing operates in practice, from the perspectives of police officers and affected drug market actors. Attention is given to how specific drugs policing activities such as crackdown operations, the execution of drug warrants, responding to new threats, and attempting to safeguard 'vulnerable' populations can be considered symbolic in terms of how they are performed and their outcomes. Recognising that symbolism is inescapable in how drugs policing is undertaken and represented, the chapter concludes by putting forward recommendations for how the communications and signals sent out may be reconfigured to help promote practices that align with harm reduction principles.

Continuity, change, and the prospect of reform

The next three chapters explore continuity, change, and the prospect of reform in drugs policing.

In Chapter 5, James Martin, Ian Warren, and Monique Mann examine the ideological challenges and principal enforcement tactics associated with policing cryptomarkets. Focusing on legal developments in the United States and Australia, the authors draw on the concept of moral panic to help explain the constant expansion of state power into new and problematic territories. In particular, they demonstrate how permissive organised crime, conspiracy, and surveillance laws provide the basis for sanctioning interventions that undermine human rights and civil liberties but do little to reduce the size of the market or the harms caused by illicit drug distribution on the dark web. The authors argue that the policing of cryptomarkets is a digital manifestation and expansion of the war on drugs that is strikingly similar in terms of its limited effectiveness and damaging impact.

Although many parts of the world are experiencing shifts in rhetoric, discourse, and policy regarding the policing of drugs, Matthew Bishop and Dylan Kerrigan consider the difficulties faced by many Caribbean states in moving towards approaches based on harm reduction principles. Chapter 6 explores the distinctive nature of the 'drug problem' in the Caribbean in three main sections. First, the authors discuss how the barriers that exist reflect both enduring legacies of colonial brutality in which policing systems were established to maintain order in deeply racially stratified societies and a post-independence settlement that coincided with intense anti-drug surveillance led by the United States. Second, they explain the changing geopolitical context since the dawn of independence, showing how Caribbean policing systems have evolved in tandem with US-driven security interventions, entrenching structural dynamics which inhibit them from either emulating legal shifts elsewhere or developing more humane criminal justice systems. Third, they examine how the securitising, militarising, and privatising of 'hard' interventions on the basis of imported policing models that sit uneasily with local culture, in tandem with deteriorating public infrastructure for 'soft' policy geared towards social transformation, have exacerbated this picture, leading to sustained antagonism between police and marginalised populations.

Chapter 7 illuminates aspects of the risk environment within which drugs are consumed and policed in Scotland, a country that is in urgent need of reform to reduce the negative health, social, and legal impacts of drug use, not least because drug-related deaths are at record levels. Maria Fotopoulou and Liz Aston start by critically analysing the policy environment. They explain how the 1971 Misuse of Drugs Act has created enabling conditions for criminal justice responses but impedes the establishment of harm reduction interventions, such as drug consumption rooms. They also explain how, as a devolved administration, Scotland has its own drug strategy, which recognises drug use as a public health issue and aims to focus on a holistic, human rights-based approach to drug problems. The organisational policies of Police Scotland are also conducive to harm reduction policing. However, while the language of the police signals a progressive approach, the authors argue that there is a gap between policy and practice, which they demonstrate through their analysis of contemporary policing practices. They conclude with suggestions for fundamental shifts in the field to move beyond the stalemate produced by heavily prohibitionist policies.

Drug diversion schemes

The next section of the book focuses on police-led diversion and includes studies of drug diversion schemes in England (Chapter 8), Denmark (Chapter 9), and the United States (Chapter 10). Diversion is a key element of the harm reduction agenda that has generated significant interest and is being increasingly employed internationally. These chapters examine different models of diversion and assess their aims, benefits, risks, and the challenges associated with implementation.

In Chapter 8, Wojciech Spyt and Jason Kew examine the rationale for the development of two separate drug diversion pilots that have been implemented by Thames Valley Police, a regional police force operating in England and Wales.

Written by two serving police officers, this chapter offers a unique and valuable insight into police decision-making processes and the various factors that are driving change in how the police deal with people who use drugs, including a greater emphasis on evidence-based policing amid record levels of illicit drug use, dependency, and drug-related deaths. It also provides a detailed overview of different models of diversion, a critique of deferred prosecution schemes, and an evaluation of the West Berkshire pre-arrest voluntary referral scheme pilot. The authors conclude that there is appetite within the police to treat drug use as a public health issue and that the trend towards diversion is likely to continue.

In Chapter 9, Tobias Kammersgaard, Esben Houborg, Thomas Søgaard, and Sidsel Schrøder provide an account of the first police-led diversion scheme in Denmark for young people caught in possession of illicit drugs. Based on survey, interview, and focus group data, the authors reveal that referral to treatment and social services was viewed by police officers as 'another tool in the toolbox' instead of an alternative to criminal sanctions. As a result, it is suggested that the diversion scheme is indicative of a new dual approach to policing youth drug use, which involves the use of traditional punitive deterrence in combination with demand or harm reduction measures. The authors also engage with the concept of 'treatmentality' (Jöhncke 2009) to explain why even progressive forms of drugs policing might still maintain a range of problematic assumptions about drug use and the appropriateness of treatment interventions.

In Chapter 10, Katherine Beckett, Monica Bell, and Forrest Stuart evaluate the current state of the drug war in the United States and describe the emergence and evolution of community-based alternative responses to drug use and drug markets. In particular, the authors account for the shift towards – and beyond – harm reduction policing that has taken place in Seattle, Washington. Their account starts with the adoption, benefits, and challenges of LEAD 1.0 (Law Enforcement Assisted Diversion), a pre-booking diversion scheme for people arrested on drug and prostitution charges. It continues by explaining how and why this framework was adapted – in the context of the COVID-19 pandemic – to become LEAD 2.0 (Let Everyone Advance with Dignity), in which police no longer serve as gatekeepers to services. Beckett et al. hope that this trend may help decentre the police and render extreme poverty, homelessness, and behavioural health issues 'unpoliceable'.

Partnerships and policy networks

In the final section, the chapters are concerned with partnerships and policy networks and illustrate how multiple sectors have come together to forge new directions in the policing of drug-related issues.

Chapter 11 examines law enforcement and public health partnerships, drawing on the development of a pre-booking diversion programme in Philadelphia. Evan Anderson and Ruth Shefner focus on the complexity and implementation challenges of aligning police and public health activities. They demonstrate that diversion is not sufficient to improve individual and community health if the resources and services needed to satisfy unmet social and health needs are lacking. They also explain how diversion can perpetuate the medicalisation of drug use, homelessness, and other social distress, not only producing substantial incidental harm but also obscuring more effective upstream strategies for promoting health. Accounting for local context, the authors contend, is essential to understanding the potential value and pitfalls of pre-booking programmes as a replacement for many current drugs policing practices.

Chapter 12 presents a case study of how police and low-threshold social and harm reduction services went from being opponents to partners in a joint effort to reduce drug-related harm associated with an open drug scene in Copenhagen. Using the concept of 'policy network' (Carlsson 2000) and actor-network theory (Latour 1993), Esben Houborg, Tobias Kammersgaard, and Thomas Søgaard explore the work that went into interesting and enrolling local actors into collective action. Aside from providing insights into the networking processes involved in the development of harm reduction policing, the authors also show how the scheme created new ways of working for the various actors involved and made new types of action possible. The chapter shows that there does not have to be a contradiction between policing and harm reduction, which has often been the case in this area of drug policy.

Finally, Chapter 13 argues that, in England and Wales, directly elected police and crime commissioners (PCCs) have become 'drug policy actors' and enablers of harm reduction through their convening power in policy networks. Meg Jones and Ben Twomey explore the PCC role in police governance and the journey to develop and deliver a harm reduction approach to drug policy in the West Midlands, where local initiatives include diversion, naloxone provision, heroin assisted treatment, drug safety testing, and drug consumption rooms. Drawing on their extensive experience working for PCCs and promoting harm reduction policing, the authors provide a rare account of the inner workings of the policymaking process and share their insights on how to overcome barriers to drug policy reform. They conclude by offering practical guidance for policymakers, practitioners, and the general public on how to achieve change.

Conclusion

With all of its contributions combined, this edited collection augments and significantly advances drugs policing scholarship, representing a notable landmark in the emerging body of literature on harm reduction policing. In so doing, it also makes a valuable contribution to the broader but still relatively new field of law enforcement and public health, which is fast finding itself at the forefront of much policing research (Punch and James 2017; van Dijk and Crofts 2017; van Dijk et al. 2019). Collectively, the authors critically examine empirical findings on drugs policing in various contexts; explore the conceptual and practical advantages, challenges, and risks of harm reduction approaches; and provide fresh perspectives on drug policy debates by fleshing out options for what can and should be done to reform the policing of drugs. Importantly, thinking critically about addressing inequality provides an overarching theme that lies at the heart of much of the discussion. In its traditional manifestations alongside broader policy regimes, drugs policing has often played a role in exacerbating inequality. But a central contention of this collection is that there is potential for progressive change.

While covering a range of countries, localities, and contexts, inevitably this edited collection does not provide an exhaustive overview of drugs policing throughout the world. Nevertheless, several core messages span the chapters: (1) 'drug war'-style forms of policing that follow the logic of prohibition in pursuing blunt, punitive interventions are generally both ineffective and counterproductive; (2) harm reduction policing provides a workable alternative that can reduce the adverse health, social, and economic consequences associated with drug use, drug markets, and efforts to control them through the criminal justice system; and (3) the path towards harm reduction policing is fragile, challenging to navigate, and almost insurmountable in some situations. With these as a starting point, there is undoubtedly a need for more research to be undertaken. Conceptually, there remains significant scope to develop our ideas, understandings, and explanations. The contributions of this book are largely concerned with policing people who use drugs and local drug distribution. More research is needed to explore harm reduction approaches to suppressing supply further up the chain and countering organised crime groups for whom drugs are one of a range of criminal activities. Empirically, as changes in the strategic direction of drugs policing continue and the contexts in which it operates shift, the need to gather and analyse data will be vital in continuing to improve our knowledge. Hopefully this book can play a part in this research agenda. As well as informing and giving critical insight into the present state of affairs, we hope it will inspire and guide the drugs policing scholarship of the future.

References

Bacon, M. (2016) *Taking Care of Business: Police Detectives, Drug Law Enforcement and Proactive Investigation*. Oxford: Oxford University Press.

Bacon, M. (2022) 'Desistance from criminalisation: Police culture and new directions in drugs policing'. *Policing and Society*. 32(4): 522–539.

Beckett, K. (2016) 'The uses and abuses of police discretion: Toward harm reduction policing'. *Harvard Law and Policy Review*. 10: 77–100.

Black, C. (2020) *Review of Drugs: Phase One Report*. London: Home Office.

Black, C. (2021) *Review of Drugs: Phase Two Report*. London: Home Office.

Bowling, B., Reiner, R. and Sheptycki, J. (2019) *The Politics of the Police*. 5th edn. Oxford: Oxford University Press.

Braithwaite, J. (2011) 'The essence of responsive regulation'. *University of British Columbia Law Review*. 44(3): 475–520.

Carlsson, L. (2000) 'Policy networks as collective action'. *Policy Studies Journal*. 28(3): 502–520.

Caulkins, J. and Reuter, P. (2009) 'Towards a harm-reduction approach to enforcement'. *Safer Communities*. 8(1): 9–23.

Collison, M. (1995) *Police, Drugs and Community*. London: Free Association Books.

Coomber, R., Moyle, L. and Mahoney, M. (2019) 'Symbolic policing: Situating targeted police operations/'crackdowns' on street-level drug markets'. *Policing and Society*. 29(1): 1–17.

Dorn, N. and South, N. (1990) 'Drug markets and law enforcement'. *British Journal of Criminology*. 30(2): 171–188.

Eastwood, N., Fox, E. and Rosmarin, A. (2016) *A Quiet Revolution: Drug Decriminalisation Across the Globe*. London: Release.

EMCDDA (2021) *European Drug Report: Trends and Developments*. Lisbon: EMCDDA.

Felbab-Brown, V. (2021) 'Pipe dreams: The Taliban and drugs from the 1990s into its new regime'. *Small Wars Journal*.

Goffman, E. (1959) *The Presentation of Self in Everyday Life*. New York: Doubleday Anchor.

HM Government (2021) *From Harm to Hope: A 10-Year Drugs Plan to Cut Crime and Save Lives*. London: HM Government.

Jöhncke, S. (2009) 'Treatmentality and the governing of drug use'. *Drugs and Alcohol Today*. 9(4): 14–17.

Kammersgaard, T. (2019) 'Harm reduction policing: From drug law enforcement to protection'. *Contemporary Drug Problems*. 46(4): 345–362.

Latour, B. (1993) *The Pasteurisation of France*. Cambridge, MA: Harvard University Press.

Loader, I. (1997) 'Policing and the social: Questions of symbolic power'. *British Journal of Sociology*. 48(1): 1–18.

Loader, I. (2020) *Revisiting the Police Mission*. London: Police Foundation.

Manning, P. (1997) *Police Work: The Social Organization of Policing*. 2nd edn. Prospect Heights, IL: Waveland Press.

Manning, P. (2004) *The Narcs' Game: Organizational and Informational Limits on Drug Law Enforcement*. 2nd edn. Cambridge, MA: MIT Press.

Maher, L. and Dixon, D. (1999) 'Policing and public health: Law enforcement and harm minimization in a street-level drug market'. *British Journal of Criminology*. 39(4): 488–512.

Paes-Machado, E. and Birkbeck, C. (2016) 'Introduction'. *Police Practice and Research*. 17(4): 303–305.

Perrone, D., Malm, A. and Magaña, E. (2022) 'Harm reduction policing: An evaluation of Law Enforcement Assisted Diversion (LEAD) in San Francisco'. *Police Quarterly*. 25(1): 7–32.

Punch, M. and James, S. (2017) 'Researching law enforcement and public health'. *Policing and Society*. 27(3): 251–260.

Rhodes, T. (2002) 'The "risk environment": A framework for understanding and reducing drug-related harm'. *International Journal of Drug Policy*. 13(2): 85–94.

Ritter, A. and Stevens, A. (2017) 'Improving knowledge on law enforcement in drug policy'. *International Journal of Drug Policy*. 41: 89–90.

Rolles, S., Murkin, G., Powell, M., Kushlick, D., Saunter, N. and Slater, J. (2016) *The Alternative World Drug Report: Counting the Costs of the War on Drugs*. 2nd edn. Bristol: Transform Drug Policy Foundation.

Shiner, M. (2016) 'Drug policing: What is it good for?' In Collins, J. (ed.) *After the War on Drugs*. London: LSE Expert Group on the Economics of Drug Policy: 56–66.

Spicer, J. (2021) *Policing County Lines: Responses to Evolving Provisional Drug Markets*. London: Palgrave.

Stevens, A. (2013) *Modernising Drug Law Enforcement: Applying Harm Reduction Principles to the Policing of Retail Drug Markets*. London: International Drug Policy Consortium.

UNODC (2021) *World Drug Report*. Vienna: UNODC.

van Dijk, A. and Crofts, N. (2017) 'Law enforcement and public health as an emerging field'. *Policing and Society*. 27(3): 261–275.

van Dijk, A., Herrington, V., Crofts, N., Breunig, R., Burris, S., Sullivan, H., Middleton, J., Sherman, S. and Thomson, N. (2019) 'Law enforcement and public health: Recognition and enhancement of joined-up solutions'. *The Lancet*. 393(10168): 287–294.

1

HARM REDUCTION POLICING

Conceptualisation and implementation

Matthew Bacon and Jack Spicer

Introduction

Of all the features comprising the contemporary policing landscape, drugs is arguably one of the most intriguing, complicated, and contentious. It is a domain that brings into sharp focus the multifaceted nature of the police role in society, characterised by a miscellany of tasks, goal conflicts, and policy trade-offs. Under the drugs umbrella, those undertaking policing functions can be exposed to anything from violent organised crime groups to drug overdose deaths. Drugs policing is undoubtedly faced with an 'impossible mandate' (Manning 1997). Central to this is how drugs cut across so many societal issues, presenting complex, compounding challenges that are intertwined with a range of wicked problems. Poverty, crime, addiction, inequality, homelessness, personal trauma, and mental health conditions are all regularly connected in various ways to the use, supply, and presence of drugs in communities. At the same time, while no drug use is entirely harmless, drugs are a source of pleasure for many and can often be used with minimal risk to both the user and the general public. Consequently, drugs and their control are bound up in thorny moral and politically charged debates that are difficult to reconcile. Policing is often caught up in this wrangling, being heavily disparaged by some, while 'fetishised' by others (Bowling et al. 2019).

Aligning with the ideologies and institutions of the global prohibition regime, drugs policing is firmly centred on law enforcement and punitive interventions. The core aim has long been to reduce – or even eliminate – the production, supply, and use of controlled substances through deterrence and criminal sanctions (MacCoun and Reuter 2001). This rather myopic view has tended to obscure the wider purpose that drugs policing could be oriented around and the harm reduction functions that the police could potentially achieve. While undoubtedly sometimes distorted, exaggerated, and misunderstood, drugs and their supply

DOI: 10.4324/9781003154136-2

are causal factors in a multitude of serious and 'real' harms. There are a variety of enforcement interventions that can effectively reduce drug crime and associated problems (see e.g. Mazerolle et al. 2007, 2020). But it should also be recognised that there are changes and reforms that can be made to policing to reduce or contribute to the reduction of a broader range of drug harms.

There is emerging evidence that drugs policing is moving away from traditional enforcement interventions towards a greater focus on harm reduction (Bacon 2016; Beckett 2016; Cloud and Davis 2015; Kammersgaard 2019; Krupanski 2018; Monaghan and Bewley-Taylor 2013a; Perrone et al. 2022; Spicer 2021; Spooner et al. 2004; Stevens 2013; UKDPC 2009). For the purposes of this chapter, 'harm reduction policing' is broadly defined as policing measures that aim to reduce the adverse health, social, and economic consequences of drug use, drug markets and the efforts to control them through the criminal justice system. Signs of a shift are apparent in burgeoning police-led diversion schemes. Other indicators include the carrying of naloxone by frontline officers and police support for harm reduction services, such as needle exchange programmes, heroin-assisted treatment, drug consumption rooms, and drug safety testing. Indeed, many proponents of harm reduction increasingly identify the police as a key partner when it comes to implementing harm reduction programmes (Houborg et al., this volume). It therefore appears timely to provide clarity to this area by considering exactly what harm reduction policing is and how it works in practice.

This chapter examines the origins, development, and current standing of harm reduction policing. It synthesises the extant literature on the topic and offers a detailed overview of developing trends and specific examples from across the globe. Our aim is to bring together this growing body of work coherently for the first time, conceptualise harm reduction policing as a distinct policing model, and provide a framework for future research. While much of this research might – often quite rightly – be explicitly critical by drawing attention to the direct and indirect harms that drugs policing causes, we argue that there is also a need for a pragmatic focus on how it may be (re)configured to reduce drug harms. The chapter begins by sketching out the wider drug policy context. It offers an overview of enforcement-led prohibition and its shortcomings, before outlining the origins and development of the harm reduction movement that emerged in response. While by no means an exhaustive account, such context is important, especially for those who come to this topic from a policing standpoint and might not be overly conversant with the drugs field. The chapter then turns its attention to the topic of harm reduction policing. It suggests that the underpinning ideas represent a continuation of themes visible in earlier drugs policing research, before going on to consider more contemporary conceptualisations and the types of drug harm with which this policing model is concerned. Drawing conceptually on the ideas of the 'risk environment' (Rhodes 2002) and 'responsive regulation' (Braithwaite 2011), the chapter moves on to discuss theoretical tools that can be employed to inform harm reduction policing. We conclude by considering its prospects, including the barriers and facilitators to its expansion. By doing so, we hope to add some much needed clarity to the discourse on harm reduction policing and inform its continued advancement.

Drug policy, prohibition, and policing

The drug policy spectrum

To understand the nature and standing of harm reduction policing, it is essential to situate it within the wider drug policy context. Drug policy refers to the 'laws, decisions, funding programmes, and instructions by which the state affects discourses and practices on illicit drugs' (Stevens 2017, p. 826). There is a spectrum of policy frameworks for regulating the production, supply, and use of drugs (Nadelmann 1992). Globally, however, drug prohibition is (almost) universal, albeit with differences in implementation. This variation

> reflects differences in attitudes toward drug use itself, toward individual rights, and toward the role of government. It also reflects the nature and history of national drug problems, the broader political structure of a country, and the different ways in which drugs affect a nation.
>
> *(Babor et al. 2010, p. 221)*

The drug policy of a state has significant implications for a wide range of stakeholders and society more broadly. For the police, it has specific consequences as they are tasked with enforcing the law and sustaining politically defined order. Drug policy sets the framework in which policing operates; it simultaneously enables and constrains what individual officers and police organisations do in relation to drugs. Because they are the most visible criminal justice institution and manifestation of state power, the police also frequently find themselves as the face of drug policy.

At one end of the policy spectrum are those who wage a ruthless 'war on drugs'. 'Zero tolerance' approaches and the meting out of harsh punishments on those found transgressing drug laws are common. Thirty-five countries still retain the death penalty for drug offences. Every year, hundreds of people are executed for non-violent drug offences, and thousands more are subject to fair trial violations and inhumane treatment (Larasati and Girelli 2021). The drug war in Latin America has seen decades of violence, corruption, and human rights abuses (Lessing 2018). In the United States, the phenomenon of mass incarceration, with all its associated social consequences, has been driven by highly punitive drug laws, sentences, and enforcement (Alexander 2010; Beckett 2022). President Duterte's drug war in the Philippines represents a particularly vicious recent manifestation of prohibition, with thousands of citizens killed through extrajudicial police executions and government-sanctioned vigilante attacks (Johnson and Fernquest 2018).

However, there are diverging views on drug policy among the international community and change is afoot in many parts of the world (Bewley-Taylor 2012; Hall 2018). The drug policy spectrum includes alternatives to criminalisation via a range of depenalisation, diversion, and decriminalisation measures (Stevens et al. 2022). In Europe, Colson and Bergeron (2017) trace a gradual policy convergence and the emergence of a model favouring public health strategies over a strictly penal approach to drug problems. Portugal is perhaps the most prominent example, where personal possession of all drugs was decriminalised as part of a wider re-orientation of policy towards a health-led approach. Elsewhere, cannabis prohibition has become progressively fragmented, since Uruguay, Canada, and numerous states in the United States decided to regulate the market for recreational use (Seddon and Floodgate 2020).

The (in)effectiveness and (un)intended consequences of prohibition

As intensely as the police and others have waged the war on drugs, there has been little success in achieving the aims of prohibition. If the purpose of this policy regime is to create a 'drug free society' by eradicating the production, supply, and use of illicit drugs, most people would concede that it has not only failed but cannot succeed (Rolles 2020). Tasked with playing a central role, the police have processed millions of people through the criminal justice system for drug offences and seized a never-ending quantity of drugs at borders, in warehouses, and out on the streets. More recently, the drug war continues to widen its purview, focusing now, for example, on some of the clandestine corners of the internet (Martin et al., this volume). Yet, however intensely these strategies have been used against illicit drug markets, they have failed to have a sustainable impact on supply or demand.

Drug markets have proven to be highly resilient, demonstrating a remarkable capacity for adaptation in response to actions taken against them by law enforcement. While there are plenty of arrests of drug market actors, even occasionally of those situated towards the higher echelons, the markets themselves remain buoyant, often at least one step ahead of enforcement efforts. In the United Kingdom, the exceptional social restrictions placed on citizens as a result of the COVID-19 pandemic, combined with the high-profile international policing operation labelled 'Operation Venetic', provided a good case study of market resilience. The police were able to sweep up significant numbers of low-level dealers who became highly visible on otherwise deserted streets, while unique intelligence gathered by infiltrating the 'Encrochat' messaging system allowed them to arrest a significant number of those operating at the upper levels of the market. Yet, faced with this potentially existential crisis, the drug market has remained robust (Aldridge et al. 2021).

This recent experience corresponds with wider observations that levels of enforcement activity appear to bear little to no direct relationship to levels of drug availability or use. In their synthesis of the literature assessing the relationship between drug enforcement intensity and drug prices, Pollack and Reuter (2014) found that, while prohibition itself may push prices above those likely to pertain in legal markets and therefore hold down drug use, there is little evidence that raising the risk of arrest, incarceration, or seizure at different levels of the distribution system will raise prices, at least for established drugs. While drug laws reinforced through enforcement approaches shape the environments in which illicit drugs are produced, sold, and used, more enforcement does not appear to reduce drug problems. There is no research showing that tougher enforcement, more prevention, or even increased treatment has substantially reduced the extent of drug use and addiction in a nation (Reuter 2009). Werb et al.'s (2013) audit of international drug surveillance databases also indicates that the availability and purity of drugs have generally increased, while the price of drugs has remained stable or declined, the precise opposite of what would be expected if enforcement measures were effective as a market reduction instrument.

The criticisms of enforcement-led prohibition do not stop at its ineffectiveness. As anyone studying this area soon learns, not only has the current policy position failed in its aims, but the associated efforts at achieving them also drive a range of significant harms (Csete et al. 2016; Rolles et al. 2016). It is important to recognise that being criminalised and subsequently punished is itself a harmful process rooted in the intentional infliction of pain. For those convicted of drug offences, consequences can include stigmatisation, social exclusion, the restriction of education, employment, and housing prospects, as well as disrupting health care provision and increasing risk behaviour associated with infectious disease transmission and overdose (Baker et al. 2020; Kerr et al. 2005). There are strong arguments questioning whether there is ever moral justification for criminalising individuals for what they choose to consume or do with their bodies (e.g. Szasz 1974). But even if it was accepted that this might be justifiable under certain circumstances, evidence suggests that the harms of criminalising people who use drugs are not counterbalanced by reductions in drug use. Furthermore, while there is a lack of evidence that vigorously enforcing prohibition serves as a deterrent to drug use, there is an abundance on the harmful consequences of repressive policing and criminalising people for possession offences. This is compounded considering that criminalisation is unevenly distributed across society. Shiner et al. (2018) show how drugs policing, particularly involving the use of stop and search, drives ethnic disparities through the criminal justice system in England and Wales. Similar observations have been made in the United States, with Vitale (2017, p. 129) arguing that the end of drug war policing 'would be a major positive step toward radically redefining the role of police in society and improving racial justice'.

In addition to those harms typically associated with being criminalised, a further concern relating to the harmful consequences of drugs policing is the association between enforcement and increased drug market violence. Evidence from various countries and market contexts points to this relationship (e.g. Atuesta and Ponce 2017; Moeller and Hesse 2013). Some of the strongest evidence comes from Werb et al. (2011), whose systematic review found that intensified drug law enforcement interventions were actually associated with an increase in drug market violence, with underlying mechanisms including the destabilisation of markets, contributing to significant levels of serious violence. Such findings are of significant concern, not least because desires to reduce violence are regularly used to justify why such enforcement actions are undertaken. With this and the above-mentioned evidence combined, it is unsurprising that, in a frank assessment of drug law enforcement as part of the evaluation of the UK's 2010 Drug Strategy, HM Government (2017) concluded that it had little measurable impact on the prevalence of use or other metrics of performance, while conceding that there are often a range of negative outcomes.

Harm reduction: origins, development, and definition

The ineffective and often harmful outcomes of drug war–style policies and practices have long been recognised by stakeholders in the drug field. It was against this backdrop that the notion of 'harm reduction' emerged and has continued to develop. Rooted in the public health tradition (Erickson 1995), harm reduction typically denotes policies and programmes that seek to promote positive health outcomes and minimise the various harms (and/or risks) associated with drug use. The harm reduction movement, as widely recognised today, emerged in the mid-1980s and was triggered by two major factors: first and foremost, the need for effective strategies for minimising the risk of HIV transmission among injecting drug users; and, secondly, the increase in 'normalised' recreational drug use among young people (Berridge 1996; Newcombe 1987). Although the reduction of drug-related harm was by no means a new paradigm (Berridge 1993), a series of international conferences beginning in Liverpool in 1990 marked the start of what may formally be called a 'harm reduction approach' to drug policy (Erickson et al. 1997; Heather et al. 1993; O'Hare et al. 1992). Since then, harm reduction has become a crucial pillar of contemporary drug control efforts worldwide, sitting alongside prevention, treatment, and enforcement, as well as the aims of demand and supply reduction. It encompasses a range of health and social services. Well-recognised examples include needle and syringe programmes, naloxone, drug consumption rooms, drug safety testing, opioid agonist therapy, outreach, and education (Hunt 2003; Ritter and Cameron 2006).

There is no universally accepted definition of harm reduction and the term has been subject to robust debate (King 2020). This is partly due to it referring to a philosophical approach based on a set of principles, as well as specific types of interventions justified on consequentialist grounds of aiming to reduce net harms. The term originally referred to only those policies and programmes that attempted to reduce the risk of harm among people who used drugs. However, there are now broader, more inclusive definitions encompassing any measures aimed at reducing drug-related harm (Lenton and Single 1998). An explicit goal stated by Harm Reduction International (2022) is to 'improve drug laws, policies and law enforcement practices, so that they are not detrimental to the health and wellbeing of people who use drugs and their communities'. This broadening of the harm reduction agenda recognises a wider range of measures that aim to minimise the negative health, social and economic impacts associated with drug use, markets, and policies.

Key to harm reduction is its grounding in justice and human rights. In contrast to abstinence-oriented prohibitionism, with its roots in social control and medical and religious paternalism, the harm reduction perspective is deeply rooted in humanitarianism and libertarianism (Hathaway 2001; Newcombe 1992). For King (2020, p. 328), harm reduction 'is driven by compassion and a de facto prioritarian sense of justice, not a utilitarian calculus'. It is caring, non-judgemental, and avoids marginalising or stigmatising drug users. Importantly, it is also committed to collaborating with people who use drugs in designing, implementing, and evaluating policies and programmes. Since drug use and people who use drugs are not defined as intrinsically problematic, the focus is on problems, or harmful consequences resulting from use, rather than on use directly. It is consequently free from 'moral, legal, or medical-reductionist strings' (Erickson et al. 1997, p. 7). Harm reduction recognises that many people are unable or unwilling to stop using illicit drugs. It also recognises that many do not require treatment. People who use drugs are treated with compassion and dignity. They are regarded as capable of making choices about their life and taking responsibility for their actions, while acknowledging that agency is shaped and constrained by the environments in which drug use occurs (Rhodes 2002).

Harm reduction generally eschews simplistic and sometimes unhelpful dichotomies between prohibition and legalisation. By neither denouncing nor promoting drug use, harm reduction programmes are able to be pragmatic and consider which policies are likely to be most effective for reducing specific drug-related harms. Harm reduction policies and practices aspire to be evidence based, with advocates committed to achievable goals. This approach to harm reduction both avoids and problematises moralistic influences that are often prevalent in drug policy (Keane 2003; Stevens 2019). Of course, taking this position can put harm reduction at odds with the dominant legal sanction–based policy. Roe (2005, p. 245) stresses the activist origins of harm reduction, conceptualising it as 'ideological and oppositional', with a 'political and moral commitment to altering the material and social conditions for drug users'. Yet, the pragmatic nature of harm reduction measures makes it possible for certain strategies to be tolerated, accepted, or even actively incorporated into existing drug policies, without completely dismantling the legal framework. Erickson (1995, p. 284) reminds us that drug '[l]aws are not moral absolutes, but are instruments used to achieve health objectives that reduce risk for individuals, communities and society'. Making drugs illegal has not stopped people from using them or reduced their harms. Legalising drugs overnight is unlikely to represent a silver bullet either.

Pragmatically transcending the space in between, harm reduction provides a pathway for genuinely effective responses to drugs to be designed and delivered.

Towards harm reduction policing

Back to the future: the empirical foundations of harm reduction policing

It is against the backdrop of the deficiencies of enforcement-led prohibition, combined with the value of harm reduction, that an approach to drugs policing which applies harm reduction principles can be situated. Considerations of how the paradigm of harm reduction could be aligned with drugs policing is a relatively new and growing movement (Bacon 2016; Beckett 2016; Cloud and Davis 2015; Kammersgaard 2019; Krupanski 2018; Monaghan and Bewley-Taylor 2013a; Perrone et al. 2022; Spicer 2021; Spooner et al. 2004; Stevens 2013; UKDPC 2009). Certainly, the concept of harm reduction has less frequently been applied to policing than other areas in the drugs field. Yet, importantly, there is some significant precedent. Earlier drugs policing researchers both implicitly and more explicitly recognised that harm reduction was the only feasible outcome of work in this area. Going back to these studies provides a foundation for harm reduction policing, as well as recognition that contemporary drugs policing scholarship is building on what has come before. Harm reduction policing can thus be considered a progressive development, rather than a radical departure from the past.

Returning to the work of Manning (2004), for example, who provided one of the first in-depth accounts of drugs policing by studying two police drug units located in metropolitan areas in the United States in the spring of 1975, is instructive. His conclusions were critical of attempts to punish drug offenders through the criminal law. As an alternative, he suggested that drug use and supply could be approached through the lens of public health, with 'the risk and disease-causing factors related to drug use as matters to be mitigated, reduced, or prevented' (p. 265). Also explicitly invoking the logic of harm reduction, Dorn and South (1990, p. 186) suggested:

> It may now be time to discuss harm minimization in relation to drug distribution. The question is, given that we cannot totally prevent illegal drug markets … what sort of markets do we least dislike, and how can we adjust the control mix so as to push markets in the least undesired direction.

A similar argument was made shortly after by Pearson (1992, p. 15), who, acknowledging the potential role of harm reduction in this area, stated that 'there is a pressing need that the concept should be expanded to include drug enforcement, criminal justice and the penal system'. Also central to his argument was the value in minimising the use of 'counter-productive aspects of enforcement strategies through arrest-referral schemes, diversion programmes and other community-based activities which avoid the excessive use of custodial measures' (p. 17), something also championed by Collison (1995) and Murji (1998). Recognising this wider application of harm reduction set a platform for considering how drugs policing could be more reflexive, pragmatic, and humane.

Findings from studies grounded in the perspectives of those subjected to, rather than undertaking, drugs policing also made significant contributions in setting the scholarly foundations for harm reduction policing. Maher and Dixon's (1999) study of Sydney's principal heroin market highlighted tensions between commitments to law enforcement and harm minimisation. Identifying a number of drug-related harms that were (re)produced by drugs policing measures, their findings integrated perspectives from policing and public health research, ultimately arguing for a shift in policing priorities towards public health and community safety, while rejecting suggestions that the law constrains the ability of the police to subordinate enforcement to other objectives. Lying at the heart of this argument is the emphasis on the capacity of the police to use their discretion in a way that reduces harm. Similarly, based on ethnographic observation in New York City, Curtis and Wendel (2007) argue that police interventions can effectively reconfigure markets by 'training' them to act in ways less likely to produce violence and social disorder.

Contemporary conceptualisations of harm reduction policing

The move towards harm reduction policing is not only a logical progression in the harm reduction approach to drug policy. Fundamentally, it should also be situated in debates about the nature and boundaries of the contemporary police 'mission' (Loader 2020). Notwithstanding the intersections, in-betweens, and shades of grey, the crux of the matter is the long-standing but oversimplified question of whether the police are best defined as a law enforcement agency tasked with fighting crime or a social service doing whatever is necessary to improve public safety and well-being. History reveals that the policing pendulum constantly swings between 'force' and 'service' roles (Bowling et al. 2019). Inevitably, this has implications for drugs policing.

As previously outlined, the policing of drugs is usually conceptualised primarily as a matter of law enforcement: drugs are prohibited and it is a role of the police to enforce the law and bring offenders to justice. This narrow definition overlooks and undervalues the wider purpose of (drugs) policing, 'to protect public and individual safety, security, order, and rights' (Krupanski 2018, p. 5). While enforcement is certainly a core element of the police mandate, adopting a harm reduction perspective, it should be viewed as a means to an end rather than an end in itself. Put simply, the law is a resource that can be enforced as a means of promoting order and ensuring the safety of the community by reducing harms to its members. Treating enforcement as the end goal encourages the police to measure success through the process and largely symbolic outcomes of arrests and seizures (Coomber et al., this volume). Recognising this conceptual issue, Caulkins and Reuter (2017, p. 113) suggest that remembering that 'the principal purpose of prohibition is to protect people… may insulate against a mentality of having to burn the village in order to save it'.

Correspondingly, harm reduction policing might be viewed as part of broader trends in modern policing that have resulted in a more expansive and proactive conception of police work. These include the rise of intelligence-led approaches and problem-oriented strategies, as well as the emphasis on community engagement and multi-agency partnerships. One of the reasons Goldstein (1979) formulated problem-oriented policing was to counter the 'means over ends' syndrome that can afflict policing. He challenged the prevailing view of police work as a series of discrete incident responses and instead advocated refocusing on the problems that connected them. Evidence indicates that suitably conceived and implemented policing interventions that integrate problem-oriented, geographical targeting with efforts to create and sustain partnerships between key stakeholders can help to create positive outcomes in relation to drug markets and related harms (Mazerolle et al. 2007, 2020). Increasing emphasis on the intersections between law enforcement and public health has also seen the promotion of partnerships to address complex and interrelated social issues with health, safety, well-being, and security impacts and implications (van Dijk et al. 2019).

The concept of harm reduction policing has begun to develop into a model with identifiable values, objectives, and norms. It is, however, one policing model among many and must operate alongside, combine, compete, or conflict with, alternatives. With regard to policing social marginality, for example, Herbert et al. (2018) examine contrasting approaches to insecurely housed people with drug use and/or mental health issues: aggressive policing (i.e. 'zero tolerance'); coercive benevolence, whereby officers use the threat of arrest to compel individuals to make 'better' choices; and officer-assisted harm reduction. For them, harm reduction policing differs from the other approaches in several important ways. Chief among them is that, rather than pursuing arrests to enhance deterrence, officers use their discretion to channel people out of the criminal justice system and towards services based on the principles of harm reduction. Unless there is an immediate threat to public safety, arrest and punishment are deemed inappropriate responses to low-level criminal behaviours that are understood as having their roots in structural failings.

Just as with more established harm reduction interventions, harm reduction policing recognises that the core mission of the police is to protect human life. As a model, it promotes the benefits of reducing the reliance on enforcement and refining the roles and objectives of policing within the context of drug prohibition. In contrast to other policing strategies, it is novel in recognising that 'the level of harm is more important than the size of the market' (Stevens 2013, p. 12). The underlying logic is that strategically nuanced policies aimed at lessening the negative consequences of risky behaviours – especially those addressing the needs of people who use drugs and engaging communities in a manner that builds trust

(Krupanski 2018) – may reduce harm more than blunt policies aimed at eradicating such behaviours. Focusing on primary activities for which the police are the lead agency, Caulkins and Reuter (2009) distinguish four broad pathways to harm reduction policing: reducing drug use; reducing the harm that users experience per unit of drugs used; reducing the harms that users impose on others; and reducing the harms caused by the production, trafficking and distribution of drugs. Kammersgaard (2019) additionally argues that harm reduction policing should seek to reduce the harms that others impose on drug users since they are much more prone to be victims of violence, threats, and harassment than the general population. Another important pathway is reducing the harm caused by drug policies and policing interventions. Combined, this moves towards a framework for balancing trade-offs and taking into account both the positive outcomes and potential adverse effects of efforts to control drug problems through the criminal justice system. It also appreciates that there are progressive policies and reforms that can be implemented without legislative change 'to help better align the mission, culture, and practices of law enforcement, public health agencies, and harm reduction organizations' (Cloud and Davis 2015, p. 9). This may therefore spur innovation in the creation and diffusion of new strategies and tactics.

Harm reduction policing in theory and practice

Meaning and types of 'harm'

One of the more complicated analytic tasks when thinking about harm reduction and the role it can play in drugs policing concerns establishing the meaning and types of 'harm' it covers. Some lessons can be taken from other relevant disciplines. Social harm scholars have focused on the structural determinants of preventable harms (Pemberton 2015). Zemiologists have made strong arguments for taking into account all the harms people might experience from the cradle to the grave, rather than only those defined as criminal (Hillyard et al. 2004). Some evidence-based policing researchers also stress how different crimes are responsible for significantly different levels of harm (Sherman 2007). Nevertheless, 'harm' remains a slippery concept. Complex and multidimensional, it encompasses health, social, and economic components. As previously mentioned, specifically for drug harm reduction, sometimes 'harm' is used only to refer to health harms for users, what Nadelmann (1993) identifies as 'primary harms'. Yet, while a core part of drug harms relates to drug use directly, others include those associated with markets and drug-related crime. As Caulkins and Reuter (2009, p. 9) argue, 'harm reduction has potentially much broader application when applied to the entire suite of harms generated by the production, distribution, consumption, and control of drugs, not just drug use'. If harm reduction can therefore be concerned with such 'secondary harms' (Blaustein et al. 2017), as well as those arising from drug policies, this opens the door to a range of issues relevant to policing.

A number of conceptual frameworks of harm reduction have been developed. Newcombe's (1992) widely cited work distinguishes drug harm at different levels: individual, community, and societal. Three different types of harm are also identified: health, social, and economic. Arguably the most useful for harm reduction policing is MacCoun and Reuter's (2001) multidimensional 'taxonomy of drug-related harms'. This includes four categories of harm (health, social and economic functioning, safety and public order, criminal justice); six groups that bear the cost (users, dealers, intimates (family, partners, friends), employers, neighbourhood, and society); and three sources of harm (use, illegal status, and enforcement). The sheer number of harms listed highlights the scale and complexity of drug problems. Examples of harms that are most directly related to policing include the elevated price of substances, acquisitive crime, violence, fear, and the sense of disorder. Paying attention to the possible bearers of harm/risk stresses their heterogeneity and encourages us to think about their distribution across different groups under different policies. The inclusion of the primary source of harm in MacCoun and Reuter's taxonomy is also useful for harm reduction policing purposes as it recognises that 'among the costs of prohibition are the side effects of what is necessarily imperfect and incomplete enforcement of the law' (p. 109). Harms attributed to enforcement include systemic crime, infringement on liberty, stigma of criminal record, devaluation of arrest as moral sanction, and inhibition of voluntary pursuit of treatment. As with harm reduction strategies more generally, through this framework drugs policing should aim to demonstrate that, on the balance of probabilities, it is likely to result in a 'net' reduction in drug-related harm. Of course, this is not easily measured. Drugs policing strategies can have multiple effects, potentially decreasing some harms while increasing others. Ultimately, however, harm reduction policing measures can reasonably be considered successful if net harm is minimised.

Policing the 'risk environment'

A clear understanding of harm and a framework for harm reduction in the context of drugs policing allow for harms to be identified, understood, and analysed further by adopting other complementary theoretical lenses. The 'risk environment' (Rhodes 2002) is a useful framework for understanding and reducing drug-related harm. Rhodes (2002, p. 88) defines a risk environment as 'the space – whether social or physical – in which a variety of factors interact to increase the chances of drug-related harm'. Within this broad definition, there is the need to delineate the environmental factors associated with harm production and reduction. Rhodes (2002) suggests that a basic framework of the risk environment comprises 'ideal types' of environment (physical, social, economic, policy) and levels of environmental influence (micro, macro). Studies have unpacked the nature of risk environments in relation to varied contexts and drug-related harms, including heroin use initiation (Mayock et al. 2015), drug injecting (Rhodes et al. 2003), and overdose (McLean 2016).

A risk environment approach places primacy on context and understanding the environmental determinants of harm as a means to create or enhance 'enabling environments' for harm reduction. Individual behaviour change is considered possible only if the environment enables it. Emphasis is also placed on understanding how risk environments shape the introduction, implementation, and impact of policies and interventions. For Rhodes (2002, p. 91), a critical feature of a risk environment approach is that it 'seeks to shift both the responsibility for harm and the focus for change from individuals alone to the social situations and structures in which they find themselves'. It therefore aims to help overcome the constraints of individualism that are typical of many harm reduction interventions, stressing the often overlooked role of social and political institutions in harm production.

A substantial amount of literature documents how drug laws and enforcement practices contribute to the risk environment of drug use. The bulk of the empirical evidence indicates that policies based solely on enforcement – without taking into account public health and human rights considerations – produce harmful health and social impacts for users (Baker et al. 2020; Kerr et al. 2005; Strathdee et al. 2015). To demonstrate the value of considering harm reduction policing through the lens of the risk environment, here we will briefly consider two contexts with distinct social and physical spaces: street injecting drug use and the night-time economy and festivals. For both, we consider how the police can generate harm through their role in the risk environment and then how policing can be (re)oriented around harm reduction principles to create enabling environments that reduce harm.

International research has consistently shown that drug law enforcement in the context of street injecting has both direct and indirect effects on behaviours that increase the risk of HIV and blood-borne infections. In studies considering the risk environments relating to HIV and drug injecting, local policing activities are identified as a structural determinant of harm, as well as a direct social risk (e.g. Rhodes et al. 2003; Small et al. 2006). In their systematic review, Baker et al. (2020) provide a synthesis of policing practices that can act as structural risk factors for HIV infection and risky injection behaviours. Robust evidence shows that HIV infection is significantly associated with syringe confiscation, reluctance to buy/carry syringes for fear of police, and rushed injection due to police presence. These practices increase the risk of needle sharing and overdose mortality. Street policing shapes the risk environment when people who inject drugs avoid harm reduction services and accessing voluntary treatment because of (fear of) negative encounters with the police. Studies also reveal that mistrust and fear of arrest deter people who use drugs from calling emergency services in the event of an overdose (Green et al. 2009; Selfridge et al. 2020).

Burris et al. (2004) were among the first to stress the need to incorporate policing into public health research and action. Focusing on people who inject drugs, they argue that examining the role of the police in creating risk provides new opportunities for harm reduction through structural interventions that alter the risk environment. Regarding drug injecting and overdose, there are various measures the police can adopt to create and enhance enabling environments for harm reduction. A basic policing measure is 'to identify operational practices that may impede access to lifesaving services and adjust these practices to prioritize the lives and health of vulnerable populations' (Krupanski 2018, p. 10). An obvious way to achieve this is through cooperation or collaboration with harm reduction services that provide sterile injecting equipment and supervised injection facilities. Police can enter into agreements not to conduct drug searches or arrests for drug consumption or personal possession at or near service locations (see e.g. Watson et al. 2018). They can also train in overdose resuscitation, carry naloxone, and implement policies that exempt people who call emergency services from being charged for possession.

Policing drugs can also be associated with harm in the risk environments of the night-time economy and at festivals. In her ethnographic research on New York City 'club kids', Perrone (2009) found that criminalising drug users dismantles their social support networks and reduces their economic opportunities, which are necessary for maintaining controlled drug use and employing methods to reduce harms. Cristiano (2020) found that the unpredictability of responses to drug use and supply by the police, private security, and other venue staff was important for shaping risk and risk management practices. For example, when confronted with a heightened police presence at an event or festival, some attendees engaged in drug binges and did not adhere to harm reduction advice to regulate doses. Participants in Cristiano's study were also hesitant to ask for help when needed because of uncertainty about how the police and security would react. Finally, while research suggests that the use of drug detection dogs as a policing strategy at festivals fails to act as a significant deterrent, their use has been found to contribute to risky drug using practices such as consuming drugs before entering and buying drugs from unknown sources when inside (Hughes et al. 2017; Grigg et al. 2018).

Again, after considering their detrimental role in these risk environments, there are policing practices that can help promote enabling environments for harm reduction in night-time economy and festival contexts. Ensuring that the police do not undermine harm reduction policies and programmes appears crucial. Measham and Turnbull (2021) conclude that event-based drug checking services can access and engage productively with young adults through tailored polydrug brief interventions. Rapid identification of substances of concern, dissemination of test results, and associated risk communication during and after events through friendship networks, support services, and early warning systems suggest that the benefits of drug checking can extend beyond the point of intervention. Facilitating such services could be considered a classic example of harm reduction policing. Additionally, the police can also play an active role in promoting harm reduction. They can work in partnership to adopt the '3Ps: Prevent, Pursue, Protect' drug policy as a pragmatic alternative to zero tolerance. The policy directs priorities towards preventing drugs from entering a venue or site, pursuing those suspected of supplying drugs therein, and protecting people from drug-related harm. A final example of an enabling harm reduction police role in these environments is to enforce breaches of licensing regulations that can endanger drug users (Fisher and Measham 2018).

Policing as drug market regulation

If, as has been previously argued, it is accepted that the suppression of drug markets is an impossible mandate, the task of policing inevitably becomes regulation (Bacon 2016; Canty et al. 2000; Caulkins and Reuter 2009; Curtis and Wendel 2007; Maher and Dixon 1999). In this section, harm reduction policing is considered through the lens of regulation to further enhance our conceptual toolkit and build upon the ideas of researchers who have applied regulatory theory to drug policy. Much can be learned from regulatory scholarship to help us rethink drugs policing and develop more effective, compassionate, and creative responses to drug problems (Ritter 2010; Seddon 2010, 2020).

Rather than taking a narrow view of regulation, as the actions of the state to govern through laws, systematic monitoring, and enforcement of sanctions for their breach, from our standpoint it is a capacious concept that means 'influencing the flow of events' (Parker and Braithwaite 2003, p. 119). We adopt Black's (2002, p. 26) definition of regulation as the 'sustained and focused attempt to alter the behaviour of others according to defined standards or purposes with the intention of producing a broadly defined outcome or outcomes'. Applied to harm reduction policing, this translates to attempting to alter the behaviour of people who use, supply, and/or police drugs according to the principles of harm reduction with the intention of reducing the adverse health, social, and economic consequences associated with drug use, drug markets, and efforts to control them through the criminal justice system. Approaching drugs policing as a regulation problem heightens our awareness and understanding of the forms and functions of regulation in diverse fields. Moreover, Seddon (2010, pp. 100–121) argues that it highlights the need to look 'beyond the state', decentring it both in our analyses and in our prescriptions for action, and 'beyond the law', as steering the flow of events requires a much wider range of tools than just legal instruments. This opens up new ways of thinking about the possibilities for harm reduction policing that challenge the dominant role of the police and seek to utilise the regulatory resources and capabilities of multiple actors with a stake in reducing drug harms.

What we are proposing here is an approach to harm reduction policing that incorporates the principles of 'responsive regulation'. The most influential presentation of the theory is by Ayres and Braithwaite (1992), who pulled together insights from earlier studies on corporate crime, mine safety, and business regulation. In a nutshell, the essence of responsive regulation is that regulators need to be responsive to the behaviour of those they are seeking to regulate and highly attuned to the context in which they are operating.

The idea of pyramids of supports and of sanctions is at the heart of responsive regulation. A key premise is that dynamic regulatory efforts should begin at the base of the pyramid, with the most restorative, dialogue-based remedies available. When a regulatory incident occurs, affected parties should have 'an opportunity to discuss how they have been hurt by it, their needs, and what might be done to repair the harm and prevent recurrence' (Braithwaite 2011, p. 485). In discussing motivation, Braithwaite (2011, p. 497) argues that the regulatee, rather than the regulator, should 'voice the arguments for change' and develop the 'change plan'. To effect this change, the regulator should 'listen with empathy, minimize resistance, and nurture hope and optimism'. Most of the regulatory action can fall within a 'pyramid of supports' for compliance and continuous improvement. This strengths-based pyramid seeks to try one strategy after another that might further build strengths on a foundation achieved at lower levels of the pyramid. Regulators should not rush to enforcement solutions to problems. Only if the supportive 'carrot' measures fail, should regulators move up the 'pyramid of sanctions' to increasingly more demanding, coercive, or punitive interventions, culminating in the biggest 'stick' at the apex. The knowledge that escalated enforcement is the consequence of non-compliance should be sufficient to drive down most of the regulatory action towards the lower levels of the pyramid. Indeed, the paradox of responsive regulation is that by having the capability to escalate to tough enforcement, most regulation can be about 'collaborative capacity building' (Braithwaite 2011, p. 475). It is also worth noting that compliance is more likely as responsive regulation strategies are generally viewed as more legitimate and procedurally fair.

There are numerous areas of drugs policing where responsive regulation is either currently observable or potentially applicable. One of the most obvious is alternatives to arrest and prosecution for minor cannabis offences. In England and Wales, for example, the approach to cannabis possession for personal use is generally guided by a policy of escalation: people found in possession are issued a cannabis warning for their first offence, a fine for their second, and face the possibility of arrest if caught for a third time (Monaghan and Bewley-Taylor 2013b; Lloyd, this volume). Visible in this example is the limited application of responsive regulation in that it has a pyramid of sanctions but no opportunity for dialogue or support. A fuller package of regulatory mechanisms is discernible in diversion schemes that aim to minimise the harmful effects of criminal justice interventions and provide opportunities to address drug use/offending through education, treatment, and social services. In Australia, police diversion programmes are a well-utilised policy intervention for cannabis offences. Hughes and Ritter (2008) identify two main mechanisms of cannabis diversion: cannabis cautioning and cannabis expiation. The former involves an 'on the street' formal caution, provision of educational information, and optional referral to an education session or brief intervention. The latter provides offenders with opportunities to avoid a criminal record through the payment of an expiation fee.

Another example that bears the hallmarks of responsive regulation is Checkpoint, a 'deferred prosecution' scheme operating in Durham Constabulary (Weir et al. 2021). Durham's diversion scheme engages low-level offenders – including anyone caught in possession of drugs and users who commit acquisitive crimes or sell drugs to fund their addiction – entering the criminal justice system and offers them an alternative to prosecution. The scheme targets the reasons why people commit crime by assessing their individual needs to provide tailored interventions that support their recovery and desistance. These interventions harness the expertise of partner agencies in tackling the social determinants of crime. Independent 'navigators' are employed as case managers. They complete the needs assessment, agree a 'contract to engage' following dialogue with the subject – the 'change plan' (Braithwaite 2011) – and provide them with practical and emotional support. Completion of Checkpoint results in an exit from the criminal justice system and no criminal conviction. If subjects reoffend or do not engage while on the programme, they are subject to a pyramid of sanctions that culminates in prosecution. From a harm reduction perspective, however, a criticism of deferred prosecution schemes is that they are overly reliant on mechanisms of coercion. Grounded in theories of deterrence, this model of diversion is built around the idea that the threat and certainty of punishment can act as an incentive for compliance. Coerced treatment is widely considered to be both unethical and less effective (Stevens 2012), so care needs to be taken to encourage and provide routes into engagement with services, while not alienating people from them by use of threats. This was one of the reasons why Thames Valley Police developed their own diversion pilot for people caught in possession of drugs, which allows for pre-arrest diversion, makes the process of referral voluntary, and does not require an admission of guilt (Spyt et al. 2019; Spyt and Kew, this volume).

A comparable model of diversion from the United States is Law Enforcement Assisted Diversion (LEAD), which originated in Seattle but has since been rolled out in many other jurisdictions. LEAD is a pre-booking, whole system approach to diverting people who would otherwise be arrested on misdemeanour charges into a community-based intervention that is guided by harm reduction principles (Beckett 2016; Perrone et al. 2022). Meaningful involvement of persons with lived experience is core to the local approach. Like Durham's Checkpoint, case managers work closely with participants to create an individual intervention plan that is tailored to people's particular needs and goals, which might include support with treatment, housing, education, job training, transportation, childcare, or other services. LEAD protocol does not authorise any sanctions for non-compliance though, as bringing charges might undermine therapeutic progress. Beckett et al. (this volume) describe the recent evolution of the LEAD model, whereby police no longer serve as gate-keepers, service provision has been enhanced, and there is greater access to medication-assisted treatment and health care more generally.

With regard to drug supply, Caulkins and Reuter (2009, p. 16) suggest that a harm reduction approach to regulating market-related harms 'seeks to push or mould the market into less harmful distribution practices'. Put differently, policing should focus on the characteristics of drug markets that are causing the most problems to communities. An intervention that might be employed to achieve this form of market regulation is the 'focused deterrence' or 'pulling levers' strategy (Braga et al. 2018; Kennedy and Wong 2012). Pioneered in Boston as a problem-oriented policing project to halt serious gang violence during the 1990s, the basic principles of the focused deterrence approach have also been applied to overt drug market problems and repeat offending by drug using probationers. In the 'High Point model' (Kennedy and Wong 2012), for example, which has been rolled out as the 'drug market intervention' strategy, the process starts with dialogue between law enforcement and members of the community in order to address the 'norms and narrative' of each group. Police officers gather sufficient evidence to prosecute targeted drug dealers, 'bank' the cases, and then show the individuals in question that they will face swift and certain punishment unless they change their criminal behaviour. The next stage of the intervention is the 'call-in'. Targeted individuals are invited to attend a meeting at which the police, service providers, community, and family members explain the purpose of the intervention and deliver a clear message about what behaviours are liable to receive a more punitive response. Defining the problems together – which often includes racial conflict between the public and the police – and considering harms to all parties provide a platform for developing coordinated action to deal with the issues through 'collaborative capacity building' (Braithwaite 2011).

In much the same way as deferred prosecution schemes, however, focused deterrence strategies can be criticised for relying primarily on enforcement and the threat of punishment. Vitale (2017) argues that the supports offered tend to be limited and do little to create real opportunities for people. Instead, they reinforce 'an ethos of "personal responsibility" that often ends up blaming the victims for their unemployment and educational failure in communities that are poor, under-serviced, segregated, and dangerous' (p. 168). Such observations can take us back to the risk environment framework, which is predicated on a critique of responses that over-rely on individual behaviour change. By recognising the limitations of interventions that fail to account for structural factors external to targeted individuals, this stresses the need for regulatory policing measures to be more responsive to environmental determinants of harm in order to create and enhance enabling environments for harm reduction.

Conclusion: barriers, facilitators, and the expansion of harm reduction policing

This chapter has detailed the model of harm reduction policing by tracing its origins and drawing on pertinent theoretical perspectives to understand and inform its contemporary standing. Various international examples of harm reduction policing operating in practice have also been cited. To date, however, the application of harm reduction has only been realised to a limited extent in response to drug use, drug markets, and efforts to control them through the criminal justice system. Despite the theoretical potential, emerging evidence of its benefits, and arguable moral imperative, there are barriers to wider implementation that need to be overcome. To conclude, we consider some of these barriers and the facilitators likely to be encountered in the development and implementation of harm reduction policing.

Police culture is regularly identified as a barrier to reform, with attempts at introducing new policies or modifying existing practices often thwarted by some of the engrained values, norms, and outlooks that permeate the world of policing (Bacon 2016; Spooner et al. 2004). Harm reduction policing requires a shift in how the police understand and make sense of drug problems, their role and impact. While there are manifest continuities with drug war mentalities and traditional patterns of enforcement, recent empirical studies indicate that cultural change is happening as police officers reflect on their experiences and engage with evidence of what works in drugs policing (Bacon 2022; Kammersgaard 2019; Krupanski 2018; Marks et al. 2017). A policy implication of these findings is that cultural change could be furthered through experiential learning and critical reflective practice approaches to police education. This could include critical reflection on the complexities of drugs policing, moral dilemmas, and perspectives on successful outcomes, as well as deliberative engagement with people with lived experience of drug problems and the criminal justice system. Such an approach to education could help tackle stigma and challenge institutional myths and misconceptions, breaking down some of the potential cultural resistance to forms of drugs policing less familiar to officers. Police understanding and uptake of practices that are more congruent with harm reduction can also be facilitated through relevant harm reduction training (Khorasheh et al. 2019).

The structural conditions of police organisations also require change to foster and facilitate harm reduction policing. As outlined throughout this chapter, policing is shaped by legal frameworks and drug policies. Kammersgaard (2019), for example, argues that the partial decriminalisation of drug possession that followed the introduction of drug consumption rooms in Copenhagen enabled a shift in the logic of policing whereby people who use drugs could be more readily perceived as citizens with rights, rather than simply offenders. Structural change should also include a shift in police organisational policy and operational guidance towards strategies and tactics that are aligned with harm reduction principles. As Skogan (2008, p. 26) makes clear in relation to police reform, abstract concepts 'must be turned into lists of practical, day-to-day activities and then enshrined in enforceable orders to which officers in the field can fairly be held accountable'. Keeping this in mind would appear essential if attempts at introducing harm reduction policing are to be meaningful and enduring. Finally, another practical challenge is developing new performance measures that value harm reduction, remove the emphasis on criminal justice outputs, and incentivise officers to adapt their practices. As Bear (2016) has shown, the lure of traditional measures of drugs policing success such as arrests and seizures can (re)produce drug harms and damage community relations. Instead, more fruitful measurable outcomes might include lives saved through overdose prevention, the number of police referrals to community health and social services, and public satisfaction with policing interventions.

Much the same could be said about the wider political environment in which the police operate. Political actors often expect the police to act in particular ways in response to drugs. For this reason, 'any police reform efforts will likely fail unless key political actors are supportive for long enough to allow change to take hold' (Herbert et al. 2018, p. 1493). Harm reduction has been subject to considerable political debate. It has also been criticised as condoning dangerous or morally wrong behaviour by prohibitionists, as well as those who advocate abstention. Such a view has raised concerns that accepting that drug use will occur will encourage use by undermining the social signal of prohibition. There is anxiety that harm reduction 'may "enable" drug use and keep people stuck within a pattern of addiction' (Hunt 2003, p. 7). There have also been concerns that harm reduction policy and practice may operate as a 'Trojan horse' for legalisation (pp. 8–9). Any signs of the police not acting in accordance with the politically charged position of prohibition therefore potentially renders them vulnerable to critique. Yet, as has been demonstrated since its original formulation, not only can harm reduction prove lifesaving for individuals and invaluable for communities and society, but it is also possible for it to function successfully within the framework of prohibition. At national and local levels, bravery is required from political actors who are prepared to resist the temptation of scoring easy political points by superficially posturing as being 'tough on drugs' and instead support efforts to genuinely reduce drug harms (Jones and Twomey, this volume).

Finally, it is important to recognise that any police efforts to reduce drug-related harms are fundamentally limited. These arise from a complex web of social factors that are far beyond the ability of the police to address on their own. For all of its potential, harm reduction policing does not hold all of the answers and nor should it be suggested otherwise. Even if the various barriers in the way of its successful implementation are overcome, drug-related harms will still exist. Drawing on arguments made in the realist criminological literature (e.g. Matthews 2014), pursuing harm reduction policing could be considered as a pragmatic option for what *can* be done to deal with contemporary drug problems, but also what *must* be done both now and in the future to reduce drug harms and help to deliver positive change. But it is crucial that harm reduction policing and those engaged in it do not set themselves up for failure by over-promising. The continued presence of drug-related harms where forms of harm reduction policing are pursued should not be interpreted as evidence of its failure. Similarly, examples of the pursuit of harm reduction policing should not be considered 'enough' of a response to drug problems. Instead, harm reduction policing should be viewed as just one piece of a much larger societal puzzle. Only structural changes can alleviate many of the serious drug-related harms that nations around the world currently face. In the meantime, the best the police can do is to organise themselves in ways that minimise harms they might generate, avoid impeding measures aimed at addressing drug-related harms, and actively facilitate interventions that reduce them.

References

Aldridge, J., Garius, L., Spicer, J., Harris, M., Moore, K. and Eastwood, N. (2021) *Drugs in the Time of COVID: The UK Drug Market Response to Lockdown Restrictions*. London: Release.

Alexander, M. (2010) *The New Jim Crow: Mass Incarceration in the Age of Colorblindness*. New York: The New Press.

Atuesta, L. and Ponce, A. (2017) 'Meet the Narco: Increased competition among criminal organisations and the explosion of violence in Mexico'. *Global Crime*. 18(4): 375–402.

Ayres, I. and Braithwaite, J. (1992) *Responsive Regulation: Transcending the Deregulation Debate*. Oxford: Oxford University Press.

Babor, T., Caulkins, J., Edwards, G., Fischer, B., Foxcroft, D., Humphreys, K., Obot, I., Rehm, J., Reuter, P., Room, R., Rossow, I. and Strang, J. (2010) *Drug Policy and the Public Good*. Oxford: Oxford University Press.

Bacon, M. (2016) *Taking Care of Business: Police Detectives, Drug Law Enforcement and Proactive Investigation*. Oxford: Oxford University Press

Bacon, M. (2022) 'Desistance from criminalisation: Police culture and new directions in drugs policing'. *Policing and Society*. 32(4): 522–539.

Baker, P., Beletsky, L., Avalos, L., Venegas, C., Rivera, C., Strathdee, S. and Cepeda, J. (2020) 'Policing practices and risk of HIV infection among people who inject drugs'. *Epidemiologic Reviews*. 42(1): 27–40.

Bear, D. (2016) 'The need to create a narrative: Examining justifications police used to target drugs in the led up to the 2011 London riots'. *Police Practice and Research*. 17(4): 317–328.

Beckett, K. (2016) 'The uses and abuses of police discretion: Toward harm reduction policing'. *Harvard Law and Policy Review*. 10: 77–100.

Beckett, K. (2022) *Ending Mass Incarceration: Why it Persists and How to Achieve Meaningul Reform*. Oxford: Oxford University Press.

Berridge, V. (1993) 'Harm minimization and public health: A historical perspective'. In Heather, N., Wodak, A., Nadelmann, E. and O'Hare, P. (eds.) *Psychoactive Drugs and Harm Reduction: From Faith and Science*. London: Whurr Publishers: 55–64.

Berridge, V. (1996) *AIDS in the UK: The Making of Policy, 1981–1994*. Oxford: Oxford University Press.

Bewley-Taylor, D. (2012) *International Drug Control: Consensus Fractured*. Cambridge: Cambridge University Press.

Black, J. (2002) 'Critical reflections on regulation'. *Australian Journal of Legal Philosophy*. 27(1): 1–36.

Blaustein, J., McLay, M. and McCulloch, J. (2017) 'Secondary harm mitigation: A more humanitarian framework for international drug law enforcement'. *International Journal of Drug Policy*. 46: 66–73.

Bowling, B., Reiner, R. and Sheptycki, J. (2019) *The Politics of the Police*. 5th edn. Oxford: Oxford University Press.

Braga, A., Weisburd, D. and Turchan, B. (2018) 'Focused deterrence strategies and crime control: An updated systematic review and meta-analysis of the empirical evidence'. *Criminology and Public Policy*. 17(1): 205–250.

Braithwaite, J. (2011) 'The essence of responsive regulation'. *University of British Columbia Law Review*. 44(3): 475–520.

Burris, S., Blankenship, K., Donoghoe, M., Sherman, S., Vernick, J., Case, P., Lazzarini, Z. and Koester, S. (2004) 'Addressing the "risk environment" for injection drug users': The mysterious case of the missing cop. *Milbank Quarterly*. 82(1): 125–156.

Canty, C., Sutton, A. and James, S. (2000) 'Models of community-based drug law enforcement'. *Police Policy and Research*. 2(3): 171–187.

Caulkins, J. and Reuter, P. (2009) 'Towards a harm-reduction approach to enforcement'. *Safer Communities*. 8(1): 9–23.

Caulkins, J. and Reuter, P. (2017) 'Dealing more effectively and humanely with illegal drugs'. *Crime and Justice*. 46(1): 95–158.

Cloud, D. and Davis, C. (2015) *First Do No Harm: Advancing Public Health in Policing*. New York: Vera Institute.

Collison, M. (1995) *Police, Drugs and Community*. London: Free Association Books.

Colson, R. and Bergeron, H. (eds.) (2017) *European Drug Policies: The Ways of Reform*. Abingdon: Routledge.

Cristiano, N. (2020) *Managing Risk Environments: An Ethnographic Study of Club Drug Use and Harm Reduction in the EDM Scene*. Toronto: York University.

Csete, J., Kamarulzaman, A., Kazatchkine, M., Altice, F., Balicki, M., Buxton, J., Cepeda, J., Comfort, M., Goosby, E., Goulão, J., Hart, C., Horton, R., Kerr, T., Madrazo Lajous, A., Lewis, S., Martin, N., Mejía, D., Mathiesson, D., Obot, I., Ogunrombi, A., Sherman, S., Stone, J., Vallath, N., Vickerman, P., Zábranský, T. and Beyrer, C. (2016) 'Public health and international drug policy'. *The Lancet*. 387(10026): 1427–1480.

Curtis, R. and Wendel, T. (2007) '"You're always training the dog": Strategic interventions to reconfigure drug markets'. *Journal of Drug Issues*. 37(4): 867–891.

Dorn, N. and South, N. (1990) 'Drug markets and law enforcement'. *British Journal of Criminology*. 30(2): 171–188.

Erickson, P. (1995) 'Harm reduction: What it is and is not'. *Drug and Alcohol Review*. 14(3): 283–285.

Erickson, P., Riley, D., Cheung, Y. and O'Hare, P. (eds.) (1997) *Harm Reduction: A New Direction for Drug Policies and Programs*. Toronto: University of Toronto Press.

Erickson, P., Riley, D., Cheung, Y. and O'Hare, P. (1997) 'Introduction: The search for harm reduction'. In Erickson, P., Riley, D., Cheung, Y. and O'Hare, P. (eds.) *Harm Reduction: A New Direction for Drug Policies and Programs*. Toronto: University of Toronto Press: 3–14.

Fisher, H. and Measham, F. (2018) *Night Lives: Reducing Drug-Related Harm in the Night Time Economy*. London: Volteface.

Goldstein, H. (1979) 'Improving policing: A problem-oriented approach'. *Crime and Delinquency*. 25(2): 236–258.

Green, T., Grau, L., Blinnikova, K., Torban, M., Krupitsky, E., Ilyuk, R., Kozlov, A. and Heimer, R. (2009) 'Social and structural aspects of the overdose risk environment in St. Petersburg, Russia'. *International Journal of Drug Policy*. 20(3): 270–276.

Grigg, J., Barratt, M. and Lenton, S. (2018) 'Drug detection dogs at Australian outdoor music festivals: Deterrent, detection and iatrogenic effects'. *International Journal of Drug Policy*. 60: 89–95.

Hall, W. (2018) 'The future of the international drug control system and national drug prohibitions'. *Addiction*. 113(7): 1210–1223.

Harm Reduction International. (2022) *What is Harm Reduction?* Available from: https://www.hri.global/what-is-harm-reduction.

Hathaway, A. (2001) 'Shortcomings of harm reduction: Toward a morally invested drug reform strategy'. *International Journal of Drug Policy*. 12(2): 125–137.

Heather, N., Wodak, A., Nadelmann, E. and O'Hare, P. (eds.) (1993) *Psychoactive Drugs and Harm Reduction: From Faith to Science*. London: Whurr Publishers.

Herbert, S., Beckett, K. and Stuart, F. (2018) 'Policing social marginality: Contrasting approaches'. *Law and Social Inquiry*. 43(4): 1491–1513.

Hillyard, P., Pantazis, C., Tombs, S. and Gordon, D. (eds.) (2004) *Beyond Criminology: Taking Harm Seriously*. London: Pluto.

HM Government. (2017) *An Evaluation of the Government's Drug Strategy 2010*. London: HM Government.

Houborg, E., Frank, V. and Bjerge, B. (2014) 'From zero tolerance to non-enforcement: Creating a new space for drugs policing in Copenhagen, Denmark'. *Contemporary Drug Problems*. 41(2): 261–291.

Hughes, C., Moxham-Hall, V., Ritter, A., Weatherburn, D. and MacCoun, R. (2017) 'The deterrent effects of Australian street-level drug law enforcement on illicit drug offending at outdoor music festivals'. *International Journal of Drug Policy*. 41: 91–100.

Hughes, C. and Ritter, A. (2008) *A Summary of Diversion Programs for Drug and Drug-Related Offenders in Australia*. Sydney: National Drug and Alcohol Research Centre.

Hunt, N., Ashton, M., Lenton, S., Mitcheson, L., Nelles, B. and Stimson, G. (2003) *A Review of the Evidence-Base for Harm Reduction Approaches to Drug Use*. London: Forward Thinking on Drugs.

Johnson, D. and Fernquest, J. (2018) 'Governing through killing: The war on drugs in the Philippines'. *Asian Journal of Law and Society*. 5(2): 359–390.

Kammersgaard, T. (2019) 'Harm reduction policing: From drug law enforcement to protection'. *Contemporary Drug Problems*. 46(4): 345–362.

Keane, H. (2003) 'Critiques of harm reduction, morality and the promise of harm rights'. *International Journal of Drug Policy*. 14(3): 227–232.

Kennedy, D. and Wong, S. (2012) *The High Point Drug Market Intervention Strategy*. Washington, DC: US Department of Justice, Office of Community Oriented Policing.

Kerr, T., Small, W. and Wood, E. (2005) 'The public health and social impacts of drug market enforcement: A review of the evidence'. *International Journal of Drug Policy*. 16(4): 210–220.

Khorasheh, T., Naraine, R., Watson, T., Write, A., Kallio, N. and Strike, C. (2019) 'A scoping review of harm reduction training for police officers'. *Drug and Alcohol Review*. 38(2): 131–150.

King, N. (2020) 'Harm reduction: A misnomer'. *Health Care Analysis*. 28(4): 324–334.

Krupanski, M. (2018) *Police and Harm Reduction*. New York: Open Society Foundations.

Larasati, A. and Girelli, G. (2021) *The Death Penalty for Drug Offences: Global Overview 2020*. London: Harm Reduction International.

Lenton, S. and Single, E. (1998) 'The definition of harm reduction'. *Drug and Alcohol Review*. 17(2): 213–220.

Lessing, B. (2018) *Making Peace in Drug Wars: Crackdowns and Cartels in Latin America*. New York: Cambridge University Press.

Loader, I. (2020) *Revisiting the Police Mission*. London: Police Foundation.

MacCoun, R. and Reuter, P. (2001) *Drug War Heresies – Learning From Other Vices, Times and Places*. Cambridge: Cambridge University Press.

Maher, L. and Dixon, D. (1999) 'Policing and public health: Law enforcement and harm minimization in a street-level drug market'. *British Journal of Criminology*. 39(4): 488–512.

Manning, P. (1997) *Police Work: The Social Organization of Policing*. 2nd edn. Prospect Heights, IL: Waveland Press.

Manning, P. (2004) *The Narcs' Game: Organizational and Informational Limits on Drug Law Enforcement*. 2nd edn. Cambridge, MA: MIT Press.

Marks, M., Howell, S. and Shelly, S. (2017) 'The fluidity of "police culture": Encountering the contextual complexity of policing street-level drug use'. *Policing*. 113(3): 318–331.

Matthews, R. (2014) *Realist Criminology*. Basingstoke: Palgrave Macmillan.

Mazerolle, L., Soole, D. and Rombouts, S. (2007) 'Drug law enforcement: A review of the evaluation literature'. *Policing Quarterly*. 10(2): 115–153.

Mazerolle, L., Eggins, E. and Higginson, A. (2020) 'Street-level drug law enforcement: An updated systematic review'. *Trends & Issues in Crime and Criminal Justice* (No. 599). Canberra: Australian Institute of Criminology.

Mayock, P., Cronly, J. and Clatts, C. (2015) 'The risk environment of heroin user initiation: Young women, intimate partners, and "drug relationships"'. *Substance Use and Misuse*. 50(6): 771–782.

McLean, K. (2016) '"There's nothing here": Deindustrialization as risk environment for overdose'. *International Journal of Drug Policy*. 29: 19–26.

Measham, M. and Turnbull, G. (2021) 'Intentions, actions and outcomes: A follow up survey on harm reduction practices after using an English festival drug checking service'. *International Journal of Drug Policy*. 95: 103270.

Moeller, K. and Hessee, M. (2013) 'Drug market disruption and systemic violence: Cannabis markets in Copenhagen'. *European Journal of Criminology*. 10(2): 206–221.

Monaghan, G. and Bewley-Taylor, D. (2013a) *Police Support for Harm Reduction Policies and Practices Towards People Who Inject Drugs*. London: International Drug Policy Consortium.

Monaghan, G. and Bewley-Taylor, D. (2013b) *Practical Implications for Policing Alternatives to Arrest and Prosecution for Minor Cannabis Offences*. London: International Drug Policy Consortium.

Murji, K. (1998) *Policing Drugs*. Aldershot: Ashgate.

Nadelmann, E. (1992) 'Thinking seriously about alternatives to drug prohibition'. *Dædalus*. 121(3): 85–132.

Nadelmann, E. (1993) 'Progressive legalizers, progressive prohibitionists and the reduction of drug-related harm'. In Heather, N., Wodak, A., Nadelmann, E. and O'Hare, P. (eds.) *Psychoactive Drugs and Harm Reduction: From Faith to Science*. London: Whurr Publishers: 34–45.

Newcombe, R. (1987) 'High time for harm reduction'. *Druglink*. 2(1): 10–11.

Newcombe, R. (1992) 'The reduction of drug-related harm: A conceptual framework for theory, practice and research'. In O'Hare, P., Newcombe, R., Matthews, A., Buning, E. and Drucker, E. (eds.) *The Reduction of Drug-Related Harm*. London: Routledge: 1–14.

O'Hare, P., Newcombe, R., Matthews, A., Buning, E. and Drucker, E. (eds.) (1992) *The Reduction of Drug-Related Harm*. London: Routledge.

Parker, C. and Braithwaite, J. (2003) 'Regulation'. In Cane, P. and Tushnet, J. (eds.) *Oxford Handbook of Legal Studies*. Oxford: Oxford University Press: 119–145.

Pearson, G. (1992) 'Drugs and criminal justice: A harm reduction perspective'. In O'Hare, P., Newcombe, R., Matthews, A., Buning, E. and Drucker, E. (eds.) *The Reduction of Drug-Related Harm*. London: Routledge: 15–29.

Pemberton, S. (2015) *Harmful Societies: Understanding Social Harm*. Bristol: Policy Press.

Perrone, D. (2009) *The High Life: Club Kids, Harm and Drug Policy*. Monsey, NY: Criminal Justice Press.

Perrone, D., Malm, A. and Magaña, E. (2022) 'Harm reduction policing: An evaluation of Law Enforcement Assisted Diversion (LEAD) in San Francisco'. *Police Quarterly*. 25(1): 7–32.

Pollack, H. and Reuter, P. (2014) 'Does tougher enforcement make drugs more expensive?' *Addiction*. 109(2): 1959–1966.

Reuter, P. (2009) 'Ten years after the United Nations General Assembly Special Session (UNGASS): Assessing drug problems, policies and reform proposals'. *Addiction*. 104(4): 510–517.

Rhodes, T. (2002) 'The "risk environment": A framework for understanding and reducing drug-related harm'. *International Journal of Drug Policy*. 13(2): 85–94.

Rhodes, T., Lilly, R., Fernandez, C., Giorgino, E., Kemmesis, U., Ossebaard, H., Lalam, N., Faasen, I. and Spannow, K. (2003) 'Risk factors associated with drug use: The importance of "risk environment"'. *Drugs: Education, Prevention and Policy*. 10(4): 303–329.

Ritter, A. (2010) 'Illicit drug policy through the lens of regulation'. *International Journal of Drug Policy*. 21(4): 265–270.

Ritter, A. and Cameron, J. (2006) 'A review of the efficacy and effectiveness of harm reduction strategies for alcohol, tobacco and illicit drugs'. *Drug and Alcohol Review*. 25(6): 611–624.

Roe, G. (2005) 'Harm reduction as paradigm: Is better than bad good enough? The origins of harm reduction'. *Critical Public Health*. 15(3): 243–250.

Rolles, S. (2020) 'The rise and fall of the "drug free world" narrative'. In Bewley-Taylor, D. and Tinasti, K. (eds.) *Research Handbook on International Drug Policy*. Cheltenham: Edward Elgar: 206–224.

Rolles, S., Murkin, G., Powell, M., Kushlick, D., Saunter, N. and Slater, J. (2016) *The Alternative World Drug Report: Counting the Costs of the War on Drugs*. 2nd edn. Bristol: Transform Drug Policy Foundation.

Seddon, T. (2010) *A History of Drugs: Drugs and Freedom in the Liberal Age*. London: Routledge.

Seddon, T. (2020) 'Markets, regulation and drug law reform: Towards a constitutive approach'. *Social and Legal Studies*. 29(3): 313–333.

Seddon, T. and Floodgate, W. (2020) *Regulating Cannabis: A Global Review and Future Directions*. London: Palgrave.

Selfridge, M., Greer, A., Card, K., Macdonald, S. and Pauly, B. (2020) '"It's like super structural" – Overdose experiences of youth who use drugs and police in three non-metropolitan cities across British Columbia. *International Journal of Drug Policy*. 76: 102623.

Sherman, L. (2007) 'The power few hypothesis: Experimental criminology and the reduction of harm'. *Journal of Experimental Criminology*. 3(4): 299–321.

Shiner, M., Carre, Z., Delsol, R. and Eastwood, N. (2018) *The Colour of Injustice: 'Race', Drugs and Law Enforcement in England and Wales*. London: Stopwatch.

Skogan, W. (2008) 'Why reforms fail'. *Policing and Society*. 18(1): 23–34.

Small, W., Kerr, T., Charette, J., Schechter, M. and Spittal, P. (2006) 'Impacts of intensified police activity on injection drug users: Evidence from an ethnographic investigation'. *International Journal of Drug Policy*. 17(2): 85–95.

Spicer, J. (2021) *Policing County Lines: Responses to Evolving Provisional Drug Markets*. London: Palgrave.

Spooner, C., McPherson, M. and Hall, W. (2004) *The Role of Police in Preventing and Minimising Illicit Drug Use and Its Harms*. Sydney: National Drug and Alcohol Research Centre.

Spyt, W., Barnham, L. and Kew, J. (2019) 'Diversion: Going soft on drugs?' *Thames Valley Police Journal*. 4: 44–58.

Stevens, A. (2012) 'The ethics and effectiveness of coerced treatment of people who use drugs'. *Human Rights and Drugs*. 2(1): 7–16.

Stevens, A. (2013) *Modernising Drug Law Enforcement: Applying Harm Reduction Principles to the Policing of Retail Drug Markets*. London: International Drug Policy Consortium.

Stevens, A. (2017) 'Principles, pragmatism and prohibition: Explaining continuity and change in British drug policy'. In Liebling, A., Maruna, S. and McAra, L. (eds.) *Oxford Handbook of Criminology*. Oxford: Oxford University Press: 825–845.

Stevens, A. (2019) '"Being human" and the "moral sidestep" in drug policy: Explaining government inaction on opioid-related deaths in the UK'. *Addictive Behaviors*. 90: 444–450.

Stevens, A., Hughes, C., Hulme, S. and Cassidy, R. (2022) 'Depenalization, diversion and decriminalization: A realist review and programme theory of alternatives to criminalization for simple drug possession'. *European Journal of Criminology*. 19(1): 29–54.

Strathdee, S., Beletsky, L. and Kerr, T. (2015) 'HIV, drugs and the legal environment'. *International Journal of Drug Policy*. 26: 27–32.

Szasz, T. (1974) *Ceremonial Chemistry: The Ritual Persecution of Drugs, Addicts and Pushers*. Garden City, NY: Doubleday.

UKDPC. (2009) *Refocusing Drug-Related Law Enforcement to Address Harms*. London: UK Drug Policy Commission.

van Dijk, A., Herrington, V., Crofts, N., Breunig, R., Burris, S., Sullivan, H., Middleton, J., Sherman, S. and Thomson, N. (2019) 'Law enforcement and public health: Recognition and enhancement of joined-up solutions'. *The Lancet*. 393(10168): 287–294.

Vitale, A. (2017) *The End of Policing*. London: Verso.

Watson, T., Bayoumi, A., Hopkins, S., Wright, A., Naraine, R., Khorasheh, T., Callacombe, L. and Strike, C. (2018) 'Creating and sustaining cooperative relationships between supervised injection services and police: A qualitative interview study of international stakeholders'. *International Journal of Drug Policy*. 61: 1–6.

Weir, K., Kilili, S., Cooper, J., Crowe, A. and Routledge, G. (2021) 'Checkpoint: An innovative programme to navigate people away from the cycle of reoffending – A randomised control trial evaluation'. *The Police Journal*. https://doi.org/10.1177/0032258X211018774.

Werb, D., Rowell, G., Guyatt, G., Kerr, T., Montaner, J. and Wood, E. (2011) 'Effect of drug law enforcement on drug market violence: A systematic review'. *International Journal of Drug Policy*. 22(2): 87–94.

Werb, D., Kerr, T., Nosyk, B., Strathdee, S., Montaner, J. and Wood, E. (2013) 'The temporal relationship between drug supply indicators: An audit of international government surveillance systems'. *BMJ Open*. 3(9): 1–8.

2

MORE HARM THAN GOOD

A review of the English language literature on the policing of drug possession

Charlie Lloyd

Background

In some respects, drug possession offences can appear trivial. Unlike many other offences, there is no victim directly associated with drug possession and therefore no plaintiff to report the offence. The very common and widespread use of cannabis (the possession of which makes up the large majority of possession offences) also means that its use is, to some degree, normalised and carries less stigma compared to other drugs (e.g. Hathaway et al. 2011). Furthermore, policy changes over the past 20 years in the United Kingdom and elsewhere have tended to move in the direction of downgrading the significance of drug possession offences; from legalisation in a number of US states, to attempts to deprioritise possession offences and divert offenders from the criminal justice system (CJS).

However, in other respects, drug possession offences – and the policing of them – have particular significance. Firstly, such offences are extremely common and therefore a high-volume crime. Cannabis is by far the most widely used illicit drug in England and Wales, with an estimated 2.6 million people doing so in 2019/2020. Extrapolation from survey estimates of frequency of use suggests that the number of occasions of cannabis use to be of the order of 140 million per year (ONS 2020a; b). Thus, the 'true' figure of (predominantly unrecorded) cannabis possession offences is very large indeed, making possession of this Class B drug one of the most commonly occurring notifiable offences in England and Wales, if not the most common. While the risk of a person in possession of a controlled drug being arrested is therefore very small (Caulkins and Reuter 2009; Nguyen and Reuter 2012), recorded drug possession offences are nonetheless still quite common in comparison to many other individual offences (165,450 offences in England and Wales in 2020–2021, ONS 2021).

DOI: 10.4324/9781003154136-3

The low proportion of drug users caught in possession, combined with the street-level location of most offences that come to light, has meant that there is a particularly high level of discretion in drug possession cases – even where effort has been made to structure such discretion through the use of detailed guidance. This means that young people, who tend to spend more time in public spaces, are often picked up for possession offences, with such encounters frequently representing their first enforcement contact with the police. As Warburton et al. point out, 'Mishandled, cannabis policing could alienate significant sections of the population, especially the young' (2005, p. 126). Furthermore, there have been persistently and disproportionately high rates of stop and search for suspected drug possession among Black and Minority Ethnic (BAME) groups in the United Kingdom and the United States (Beckett et al. 2005; Eastwood et al. 2013; Geller and Fagan 2010; May et al. 2007; Shiner et al. 2018): a situation that has seriously affected relations between the police and Black communities.

Thus, there are many reasons to focus on the policing of drug possession, and in England and Wales, there has been a particularly strong focus on the policing of cannabis possession, which has been subject to three different sets of guidance over the 2000s, each in response to amended or new legislation. This policy ferment and the unremitting coverage of the issue in the media over this period (Lloyd 2010) – recently resurfacing in discussions of stop and search (Guardian 2021), medicinal cannabis products (BBC News 2021), and legalisation in North America (BBC News 2019) – have undoubtedly been related to the potential for cannabis possession to be ultimately decriminalised in the United Kingdom. Part of the importance of the topic of policing drug possession therefore relates to its potential to either erode or shore-up the current system of drug prohibition. This makes it a highly sensitive issue in many countries, with many claims and counterclaims, and therefore one where, arguably, the evidence base should be examined particularly thoroughly.

It is therefore somewhat surprising that there has been limited research focused exclusively on the policing of drug possession. A substantial body of work has looked at the policing of drug markets (see Mazerolle et al. 2007), with a smaller body of detailed ethnographic work on drug squads (see Bacon 2016; Spicer 2021). However, the author is unaware of any previous review that has attempted to bring together the literature on policing drug possession. There is therefore considerable need for such a review.

Aims

The central aim of this review was to bring together the English language research undertaken on the policing of drug possession. Once begun, two things quickly became clear. First, as stated above, no such review had been undertaken previously. Second, there were definitional issues surrounding what counted as a study of the policing of drug possession. Many studies have been undertaken of policing, one element of which has involved the policing of drug possession offences. To make this review relevant and manageable, only studies that had a main focus on drug possession policing were included The most difficult area to make this differentiation was the large body of work on 'crackdowns', where the police frequently made arrests for possession as part of their attempts to disrupt drug markets. This review touches on this literature in a proportionate manner – i.e. to the degree that it focuses on policing possession – but it does not provide a full review of the wider impacts of police crackdowns, which have been reviewed elsewhere (Kerr et al. 2005). Also excluded despite partial relevance were those studies referred to earlier on specialist drug police agencies ('drug squads'). These have been reviewed by Bacon (2016) and concentrate on the proactive policing of *supply*. A further exclusion has been the sizeable body of work on drug referral and diversionary programmes either at street level or in custody suites. Treatment referral from police custody has been reviewed elsewhere (Mazerolle et al. 2007) and police referral is covered elsewhere in this volume (see Anderson and Shefner, this volume; Beckett et al. 2005; Kammersgaard 2019; Spyt and Kew, this volume). Lastly, the fact that cannabis policing lies at the heart of the ongoing debate about the role of the state in controlling psychoactive substances means that there is a much wider literature on the legalisation and decriminalisation of cannabis around the world. However, unless explicitly focused on the implications for policing possession, such commentaries have not been included here.

Methods

Systematic searches of the Medline, ASSAI, Web of Science, and PsychINFO databases were carried out in April 2021. Titles and abstracts were read for potential relevance and copies of papers were obtained where relevant to the review focus. Further relevant articles were identified through 'snowballing' from article reference lists. A large majority of the resulting texts were peer-reviewed journal articles. However, some published reports from the United Kingdom were included, one of which was central to the aims of this review (May et al. 2007).

Fifty-five relevant papers and published reports were read and detailed notes taken. While these have provided the main focus, the author has chosen not to be hamstrung by this process. Where the review has raised questions that relate to fundamental policing issues, such as deterrence and discretion, forays were made into these literatures to make links with broader themes.

The themes below that structure the findings from these studies emerged from reading and re-reading the notes taken on each text and identifying links between them. The process was akin to coding qualitative data, with common themes identified and relevant sections of articles brought together for secondary analysis and assimilation into the text that follows. Again, reflecting qualitative analysis, what follows is not an exhaustive account of the identified themes – many of which overlapped in terms of the studies associated within them.

Rather, it is an account of what the author identified as the most salient themes, all of which were addressed in multiple papers and reports.

The variable impacts of policy change around the world

A sizeable body of work has focused on changes in policy (whether national or local), including the introduction of policing guidance. In the United Kingdom, a number of studies and commentaries (May et al. 2002, 2006, 2007; Shiner 2015; Turnbull 2009; Warburton et al. 2005) have focused on the decision to reclassify cannabis from Class B to Class C in 2003, and then back again to Class B in 2009, and the three sets of guidance on policing cannabis that were introduced over this period by the Association of Chief Police Officers[1] (ACPO) (ACPO 2003, 2007, 2009). Two quite recently published studies focused on what has been widely referred to as 'the Lambeth Experiment', whereby police in the London borough of Lambeth ceased to arrest for cannabis possession for 13 months over 2001–2002 (Adda et al. 2014; Kelly and Rasul 2014). Studies elsewhere in the world have focused on legislative changes in Jamaica (Davenport and Pardo 2016), Mexico (Arredondo et al. 2018; Gaines et al. 2015), the United States (Geller and Fagan 2010; Johnson et al. 2008; Ross and Walker 2016; Wiens et al. 2018), Belgium (Gelders and Vander Laenen 2007), and Denmark (Houberg et al. 2016; Kammersgaard 2019; Moeller 2009).

The 'Lambeth Experiment' in London: liberating police time and reducing criminalisation

In 2000, the Independent Inquiry into the Misuse of Drugs Act produced its report (Independent Inquiry 2000), recommending that cannabis be moved from Class B to Class C under the three categories of descending harm (A, B, C) defined by the Misuse of Drugs Act (1971). This would have meant that cannabis possession would cease to be an arrestable offence. Following this report, the Metropolitan Police Service (MPS) published its own report, focusing on ways to save police time by introducing alternatives to arrest for a number of minor offences, including cannabis possession. This idea was later adopted by the police commander of the London Borough of Lambeth, Brian Paddick, in response to the high rates of violent crime in Lambeth, alongside a temporary shortage of staff (Dark and Fuller 2002). Paddick consulted officers on the potential for a cannabis warning scheme, which was implemented in 2001 in the form of 'the Lambeth Cannabis Warning Scheme' (LCWS), widely known as 'the Lambeth Experiment'. Under this initiative, people found in possession of small amounts of cannabis had their drugs confiscated and were given a formal warning, rather than being arrested – although the offence was recorded by the police. This radical change was achieved through local police policy and practice, rather than any change in legislation. The policy was initially intended to run as a six-month pilot, with the aim of reducing time spent on cannabis possession and increasing time devoted to serious offences, including Class A drug offences (Dark and Fuller 2002). Unfortunately, no independent evaluation of the initiative was commissioned and this has restricted what can be learnt from this experiment. However, the LCWS was internally evaluated and a public opinion survey was also commissioned (Dark and Fuller 2002). In more recent times, two further studies have used routinely collected data to explore the impact of the LCWS: one focusing on its impact on other recorded crime (Adda et al. 2014); the other on the impact on drug-related hospital admissions (Kelly and Rasul 2014). Only the former is covered here. This, the internal evaluation and the opinion survey are drawn on in considering the impact of the LCWS.

With regard to implementation, the internal Policy Review and Standards Consultancy Group reported that over the first six months, officers issued 450 warnings for possession, which they associated with at least 1,350 hours of liberated officer time (by avoiding arrest, custody procedures, and interviewing), equivalent to 1.8 full-time officers per annum (Dark and Fuller 2002). Data analysed by Adda et al. (2014) show that recorded cannabis offences (and therefore, presumably, warnings) increased dramatically following the announcement of a second six months of the trial: an increase that was much higher than those seen in other London boroughs. These authors state that 'our evidence strongly suggests that .... cannabis use in Lambeth increased substantially following the implementation of the LCWS' (p. 13). While this is a logical possibility, the authors appear unaware of the widespread use of informal disposals[2] reported elsewhere (May et al. 2002). Another, perhaps more plausible explanation for the increase in cannabis possession offences is that police officers simply began to record offences that they previously would not have recorded – especially when they realised that this was an ongoing initiative, rather than a one-off six-month trial. Such a possibility raises questions about the amount of police time saved. Where formal warnings (which were still quite burdensome according to Dark and Fuller 2002) replaced informal warnings, there would be an increase in police time.

The main aim of the LCWS was to reduce violent and other serious crime, through liberating police time. Drawing on the internal evaluation, Dark and Fuller (2002) report a reduction in street crime in Lambeth over the pilot period, although they also note that the concurrent 'Safer Streets' initiative could have been responsible for this. Adda et al. (2014) undertook a sophisticated time-series statistical analysis to explore the impact of the LCWS on other crimes and house prices. However, the lack of detailed information on the extent to which initiatives such as Safer Streets were successfully implemented in different boroughs, makes interpretation difficult. Moreover, it is not very clear from the available LCWS documentation exactly how the progenitors of the LCWS saw the liberation of police time from policing cannabis resulting in lower rates of serious crime. To explore such complex links, one would really need observation work on the ground and interviews with officers.

In conclusion, the LCWS represents a wasted opportunity: there was the scope to undertake a rigorous evaluation, made more robust by the fact that the experiment only took place in one borough, providing the potential for comparative evaluation. However, the experiment demonstrated the potential for the police to adopt approaches that reduced the criminalisation of those caught in possession of cannabis and saved police time.

Reclassification: full of sound and fury, signifying little

In July 2002, the new home secretary, David Blunkett, announced that cannabis would be reclassified from Class B to Class C and, finally, in January 2004, cannabis became a Class C drug. However, at the same time, the 2003 Criminal Justice Act also came into effect, which made the possession of cannabis (but no other Class C drug) an arrestable offence. The Act also increased the maximum sentence for all Class C trafficking and supply offences from 5 to 14 years – the same as the maximum for Class B offences. Therefore, despite the media furore that surrounded reclassification, the only legal difference was that the maximum sentence for possession received at the Crown Court was reduced from five to two years imprisonment and, as very few people receive prison sentences for simple cannabis possession, this was a very minor change (Lloyd 2008). The process of reclassification and the ensuing media backlash (Warburton et al. 2005) has therefore been described as 'full of sound and fury, signifying nothing' (Lloyd 2008). However, reclassification did result in significant changes on the ground, through new ACPO guidance on policing cannabis possession, including the introduction of street warnings for cannabis possession (ACPO 2003).

Some of the most detailed research on cannabis policing has been undertaken by May and colleagues (May et al. 2002, 2007). Data collected in 2000 and 2004/2005 acted as a 'before and after' design, examining the impact of reclassification (which took effect in January 2004) and the accompanying ACPO guidance. Detailed data were collected in four police divisions, within two English police forces, including observations with operational police officers, interviews with 150 police officers, and interviews with 61 young cannabis users in each study. With regard to overall impact, the authors concluded that reclassification 'had a smaller impact than advocates of the change hoped for, and than opponents feared' (May et al. 2006, p. 30). Drawing on national statistics, the authors found that the introduction of the street warning for cannabis possession in 2004 was associated with a considerable drop in cautions and convictions for cannabis possession offences: from 77,500 in 2003 to 45,490 in 2004. They estimated that there were also 36,693 street warnings in 2004, making a total of 82,183 offences: a marked increase on 2003. The authors suggest that part of this increase may have been due to offenders receiving street warnings who would otherwise have been dealt with informally. In both years, officers were asked if they had ever dealt informally with cannabis possession – i.e. got rid of the cannabis, giving the offender an informal warning, and not recording the offence.

Of the officers in 2000, 69% said that they had and 48% in 2004/2005. Thus, while street warnings certainly appear to have been substituting for cautions and convictions, there is also the likelihood that some cases previously dealt with informally were given formal street warnings (see also Shiner 2015, below).

Comparing police data across the four sites, there was considerable variation. The proportion of cases dealt with through street warnings over the 12-month period in 2004/2005 was considerably lower in Site 1 (22%) compared with the other three (37–41%). This seemed to be associated with the presence of two 'open' street-based drug markets in Site 1 and the associated policy of arresting people found in possession in these areas. In Sites 1 and 2, there was a similar total number of cannabis offences between 2000 and 2004/2005 and street warnings appeared to have substituted for cautions (which went down considerably between the two periods of time). In Sites 3 and 4, street warnings appeared to be substituting for both cautions and charges. There was also considerable variation in how offences came to light, with 56% of cases in Site 1 resulting from stop and search, compared with 5–17% in the other three sites, where cannabis possession most often came to light in the course of investigating another offence. The researchers also explored whether resources had been saved as a result of the introduction of street warnings. Using estimates of time spent on arrests versus time spent on warnings, a total of £38,000 was estimated to have been saved across the four sites over the 12-month study period, equivalent to 3,000 hours of police time.

The extent to which street warnings (which became 'cannabis warnings' in the 2007 ACPO guidance) were substituting for arrests or informal disposals was also explored by Shiner (2015), using national statistics to explore the potential 'net-widening' effect of formal warnings. The abrupt drop in cautions for cannabis possession in 2004 noted by May and colleagues (2007), plateaued out and remained at this low level until 2011. The number found guilty of an offence in court remained low over 2004–2006 but then increased back to 2003 levels over 2007–2011. However, street warnings increased dramatically over 2004–2008: from the 36,693 estimated in 2004 to over 100,000 in 2008. Shiner concludes that this dramatic increase represents net widening – i.e. the capturing of a wider set of people within the criminal justice system – partly as a consequence of the increased focus over this period on performance targets associated with 'sanction detections'. At this time, formal warnings for cannabis counted as sanction detections – offences that are detected and resolved through formal disposal. Indeed, officers in May et al.'s (2007) study reported being under considerable pressure to increase the number of street warnings in order to meet such local targets. As Turnbull (2009) has stated, the increase in street warnings over this period therefore has two possible explanations: an increased targeting of cannabis users (presumably to meet targets) or the police ceasing to use informal methods and adopting formal warnings instead. Ultimately, while it is impossible to be certain about such questions, it may well be that the rapid escalation in formal warnings stemmed from both of these processes.

There have been further policy developments in the United Kingdom since: the second reclassification of cannabis (back to Class B) and two further sets of ACPO guidance, the first taking account of the Serious Organised Crime and Police Act of 2005 and replacing 'street warnings' with 'cannabis warnings' (ACPO 2007); and the second introducing the three-point escalating response to cannabis possession that is operational at the time of writing in some police forces (ACPO 2009). The latter introduced penalty notices for disorder (PNDs) as a disposal for a second cannabis possession offence, the first offence to receive a cannabis warning and the third arrest. The author is unaware of any independent evaluations of the current guidance.

In concluding from these studies, the history of reclassification in the United Kingdom has been marked by media clamour and political drama on the one hand, and on the other, limited impact on both the legislature and on the ground. It demonstrates how, perhaps particularly in the United Kingdom, cannabis has served as a totem for legalisers and prohibitionists alike, with a lot of heated debate but surprisingly little actual change. The Lambeth Experiment has shown how the fraught, central government politics of drug policy change can be side-stepped by the application of quite radical approaches at the local level.

Radical policy changes in the United States: racial disproportionality in enforcement and the promise of decriminalisation

Perhaps the most closely studied change in cannabis policing policy has been that associated with the order maintenance policing (OMP)[3] policy associated with Mayor Giuliani and New York Police Department Commissioner William Bratton. The idea of OMP grew out of the 'broken windows' theory (Wilson and Kelling 1982), which proposed that serious, violent crime could be prevented by the aggressive policing of 'the little things', such as public disorder and cannabis possession. A central plank of the OMP was the use of stop, question, and frisk (SQF), primarily to uncover possession of weapons (Geller and Fagan 2010). Considerable efforts were also made to target the public use of marijuana or 'marijuana in public view' (MPV).

Three key studies of the impact of changes are included here (Elliott et al. 2012; Geller and Fagan 2010; Golub et al. 2007). In their detailed study of MPV arrests over 1980–2003, Golub et al. (2007) found that arrests for such offences increased dramatically over the 1990s and by 2000 accounted for 15% of all New York City (NYC) adult arrests. The researchers found pronounced disparities in the expected proportion of arrestees from different BME groups. Of arrestees, 52% were Black, while only 23% of the NYC resident population was Black. Black arrestees were also more than two-and-a-half times more likely to be detained than their White counterparts, and Blacks and Hispanics were more likely to be convicted and receive a prison sentence. A multivariate analysis, which controlled for prior arrests and demographics, found that Blacks and

Hispanics were still significantly more likely to receive a prison sentence than Whites. The authors conclude that 'the growth in MPV arrest activity has had a substantial and disproportionate impact on Black and Hispanic communities, especially on young Black and Hispanic men' (p. 14).

The second study from the same research institute focused on the impact of MPV policing on 90 cannabis users interviewed as part of a longitudinal study of cannabis use in low-income neighbourhoods (Elliott et al. 2012). They found that the large majority of participants referred to the police as a major factor affecting where they chose to use, with many citing the change in policing policy. Users avoided high-profile locations like Times Square and Washington Square and moved their cannabis smoking to lower profile public spaces. The study also identified other important factors that could override concerns about law enforcement: in particular, family pressures that made smoking at home impossible and the prioritisation of being with friends, even if that meant smoking cannabis in public spaces, with attendant risks.

The third and final study of the changes brought about by OMP (Geller and Fagan 2010) examined data on SQF activity for cannabis possession over 2004–2008. The authors examined such stops across the 123 New York police precincts, controlling for socio-economic conditions, crime levels, and the total number of police stops (for whatever reason). Stops and arrests for cannabis possession were found to take place disproportionately in precincts with large ethnic minority populations. Geller and Fagan conclude that 'The deep reach of OMP into the city's minority communities has serious social costs, undermining perceived police legitimacy' (p. 624).

More recently, research has been undertaken to explore whether various decriminalisation initiatives have differentially impacted on ethnic groups. California's Proposition 47 was introduced in 2014 and reduced the possession of drugs from felony to misdemeanour offences. Studying over a million drug arrests from 2011 to 2016, Mooney et al. (2018) found that the policy led to substantially fewer drug arrests across all racial/ethnic groups and that the longstanding disproportionality across Black and White people decreased. Likewise, a comparative study of the 2014 reclassification of cannabis possession as a 'civil infraction' in Philadelphia found an immediate reduction in arrest rates for cannabis possession, a reduction that was considerably greater among Blacks than Whites. Other studies that have not focused on race have shown decriminalisation approaches that have deprioritised or downgraded cannabis possession offences to be associated with general reductions in drug-related arrests (Grucza et al. 2018; Ross and Walker 2016).

Finally, recent research has focused on the impacts of legalisation in the United States. Despite legalisation in an increasing number of states, the police still have a role to play, as illicit markets still exist and laws concerning age limits still need to be enforced. Firth et al.'s (2019) recent study on the impact of legalisation on cannabis arrest disproportionalities after the legalisation of cannabis in Washington State concluded that while arrest rates dropped dramatically across the board, residual arrests were even more disproportionate across race than prior to legalisation. The authors suggest that this may be due to differences in the numbers of possession with intent to supply offences and relatedly, disproportionate access to legitimate jobs in the cannabis growing, manufacturing, and sales industry.

The overriding finding from the US studies is the disproportionate impact of the dramatic increase in cannabis offence enforcement on minority ethnic communities, which occurred as a result of the OMP initiative in New York City. While perhaps not a complete panacea, decriminalisation and legalisation do appear to be at least reducing the long-standing blight of disproportionality in simple cannabis possession arrests.

Policy changes elsewhere in the world

Looking beyond the United Kingdom and the United States, the impact of policy changes on cannabis policing has been examined in Denmark, Jamaica, Australia, and Mexico. In 1971, an unoccupied area of Copenhagen was taken over by squatters who claimed it as an independent, self-governing society: 'Freetown Christiania'. Despite the open supply of cannabis, the development was tolerated by the government and the police. However, in 2003, the Fight Against Drugs strategy was introduced by the Danish government along with new legislation in 2004, which increased the penalties for cannabis possession and supply (Houborg et al. 2016; Moeller 2009). The associated crackdown in Christiania was aimed at discouraging people from buying cannabis there (Moeller 2009). Dealers were arrested and many were imprisoned. Moeller (2009) describes the immediate impacts as a reduction in the daily sales of cannabis, the replacement of dealers, and increased drug-related violence. Houborg et al. (2016) have examined the wider impacts of the Fight Against Drugs strategy on four police districts in Denmark. Analysing district-level statistics, a sample of drugs possession cases from police files, and qualitative interviews and focus groups with police officers, they found a gradual increase in drug possession offences over 2002–2005, and no marked increase associated with the introduction of the new strategy over 2004–2005. However, over this latter period, there was a clear decrease in the use of cautions and a concomitant increase in 'sanctions' – which presumably involved charge and conviction.

Accompanying the introduction of official drug consumption rooms (DCRs) in Copenhagen in 2012, the law was changed such that in the vicinity of the DCRs the police would no longer arrest adults with drug problems in possession of drugs for their own use. Kammersgaard (2019) undertook observation and interviews with key stakeholders to explore this de facto decriminalisation. While some police continued to arrest users and confiscate their drugs, drug possession ceased to be a target in itself and there was greater scope for harm reduction approaches. Interestingly, the decriminalisation of possession enabled users to be seen as 'citizens with rights' (p. 355) who had their own claims on police services and the protection they conferred.

Davenport and Pardo (2016) focused on the implementation of the Dangerous Drugs Act Amendment in Jamaica in 2015, which decriminalised personal possession and use of cannabis, and allowed home cultivation for medicinal and, uniquely, sacramental purposes (reflecting the use of cannabis in Rastafarianism). They see this radical change as stemming from concerns about the rights of Rastafarians to practice their faith, the waste of limited criminal justice resources, and the negative impacts of gaining a criminal record. The researchers cite police data showing a dramatic reduction in arrests for cannabis possession: from 10,223 in 2014 to 2,389 in 2015.

There is a long and complex history of cannabis policy change and variation across jurisdictions in Australia (Hughes et al. 2019). Some comparative studies are included below, but relevant here is a recent study of the experimental introduction of on-the-spot fines (criminal infringement notices, CINs) for drug possession offences at music festivals in New South Wales (Sutherland et al. 2020). This study found that CINs were largely issued for ecstasy possession, with an estimated saving to the criminal justice system of 200,000 AUD. However, as the authors point out, the use of fines carries implications for their differential impact across income and disadvantage.

Finally, two studies (Arredondo et al. 2018; Gaines et al. 2015) report on the decriminalisation of the possession of small amounts of cocaine, heroin, methamphetamine, and cannabis for personal use in Mexico, with the aim of 'refocusing law enforcement resources on drug dealers and traffickers' (Gaines et al. 2015, p. 339): a similar motivation to that described for the reclassification of cannabis to Class C in 2003 (Lloyd 2010). The 2009 law (also referred to as the *narcomenudeo* reforms) introduced police warnings for those found in possession and an escalating approach so that for the third offence, the offender is required to enter addiction treatment within 90 days or face imprisonment. The first study focused on a survey of people who inject drugs (PWID) in the Tijuana region of Mexico. The researchers used outreach workers and 'targeted sampling' to recruit PWID in areas with high concentrations of drug users. Of the sample of 711, 461 (65%) reported experiencing law enforcement in 2011 and half of the 461 reported multiple experiences. Of the 736 such incidents, over half involved being stopped by the police but not arrested and a third involved 'extra-judicial' incidents – usually where participants had been stopped and not arrested. Respondents reported 38 incidents involving coerced sexual activity, 136 incidents of physical assault, 26 incidents of extortion, and 7 incidents of syringe confiscation. The authors conclude that despite the changes in the law, PWID 'continued to experience substantial and persistent burden of law enforcement encounters' (p. 344) and that drug treatment diversion was not implemented. One issue raised by this shocking study (but not addressed in the journal article) is the extent to which the reduction in the use of arrest led to more abuse by police officers, given the greater discretion available to them. Because the study did not include data from prior to the implementation of the 2009 law, this could not be addressed. The second, recent study (Arredondo et al. 2018) considered the same policy change through an examination of monthly arrest data for drug possession and violent and non-violent crimes. The authors adjusted for a range of factors in a hierarchical analysis examining arrest rates within police precincts but found no significant association between the implementation of the *narcomenudeo* reforms and drug possession arrests.

These studies offer further evidence of how policy change has varied around the globe, from the decriminalisation of cannabis possession in Jamaica to the crackdown in Christiania. Throughout this section on policy change, the gap between national policy and local implementation has been clear: offering the space for experimentation. However, the experience from Mexico shows how this gap can have terrible consequences in countries where some police officers appear to be largely untrammelled by official policy and accountability.

Weighing up the impacts of drug possession policing

The negative impacts of drug possession policing on police legitimacy

As outlined in the introduction, as common offences that often represent someone's first contact with the police as a potential suspect, experiences of being policed for cannabis possession can be very significant – especially as many suspects will see the offence as trivial and the policing unnecessary. Cannabis policing therefore has implications for police legitimacy. As May et al. (2002) state:

> cannabis possession is one of the offences that are most likely to bring people into 'adversarial' contact with the police. The scope for erosion of police legitimacy is obvious. If the laws that the police most frequently enforce are regarded by the policed as unreasonable and unnecessary, it is unlikely that police powers will be regarded as legitimate.
>
> *(p. 33)*

This is particularly relevant to stop and search practice, and the sense of injustice felt by the over-represented groups targeted in stop and search: young people and visible ethnic minorities. To address the impact of policing cannabis on the policed, May et al. (2002) interviewed 61 young people aged 11–24 years who had been stopped and searched for drugs and/or arrested for a cannabis offence. Between them, this group had been stopped and searched approximately 500 times, usually on the grounds of drug possession, and two-thirds had been stopped within the previous three months. When asked how they had been treated, around a third were happy with the way the police had dealt with them, having been given a clear explanation for the stop and treated with respect. However, another third felt that the police had been rude or aggressive and given no proper reason for the stop; and another third felt that they had been targeted unfairly because they were already known by the police to be cannabis users. Nonetheless, only two mentioned that their attitude toward the police had become more negative as a result.

May et al. (2002) also provided an analysis of the British Crime Survey (now the Crime Survey for England and Wales) data on police-initiated contact. Comparing people who reported using cannabis with those who did not, users were four times as likely to report having been stopped on foot and twice as likely to have been stopped in a car. In a multivariate analysis, self-reported cannabis use remained a strong predictor of being stopped, even controlling for factors such as age, gender, ethnicity, and going out at night. This begs questions about the nature of this association: how could being a cannabis user lead to being stopped by the police (other than in instances where people are publicly smoking cannabis)? As the authors surmise, the most likely explanation is that cannabis users have other, visible, 'suspicious' attributes or behaviours that result in their increased contact with the police (such as particular clothing or avoidance of initial police attempts to speak to them).

Two studies from Australia (Lenton et al. 2000; Shanahan et al. 2017a) sought to compare the experiences and attitudes of people dealt with in different ways for cannabis possession offences, including 'expiation', whereby cannabis offenders pay a fine and receive no conviction. Shanahan et al. (2017a) utilised an online survey and contacted their sample of 998 participants through social media, divided into those who received an informal warning, an expiation notice, a cannabis caution, or a criminal charge. Lenton et al. (2000) compared a sample of people given expiation notices for cannabis possession in Southern Australia (SA) with a sample of people convicted of cannabis possession in Western Australia (WA) – where expiation notices had not been introduced – accessing them through media coverage, advertisements, and snowball sampling. A total of 127 people were interviewed. Both studies were limited in their ability to ascribe differences to a disposal group, given the considerable other differences between the samples. However, they both collected data on attitudes to the police and a range of life impact measures (covered below). Overall, only 21% of Shanahan et al.'s (2017a) sample perceived the police as legitimate, and there were differences across the four groups, with those charged being least likely (15%) and the expiation and caution groups most likely (22% and 24%, respectively). In Lenton et al.'s study (2000), 49% of the WA group reported that they had become less trusting of the police, compared with 18% of expiators.

Thus, there is a disproportionate tendency for cannabis users (who may already hold anti-police attitudes) to come into contact with the police and for their trust in the police to be eroded through these contacts. This process is all the more prominent among young Black men. The much larger literature on the over-representation of Black men among those subjected to stop and search cannot be wholly included here. However, some studies have focused specifically on drug possession and these studies are described below.

May et al.'s (2007) study described above looked at the police recorded ethnicity of cannabis possession offenders. They found that, allowing for the racial composition of the area, BAME groups were 'heavily over-represented' in three of the sites and 'somewhat over-represented' in the other. Eastwood et al. (2013) used routine data from the UK Home Office and Ministry of Justice, and detailed data from the MPS to look at disparities across race in the policing and prosecution of drug offences in England and Wales in 2009/2010. They found that the rate of police drug stops per 1,000 of the population varied from 45 for Black people to 7 for White people (6.4 times as many). This disproportionality was more marked in some individual forces. In Dorset, for example, the population-adjusted rate among Black people was 17 times higher than among White people. Disproportionality in London as a whole was lower: rates of 66 for Black people and 24 for White people,[4] however, looking at individual London boroughs, Black people were stopped and searched on the grounds of drug possession at 4 or more times the rate of White people in 7 of the 32 boroughs for which the MPS was responsible. This analysis was updated by Shiner et al. (2018), focusing on 2016/2017 and found that while the use of stop and search had fallen sharply since the previous study, disproportionality had increased, with approximately 18 drug stops per 1,000 among Black people and 2.5 among White people (8.7 times as many). Again, the Dorset drug stop rate was far higher among Black people – 26.5 times higher – and there was wide variation across forces.

In addition to the North American evidence considered above under changes in policy, studies have focused on racial disproportionality in drug arrests in St Louis, San Francisco, Seattle, and Canadian cities (Beckett et al. 2005; Gaston 2019; Lynch et al. 2013; Owusu-Bempah and Luscombe 2021): all finding greater rates of arrest among Black groups. Gaston (2019) provides a detailed, qualitative exploration of the reasons behind these disparities, concluding that a key explanation is the targeting of neighbourhoods with high crime rates leading to 'place based discrimination that differentially criminalises people and places of colour' (p. 444).

This body of research has shown how cannabis policing is, in many areas, a race issue. The substantial disproportionality in the application of this highly intrusive form of policing across ethnic groups forms an important part of the wider feelings of injustice and suspicion towards the police among many BAME communities around the world. It is likely that such feelings are all the more amplified when the reason for stopping members of the public and searching them in the street is the suspicion that they may be in possession of cannabis. As we have seen earlier, decriminalisation policies carry the potential to substantially reduce this long-standing and unacceptable disproportionality.

Other negative social impacts

A number of commentators refer to the broader impacts of policing for cannabis possession, particularly on the young: that 'otherwise law-abiding, mainly young people are… being criminalised to the detriment of their future' (Shiner 2015, p. 701); that convictions for drug possession contribute to a 'tariff escalation', putting people at risk of more serious sanctions if convicted of offences at a later date (Ward 2013); and that if 'mishandled, cannabis policing could alienate significant sections of the population, especially the young' (to repeat Warburton et al.'s 2005, p. 126 statement).

However, studies that have attempted to measure these impacts are rare, probably because they are difficult to undertake, necessitating the identification of a community sample of people who have been policed for drug possession. Nonetheless, the two Australian studies described above (Lenton et al. 2000; Shanahan et al. 2017a) included questions relating to social impact. Lenton et al. (2000) found a much larger number of adverse employment consequences associated with arrest for cannabis possession among the WA group (32%) compared to the SA group (1.7%), including a substantial group reporting that they had not got jobs due to their cannabis conviction. Of the WA group, 21% also reported adverse relationship consequences, such as family disputes, and 16% accommodation consequences, such as a forced change of accommodation. Similarly, Shanahan et al. (2017a) found that self-reported relationship problems (two-thirds of which were attributed to the police encounters) and employment problems (half of which were so attributed) were significantly more common among the charge group, compared to the caution/expiation/warning groups.

The wider literature on the impact of crackdowns was referred to in the introduction. As described there, the health impacts are beyond the scope of this review. However, some studies have focused more explicitly on the impact of crackdowns on drug possession. Werb et al. (2008) compared the 130 people in the Vancouver Injection Drug Users Study (VIDUS)[5] who had been stopped/searched/detained by the police in the past six months with the 335 people who had not. A logistic regression analysis found that homelessness, recent incarceration, frequent crack use, needing help injecting, and lending syringes were positively associated with being stopped by the police. Of the 130 people stopped, 34% had their drugs confiscated. Of these, 70% immediately acquired more drugs. The authors conclude that homeless high-risk users who spend their time in public spaces are more likely to be policed and therefore more likely to have their drugs confiscated (see also similar results from the At-Risk Youth Study in Vancouver from Ti et al. 2013).

Positive impacts?

Hitherto, this section has reflected the majority of the literature in focusing on the negative impacts of enforcement. What of potentially positive impacts? In thinking about positive effects, it is important to try to separate the impacts of drug control legislation from the impacts of policing. There are numerous functions of drug laws, some of which lie outside the process of their application. These are the expressive, communicative, and symbolic functions which effectively mark cannabis and other drug use as a prohibited behaviour and therefore 'wrong'. Drug laws might therefore be assumed to have a deterrent effect of themselves, however enforced. As this chapter has shown, studies of policy changes have frequently demonstrated the considerable gap that exists between laws as they exist 'on the books' and law as enforced on the ground. The Lambeth Experiment, reclassification, police crackdowns, and Dutch 'coffeeshops' all demonstrate the crucial disconnect between drug laws and their enforcement. What, therefore, might be the separate, positive effects of the policing of cannabis possession?

An Australian study has explored the potential deterrent effect of different types of policing on illicit drug possession among music festival attendees by conducting an online survey and asking festival-attending respondents how they would react in the face of five hypothetical policing vignettes (Hughes et al. 2017). The hypothetical policing approaches consisted of drug detection dogs, high visibility policing, riot policing, collaborative policing, and no police presence. Participants were randomly assigned to consider two of the five vignettes and were asked if they would possess a number of different recreational drugs if they knew about the policing approach in advance of the music festival. The findings showed that any police presence was associated with a reduction of 10% in projected drug possession compared with no police presence (53% versus 63%). Drug detection dogs had the largest deterrent effect on possession (47%). Other Australian studies have shown little or no impact of drug detection dogs, arrest, or diversion on levels of cannabis use.

As the authors point out, an obvious limitation to the study is its focus on hypothetical situations: would such predictions be reflected in reality? While there is no simple way to address this question, these findings and those from other Australian studies that have looked at the impact of enforcement on self-reported drug use (Hickey et al. 2012; Shanahan et al. 2017b) suggest either a limited deterrent effect or no deterrent effect of policing on drug possession. One important, broader implication of Hughes et al.'s study is the importance of public spaces. The focus of this study on music festivals is significant because the large majority of drug possession policing occurs in public places. Of course, some arise in the course of searches of private properties but only a minority (Lloyd et al. 2018; May et al. 2007). If there is a deterrent effect of the policing of drug possession, it is likely to be specifically on the possession of drugs in a public place. It seems much less likely that it would have a broader impact on possession in private locations – or indeed on drug use in these locations. Similar to the findings from studies of the impact of police crackdowns on Class A drug users, we might also expect a crackdown on drug possession to lead to much more careful hiding of the drug, such that it would not be found in the course of a search conducted on the street – or on entry to a festival.

Another potential positive impact of enforcement is the discovery of other, more serious offences. Officers in Bear's detailed ethnographic study of the policing of drug possession in the MPS found this to be one of the reasons officers gave for targeting cannabis possession offences (Bear 2016). Similarly, officers in Bacon's (2022) recent study (see below) spoke of the importance of possession policing in providing intelligence about dealers. As part of their evaluation of the cannabis reclassification from B to C, May et al. (2007) explored police officers' views on reclassification. That cannabis possession offences lead to the detection of more serious offences was a common reason given by those who thought that the government was wrong to move cannabis from Class B to Class C. Accordingly, May and colleagues (2006, 2007) undertook an analysis of 30,000 custody records and found that 'less than one per cent of simple possession offences "opened the door" to the discovery of more serious offences', thus challenging 'the widespread view that cannabis arrests frequently lead to the detection of more serious offences' (2006, p. 32).

In terms of other police perspectives on positive impacts, Bacon's (2022) recent work involving interviews with 46 officers across 11 police forces also shows how police attitudes are changing, with decreasing faith in the deterrent impact of enforcement and a developing interest in rehabilitation and recovery (although such views were not universal). Through contact with dependent Class A drug users in particular, low-level street policing has the potential to divert (potentially reluctant) users into treatment and recovery. For those arrested for possession, there is also the potential for later diversion into treatment through the CJS. However, dependent drug users are usually arrested for offences other than drug possession (e.g. Bennett and Holloway 2005). Thus, if the police stopped arresting for possession offences, this might have a more limited effect on police custody diversion than might be expected.

Finally on police perspectives, Bear describes how, while policing frequently does not result in tangible outcomes, 'finding a bit of cannabis allowed the officer to hold up their "trophy" to their colleagues' (p. 7). Thus, cannabis policing may also serve functions for police officers that have little to do with the impact on users or wider society.

Selective enforcement: the partiality of discretion in drug possession policing

While generally thought of at the level of the officer on the street, 'discretion' can be seen to be enacted at all levels of the drug law enforcement policy/practice continuum, up to the interpretation and implementation of the United Nations drug conventions. Belackova et al. (2017) provide an interesting analysis of the degree of concordance between drug laws as they exist 'on the books' and as they are enforced on the ground. The UN conventions leave considerable 'room for manoeuver' (Dorn and Jamieson 2000), and national legislation therefore varies considerably. Moreover, as Belackova et al. (2017) point out, further potential for variation exists in the enforcement of these laws. These authors compared the Czech Republic, Florida USA, and New South Wales, Australia on the relative leniency of their drug laws and went on to compare the drug offence arrest rate, prosecution, and sentencing in these countries. Of relevance here, they found that per capita arrest rates did follow the relative leniency of the national drug laws, so that Florida had the most prohibitive laws and the highest arrest rate, followed by New South Wales and the Czech Republic.

Nonetheless, most authors focus on discretion further down the CJS. In his report that followed the Brixton riots in London in 1981, Lord Scarman stated that: 'Neither politicians nor pressure-groups nor anyone else may tell the police what decisions to take or what methods to employ, whether to enforce the law or not, in a particular case' and went on to say that 'the exercise of police judgement has to be as independent as the exercise of professional judgement by a doctor or a lawyer' (p. 104). As Scarman also pointed out, however, this independence has to be coupled with operation within the law and the support of the community. An important feature of possession cases in this context is the lack of a direct victim or aggrieved party, which provides particular scope for police discretion (Bacon 2016; Beckett et al. 2005; Houberg et al. 2016; Shiner 2015; Warburton et al. 2005). Given the widespread, 'victimless', and usually hidden nature of the use of controlled drugs, the police have little choice but to be selective in their enforcement of drug laws. This selective enforcement is an area in which police independence can come into conflict with local communities, as it did in Brixton in 1981.

A number of studies have provided valuable insights into the ways that officers employ discretion in their policing of drug possession. Perhaps the most detailed and thoughtful account comes from Warburton et al. (2005) in their analysis of the findings from the first of the two studies undertaken by May and colleagues (described above). While a third of the 150 patrol officers in this study reported always arresting someone in possession of cannabis, the others said that they did not always arrest. Demeanour was important for many: 'If you stop someone and they are not aggressive or abusive and they don't have a criminal record, I can't see the point in giving them a criminal record for a bit of cannabis' (p. 118). Others never arrested anyone: 'I never nick anyone for cannabis, and never will, unless it's a van load' (p. 119). The importance of honesty also came out strongly: those who made no attempt to conceal or deny the offence were more likely to be dealt with sympathetically. Warburton et al. (2005) also looked at the issue of consistency across the areas included in the research: an issue also picked up in the second study (May et al. 2007). Comparing the four sites, there was pronounced variation in practice, with 27 out of 38 officers interviewed in one site reporting that they had dealt with cannabis possession informally (i.e. confiscated the drug and taken no formal action), while in another, predominantly rural site, 14 out of 36 offices reported informal practices (Warburton et al. 2005). The researchers suggest that rural officers may 'consider cannabis a harmful or gateway offence' (p. 122) and that the lower levels of recorded crime and associated pressures may allow rural officers to take formal action where officers in metropolitan areas would not. In the second study, May et al. (2007) found that the proportion of apprehended offenders given street warnings varied across sites, from 22% to over 40%. These studies therefore demonstrate a considerable variation across

England in how cannabis possession is policed both at the individual officer and force division levels – at least within the four divisions and the two points in time within which these studies were undertaken.

In a detailed study of drug policing in four Danish police districts, Houberg et al. (2016) explored the potential for drug control to be used selectively to control marginalised young men. They emphasised the importance of 'suspicion formation' in discretion, whereby police officers draw on intelligence, appearance, behaviour, time, and location in selecting who to approach on the street. The study involved interviews with senior police officers and analysis of case records relating to 317 randomly selected possession cases and focus groups. Compared to a general population comparison group, offenders were found to be more likely to be male, young, less educated, unemployed, and have a criminal record. They went on to categorise the 317 possession cases on the basis of the nature of the initial police contact and found that, in 27% of cases, the offence was a by-product of police work unrelated to drugs – the majority being initially suspected of a non-drug-related offence – and in 33% of cases, information had come from a member of the public or bar/nightclub staff. The authors describe these 60% of cases as involving 'reactive' policing, i.e. they had not been sought out. In another 29% of cases, described as 'proactive', officers had formed suspicions about people, including cases where they were known to the police or were behaving suspiciously. In interviews, officers talked about who they would approach proactively and described two types: 'young guys, scruffy, unhealthy, slight of build' and muscular men 'with tattoos and gold chains' who could be involved in gangs. They also referred to particular kinds of cars – 'old, big cars' – and particular kinds of driver arousing suspicion. The authors conclude that the disproportionate criminalisation of unemployed young men for drug offences is, at least in part, associated with the fact that 'these people get into circumstances where they attract the attention of the police' (p. 338).

Lastly, Sarang et al. (2010) interviewed 209 injecting drug users in three Russian cities about their experiences of being policed. Interviewees described how they saw the police as having unlimited powers to detain/arrest users. Extortion and having drugs planted on them were described as 'routine' and physical violence was also reported as quite common, including beating people for confessions. Instances of torture and rape were also reported.

As described in the introduction, drug possession is an extremely common offence. However, only a tiny proportion of these occasions of possession come to the notice of the police and, from the studies reviewed above, this often appears to be accidental: through stop and search for other offences or on the basis of quite vague suspicions relating to how people look and behave. Those who carry drugs on their person in public places and those who are regularly policed – either because of their appearance/behaviour or previous record – tend to make up the very small percentage who are policed for their drug possession. The huge majority who use it at home and are unlikely to be searched when out of the home, are very unlikely to appear in the offence statistics. The corollary of this is that the type of profile described by Houberg et al. (2016) becomes something of a self-fulfilling prophecy: those policed for drug possession are likely to be young, male, and economically marginalised: at least in part because this is the group most likely to come to the attention of the police (e.g. Quinton et al. 2000).

Conclusions: more harm than good

A number of strong themes have stemmed from this review. A central issue has been the disconnect between centrally formulated policy and drug possession policing on the ground. Of course, this is not a surprising finding: it is a finding that resonates across a broad swathe of social policy, frequently understood in terms of the powers held by the street-level bureaucrat (Lipsky 1980). However, it is of particular significance in the drug policing context, where vast numbers of people are in possession at any one point in time, only a very small proportion of whom will come to the attention of the police. This leaves space for the adoption of different local approaches, and the way in which drug laws are enforced has therefore been subject to experimentation at city, force, and divisional level. The Lambeth Experiment has been very influential, despite the lack of evaluation, and there appears to be another wave of experimentation currently under way in the United Kingdom concerning different approaches to diversion and referral (Spyt and Kew, this volume). It is vitally important that we learn what we can from such experiments and that they are independently evaluated and findings published. However, taking a global perspective, it should also not be forgotten that the leeway that exists between the law and policing as enacted on the ground can also result in terrible abuses in some countries around the world.

The ubiquity of drug possession has meant that apprehension by the police is not only rare but also often accidental, in the sense that a drug is found in the course of approaching people on the street or in cars, on the basis of suspicions relating to how people look, where they are, and the time of day or night. Those select few on the receiving end therefore tend to be people in public spaces who arouse suspicion and, at least in the United Kingdom and the United States, this seems to translate not only as young men – and in particular, Black young men – but also homeless, dependent drug users, who have no choice but to spend much of their time in public spaces. The selective nature of the policing of a largely victimless offence carries important implications for procedural justice and police legitimacy – and raises questions about the balance of negative and positive impacts associated with policing possession.

This review has taken a careful and detailed approach to analysing the evidence of the positive and negative impacts of the policing of drug possession. In weighing these against each other, it is clear that the scales dip abruptly towards the latter. The evidence shows that there is a clear divide in the literature between the policing of dependent drug users and the policing of recreational drug users. Research from Mexico and Russia has revealed some of the extreme, negative impacts of experiences of 'policing' on dependent users in those countries. Additionally, in a very different context, research from Vancouver has shown not only how it is the high-risk users who tend to be on the receiving end of street policing but also how confiscation of drugs has very little effect on use. With regard to recreational users, evidence suggests that a significant minority of young people in the United Kingdom have found the police to be rude or aggressive when being stopped and searched for suspected drug possession. Disaffection with the police, including reduced trust, has also been found in a number of Australian studies that have focused on people's experiences of being apprehended for cannabis possession offences. Other impacts of more criminalising approaches to possession have included negative employment, accommodation, and relationship consequences. But by far the largest weight on the negative side of the scale is the gross over-representation of young Black men among those stopped and searched on suspicion of drug possession – either in the course of regular policing or as part of a policing initiative. This ongoing injustice has had a major impact on relations between the police and Black communities in North America and the United Kingdom. On the other side of the balance, there is some evidence that more intensive policing efforts may have a small impact on drug possession – although only through users avoiding certain places at certain times or concealing drugs more carefully, rather than any impact on use. The policing of possession also provides opportunities for referral to treatment for dependent users. However, here it should be noted that the large majority of possession cases involve cannabis[6] and the large majority of cannabis users are recreational users.

In conclusion, this review of the evidence in this neglected field has led the author to the inescapable conclusion that the current approach to policing drug possession in the United Kingdom does considerably more harm than good. There are certainly other options: cannabis decriminalisation and legalisation in North America have been associated with decreasing harms – in particular (other than in one study) a decline in the perennial social ill of racial disproportionality. Alternatively, reflecting the local room for manoeuvre, a potential first step would be to cease to stop and search simply for cannabis possession and to stop taking any action (including seizure of the drug) when small amounts of cannabis are found in the course of police action aimed at other objectives. Such an approach would serve to prevent the needless criminalisation of people – disproportionately young Black people – who are apprehended for possession of a small quantity of cannabis. Together with the national roll out of effective diversionary projects, such developments would start to reset the balance, leading to more effective, more humane policing of possession.

Notes

1 Since replaced by the National Police Chiefs' Council (NPCC).
2 Situations where the police dispose of the drugs and take no further action.

3 Also referred to as quality of life (QOL) policing and zero-tolerance policing.
4 Indeed, if the authors had taken the MPS figures out of the national statistics, the disproportionality would have been even more marked for the rest of the country.
5 The VIDUS is a prospective cohort study of injecting drug users residing in Greater Vancouver (see Kerr et al. 2004).
6 81% of recorded possession offences in 2020/2021 were for cannabis (ONS 2021). Moreover, a large proportion of the other possession offences will be for drugs used recreationally.

References

Adda, J., McConnell, B. and Rasul, I. (2014) 'Crime and the depenalization of cannabis possession: Evidence from a policing experiment'. *Journal of Political Economy.* 122(5): 1130–1202.

Arredondo, J., Gaines, T., Manian, S., Vilalta, C., Bañuelos, A., Strathdee, S. and Beletsky, L. (2018) 'The law on the streets: Evaluating the impact of Mexico's drug decriminalization reform on drug possession arrests in Tijuana, Mexico'. *International Journal of Drug Policy.* 54: 1–8.

Association of Chief Police Officers. (2003) *The ACPO Cannabis Enforcement Guidance.* London: ACPO.

Association of Chief Police Officers. (2007) *Guidance on Policing Cannabis – Use of Cannabis Warnings.* London: ACPO.

Association of Chief Police Officers. (2009) *ACPO Guidance on Cannabis Possession for Personal Use: Revised Intervention Framework.* London: ACPO.

Bacon, M. (2016) *Taking Care of Business: Police Detectives, Drug Law Enforcement and Proactive Investigation.* Oxford: OUP.

Bacon, M. (2022) 'Desistance from criminalisation: Police culture and new directions in drugs policing'. *Policing and Society.* 32(4): 522–539.

BBC News. (2019) 'Cannabis "to be legalised in the UK" within five to ten years, say MPs'. Available from: https://www.bbc.co.uk/news/newsbeat-49073222 [Accessed 20 July 2021].

BBC News. (2021) 'Medical cannabis "saved my life"'. Available from: https://www.bbc.co.uk/news/health-57098858 [Accessed 20 July 2021].

Bear, D. (2016) 'The need to create a narrative: Examining the justifications police used to target drugs in the lead up to the 2011 London riots'. *Police Practice and Research.* 17(4): 317–328.

Beckett, K., Nyrop, K., Pfingst, L. and Bowen, M. (2005) 'Drug use, drug possession arrests, and the question of race: Lessons from Seattle'. *Social Problems.* 52(3): 419–441.

Belackova, V., Ritter, A., Shanahan, M. and Hughes, C. (2017) 'Assessing the concordance between illicit drug laws on the books and drug law enforcement: Comparison of three states on the continuum from "decriminalised" to "punitive"'. *International Journal of Drug Policy.* 41: 148–157.

Bennett, T. and Holloway, K. (2005) *Understanding Drugs, Alcohol and Crime.* Maidenhead: Open University Press.

Caulkins, J. and Reuter, P. (2009) 'Towards a harm-reduction approach to enforcement'. *Safer Communities.* 8(1): 9–24.

Dark, S. and Fuller, M. (2002) *The Lambeth Cannabis Warning Pilot Scheme*, MPA Report 17. Available from: http://policeauthority.org/metropolitan/committees/mpa/2002/020926/17/index.html [Accessed 1 September 2021].

Davenport, S. and Pardo, B. (2016) 'The dangerous drugs act amendment in Jamaica: Reviewing goals, implementation, and challenges'. *International Journal of Drug Policy*. 37: 60–69.

Dorn, N. and Jamieson, A. (2000) *Room for Manoeuvre*. London: DrugScope.

Eastwood, N., Shiner, M. and Bear, D. (2013) *The Numbers in Black and White: Ethnic Disparities in the Policing and Prosecution of Drug Offences in England and Wales*. London: Release.

Elliott, L., Golub, A. and Dunlap, E. (2012) 'Off the street and into "the cut": Deterrence and displacement in NYC's quality of life marijuana policing'. *International Journal on Drug Policy*. 23(3): 210–219.

Firth, C., Maher, J., Dilley, J., Darnell, A. and Lovrich, N. (2019) 'Did marijuana legalization in Washington State reduce racial disparities in adult marijuana arrests?' *Substance Use and Misuse*. 54(9): 1582–1587.

Gaines, T., Beletsky, L., Arredondo, J., Werb, D., Rangel, G., Vera, A. and Brouwer, K. (2015) 'Examining the spatial distribution of law enforcement encounters among people who inject drugs after implementation of Mexico's drug policy reform'. *Journal of Urban Health: Bulletin of the New York Academy of Medicine*. 92(2): 338–351.

Gaston, S. (2019) 'Producing race disparities: A study of drug arrests across place and race'. *Criminology*. 57(3): 424–451.

Gelders, D. and Vander Laenen, F. (2007) '"Mr Police Officer, I thought cannabis was legal" – Introducing new policy regarding cannabis in Belgium: A story of good intentions and Babel'. *Drugs: Education, Prevention and Policy*. 14(2): 103–116.

Geller, A. and Fagan, J. (2010) 'Pot as pretext: Marijuana, race, and the new disorder in New York City street policing'. *Journal of Empirical Legal Studies*. 7(4): 591–633.

Golub, A., Johnson, B. and Dunlap, E. (2007) 'The race/ethnicity disparity in misdemeanour marijuana arrests in New York City'. *Criminology and Public Policy*. 6(1): 131–164.

Grucza, R., Vuolo, M., Krauss, M., Plunk, A., Agrawal, A., Chaloupka, F. and Bierut, L. (2018) 'Cannabis decriminalization: A study of recent policy change in five U.S. states'. *International Journal of Drug Policy*. 59: 67–75.

Guardian. (2021) 'Met may change stop and search tactics on cannabis possession'. Available from: https://www.theguardian.com/law/2021/mar/18/met-may-change-stop-and-search-tactics-on-cannabis-possession [Accessed 20 July 2021].

Hathaway, A., Comeau, N. and Erickson, P. (2011) 'Cannabis normalization and stigma: Contemporary practices of moral regulation'. *Criminology and Criminal Justice*. 11(5): 451–469.

Hickey, S., McIlwraith, F., Bruno, R., Matthews, A. and Alati, R. (2012) 'Drug detection dogs in Australia: More bark than bite?' *Drug and Alcohol Review*. 31(6): 778–783.

Houborg, E., Kammersgaard, T. and Pedersen, M. (2016) 'Drug policing in four Danish police districts'. *Police Practice and Research*. 17(4): 329–340.

Hughes, C., Moxham-Hall, V., Ritter, A., Weatherburn, D. and MacCoun, R. (2017) 'The deterrent effects of Australian street-level drug law enforcement on illicit drug offending at outdoor music festivals'. *International Journal of Drug Policy*. 41: 91–100.

Hughes, C., Seear, K., Ritter, A. and Mazerolle, L. (2019) *Criminal Justice Responses Relating to Personal Use and Possession of Illicit Drugs: The Reach of Australian Drug Diversion Programs and Barriers and Facilitators to Expansion*. Sydney: NDARC.

Johnson, B., Golub, A., Dunlap, E. and Sifaneck, S. (2008) 'An analysis of alternatives to New York City's current marijuana arrest and detention policy'. *Policing*. 31(2): 226–250.

Kammersgaard, T. (2019) 'Harm reduction policing: From drug law enforcement to protection'. *Contemporary Drug Problems*. 46(4): 345–362.

Kelly, E. and Rasul, I. (2014) 'Policing cannabis and drug related hospital admissions: Evidence from administrative records'. *Journal of Public Economics*. 112: 89–114.

Kerr, T., Palepu, A., Barnes, G., Walsh, J., Hogg, R., Montaner, J. Tyndall, M. and Wood, E. (2004) 'Psychosocial determinants of adherence to highly active antiretroviral therapy among injection drug users in Vancouver'. *Antiviral Therapy*. 9(3): 407–414.

Kerr, T., Small, W. and Wood, E. (2005) 'The public health and social impacts of drug market enforcement: A review of the evidence'. *International Journal of Drug Policy*. 16(4): 210–220.

Lenton, S., Hueniuk, R., Heale, P. and Christie, P. (2000) 'Infringement versus conviction: The social impact of a minor cannabis offence in South Australia and Western Australia'. *Drug and Alcohol Review*. 19(3): 257–264.

Lipsky, M. (1980) *Street-Level Bureaucracy: Dilemmas of the Individual in Public Services*. New York: Russell Sage Foundation.

Lynch, M., Omori, M., Roussell, A. and Valasik, M. (2013) 'Policing the "progressive" city: The racialized geography of drug law enforcement'. *Theoretical Criminology*. 17(3): 335–357.

Lloyd, C. (2008) *The Cannabis Classification Debate in the UK: Full of Sound and Fury, Signifying Nothing*. Paper presented to the second annual conference of the International Society for the Study of Drug Policy, ISDDP.

Lloyd, C. (2010) 'Cannabis'. In Lloyd, C. and McKeganey, N. (eds.) *Drugs Research: An Overview of Evidence and Questions for Policy*. York: Joseph Rowntree Foundation: 7–21.

Lloyd, C., Page, G., Grace, S. et al. (2018) *Policing Cannabis in North Yorkshire*. Available from: https://n8prp.org.uk/wp-content/uploads/2018/09/Policing-Cannabis-in-North-Yorkshire.pdf [Accessed 3 August 2021].

May, T., Warburton, H., Turnbull, P. and Hough, M. (2002) *Times They Are A-Changing: Policing of Cannabis*. York: Joseph Rowntree Foundation.

May, T., Duffy, M. and Hough, M. (2006) 'Policing cannabis as a Class C drug: An arresting change?' *Drugs and Alcohol Today*. 6(4): 30–36.

May, T., Duffy, M., Warburton, H. and Hough, M. (2007) *Policing Cannabis as a Class C Drug: An Arresting Change?* York: Joseph Rowntree Foundation.

Mazerolle, L., Soole, D. and Rombouts, S. (2007) 'Drug law enforcement: A review of the evaluation literature'. *Police Quarterly*. 10(2): 115–153.

Moeller, K. (2009) 'Police crackdown on Christiania in Copenhagen'. *Crime, Law and Social Change*. 52(4): 337–345.

Mooney, A., Gianella, E., Glymour, M., Neilands, T. B., Morris, M. D., Tulsky, J. and Sudhinaraset, M. (2018) 'Racial/ethnic disparities in arrests for drug possession after California proposition 47, 2011–2016'. *America Journal of Public Health*. 18(8): 987–993.

Nguyen, H. and Reuter, P. (2012) 'How risky is marijuana possession? Considering the role of age, race, and gender'. *Crime & Delinquency*. 58(6): 879–910.

Office for National Statistics. (2020a) *Drug Misuse in England and Wales: Year Ending March 2020*. London: ONS.

Office for National Statistics. (2020b) *Drug Misuse in England and Wales: Appendix Table*. Table 2.02. Available from: https://www.ons.gov.uk/peoplepopulationandcommunity/crimeandjustice/datasets/drugmisuseinenglandandwalesappendixtables [Accessed 16 July 2021].

Office for National Statistics. (2021) *Crime in England and Wales: Appendix Tables*. Available from: https://www.ons.gov.uk/peoplepopulationandcommunity/crimeandjustice/datasets/crimeinenglandandwalesappendixtables [Accessed 16 July 2021].

Owusu-Bempah, A. and Luscombe, A. (2021) 'Race, cannabis and the Canadian war on drugs: An examination of cannabis arrest data by race in five cities'. *International Journal of Drug Policy*. 91: 102937.

Quinton, P., Bland, N. and Miller, J. (2000) *Police Stops, Decision-Making and Practice*. Home Office Police Research Series, Paper 130. London: Home Office.

Ross, A. and Walker, A. (2016) 'The impact of low-priority laws on criminal activity: Evidence from California'. *Contemporary Economic Policy*. 35(2): 239–252.

Sarang, A., Rhodes, T., Sheon, N. and Page, K. (2010) 'Police drug users in Russia: Fear and structural violence'. *Substance Use and Misuse*. 45(6): 813–864.

Shanahan, M., Hughes, C. and McSweeney, T. (2017a) 'Police diversion for cannabis offences: Assessing outcomes and cost-effectiveness'. *Trends and Issues in Crime and Criminal Justice* No. 532. Canberra: Australian Institute of Criminology.

Shanahan, M., Hughes, C., McSweeney, T. and Griffin, B. (2017b) 'Alternate policing strategies: Cost-effectiveness of cautioning for cannabis offences'. *International Journal of Drug Policy*. 41: 140–147.

Shiner, M. (2015) 'Drug policy reform and the reclassification of cannabis in England and Wales: A cautionary tale'. *International Journal of Drug Policy*. 26(7): 696–704.

Shiner, M., Carre, Z., Delsol, R. and Eastwood, N. (2018) *The Colour of Injustice: 'Race', Drugs and Law Enforcement in England and Wales*. London: StopWatch, London School of Economics and Release.

Spicer, J. (2021) *Policing County Lines: Responses to Evolving Provincial Drug Markets*. London: Palgrave.

Sutherland, R., Weatherburn, D. and Dagenhardt, L. (2020) 'A trial of criminal infringement notices as an alternative to criminal penalties for illicit drug offences in New South Wales, Australia: Estimated savings'. *Drug and Alcohol Review*. 40(1): 93–97.

Ti, L., Wood, E., Shannon, K, Feng, C. and Kerr, T. (2013) 'Police confrontations among street-involved youth in a Canadian setting'. *International Journal of Drug Policy*. 24(1): 46–51.

Turnbull, P. (2009) 'The great cannabis classification debacle: What are the likely consequences for policing cannabis possession offences in England and Wales?' *Drug and Alcohol Review*. 28(2): 202–209.

Warburton, H., May, T. and Hough, M. (2005) 'Looking the other way: The impact of reclassifying cannabis on police warnings, arrests and informal action in England and Wales'. *British Journal of Criminology*. 45(2): 113–128.

Ward, J. (2013) 'Punishing drug possession in the Magistrates' Courts: Time for a rethink'. *European Journal on Criminal Policy and Research*. 19(4): 289–307.

Wiens, T., Lenk, K., Fabian, L. and Erickson, D. (2018) 'Law enforcement practices in the first two states in U.S. to legalize recreational marijuana'. *International Journal of Drug Policy*. 61: 38–43.

Wilson, J.Q. and Kelling, G. (1982) 'Broken windows: The police and neighborhood safety', *Atlantic Monthly*, 249(3): 29–38.

Werb, D., Wood, E., Small, W., Strathdee, S., Li, K., Montaner, J. and Kerr, T. (2008) 'Effects of police confiscation of illicit drugs and syringes among injection drug users in Vancouver'. *International Journal of Drug Policy*. 19(4): 332–338.

3

DRUGS, RACE, AND DEFUNDING THE POLICE

Daring to dream

Benson Egwuonwu, Habib Kadiri, and Michael Shiner

Introduction

On 30 May 2020, Black Lives Matter (BLM 2020) launched a petition in the United States demanding 'acknowledgment and accountability for the devaluation and dehumanization of Black life at the hands of the police'. Identifying George Floyd's violent death as a 'breaking point', it stated:

> 'We call for a national defunding of police. We demand investment in our communities and the resources to ensure Black people not only survive, but thrive'.

Calls to defund the police gained most immediate traction in Minneapolis where Floyd was killed, in what was later ruled a homicide, while he was being restrained by law enforcement (Stelloh 2020). The four officers involved were sacked the next day as protests erupted and bystander videos, showing an officer kneeling on Floyd's neck for more than nine minutes, went viral (New York Times 2021). Within 13 days, a majority of the city council had pledged to dismantle the city police department and replace it with new systems for public safety (Searcey and Eligon 2020). One of the former officers involved, Derek Chauvin, was convicted of two counts of murder and one of manslaughter for killing Floyd, while his three former colleagues received prison sentences for aiding and abetting second-degree manslaughter and violating Floyd's civil rights (Associated Press 2022). Chauvin's conviction has been described as a 'milestone' and a sign, perhaps, that the United States has moved towards greater accountability for police abuses and greater equality under the law (Bogel-Burroughs and Arango 2021). Minneapolis city council's appetite for reform has 'collapsed', however, and its 'once sweeping ambitions' have 'given way, once again, to incremental change'

DOI: 10.4324/9781003154136-4

(Dickenson 2020; Herndon 2021; Oladipo 2021). In February 2021, the council approved an additional $6.4 million funding for the police department to hire new recruits amid reports of a shortage of officers following a large number of departures, slow response times to emergency calls, and a surge in violent crime (Lapin 2021). On the first anniversary of Floyd's death, it was reported that plans for reform in Minneapolis had 'softened' and would retain a police department, albeit one that would form part of a broader focus on 'public safety' and be subject to greater civilian oversight (Sepic 2021). Although Minneapolis has struggled to realise its radical vision, many other cities have shown that divesting from police departments is possible by reducing police numbers, cutting expenses, decreasing overtime, and redirecting funding to other public services (Racial Justice Coalition 2021). Such developments have been sharply contested, of course, but municipalities across the United States are making changes in line with the defund police movement, with one commentator recently describing the situation thus:

> while the word 'reallocate' may be a more palatable, digestible word on the House floor or at a city council meeting, 'defund' surely gets more attention on a protest sign. And more importantly, it seems to be having an impact.
>
> *(Ray 2020)*

The situation in the United Kingdom is rather different as calls to defund the police have been met with widespread derision and hostility from the political establishment. One of the problems with such calls is that they may appear more radical than they actually are (Hersh 2020), playing into a well-established dynamic whereby black political thought is delegitimised on the grounds that it is simultaneously 'dangerous' yet 'naïve'. On 9 June 2020, Keir Starmer, leader of the Labour Party, took a knee in an act of apparent solidarity with BLM, but then went on to describe the case for defunding as 'just nonsense', saying: 'Nobody should be saying anything about defunding the police' (Shand-Baptiste 2020). Priti Patel, the then home secretary, went further, describing the BLM protests as 'dreadful' and stating her disagreement with the gesture of taking the knee (Parveen 2021). In response, advocates argued that critics had misunderstood what defunding the police really means, insisting it amounts to a realistic and serious policy approach: 'Campaigns to defund the police and prison system do not argue that every prison should close tomorrow and every police officer be sacked the day after – they argue that social problems are better addressed through social responses' (Elliot-Cooper 2020; see also Henderson and Yisrael 2021; Vitale 2017).

This chapter considers whether calls to defund the police should be taken more seriously in the United Kingdom. We begin in the United States and examine the role of drug policing in relation to both the case that has been made for defunding, and in generating the underlying problems that these calls seek to address. We then focus on England and Wales, arguing that there are sufficient parallels with the United States for the case for defunding to be taken more seriously.

The American drug wars

Black Lives Matter has been surprisingly quiet on the issue of drug policy reform and the end of the war on drugs has been 'curiously absent' from its list of demands (Werleman 2020). Although George Floyd's final, fatal, encounter with the police was not directly drug related, it might well have been. Floyd was arrested on suspicion of paying for cigarettes with a counterfeit $20 bill, but the subsequent autopsy found fentanyl and methamphetamine in his system (Stelloh 2020). We later learnt that Floyd had served jail time for a $10 drug deal having been apprehended by a narcotics officer whose arrests were under review for possible false testimony (Fernandez 2020).

Critics have long argued that the US drug war is 'basically a technique for controlling dangerous populations and doesn't have much to do with drugs' (Chomsky 2003, p. 57). When Richard Nixon officially declared the 'War on Drugs' in 1971, he did so as part of the 'Southern Strategy' devised by Republican campaigners: the aim was to appeal to white voters through coded, subliminal, appeals to anti-black sentiment that linked black civil rights to growing anxieties about rising crime and urban disorder (Alexander 2010). Although the Nixon administration invested heavily in drug treatment and methadone maintenance, rather than rely on law enforcement, it deployed the rhetoric of the 'War on Drugs' in a politically calculated manner. As John Ehrlichman, special counsel to President Nixon, admitted years later (cited by Baum 2016):

> You want to know what this was really all about? The Nixon campaign in 1968, and the Nixon White House after that, had two enemies: the anti-war left and black people. You understand what I'm saying? We knew we couldn't make it illegal to be either against the war or black, but by getting the public to associate the hippies with marijuana and blacks with heroin, and then criminalizing both heavily, we could disrupt those communities. We could arrest their leaders, raid their homes, break up their meetings, and vilify them night after night on the evening news. Did we know we were lying about the drugs? Of course we did.

President Reagan renewed the war on drugs shortly after taking office in 1981. The effect on African-American communities was 'devastating' (Nunn 2002, p. 381). Prisoner numbers began to sky-rocket, not because of a surge in violent crime, but because of a series of policy choices, including a more punitive approach to drug offences (Tonry 2011). The number of inmates in state prisons convicted of drug crimes increased 17-fold between 1979 and 2006 as drug arrests translated into prison sentences at a much higher rate (Bobo and Thompson

2006; Tonry 2011). By 2007, approximately half a million people were in prison or jail for drug offences across the United States, exceeding the number who had been incarcerated for any offence in 1980 (Alexander 2010). Black people were imprisoned at five to seven times the rate of white people throughout this period (Tonry 2011) and 'mass imprisonment' came to be defined partly by the 'social concentration' of its effects among 'young black males in large urban centres' (Garland 2001, p. 6). Nunn (2002, p. 382) noted that 'more African American men go to prison than go to college' and, by 2005, approximately a third of young black men were in prison or jail or on probation or parole on an average day (Nellis 2016; Tonry 2011). African-American communities were not devastated by the war on drugs because of a particular propensity to use or supply drugs, but because of the way the war was fought (Mauer 2009; Tonry 2011). After exhaustive statistical analysis, Tonry (2011, p. 53) observed: 'No honest observer can deny that racial disparities in imprisonment are substantially attributable to the War on Drugs'. Using arrests as a proxy for criminal behaviour, he found racial differences in offending may have been the primary cause of imprisonment disparities in 1979, but were no longer so by 2004. Setting these disparities in their historical context, Tonry (2011, p. 99) concluded that contemporary drug and crime control policies 'are in large part products of unconscious efforts by the white majority to maintain political, social and economic dominance over blacks', perpetuating centuries-old patterns of racial disadvantage.

The continuities linking mass imprisonment and the war on drugs to earlier, explicitly racist, systems of social control are laid bare by Alexander (2010, p. 3), who demonstrates how: 'In each generation, new tactics have been used for achieving the same goals'. Mass incarceration, she argues, emerged out of opposition to the civil rights movement as a 'stunningly comprehensive and well-disguised system of racialized social control' with striking similarities to the Jim Crow system of segregation that maintained white dominance after the collapse of slavery (p. 4). The impact of this system extends well beyond the prison wall as millions of Americans are on probation or parole, primarily for non-violent offences. At the heart of the system, the war on drugs convicts people of colour for drug offences at rates that are out of all proportion to their drug crimes under the guise of a race-neutral approach (p. 2):

> What has changed since the collapse of Jim Crow has less to do with the basic structure of our society than with the language we use to justify it. In the era of colorblindness, it is no longer socially permissible to use race, explicitly as a justification for discrimination, exclusion and social contempt. So we don't. Rather than rely on race, we use our criminal justice system to label people of color 'criminals' and then engage in all the practices we supposedly left behind. Today it is perfectly legal to discriminate against criminals in nearly all the ways that it was once legal to discriminate against African Americans. Once you're labelled a felon, the old form of discrimination – employment discrimination, housing discrimination,

> denial of the right to vote, denial of educational opportunity, denial of food stamps and other public benefits and exclusion from jury service – are suddenly legal.

Neither Alexander nor Tonry believe that the gross racial disparities they identify can be plausibly explained by 'old-fashioned racism' (Alexander 2010, p. 101) or 'racism in its most blatant forms' (Tonry 2011, p. 77). But both maintain that such disparities were entirely predictable and provide systemic explanations that highlight the role of policing. Tonry argues that tactical decisions to concentrate police resources on street-level drug supply in inner-city neighbourhoods inexorably narrowed the focus onto black and other racialised minorities because these are the markets they are most likely to participate in, while doing little to restrict the availability of drugs. He also points to widespread racial profiling, which means the police stop black people much more often than can be justified on the basis of objective, race-neutral criteria. Legislative decisions to mandate 'breathtakingly long prison sentences for many drug crimes' were a second tactical 'mistake' that has had a hugely disparate impact (Tonry 2011, p. 54).

But why did police leaders and policymakers continue to pursue these policies and practices even in the face of such striking disparities? The answer, according to Tonry, lies in the interaction of three powerful forces: a psychology of race relations characterised by stereotypes of black criminals, unconscious preferences for whiteness, and a lack of empathy among whites for black offenders and their families; a three-centuries-old pattern of economic, political, and social dominance of blacks by whites; and the Republican Southern Strategy of using stereotypes of black criminals and tough crime policies to appeal to white voters. To explain how the war on drugs operates in such a discriminatory manner without widespread support for explicit race discrimination, Alexander (2010, p. 103) identifies a simple two-stage design that 'has helped to produce one of the most extraordinary systems of racialized social control the world has ever seen'. The *first step* was to grant law enforcement officials extraordinary discretion over who to stop, search, arrest, and charge for drug offences, ensuring conscious and unconscious racial beliefs and stereotypes are given free rein. The *second*, 'damning', step was to 'close the courthouse doors' to claims of discrimination against the criminal justice system by insisting claimants have clear proof of intentional racial discrimination. Such proof 'will almost never be available in the era of colorblindness, because everyone knows – but does not say – that the enemy in the War on Drugs can be defined by race' (loc. cit).

Although individual bias provides a common reference point for explanations of racial disparities in US policing and criminal justice, recent analysis suggests situational factors may be more important. Given the strength of the evidence pointing to widespread unintentional and unconscious racial biases across the US population, Tonry (2011, p. 90) argues that it would be 'remarkable' if criminal justice practitioners were not similarly affected, and there is some indication that police officers are subject to such biases (Correll et al. 2014). Alexander (2010) also draws on decades of cognitive bias research to support her analysis, while Ghandnoosh (2015) identifies racial bias among criminal justice professionals as one of four key sources of unwarranted racial disparities. Others have questioned the focus on individual bias on the grounds that external situational factors have much greater influence on human behaviour. Pryor et al. (2020) argue that racially disparate policing practices are unlikely to arise solely, or even mainly, from officers' individual biases and identify five situational risk factors that have been shown to heighten the risk of discriminatory behaviour: discretion, inexperience, salience of crime, cognitive demand, and identity threat. These factors, they argue, especially in combination, can aggravate the risk that officers will exercise their judgment in discriminatory ways. Discretion and the salience of the black-criminality stereotype are particularly pertinent to drug policing and are likely to be important drivers of discrimination.

Drug policing in England and Wales

Although the US model of drug-fuelled mass incarceration stands out for its scale and severity, the underlying dynamics are mirrored in many other countries, reproducing and reinforcing a global 'colour line' (Koram 2019, p. 2). The United Kingdom offers an 'immediate parallel' where the uneven enforcement of drug laws has helped to produce ethnic disparities that are larger than those in the United States (p. 6). Disparities in policing, from stop and search through to deaths after police contact, have been cited as evidence that the United Kingdom is not innocent of the charges laid by BLM (Joseph-Salisbury et al. 2021, p. 21). Two months after Derek Chauvin was convicted of the murder of George Floyd, PC Benjamin Monk was convicted of the manslaughter of Dalian Atkinson, a former professional footballer, becoming the first police officer in 35 years to be convicted of murder or manslaughter following a death in police contact or custody in England and Wales (INQUEST 2021). Atkinson was suffering an acute mental health crisis when PC Monk tasered him for 33 seconds – six times longer than is standard – and kicked him twice in the head as he lay on the ground. After sentencing, Atkinson's family paid tribute 'to all the bereaved families of black men who have died at the hands of the police and whose fight for justice has not led to successful prosecutions' (Dodd 2021a).

Racial disparities in an era of colour-blindness

Despite the advent of apparently colour-blind policing in the United Kingdom and the virtual elimination of explicitly racist language, 'police culture continues to impact adversely on minority groups in ways identified in earlier research' (Loftus 2009, p. 127). Analysis by the Ministry of Justice to identify key pinch points in the criminal justice system, where ethnic disparities become more pronounced, confirmed that policing is the main driver of disproportionality (Uhrig 2016). Large ethnic disparities were identified at the point of arrest with small contributions emerging at later stages. The analysis also confirmed that such disparities are especially marked in relation to drug offences, reinforcing previous findings that black and minority ethnic young people are considerably more likely than their white counterparts to be arrested as a result of proactive police work that focuses on robbery and drug offences (May et al. 2010).

Although drug policing is rhetorically dominated by supply-side activities involving criminal gangs and organised crime groups running 'county lines' and engaging in modern-day slavery, the reality is more mundane (Shiner et al. 2018). Most recorded drug crime is for cannabis possession and this reflects the focus of police activity because drug offences are typically only recorded when drugs are found and offences cleared up (Shiner 2015a). Cannabis possession for personal use accounted for approximately two-thirds (60–70%) of drug offences recorded by the police each year from 2004/2005 to 2019/2020, while possession of other controlled substances accounted for less than a quarter (16–22%) (ONS 2021a). Trafficking offences, including supply, made up no more than a fifth of all police-recorded drug offences, varying from 12 to 20% per year. Stop and search is integral to the policing of drugs, with almost two-thirds (63%) of all searches targeting such offences (Home Office 2020a). The use of these powers accounts for a third to a half of all drug arrests (ranging from 33 to 50% per year from 2006/2007 to 2019/2020) compared with a tenth (8–11%) of all arrests (ibid). While the Police and Criminal Evidence Act 1984 (PACE) requires that officers establish 'reasonable grounds for suspicion' before they may use their stop and search powers, the national inspectorate of policing has identified a series of concerns about the disproportionate and proactive nature of drug searches (HMICFRS 2021):

- Black people were stop-searched at almost nine times the rate of whites in 2019/2020 and drug searches were more disproportionate than other types of search even though 'there is no correlation between ethnicity and rates of drug use' (p. 2).
- 'Surprisingly few' stop-searches (9%) are intelligence led and most are 'self-generated' by officers based on what they see or hear (p. 33). Self-generated and 'intelligence-led' searches are overwhelmingly focused on drugs (86 and 82%, respectively) in contrast to 'third-party' searches based on information provided by others, including members of the public (32%).
- Most drug searches are for suspected possession offences and half (50%) of all searches are self-generated possession-only drug searches.
- Self-generated drug possession searches are typically based on weak grounds (80%), including some that are based solely on the smell of cannabis, in contrast to third-party and intelligence-led searches (5 and 15% of which were deemed to be weak, respectively).
- Most searches find nothing, with approximately a quarter of self-generated possession-only drug searches finding drugs.
- Black and Asian people are more likely than whites to be subject to searches that are self-generated by the officer. Drug searches on black people,

> particularly possession-only drug searches, have weaker recorded grounds than equivalent searches on white people, and fewer drug searches of black people result in drugs being found.

These disparities provide prima facie evidence of discrimination given that drug use is no more prevalent among black than white people. Detailed analysis of stop and search across the 32 London boroughs identified some of the underlying dynamics, pointing to a combination of geographic profiling, targeting deprived areas with ethnically diverse populations, and individual profiling, targeting black people (Shiner et al. 2018). This mirrors the situation in the United States because it implicates deliberate policy decisions to concentrate drug law enforcement efforts in certain neighbourhoods, and ethnic profiling. The concentration on deprived inner-city boroughs cannot be fully explained by levels of crime and fuels disproportionality because such areas tend to have a relatively large number of black and minority ethnic residents (see Gordon 2020; Stott et al. 2021). This kind of targeting of 'high-risk' areas is commonly associated with proactive policing, where the ostensible aim is to prevent crime and disrupt drug markets, often through 'systematic and aggressive enforcement of low-level violations' (Sullivan and O'Keeffe 2017, p. 730). Such an approach tends to generate large racial disparities because it promotes selective enforcement (Weisburd and Majmunder 2018). An observational study in England and Wales contrasted the 'adversarial style' of proactive policing with the more consensual, responsive approach of neighbourhood teams, noting that the former fuelled a dynamic of mutual antagonism with a group of young, mainly black, teenagers suspected of being criminally active or engaged in gang activity in a 'high crime area' (May 2010, p. 40). The accompanying statistical analysis confirmed that young people from black and minority ethnic groups were considerably more likely than their white counterparts to have been arrested as a result of this kind of proactive police work.

The London borough analysis also found that 'race' complicates and confounds the general relationship between stop and search and deprivation (Shiner et al. 2018). While white and Asian people experienced significantly higher rates of stop and search in deprived boroughs, this was not the case for black people who were exposed to similarly heightened rates regardless of deprivation levels. Because rates of stop and search are reduced for white people in affluent boroughs, but remain high for black people, it is here that racial disparities are most marked. The combination of very low rates of stop and search for white people and high rates of black/white disproportionality point to ethnic profiling because it indicates that black people are singled out for suspicion. Such decisions may reflect biases, implicit or otherwise, that highlight the salience of the black-criminality stereotype, whereby the presence of black people is considered incongruent, and therefore suspicious, in affluent neighbourhoods. Observational studies suggest that assumptions about 'race' and poverty may mean black people are deemed 'out of place' in wealthy areas, particularly if they are dressed in ways that are also considered incongruent with the location, triggering suspicion even if there are no objective indicators to support such a conclusion (Quinton 2011; see also Carroll and Gonzalez 2014).

Initial disparities due to stop and search are exacerbated by subsequent decisions, generating marked 'downstream' differences in arrest and prosecution (Stott et al. 2021). Shiner et al. (2018) identify the application of out-of-court disposals, including cannabis warnings and fines, as a key decision point. They report that the find rate from searches was similar across all ethnic groups, as was the rate at which further action was taken, but that there were notable variations in the type of action taken. Black people were less likely to be given an out-of-court disposal than white people, but more likely to be arrested. While these disparities may reflect biases in individual officer decision-making, they are the logical conclusion of existing patterns of enforcement and policies regarding the allocation of out-of-court disposals. Where such disposals are only available for a first offence (as with cannabis warnings) or are discouraged for 'repeat offenders' (as with cautions) the over-policing of particular communities is likely to create feedback loops that selectively constrain the future availability of these options. When policing is concentrated in 'high crime areas' and targeted at 'known offenders', it is inevitable that the law will be differentially enforced for volume crimes such as cannabis possession, disqualifying some 'repeat' offenders from receiving out-of-court disposals if and when they are caught in possession. The selective application of out-of-court disposals means black offenders are more likely to be prosecuted than white offenders, pushing them deeper into the criminal justice system. Disparities are particularly marked in relation to cannabis possession, for which black people were prosecuted and convicted at 12 times the rate of whites in 2017 despite similar or lower rates of use. While more black people were prosecuted for cannabis possession than supply of Class A or B substances combined (3,229 versus 2,453), the balance was reversed for whites (6,892 versus 7,955). The prevalence of cannabis possession cases among black defendants is particularly striking because it exposes and challenges the racialised discourse and practices surrounding 'gangs' and 'county lines' (Wroe 2021).

Policing under austerity

Although defunding has gained little traction in the United Kingdom, the police have had to deal with significant reductions in government funding as part of a broader programme of austerity. Annual expenditure on the police increased by 48% in real terms between 1998/1999 and 2008/2009 (Mills et al. 2010), but this trend came to an abrupt halt following the 2008 financial crash. The October 2010 Comprehensive Spending Review outlined a 20% reduction in the central government police funding grant up to 2014/2015 (HMIC 2011). Central grants actually fell by 30% in real terms from 2010/2011 to 2018/2019, and forces became increasingly reliant on income raised through local council tax bills, known as the 'police precept' (Institute for Government 2021). While increases in local funding made up some of the shortfall, overall spending on the police fell by 16% between 2009/2010 and 2018/2019. The way the police adapted to these cuts may provide clues as to their likely response to defunding more generally and its implications for crime control.

Austerity prompted a reassessment of police priorities. The cartoonish call by Theresa May, the then home secretary, for 'tough, no-nonsense crime-fighters' glossed over the complexity of the police task, which combines crime control, social service, and order maintenance functions (Millie 2014). Of the emergency and priority incidents the police responded to in 2016/2017, only 24% were crime related and approximately 12% involved anti-social behaviour, leaving 64% that were non-crime related and covered such matters as road traffic accidents, mental health incidents, and missing persons cases (Comptroller and Auditor General 2018). The national inspectorate of policing identified significant concerns about the extent to which the police are involved in responding to mental health problems, noting that they are often the only professionals available to respond 'out of hours' (HMICFRS 2018). According to Millie (2014), the police remit has extended well beyond its core task to include roles that are more suitable for other agencies, community groups, or volunteers. Attributing this development to the rise of risk-oriented approaches to social policy, he advocates less police involvement in schools work, probation, event security, immigration control, and disaster management, and calls for 'a return to the fundamental roles of the police' (p. 59). One of the benefits of less police involvement in 'wide policing' activities, Millie argues, would be the decriminalisation of aspects of social policy, leaving the police to focus on a new narrower frontline and the preservation, rather than production, of order.

The police response to austerity concentrated on filling the financial hole and protecting the 'frontline'. Forces drew on their reserves and sold-off assets, including a large number of police stations (Institute for Government 2021); and made 'material changes in how they are structured and organised' to achieve 'the necessary workforce reductions, while seeking to protect their crime-fighting capacity on the front line' (HMIC 2014, p. 36). The number of full-time equivalent police officers and police staff across England and Wales fell by 15 and 22% respectively, during the course of austerity,[1] and only started to recover when the government provided a £970 million uplift in police funding for 2019/2020 and pledged to recruit an extra 20,000 officers by 2022 (Inman 2019; Institute for Government 2021). Although forces 'continued to provide an effective service to the public', their response to austerity did have some 'adverse effects' (HMIC 2014, p. 33). The national inspectorate identified specific concerns 'about the potential erosion of neighbourhood policing, the cornerstone of British policing', citing a higher than anticipated reduction in police community support officers (PCSOs) (p. 36): the number of PCSOs continued to fall beyond the 'end of austerity', almost halving between 2010 and 2020 (Home Office 2020b). Concentrating workforce reductions on neighbourhood roles was not mandated by the government and represented a significant reorientation of the police service towards a more 'reactive' mode, prompting the inspectorate to warn: 'The service must guard against a vicious circle emerging which involves less preventive activity, more reactive policing responses and spiralling demand. It is extremely important that action is taken now to prevent this from happening' (HMIC 2014, p. 36). Others, by contrast, maintained that 'emergency order maintenance', or so-called 'fire-brigade' policing, is 'the true purpose of policework and should be protected from budget cuts', noting that the façade of community policing has been destroyed by the use of highly invasive forms of surveillance technology (Bowling et al. 2016, p. 129). For those who consider community policing a disguised attempt at intensifying surveillance and control over 'problem' populations, the erosion of neighbourhood policing is likely to be welcomed as a step towards defunding (Gordon 1984; Joseph-Salisbury et al. 2021; Williams 2018).

Although budget cuts raised concerns about effectiveness, the impact of police resourcing on crime is unclear (College of Policing 2012; Draca and Langella 2020), and is likely to be less significant than the direct economic consequences of austerity (UNODC 2012). When the House of Commons Home Affairs Committee (2007, p. 16) considered resourcing issues on the eve of the financial crash, it noted that 'the significant decrease' in crime predated 'any significant increase in police funding or in police officer numbers', concluding that 'the reduction in overall crime levels does not seem to have been directly related to additional resources'. The committee was also struck by the volume of cautions, fines, and cannabis warnings, asking 'why, despite a huge increase in resources, such a large number of offences brought to justice seem to be made up of petty offences'? (p. 12). This focus on 'petty' crime is evident from the sharp increase in police-recorded cannabis possession offences, which almost doubled between 2004/2005 and 2008/2009 (see Figure 3.1). The increase in recorded possession offences was unrelated to trends in use, which were falling, and was the unintended consequence of a target-driven culture that rewarded officers for processing minor drug offences: the introduction of cannabis street warnings in 2003 provided officers with a quick way of clearing up offences at a time when forces were under pressure to meet government targets (Shiner 2015a).

The number of police-recorded drug offences fell sharply during the course of austerity, dropping by 41% between 2009/2010 and 2017/2018. This reduction was much sharper than the overall reduction in recorded crime: the total number of offences, excluding fraud and computer misuse, fell by less than a fifth (18%) and started to climb back to pre-austerity levels much earlier, from 2014/2015. Cannabis possession made up the bulk of the reduction in recorded drug offences from 2009/2010 to 2017/2018, falling by 49% compared with a 28% reduction in possession of other controlled drugs and an 18% reduction in trafficking offences. Once again, the trend in recorded drug crime was unrelated to the trend in drug use, which was on an upward trajectory for much of this period (ONS 2020). Reductions in recorded drug crime were largely a function of a sharp downturn in stop and search, resulting from a package of government reforms introduced in the wake of the 2011 riots (Shiner and Thornbury 2019), possibly reinforced

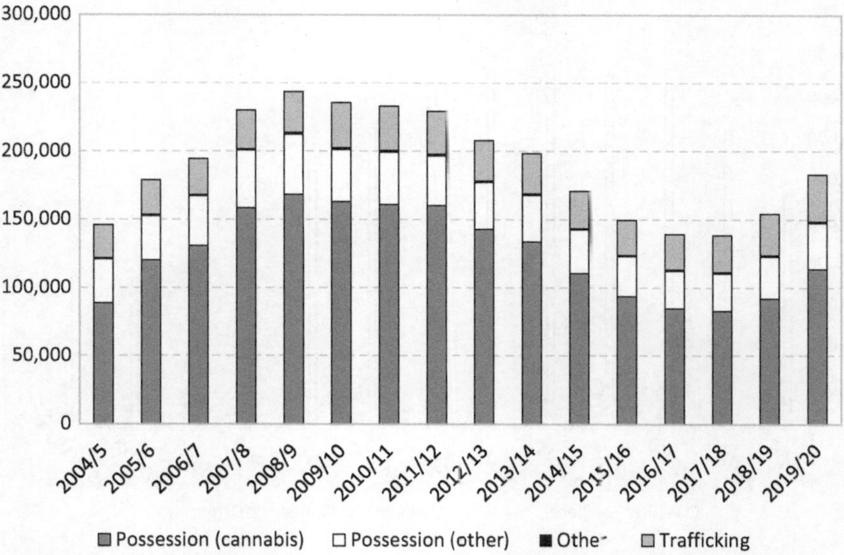

FIGURE 3.1 Police-recorded drug crime (numbers). Source: ONS (2021a) [Table A4]. Note: Possession offences refer to possession without intent to supply (i.e. for personal use); trafficking offences refer to unlawful importation as well as production, supply, and possession with intent to supply; and 'other drug offences' cover an array of offences relating to the production and supply of psychoactive substances, prejudicing an investigation, and permitting premises to be used for unlawful purposes among others (Ministry of Justice 2021).

by the effects of austerity.[2] That these developments had relatively little impact on trafficking offences reinforces the point that the 'frontline' is only peripherally involved with drug supply, despite the dominant discourse around 'county lines' and organised crime groups (Spicer 2021).

Drug arrests fell in line with recorded drug offences, almost halving between 2009/2010 and 2017/2018. These reductions were heavily concentrated among white people, who were subject to 58% fewer drug arrests in 2017/2018 than in 2009/2010 (see Figure 3.2). Black people experienced the smallest proportionate reduction and were subject to only 15% fewer drug arrests over the same period. A fifth (19%) of all drug arrests in 2017/2018 and 2018/2019 were of black people even though they make up less than 4% of the population (ONS 2018). Whatever the constraints created by austerity and the reform of stop and search, police forces adapted in ways that ensured a largely consistent flow of arrests of black people for, mainly minor, drug offences. The sharper focus on black people can be explained by increasingly polarised patterns of policing, whereby proactive interventions became more heavily concentrated in deprived, ethnically diverse, urban and inner-city neighbourhoods, while suburban and rural areas received

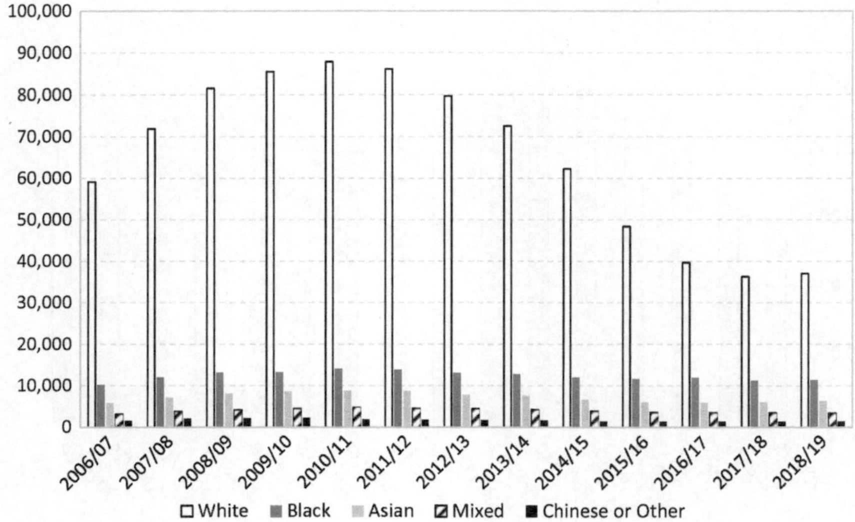

FIGURE 3.2 Drugs arrests by ethnicity (number). Source: Home Office (2020a) [Arrests open data tables]. Notes: (i) Figures for Lancashire Police were excluded from the analysis because this force was unable to provide full data for 2017/2018 and 2018/2019; (ii) figures are not shown for 2019/2020 because changes were made to the ethnic classification.

less intense forms of response policing if they were policed at all (Shiner and Thornbury 2019; Shiner et al. 2018). This bifurcated pattern of engagement institutionalises disparate patterns of enforcement because, put crudely, proactive policing treats members of the public as (potential) suspects, while response policing treats them as citizens in need of help.

Over-policing of the sort experienced by black communities constitutes a threat to citizenship, fuelling psychological and social exclusion. Unfair treatment at the hands of the police can undermine people's 'symbolic' sense of belonging (Bradford 2015; Bradford et al. 2014), while repeated experiences of proactive policing have been linked to trauma, anxiety, and distress (Borysik and Corry-Roake 2021; Geller et al. 2014; Williams 2018). Differential patterns of law enforcement also serve to reinforce social (dis)advantage by selectively criminalising black people, while maintaining white innocence even in the face of legal infractions. The targeting of large numbers of black people for cannabis possession, for example, contrasts sharply with police support of drug testing at festivals for an overwhelmingly white clientele engaging in Class A drug use (Chowdhury 2019; Measham 2019). The mainly black and Asian young people who are suspected of gang involvement live in something like 'a police state', where the 'surveillance and intelligence gathering function of the multi-agency gang management units conspires to curtail opportunities… under a guise of safeguarding and risk-management' (Williams 2018, p. 47). Being policed, under these circumstances, connotes 'unmitigated criminal and social regulation' via a series of often unknown state powers that extend into every area of life, including accommodation, education, employment, and training as well as family and friendships (loc. cit.). Ironically, perhaps, such patterns of over-policing serve to distance citizens from the police, divesting them of the right to be protected and orienting them towards alternative forms of conflict resolution, including self-help violence (Bradford 2015; Sharp and Atherton 2007). Having identified lack of trust in the police as a strong predictor of weapon carrying among young people in England and Wales, Brennan (2019, p. 588) notes:

> Although young people in high-crime neighbourhoods may be 'over-policed' in terms of 'stop and search' or the prosecution of drug-related offences, they may be 'under-policed' in terms of the protection from harm or the deterrent effect that the police offer, leading to weapon-carrying as a form of self-protection.

The literature on procedural justice attests to this dynamic by showing how unfair policing damages trust and confidence, undermining public cooperation and compliance with the law (see Jackson et al. 2013; Trinkner et al. 2018). Proactive police stops are a particular concern because they communicate suspicion of ongoing or future criminal conduct, which damages social bonds between the police and the community (Tyler et al. 2015).

Regulation and reform

The case for defunding rests partly on the claim that police reform has failed 'time and again' to address 'deeply entrenched institutional racism' (Joseph-Salisbury et al. 2021, p. 25). This is a powerful claim. Forty years ago, Lord Scarman's inquiry into the 1981 Brixton 'riots' noted 'the ill-considered, immature and racially prejudiced actions of some officers' and linked the 'disastrous impact' of stop and search to organisational policies that did not command support from the local population (Scarman 1981, 4.63). Almost two decades later, the Stephen Lawrence Inquiry did what Scarman refused to do and explicitly framed the problem as one of 'institutional racism', including stop and search among four areas where the problem was most apparent (Macpherson 1999). After the 2011 riots, Theresa May, then home secretary, told Parliament that the misuse of stop and search is 'an unacceptable affront to justice' that 'is unfair, especially to young, black men' (Hansard 2014, 831 and 833), while her colleagues denounced the disproportionate use of the powers as 'a stain on British policing' and 'probably the worst form of legal racial abuse in our country' (842–843). Police responses to this cycle of crisis and reform have been overwhelmingly defensive, highlighting 'an unavoidable central paradox, whereby the police cannot be relied upon to ensure robust regulation themselves, yet are likely to resist and subvert external efforts to this end' (Shiner 2015b, p. 147). Remarkably, stop and search became more, not less, disproportionate after both the Stephen Lawrence Inquiry and the reforms introduced by Theresa May (despite striking reductions in the overall use of the powers in the latter case) (Shiner et al. 2018). Rather than address the problem, senior police leaders have insisted that officers are scared to use their powers for fear of being accused of racism and have vowed to continue 'disproportionate' stop-searches of young black men, even stating that they are 'trying to decriminalise the word disproportionate' (Bentham 2021). This lack of moral leadership precludes meaningful reform and amounts to a form of 'institutional corruption' where failings are denied and concealed for 'reputational benefit' (O'Loan et al. 2021, p. 1060).

The government and courts are also part of the problem. Despite the introduction of statutory regulations, through PACE, the courts have been reluctant to subject police powers to detailed scrutiny and have tended to defer to the executive on such matters (Griffith 1997). Consequently, the rules covering stop and search – and other police activities – 'are not catered for at all by civil and criminal remedies', leaving officers to operate in a 'legal wilderness' (Sanders et al. 2010, p. 717). The police have also been granted several 'exceptional' powers they can use without the requirement for reasonable suspicion: Section 163 of the Road Traffic Act 1988 enables officers to stop motorists or cyclists; Section 60 of the Criminal Justice and Public Order Act 1994 enables them to stop and search anybody in a designated area; and Section 44 of the Terrorism Act 2000 made similar provisions until it was repealed in 2012. All these powers exacerbated ethnic disparities, intensifying the over-policing of minority communities (Delsol and Shiner 2015; HMICFRS 2021; StopWatch and Liberty 2017).

The courts have defended the ability of the police to conduct suspicionless searches. Although the Section 44 power was eventually deemed illegal by the European Court of Human Rights, this was only after it had been upheld domestically by the High Court, the Appeal Court, and the House of Lords (ECHR 2010). When Section 60 was challenged on the basis that there are insufficient safeguards limiting officers' discretion, leading to a risk of arbitrariness and discrimination, the power was also upheld by the domestic courts (Shiner and Delsol 2015). A striking feature of this case was the refusal of the court to consider statistical evidence pertaining to racial discrimination. According to official statistics, black people were subject to Section 60 searches at more than 20 times the rate of white people when use of the power spiked in 2008/2009, while the evidence on effectiveness – including Home Office evaluations – indicated that such interventions had no measurable impact on knife crime and serious youth violence (Shiner 2012; see also McCandless et al. 2016).[3] Presented with this evidence, the High Court objected that it could not be expected to consider disputed, 'undigested' statistical material and sought to refer the question of racial discrimination to the Equalities and Human Rights Commission (Moses and Eady 2012, 50ff). The Court of Appeal concurred (Kay et al. 2014, 32ff), stripping the case of its focus on indirect racial discrimination (Wills 2016).

Devoid of this evidential context, the Supreme Court was left to conduct a technical analysis of whether Section 60 had a legitimate basis and was in accordance with Article 8 of the European Convention of Human Rights, which protects the right to respect for private and family life, finding that it did and it was. In explaining their judgment, Lady Hale and Lord Reed made a series of unsubstantiated claims that were inconsistent with the evidence that had been excluded earlier in the case, implying any disproportionality was legitimate and Section 60 powers are effective in tackling serious violence:

> many of these gangs are largely composed of young people from black and minority ethnic groups… [and] it is members of these groups who will benefit most from the reduction in violence, serious injury and death that may result from the use of such powers.
>
> *(Hale et al. 2015, p. 4)*

By side-stepping the issue of indirect discrimination and endorsing the staggeringly disproportionate use of suspicionless stop and search, the Supreme Court has demonstrated that it is not only the United States that has 'closed the courthouse doors to claims of racial bias' (Alexander 2010, p. 138).

Conclusion

George Floyd's murder resonates with black communities in the United Kingdom and beyond because of a shared, collective, experience of injustice (Joseph-Salisbury et al. 2021) and an enduring sense that policing is 'against black people' (Institute of Race Relations 1987). According to the latest figures, almost half of black Caribbean adults in England and Wales do not have confidence in their local police (ONS 2021b). This startling figure prompted the chair of the National Police Chiefs' Council to declare that police legitimacy in black communities is so low it is damaging the effectiveness of law enforcement (Dodd 2021b). Under these circumstances, calls to defund the police warrant more serious consideration than they have been given in the United Kingdom. Although such calls have been summarily dismissed by mainstream politicians, the police have had to come to terms with shrinking budgets due to public spending cuts. The uncertainty associated with austerity provided an opportunity 'to rethink the shape of policing' and to 'create a leaner and fitter post-austerity police' (Millie 2014, p. 60), but it was an opportunity that was not taken. Forces sought to protect their frontline response capacity amid rising demand as they were called on to fill the gaps left by cuts to other services, taking on a greater safeguarding role covering missing persons and those in distress. The House of Commons Home Affairs Committee (2018, p. 6) described a police service 'under serious strain' that was 'badly overstretched', and called for greater investment in health services to reduce police involvement in mental health crisis work. While neighbourhood policing bore the brunt of the cuts, it is remarkable that, faced with these challenges, the police continued to prioritise low-level drug law enforcement in black communities to the extent that they did.

The defunding agenda is about more than funding and more than police. Much of what the police do is bound up with broader social inequalities and it is no coincidence that those who experience discrimination in this arena also suffer the most in other social spheres (Bowling et al. 2016). Institutional racism extends beyond policing and is evident across a range of sectors, including education, health, housing, and civil society (BRAP 2018; Byrne et al. 2020). Simply diverting funds from the police to other services, under these circumstances, runs the risk of reproducing the problem elsewhere, shifting the site of struggle. Left to their own devices, moreover, the police will likely adapt in ways that perpetuate existing practices and run counter to the intended purpose of defunding (see Shiner 2010, 2015b). It follows that a broader focus on structural racism and institutional transformation is required if police reform is to be successful (Kurtenbach and Ansorg 2020; Vitale 2017). Drug reform should be at the forefront of this process because enforcement of existing drug laws is driving the criminalisation of black communities and because there are viable alternatives. The decriminalisation of drug possession provides an obvious first step that would remove many enforcement-related harms, including criminalisation and discrimination, without significantly increasing direct drug-related harms (Eastwood et al. 2016; MacCoun and Reuter 2001; Shiner 2016). While there is a well-established case for decriminalisation, Black Lives Matter has highlighted the need to put racial justice at its centre. As such, decriminalisation should form part of a broader programme of reform promoting practices and strategies that expand the framework of public safety beyond arrest and prison to include community investment, therapeutic interventions, employment programmes, and public health approaches (Porter 2016; Sharkey et al. 2017; Shrotri and Scantlebury 2019).

More than anything, perhaps, Black Lives Matter's call to defund the police should be seen as a demand for full citizenship. George Floyd was a regular customer at Cup Foods, the grocery store he left shortly before his murder. The store is known locally, among the largely black community, for not calling the police and the Palestinian-American store owner, Mahmoud 'Mike' Abumayyaleh, said he wished the police had not been called in this instance (Bogel-Burroughs and Healy 2021). Abumayyaleh told reporters his employee called him crying after witnessing an officer press his knee into Floyd's neck: 'I said, "Call the police on the police. And make sure it's recorded". And she did that'. Later on, the store issued a statement that it will handle such situations without involving the police 'until they stop killing innocent people' (Sampay 2020).

Notes

1 This analysis is based on data published by the Home Office (2020; Table H3). Forces began to reduce their workforce during 2010/2011 in preparation for the cuts in

government funding that were pending and, as a result, March 2011 has been used as the benchmark to assess the impact of the cuts on the police workforce (HMIC 2011). The number of police staff fell to its lowest point in 2017, while the number of police officers fell to its lowest point in 2018.

2 Interrupted Time Series Analysis confirmed that the incidence of recorded drug crime (expressed as a rate per 1,000 population) increased from 2004/2005, but fell below the projected level in 2010/2011 and then continued to fall – in both relative and absolute terms – through to 2017/2018. These effects were no longer statistically significant ($p > 0.05$) when stop and search (expressed as a rate per 1,000 population) was included in the model, indicating that reductions in recorded drug crime during the course of austerity were largely a function of falling rates of stop and search. The independent effect associated with austerity approached statistical significance ($p < 0.10$), suggesting it may have reinforced the general trend. Police strength (measured as the number of full-time equivalent staff in the total workforce per 1,000 population) was not a significant predictor of the number of recorded drug crimes ($p > 0.05$ regardless of whether the stop and search rate was included in the model).

3 This evidence was presented in an expert witness statement provided by one of the authors of this chapter (Shiner).

References

Alexander, M. (2010) *The New Jim Crow: Mass Incarceration in the Age of Colorblindness.* New York: New Press.

Associated Press. (2022) 'Two ex-Minneapolis officers sentenced to prison over George Floyd killing'. *The Guardian*. Available from: https://www.theguardian.com/us-news/2022/jul/27/george-floyd-police-officers-j-alexander-kueng-tou-thao-sentenced.

Baum, D. (2016) 'Legalize it all: How to win the war on drugs'. *Harper's Magazine*. Available from: https://harpers.org/archive/2016/04/legalize-it-all/.

Bentham, M. (2021) 'Met Chief: We will continue "disproportionate" stop and search'. *Evening Standard*. Available from: https://www.standard.co.uk/news/uk/met-police-london-stop-and-search-racism-b918169.html.

Black Lives Matter. (2020) *#DefundThePolice*. Available from: https://blacklivesmatter.com/defundthepolice/ [Accessed 22 November 2021].

Bobo, L. and Thompson, V. (2006) 'Unfair by design: The war on drugs, race, and the legitimacy of the criminal justice system'. *Social Research*. 73(2): 445–472.

Bogel-Burroughs, N. and Arango, T. (2021) 'What to know about the trial of Derek Chauvin'. *New York Times*. Available from: https://www.nytimes.com/live/2021/derek-chauvin-trial-explained.

Bogel-Burroughs, N. and Healy, J. (2021) 'George Floyd: Inside the Minneapolis corner store whose worker made the 911 call that led to his killing'. *Independent*. Available from: https://www.independent.co.uk/news/world/americas/george-floyd-news-cup-foods-minneapolis-911-call-reopen-a9567971.html.

Borysik, B. and Corry-Roake, E. (2021) *The Knot: Lived Experience Perspectives on Policing Trauma, Poverty and Inequalities*. London: Revolving Doors Agency.

Bowling, B., Iyer, S., Reiner, R. and Sheptycki, J. (2016) 'Policing: Past, present, and future'. In Matthews, R. (ed.) *What is to be Done About Crime and Punishment?* London: Palgrave Macmillan: 123–158.

Bradford, B., Murphy, K. and Jackson, J. (2014) 'Officers as mirrors: Policing, procedural justice and the (re)production of social identity'. *British Journal of Criminology*. 54(4): 527–550.

Bradford, B. (2015) 'Unintended consequences'. In Delsol, R. and Shiner, M. (eds.) *Stop and Search: The Anatomy of a Police Power*. Basingstoke: Palgrave Macmillan: 102–122.

BRAP. (2018) *Let's Talk About Race: Civil Society and Race Equality*. Birmingham: Civil Society Futures, BRAP.

Brennan, I. (2019) 'Weapon-carrying and the reduction of violent harm'. *British Journal of Criminology*. 59(3): 571–593.

Byrne, B., Alexander, C., Khan, O., Nazroo, J. and Shankley, W. (2020) *Ethnicity, Race and Inequality in the UK: State of the Nation*. Bristol: Policy Press.

Carroll, L. and Gonzalez, M. (2014) 'Out of place: Racial stereotypes and the ecology of frisks and searches following traffic stops'. *Journal of Research in Crime and Delinquency*. 51(5): 559–584.

Chomsky, N. (2003) 'Drug policy as social control'. In Herivel, T. and Wright, P. (eds.) *Prison Nation: The Warehousing of America's Poor*. Abingdon: Routledge: 57–59.

Chowdhury, T. (2019) 'Policing the "black party": Racialized drugs policing at festivals in the UK'. In Koram, K. (ed.) *The War on Drugs and the Global Colour Line*. London: Pluto Press: 48–65.

College of Policing. (2012) *What Works in Policing to Reduce Crime: The Impact of Police Numbers on Crime Rates*. London: College of Policing.

Comptroller and Auditor General. (2018) *Financial Sustainability of Police Forces in England and Wales 2018*, Session 2017–2019, HC 1501. London: National Audit Office.

Correll, J., Hudson, S., Guillermo, S. and Ma, D. (2014) 'The police officer's dilemma: A decade of research on racial bias in the decision to shoot'. *Social and Personality Psychology Compass*. 8(5): 201–213.

Draca, M. and Langella, M. (2020) 'Law, order and austerity: Police numbers and crime in the 2010s'. *Advantage Magazine: Austerity Special*. Summer, (9): 12–15.

Delsol, R. and Shiner, M. (eds.) (2015) *Stop and Search: The Anatomy of a Police Power*. Basingstoke: Palgrave Macmillan.

Dickenson, T. (2020) 'What happened to promises to disband the Minneapolis Police?' *Rolling Stone*. Available from: https://www.rollingstone.com/politics/politics-news/what-happened-disband-minneapolis-police-1102763/.

Dodd, V. (2021a) 'Dalian Atkinson's family call for justice for others bereaved "at hands of police"'. *The Guardian*. Available from: https://www.theguardian.com/uk-news/2021/jun/29/police-officer-who-killed-dalian-atkinson-jailed-benjamin-monk.

Dodd, V. (2021b) 'Race crisis damages our legitimacy and effectiveness, says top police chief'. *The Guardian*. Available from: https://www.theguardian.com/uk-news/2021/mar/28/racial-justice-is-key-to-effective-policing-says-npcc-chief-martin-hewitt.

Eastwood, N., Fox, E. and Rosmarin, A. (2016) *A Quiet Revolution: Drug Decriminalisation Across the Globe*. London: Release.

Elliot-Cooper, A. (2020) '"Defund the police" is not nonsense: Here's what it really means'. *The Guardian*. Available from: https://www.theguardian.com/commentisfree/2020/jul/02/britain-defund-the-police-black-lives-matter.

European Court of Human Rights [ECHR]. (2010) *Case of Gillan and Quinton v The United Kingdom – Final Judgement*. Strasbourg: EHRC.

Fernandez, M. (2020) 'Probe of old drug cases raises questions about 2004 George Floyd arrest'. *New York Times*. Available from: https://www.nytimes.com/2020/06/19/us/unrest-george-floyd-houston-goines.html.

Garland, D. (2001) 'Introduction: The meaning of mass imprisonment'. *Punishment and Society*. 3(1): 5–7.

Geller, A., Fagan, J., Tyler, T. and Link, B. (2014) 'Aggressive policing and mental health of young urban men'. *American Journal of Public Health*. 104(12): 2321–2327.

Ghandnoosh, N. (2015) *U.S. Prison Population Trends: Massive Build-Up and Modest Decline*. Washington, DC: The Sentencing Project.

Gordon, D. (2020) 'The police as place-consolidators: The organizational amplification of urban inequality'. *Law and Social Inquiry*. 45(1): 1–27.

Gordon, P. (1984) 'Community policing: Towards the local police state?' *Critical Social Policy*. 4(10): 39–58.

Griffith, J. (1997) *The Politics of the Judiciary*. London: Fontana Press.

Hale, L., Clarke, L., Reed, L., Toulson, L. and Hodge, L (2015) *Judgment - R (on the application of Roberts) (Appellant) v Commissioner of Police of the Metropolis and another (Respondents)*. EWCA Civ 69. London: Supreme Court.

Hansard. (2014) *Stop and Search*, April 30 2014 (Column 832 – 846). London: UK Parliament.

Henderson, H. and Yisrael, B. (2021) '7 myths about "defunding the police" debunked', Brookings. Available from: https://www.brookings.edu/blog/how-we-rise/2021/05/19/7-myths-about-defunding-the-police-debunked/.

Her Majesty's Inspectorate of Constabulary [HMIC]. (2011) *Adapting to Austerity: A Review of Police Force and Authority Preparedness for the 2011/12–14/15 CSR Period*. London: HMIC.

Her Majesty's Inspectorate of Constabulary [HMIC]. (2014) *Policing in Austerity: Meeting the Challenge*. London: HMIC.

Her Majesty's Inspectorate of Constabulary and Fire & Rescue Services [HMICFRS]. (2018) *Policing and Mental Health: Picking up the Pieces*. London: HMICFRS.

Her Majesty's Inspectorate of Constabulary and Fire & Rescue Services [HMICFRS]. (2021) *Disproportionate Use of Police Powers: A Spotlight on Stop and Search and the Use of Force*. London: HMICFRS.

Herndon, A.W. (2021) 'How a pledge to dismantle the Minneapolis Police collapsed'. *New York Times*. Available from: https://www.nytimes.com/2020/09/26/us/politics/minneapolis-defund-police.html.

Hersh, J. (2020) 'Why defunding the police isn't such a radical idea'. *Vice News*. Available from: https://www.vice.com/en/article/889qvp/why-defunding-the-police-isnt-such-a-radical-idea.

Home Office. (2020a) *Police Powers and Procedures: England and Wales, Year Ending 31 March 2020*. London: Home Office [including open data tables].

Home Office. (2020b) *Police Workforce, England and Wales, 31 March 2020 - Data Tables*. London: Home Office [data tables].

House of Commons Home Affairs Committee. (2007) *Police Funding: Fourth Report of Session 2006–07*. London: The Stationery Office Limited.

House of Commons Home Affairs Committee. (2018) *Policing for the Future: Tenth Report of Session 2017–19*. London: House of Commons.

Inman, P. (2019) 'Has the age of austerity really come to an end?' *The Guardian*. Available from: https://www.theguardian.com/business/2019/sep/05/has-the-age-of-austerity-really-come-to-an-end-sajid-javid.

INQUEST. (2021) *Dalian Atkinson: Police Officer Found Guilty of Manslaughter*, June 24. London: Inquest.

Institute for Government. (2021) *Performance Tracker – Police*. London: Institute for Government.

Institute of Race Relations. (1987) *Policing Against Black People*. London: Institute of Race Relations.

Jackson, J., Bradford, B., Stanko, B. and Hohl, K. (2013) *Just Authority? Trust in the Police in England and Wales*. Cullompton: Willan.

Joseph-Salisbury, R., Connelly, L. and Wangari-Jones, P. (2021) '"The UK is not innocent": Black Lives Matter, policing and abolition in the UK'. *Equality, Diversity and Inclusion: An International Journal*. 40(1): 21–28.

Kay, L.J., Rafferty, L.J. and Macur, L.J. (2014) *The Queen on the application of Ann Juliette Roberts and The Commissioner of Police of the Metropolis & ors*, [2014] EWCA Civ 69. London: Royal Courts of Justice.

Koram, K. (ed.) (2019) *The War on Drugs and the Global Colour Line*. London: Pluto Press.

Kurtenbach, S. and Ansorg, N. (2020) 'What the US can learn from the Global South about police reform'. *United States Politics and Policy*. LSE USA Centre.

Lapin, T. (2021) 'Minneapolis to spend $6.4 million to hire more police officers'. *New York Post*. Available from: https://nypost.com/2021/02/14/minneapolis-to-spend-6-4-million-to-hire-more-cops/.

Loftus, B. (2009) *Police Culture in a Changing World*. Oxford: Oxford University Press.

MacCoun, R. and Reuter, P. (2001) *Drug War Heresies: Learning from Other Vices, Times, and Places*. Cambridge: Cambridge University Press.

Macpherson, W. (1999) *Inquiry into the Matters Arising from the Death of Stephen Lawrence*. London: The Stationery Office.

Mauer, M. (2009) *The Changing Racial Dynamics of the War on Drugs*. Washington, DC: The Sentencing Project.

May, T., Gyateng, T., Hough, M., Bhardwa, B., Boyce, I. and Oyanedel, J. (2010) *Differential Treatment in the Youth Justice System*. London: Equality and Human Rights Commission.

McCandless, R., Feist, A., Allan, J. and Morgan, N. (2016) *Do Initiatives Involving Substantial Increases in Stop and Search Reduce Crime? Assessing the Impact of Operation BLUNT 2*. London: Home Office.

Measham, F. (2019) 'Drug safety testing, disposals and dealing in an English Field: Exploring the operational and behavioural outcomes of the UK's first onsite "drug checking" service'. *International Journal of Drug Policy*. 67: 102–107.

Millie, A. (2014) 'What are the police for? Re-thinking policing post-austerity'. In Brown, J. (ed.) *The Future of Policing*. Abingdon: Routledge: 52–63.

Mills, H., Silvestri, A. and Grimshaw, R. (2010) *Police Expenditure 1999–2009*. London: Centre for Crime and Justice Studies.

Ministry of Justice. (2021) *Criminal Justice System Statistics Quarterly: Offence Group Classification*. London: Ministry of Justice.

Moses, L.J. and Eady, L.J. (2012) *R. (on the Application of Roberts) v Commissioner of Police of the Metropolis*, [2012] EWHC 1977 (Admin). London: High Court of Justice.

Nellis, A. (2016) *The Color of Justice: Racial and Ethnic Disparity in State Prisons*. Washington, DC: The Sentencing Project.

New York Times. (2021) *How George Floyd Died, and What Happened Next*. Available from: https://www.nytimes.com/article/george-floyd.html.

Nunn, K. (2002) 'Race, crime and the pool of surplus criminality: Or why the "war on drugs" was a "war on blacks"'. *Journal of Gender, Race, and Justice*. 381: 381–445.

Office for National Statistics [ONS] (2018) *Population of England and Wales*. London: ONS.

Office for National Statistics [ONS] (2021a) *Crime in England and Wales: Appendix Tables*. London: ONS.

Office for National Statistics [ONS] (2021b) *Confidence in the Local Police*. London: ONS.

Oladipo, G. (2021) 'Minneapolis voters reject bid to replace police with public safety department', *The Guardian*. Available from: https://amp.theguardian.com/us-news/2021/nov/02/minneapolis-police-department-vote-result.

O'Loan, N., Casale, S., Kellett, M., Morgan, R. and Pollock, S. (2021) *The Report of the Daniel Morgan Independent Panel: Volume 3.* London: House of Commons.

Parveen, N. (2021) 'Priti Patel describes Black Lives Matter protests as "Dreadful"'. *The Guardian*. Available from: https://www.theguardian.com/politics/2021/feb/12/priti-patel-hits-out-at-dreadful-black-lives-matters-protests.

Porter, N. (2016) 'Expanding public safety in the era of Black Lives Matter'. *University of Miami Law Review.* 70: 533–555.

Pryor, M., Buchanan, K. and Goff, P. (2020) 'Risky situations: Sources of racial disparity in police behaviour'. *Annual Review of Law and Social Science.* 16(1): 343–360.

Quinton, P. (2011) 'The formation of suspicions: Police stop and search practices in England and Wales'. *Policing and Society.* 21(4): 357–368.

Racial Justice Coalition. (2021) *Divestment from the Police Department is Possible.* Asheville: Racial Justice Coalition.

Ray, R. (2020) 'What does "defund the police" mean and does it have merit?'. *FixGov*, June 19. Washington, DC: Brookings Institution.

Sanders, A., Young, R. and Burton, M. (2010) *Criminal Justice.* Oxford: Oxford University Press.

Sampay, T. (2020) 'Cup foods owner on George Floyd: "I Wish the Police Were Never Called"'. *The Grio.* Available from: https://thegrio.com/2020/06/01/george-floyd-cup-foods-owner/.

Scarman, L. (1981) *Scarman Report: The Brixton Disorders, 10–12 April 2001.* London: HMSO.

Searcey, D. and Eligon, J. (2020) 'Minneapolis will dismantle its police force, council members pledge'. *New York Times*. Available from: https://www.nytimes.com/2020/06/07/us/minneapolis-police-abolish.html.

Sepic, M. (2021) 'A year after George Floyd's death, plans for Minneapolis police reform have softened'. *NPR News.* Available from: https://www.npr.org/2021/05/25/1000298293/a-year-after-george-floyds-death-plans-for-minneapolis-police-reform-have-soften?t=1639067649357.

Sharkey, P., Torrats-Espinosa, G. and Takyar, D. (2017) 'Community and the crime decline: The causal effect of local nonprofits on violent crime'. *American Sociological Review.* 82(6): 1214–1240.

Sharp, D. and Atherton, S. (2007) 'To serve and protect? The experiences of policing in the community of young people from black and other ethnic minority groups'. *British Journal of Criminology.* 47(5): 746–763.

Shand-Baptiste, K. (2020) 'Keir Starmer's dismissal of defunding the police has lost him black support: The problem is, I don't know if he cares? *The Independent.* Available from: https://www.independent.co.uk/voices/keir-starmer-black-lives-matter-defund-police-protests-labour-a9596401.html.

Shiner, M. (2010) 'Post-Lawrence policing in England and Wales: Guilt, innocence and the defence of organisational ego'. *British Journal of Criminology.* 50(5): 935–953.

Shiner, M. (2012) *Report on the Use of Section 60 of the Criminal Justice and Public Order Act 1994 by the Police.* London: StopWatch.

Shiner, M. (2015a) 'Drug policy reform and the reclassification of cannabis in England and Wales: A cautionary tale'. *International Journal of Drug Policy.* 26(7): 696–704.

Shiner, M. (2015b) 'Regulation and reform'. In Delsol, R. and Shiner, M. (eds.) *Stop and Search: The Anatomy of a Police Power.* Basingstoke: Palgrave Macmillan: 146–169.

Shiner, M. (2016) 'Drug policing: What is it good for?' In Collins, J. (ed.) *After the Drug Wars: Report of the LSE Expert Group on the Economics of Drug Policy.* London: LSEIDEAS: 59–66.

Shiner, M. and Delsol, R. (2015) 'The politics of the powers'. In Delsol, R. and Shiner, M. (eds.) *Stop and Search: The Anatomy of a Police Power.* Basingstoke: Palgrave Macmillan: 31–56.

Shiner, M., Carre, Z., Delsol, R. and Eastwood, N. (2018) *The Colour of Injustice: 'Race', Drugs and Law Enforcement in England and Wales.* London: StopWatch.

Shiner, M. and Thornbury, P. (2019) *Regulating Police Stop and Search: An Evaluation of the Northamptonshire Police Reasonable Grounds Pane.* New York: Open Society Justice Initiative.

Shrotri, M. and Scantlebury, R. (2019) 'A public health approach to serious youth violence for policy making in the London borough of Lambeth: An evidence review'. *The Lancet.* 394(2): S85.

Spicer, J. (2021) 'Between gang talk and prohibition: The transfer of blame for county lines'. *International Journal of Drug Policy.* 87: 1–8.

Stelloh, T. (2020) 'George Floyd's death ruled a homicide by medical examiner'. *NBC News.* Available from: https://www.nbcnews.com/news/us-news/george-floyd-death-ruled-homicide-medical-examiner-n1221431.

Stott, C., Radburn, M., Kyprianides, A. and Muscat, M. (2021) *Understanding Ethnic Disparities in Involvement in Crime: A Limited Scope Rapid Evidence Review.* London: Commission on Race and Ethnic Disparities.

StopWatch and Liberty. (2017) *Driving While Black: Briefing on the Discriminatory Effect of Stop and Search Powers on Our Roads.* London: StopWatch/Liberty.

Sullivan, C. and O'Keeffe, Z. (2017) 'Evidence that curtailing proactive policing can reduce major crime'. *Nature Human Behaviour.* 1(10): 730–737.

Tonry, M. (2011) *Punishing Race.* Oxford: Oxford University Press.

Trinkner, R., Jackson, J. and Tyler, T. (2018) 'Bounded authority: Expanding "appropriate" police behavior beyond procedural justice'. *Law and Human Behavior.* 42(3): 280–293.

Tyler, T., Jackson, J. and Mentovich, A. (2015) 'The consequences of being an object of suspicion: Potential pitfalls of proactive police contact'. *Journal of Empirical Legal Studies.* 12(4): 602–636.

Uhrig, N. (2016) *Black, Asian and Minority Ethnic Disproportionality in the Criminal Justice System in England and Wales.* London: Ministry of Justice.

United Nations Office on Drugs and Crime [UNODC]. (2012) *Monitoring the Impact of Economic Crisis on Crime.* Vienna: UNODC.

Vitale, A. (2017) *The End of Policing.* London: Verso.

Weisburd, D. and Majmundar, M. (2018) *Proactive Policing Effects on Crime and Communities.* Washington, DC: The National Academies Press.

Werleman, C. (2020) 'Make Black Lives Matter by ending the "War on Drugs"'. *Byline Times.* Available from: https://bylinetimes.com/2020/06/08/make-black-lives-matter-by-ending-the-war-on-drugs/.

Williams, P. (2018) *Being Matrixed: The (Over)Policing of Gang Suspects in London.* London: Stopwatch.

Wills, A. (2016) 'Case comment: R (Roberts) v Commissioner of police of the Metropolis and Anor [2015] UKSC 79'. *UK Supreme Court Blog.* http://ukscblog.com/case-comment-r-roberts-v-commissioner-of-police-of-the-metropolis-and-anor-2015-uksc-79/ [Accessed 24 June 2021].

Wroe, L. (2021) 'Young people and "county lines": A contextual and social account'. *Journal of Children's Services.* 16(1): 39–35.

4

SYMBOLIC DRUGS POLICING

Conceptual development and harm reduction opportunities

Ross Coomber, Matthew Bacon, Jack Spicer, and Leah Moyle

Introduction

> 45 arrests, dozens of cars and aircrafts seized in 'biggest ever' police sting against Brazilian-European drug ring.
>
> *(The Independent, 28 November 2020)*

> Major police operation sees 27 arrests, drugs seized and raids in Peterborough and Whittlesey.
>
> *(Peterborough Telegraph, 27 May 2021)*

Readers of this chapter will no doubt be familiar with the kind of headlines above that regularly feature in the news. They all relate to outcomes of specific police operations or drug raids that are a regular feature across the media/policing landscape. Explicit to reporting on drug market crackdowns is that there has been a coordinated set of targeted actions on the part of the police and that those actions have had a palpable outcome in terms of impacting the drug market and reducing the number of dealers supposedly embodying a distinct threat to the local community.

While police forces in the United Kingdom and elsewhere often evoke stereotyped views of drug markets and the threats they present to justify repressive measures at the local level, these can pale into relative insignificance when compared to the brutal long-term operations against drug sellers (but also users) that have been employed in some countries. In the Philippines, President Duterte's Operation Double Barrel – signifying that those at the top and the bottom of the drugs trade would be targeted – is perhaps the most ruthless manifestation of the drug war in recent years; the United Nations Human Rights Council (2020) has estimated that 8,000 people connected to the illicit drug trade have

DOI: 10.4324/9781003154136-5

been killed between 2016 and 2020, while Human Rights Watch (2020) refers to local human rights organisations that believe the number of killings (both official police and sanctioned extra-judicial 'executions') is around 24,000, with many more incarcerated (Wall Street Journal 2018). In Bangladesh, the targeted crackdown on Myanmar displaced minority Rohingya groups feared to be fuelling a growth in Yaba use has resulted not only in more than 100 police killings and 13,000 arrests but also, according to Odhikar, a Bangladeshi human rights group, more than 149 extra-judicial killings by security forces in May 2018 alone (Wall Street Journal 2018).

A less repressive international operation displaying greater levels of stealth, at least during the operation itself, was that of Operation Venetic, a multi-agency and multi-country operation that brought down various organised crime groups and individuals across Europe by infiltrating the encrypted communications of tens of thousands of criminals. In the United Kingdom alone, Operation Venetic has been reported to have directly resulted in 746 arrests and the seizure of £54 million of criminal cash, 77 firearms, and over two tonnes of drugs (National Crime Agency 2020). This kind of outcome reporting, where news reports measure the success of enforcement operations in terms of arrests and seizures and frame them as victories for the police over organised crime groups is a common trope.

Efficacy and achievement appear self-evident in these headlines, but what of the purpose and impact of such interventions in reality? It is worth reminding ourselves of the 'Peelian principles' – which are a key reference point for thinking about the fundamentals of modern Anglo-American policing (Loader 2016) – in particular, the ninth principle, to 'recognise always that the test of police efficiency is the absence of crime and disorder, and not the visible evidence of police action in dealing with them'. As we shall see, it is not always clear or evident with police operations that efficacy wins out over 'performance' or that substance wins out over style.

Police operations, crackdowns, and raids clearly provide a frame for police action that evokes a scalpel-like response cutting out rotten flesh (Bourgois and Schonberg 2009). The public imagination is encouraged to see rational, direct, and effective policing and Operation Venetic may be an example close to the top of the spectrum of success where this applies more easily. Operation Venetic was a largely technical operation involving the cracking of encrypted messaging and then monitoring communications for evidence. Most police operations, however, are, ironically, in fact more complicated because they involve interactions with day-to-day human behaviour where intent and involvement are muddied by differing levels of culpability and attributable vulnerabilities. As such, police action, like all policy action and implementation, is rarely straightforward in practice and outcome. Actions such as police crackdowns play out in complex ways. They have greater or lesser degrees of explicit and implicit intent and they can have multiple aims and outcomes, not all of which are stated or even obvious to those carrying out the acts. It is also commonly the case that the motivations and strategic intentions behind specific acts do not result in outcomes that were expected or desired. At other times, strategic intent is undermined or supported by a whole panoply of barriers and facilitators and unintended consequences. Policy and practice can be messy and 'muddling through' (Lindblom 1959) is not an uncommon aspect of policymaking in the real world. Policing is no different. Stated policy aims can be confounded by all manner of intrinsic and extrinsic variables while, at other times, normative and accepted practice may achieve practical outcomes unrelated to the specifics of the intervention or action.

In this vein, this chapter is interested in the nature of symbolic forms of policing generally, and specifically how this operates in relation to the policing of drugs and drug markets. The conceptualisation of 'symbolic policing' outlined in Coomber et al. (2019) provides a central framework through which further concepts – including Goffman's (1959) concept of 'performances', Manning's (1997) dramaturgical analysis of policing, and Loader's (1997) work on 'symbolic power' – that can help extend this perspective theoretically, are discussed. Following this, we draw on our respective empirical research to provide a critical analysis of the symbolic nature of police actions and their often counterproductive outcomes from the perspective of affected drug market actors and police officers. Attention will be given to how specific drugs policing activities such as executing warrants, responding to new threats, and attempting to safeguard 'vulnerable' populations can be considered symbolic both in terms of how they are undertaken and their outcomes. We conclude the chapter by considering the implications of symbolic policing from a harm reduction perspective and outline the importance of resisting forms of drugs policing that provide a superficial spectacle, but produce outcomes that are antithetical to public health and crime control aims. Recognising that symbolism is inescapable in how drugs policing is undertaken and represented, the chapter puts forward recommendations for how the communications and signals sent out may be reconfigured to help promote practices that align with harm reduction principles.

Symbolic (drugs) policing

Appearances matter for the police. That, of course, could be said of any institution comprising part of the criminal justice system. In fact, to a greater or lesser extent, all organisations are likely to be concerned with projecting certain images and communicating certain messages to particular audiences. But this is arguably of considerable importance for the police (Mawby 2001). From the various meanings associated with their uniforms (De Camargo 2020), through patrolling the regions of their organisation to which journalists can have access (Ericson 1989), to the selection of outputs on an individual force's Twitter feed (Crump 2011), the police give significant attention to how they present themselves and manage their public image.

The strength of this concern about being 'seen' to be active, or connectedly, about being seen in a particular light, can be considered the result of a number of pressures faced by the police and those who work within the institution. The media, the government, and the public, for example, all represent key bodies that receive communications from the police, while also holding the potential to influence the very nature of these communications themselves. As Mawby (2001, p. 44) has noted in relation to police 'image work', the optics that accompany policing can play a crucial role in 'promoting, projecting and protecting' how they are viewed. On the one hand, certain hegemonic images can boost their status, authority, and social standing. Others, however, can be subversive and risk undermining their credibility, the public's respect, and their apparent ability to police by consent. The continued cultural importance of fictional representations of the police, from the romanticised visions of Dixon of Dock Green and beyond, further reinforce their symbolic importance in society (Reiner 2010).

Goffman's (1959) dramaturgical perspective provides a popular conceptual toolkit for examining the symbolic dimensions of policing (see e.g. Bullock 2018; Manning 1997; O'Neill 2017). In a nutshell, Goffman famously uses the theatrical metaphor to analyse how actors present themselves and interact with others in social settings. His work focuses on 'performances' that are fashioned to project a desired image and influence those who observe them. Performances are delivered in the 'front region' and rehearsed or knowingly contradicted in the 'back region' (or 'backstage'). During performances, actors seek to control the signals given off in order to create and sustain a particular impression or 'front'. An 'idealised impression' is offered by accentuating certain facts and underplaying or concealing others. 'Destructive information' refers to facts that call into question the impression that the performance fosters. Goffman (1959) also explores forms of performance disruption and the 'arts of impression management' employed to prevent or mitigate the occurrence of these incidents. Members of the audience use 'frames' – heuristic devices that help people make sense of situations – to interpret signals, form impressions, and adjust their behaviour accordingly. The success of a performance depends in part on the expectations of its audience and their understanding of a particular social role.

Research on symbolism and policing emerged during the formative decades of the field of police studies. Manning's (1997) *Police Work* is the first dramaturgical analysis of the social organisation of policing. Heavily influenced by symbolic interactionism, especially the work of Goffman, as well as structuralism, this book is an attempt to articulate a perspective on policing as 'poised between instrumental, efficacious action and ritual, emotional and reductant routines that affirm the certainty and value of social order' (p. 7). Ultimately, the police are said to face an 'impossible mandate' in that they have assumed responsibility for problems beyond their control. Presentational strategies – including the rhetoric of professionalism, the bureaucratic ideal, technology, and crime statistics – are thereby used to convey the impression of effectiveness and underscore the authority and legitimacy of the police institution. Emphasis is placed on the selective presentations of police activities and how symbols are used to convey messages about the meaning of those behaviours. Such messages vary in content depending on the setting, actors, and audience. For Manning, these patterns of symbolic communication are a response to police interpretations of public expectations, designed to manage the illusion of control over crime and disorder in order to gain support for the police function. It is perhaps the diverse expectations of various audiences in a divided society that require the police role to be so full of tensions and contradictions.

While the social and cultural meanings surrounding the police may be complex, they are undoubtedly important. Despite a wealth of evidence to the contrary, police officers are regularly held up by politicians and the public as representing the solution to the 'crime problem' (Reiner 2020). As Loader (1997) argues, they hold a certain 'mythical' status and their societal role is principally affective. They are a social institution, occupy a position of authority, and bring to mind feelings of order and safety in response to the criminal 'other'. They represent suitable guardians and a way of creating ontological security, telling stories, and making sense of an uncertain world. They have the capacity to generate and communicate powerful social meanings regarding such matters as order/disorder, justice/injustice, normality/deviance, inclusion/exclusion, 'us'/'them' (see also Loader and Mulcahy 2003), which impacts on the manner in which people think, feel, and act in relation to problems of crime and disorder. Borrowing from Bourdieu's (1991) conceptual toolkit, Loader (1997) argues that the police possess 'symbolic power'. The strength of this depends, at least in part, on how associated symbols are assembled and exhibited. Signs and visions of policing, the iconography, such as handcuffs, sirens, and uniforms, interplay with the existing cultural position and perception of policing. 'Police trophy shots', Linnemann (2017) suggests – the police practice of displaying large sums of money, illicit drugs, weapons, and other seized material – are dynamic images that (re)produce police power 'by reminding state subjects of threats eliminated on their behalf and of the police who keep them safe' (p. 62). While they may not create the symbolic power of the police purely in and of themselves, they do serve to reinforce the dispositions that the public have towards the police.

It is worth noting the important symbolic qualities that operate within the police as well. As many studies on their occupational culture(s) have suggested, police officers regularly view themselves as the answer to 'fighting' crime and social ills (Bacon 2016; Loftus 2009). The communications they share and receive 'backstage' and away from the public gaze are therefore important. As Collison (1995, p. 41) detailed in his ethnography of a drug squad, the 'big busts' and exemplary displays of detective craftmanship were 'embellished and relished in the folklore of the squad as a symbolic representation' of what 'real' detective work is all about. The meanings, signals, and communications of police work and how they interplay with experiences on the ground have also been observed more widely. Taking inspiration from Bourdieu, Lande and Mangels (2017) have suggested that the making of arrests can be understood within the context of a symbolic economy. Arrests can take the form of symbolic capital, being 'gifted' to certain officers or 'stolen' from others. What such observations highlight is that, from their carefully cultivated public face to the internal dynamics behind the scenes, so much of police work is imbued, both explicitly and implicitly, with constructing meaning, sending communications, and achieving symbolic goals.

When it comes to the policing of drugs, and drug markets in particular, we can see some of this dramaturgical activity laid bare and played out clearly to full effect. In *The Narcs' Game*, Manning (2004) focuses the dramaturgical lens on drug law enforcement in the United States. The 'front', which gives extraordinary attention to spectacle-like raids, arrests, and seizures, is 'a powerful shield that obscures the facts of the ramifying costs, consequences, and impacts of policies' (p. 9). With media amplification, the public is encouraged to view drugs policing 'as a series of dramatic confrontations between good and evil' and the police as possessing 'superior resources, skill, and virtue' (p. 253). Police efforts, Manning argues, represent a mode of social control directed at marginal groups in society, not the control of drugs per se. In this sense, drug law enforcement is 'a ceremony that celebrates the interests of the powerful segments of society and their views of appropriate levels and kinds of drug use, proper lifestyles and occupations, the correct place to live, and moral commitments' (p. 254).

Drawing partially on the work of Edelman (1985, 1988), Innes (2004, 2014), and others, in Coomber et al. (2019) the idea of symbolic policing as a purposeful act is taken further and posited more directly than previously at the policing of drugs and the much-utilised practice of 'crackdown' operations that often come with media-friendly names evoking a strong action or response. Edelman (1985, 1988) had long ago suggested that much of politics was in fact about managing public fears and expectations and when some issues were intractable, to assuage public dissatisfaction by 'constructing spectacles' on which the public imagination and support could be almost guaranteed. Edelman (1988) dismantles these spectacles, describing them as a 'partly illusory parade of threats and reassurances', of which, the majority 'have little bearing upon the successes and ordeals people encounter in their everyday lives, *and some of which create problems that would not otherwise occur*' (our italics, p. 96). Edelman noted how 'the drug problem' had been consistently used in US politics, across all parties, not only as a rallying point for (re)focusing away from inconvenient aspects of American politics but also as a convenient scapegoat for the ire of dissatisfied electorates and a nod towards demonstrating a willingness to grapple with important issues. In the United Kingdom, similar observations of the nature of the drugs 'problem' and its policing are posited, with actions being suggested to have as much to do with communicating meaning about power and authority in society (e.g. Loader 1997) as preventing or solving crime.

Although the idea of symbolism has gathered some momentum in understanding the role of the police and the function of policing in society, less attention has been directed to the ground-level mechanics of this process in day-to-day police work. An important development in understanding the micro-level presentation of policing is found in Innes' (2004) study on signal crimes, which considers the messaging surrounding particular crime events, as well as the expressions, meanings, and intended effects of 'control signals'. Police work involves the transmission of control signals that are designed to deter people from engaging in acts of deviance. Others provide reassurance and protection from harm. Innes (2014, p. 137) also suggests that control signals can have negative effects 'when they defray public conceptions of security, or damage public trust and confidence in institutions of the state'. Drawing on the symbolic interactionist tradition outlined above, Innes (2014) argues that all social signals comprise three component parts: the 'expression' – that is the signifier or denotative aspect; the 'content' – what is connotatively signified; and an 'effect' – 'the change induced from the connecting of a content to an expression' (p. 3). Much like 'signal events', Innes argues that signals of control are always followed by an 'effect', namely a 'sense of progress' or an acknowledgement of a local improvement (p. 133). For Innes, a signal crime/event can therefore be defined as an incident that has a meaningful impact on the way we think, feel, and act, both at a collective and an individual level.

While Innes' (2004) study was focused on unpacking the relationship between experiences of a range of crime and disorder and criminogenic risk, findings from his ten-year programme of fieldwork suggest that drug-related crime and disorder have a fairly 'dominant position' in terms of shaping how people perceive levels of neighbourhood security (2014, p. 17). For Innes, the power of the 'signal' associated with drug-related offending is such that the 'significatory properties' (Innes et al. 2002, p. 41) of the signs of drug use are seemingly a problem equivalent with drug use itself. Public concern about drugs is therefore multifaceted, encompassing a range of expressions including drug dealing, drug houses, and signs of drug use, including discarded syringes and other drug-related litter. These findings are, of course, unsurprising considering the fear and generative anxieties triggered by visible drug use or signs of supply. Private 'recreational' drug use is rarely considered a matter for intervention. Public encounters with users of what are often labelled 'problem' drugs, however, such as heroin and crack cocaine, not only induce fear, but also represent danger, 'dirt', and are symbolic of the wider collapse of social order (Fitzgerald and Threadgold 2004). Responding to the visible signs of drug use and supply as 'signals to control' (Innes 2014) therefore has obvious value to local police forces who are able to reduce the fear of crime and bolster 'feelings' of safety, as well as increasing levels of public satisfaction with police performance (Coomber et al. 2019).

Symbolic policing case studies

So far, we have provided a critical overview and theoretical framing for symbolic policing in general, as well as how it has been applied specifically to drugs policing in relation to large-scale and/or prominent police operations or crackdowns on drug supply. Drawing on our own various research projects, we will now extend this analysis and provide some detailed empirical examples of how symbolic drugs policing might be understood to operate in both everyday practice and in regard to specific novel circumstances and conditions. Three case studies are provided, focusing on different policing responses to different parts of the illegal drug market. Each case demonstrates the symbolic nature of their respective forms of drugs policing. This includes the construction of a 'spectacle', how their ultimate outcomes related to their original stated intentions, and how they were interpreted by those officers actually undertaking it.

Crackdown operations

Although our first empirical example draws on Coomber and Moyle's (Coomber et al. 2019) research on the symbolic policing of drug market crackdowns, it does so here with an emphasis on the findings that consider the impact of crackdowns on vulnerable user-dealers. Taking inspiration from Edelman's (1985) broad focus on politics and policy as 'symbolic action' and Innes' (2014) micro-level exposition of crime signals and social control, we aimed to use these ideas to advance the conceptual framework of 'symbolic policing', offering this as a theoretical tool to make sense of targeted police operations or 'crackdowns' on street-level drugs markets. In Coomber et al. (2019), police crackdowns on drug sellers were explicitly explored as symbolic practice rather than a serious attempt to dismantle the drug market/s in any one area.

Some policing may be symbolic largely because of resource deficits, that is, it may be that a given approach, if able to be scaled up sufficiently, would be an appropriate and effective way of managing a problem. Arguably, such policing has validity on a level above and beyond simply being seen to be doing something. However, other approaches are symbolic in the sense that, rather than betraying an under-resourced but otherwise effective model, they instead reveal the inappropriate implementation of an approach that cannot achieve the known objectives of policing drug markets (i.e. either a complete dismantling or meaningful disruption) and, as such, the value they have is predominantly, rather than adjunctly, symbolic. This is even more problematic if, at the same time, the symbolic acts of crackdowns produce more harm than they resolve, such as prompting a switch to more harmful forms of acquisitive criminality (Coomber 2015; Maher and Dixon 1999), increasing adverse public health outcomes such as blood-borne disease and overdose (Wood et al. 2004), or arresting vulnerable populations (Moyle 2019). Drug market crackdowns and police operations, we have argued (Coomber et al. 2019), fall into the latter category. We will now briefly consider this impact on those most affected by crackdowns – the 'low hanging fruit' of heroin user-dealers who, typically, become embroiled in such actions.

Our research in Southend-on-Sea, Torbay, and Plymouth revealed that those arrested in police crackdowns on heroin and crack cocaine supply in those areas were either low-level drug sellers who are commonly addicted to heroin and sell to be able to buy, or earn, their own supply; young, often exploited, and vulnerable individuals recruited to be disposable to enforcement; or perhaps the category involving the lowest levels of culpability – addicted heroin and/or crack users who are enticed or entrapped into 'supplying' by undercover police officers. Operation Rasp (2012) in the seaside town of Southend-on-Sea, Operation Tucker (2010) in the peninsular area of Torbay, and Operation Bugatti (2009) in the naval city of Plymouth involved a fairly standard operating policy of using undercover police to pose as drug users to infiltrate local heroin and crack drug scenes, accumulate local, street-level 'intelligence', and make what are known as 'test purchases' from genuine local drug users and sellers to achieve multiple 'countable' arrests and, for a brief period, to remove some of the most visible aspects of drug markets (Bacon 2016; Woods 2016). Such operations had mixed results with varying levels of arrest and seizure, but each was well publicised in the local news and reported as though a meaningful success regardless of the variable outcome. Arguably, the 'idealised impressions' (Goffman 1959) being aimed at and promoted are those combining police (pro)activity, community protection and reassurance, and through (even nominal seizure or arrest outcomes) a sense of being successful in these endeavours.

Respondents in each of the research areas produced similar accounts whereby the essence of the operations involved police purposively targeting the 'low hanging fruit' of visible local heroin (and/or crack) users congregating in particular local streets, locations, and shopping areas as well as low-level user-dealers and 'runners'. Little to no action was focused on those higher up the chain of supply simply because they are less visible and have a separation from the act of actual supply and thus relative insulation from enforcement. Respondents commonly reported that those who were visible and thus easily accessed were also some of the most vulnerable, such as rough sleepers, 'known' (to the police) dependent drug users, and *Big Issue* sellers (an independent magazine sold on the streets by homeless, marginalised, and disadvantaged people). These groups were routinely approached by undercover officers as they would often be understood to be either drug users (present or past) or to be able to gain access to heroin and crack cocaine:

> These coppers, they used to go up to people doing the Big Issue because they're desperate, they're trying to get money to get their fix and they say, 'I'll buy you a bag if you go and get me one' and that's how they trick them.
>
> *(Jake [35], heroin and crack user, Plymouth)*

We have previously raised doubt (Coomber et al. 2019) that genuine, non-drug using, commercially orientated sellers would be easily enticed by such an approach and non-drug using runners would be less obviously detectable. The majority of those approached in this manner in areas such as Southend-on-Sea or Plymouth, where sales are predominantly through commercially orientated dealers (or their non-drug using runners), will therefore be those palpably visible users hanging around the streets in known areas where users congregate.

One typical encounter with two, presumed to be undercover police officers, was described by a drug user in Plymouth on the day of being interviewed for the research:

> I had two of them today, 'Oh do you know where Callum lives?' Like 'Do you know where Callum lives?' And I was like, 'No.' They was like, 'Can you score for us?' And I was like, 'No.' ...and then they asked, 'can you score for us, we're really ill?' And like they were pretending they were ill; they were like just scruffy and stuff... Pathetic, isn't it?
>
> *(Sam [25], heroin and crack user, Plymouth)*

In line with international research in this area (Aitken et al. 2002; May and Hough 2004), aside from the initial 'deterrence effect' (Sherman 1990), the medium- to long-term impacts of the undercover operations and test purchases in the local drug market were negligible. Access to heroin and crack was reported to be only nominally affected for a very short period of time for some people and each undercover operation and/or 'sweep' resulted in meaningful numbers of local heroin/crack users and sellers being arrested and charged with supply-related offences (see also Spicer 2021a). Numerous naïve, vulnerable, and often intoxicated local dependent users were regularly entrapped into the act of supplying, arguably merely emphasising how, when provided with an opportunity to ease the normatively precarious and uncertain path to paying for their next 'hit' (Moyle and Coomber 2015), a proportion of this population is willing to take the risk of supplying drugs or facilitating the supply of drugs to new 'users' on the local scene. One Southend-on-Sea respondent related how this often plays out:

> I mean the police have just finished like an undercover operation; they're quite a lot of people in Chelmsford Prison at the moment, pending further charges, to go in front of the court, for actually getting drugs and selling them to the police. Not actually being the dealers, but being the sort of middleman where they've come along, the police undercover has come along, and said, 'Oh, can you get us a bit of crack, mate?' And they're thinking, 'Oh, I might be able to make a bit of crack myself, like a couple of pipes, or make a quick £10.' 'Yeah, I can get you some crack.' Get it? And then what the police have been doing is saying to them, 'Well, here you are, look, you can use my phone, I've got plenty of credit on it... And then that's how they're all getting busted.
>
> *(Geoff [51], heroin and crack user, Southend-on-Sea)*

When this scenario is further contextualised by the fact that user-dealers are often deeply 'embedded' in the local drug market milieu (Moyle and Coomber 2016), conceiving either small supply facilitation events (acting as a broker for example) or even actually supplying to other, already dependent heroin and crack users, on occasion as a natural 'extension' to their own drug use, but also as less harmful or shameful than other crimes such as shoplifting, burglary, prostitution, and theft (see Moyle and Coomber 2015), we can see how being approached to supply would be seen as an attractive opportunity, easy money, and good fortune. The real human cost of undercover policing in local drug markets is palpable and levels of vulnerability are becoming better understood and acknowledged to be morally and ethically questionable, even by the police (Coomber and Moyle 2018; Moyle 2019; Windle et al. 2020).

Such tensions for policing are writ large in county lines policing, but vulnerability comes in many forms. Young, exploited, and vulnerable boys make up only one aspect of the spectrum of vulnerability (Windle et al. 2020), with the lived experiences of drug users regularly swept up in what are largely symbolic operations (Moyle 2019). One further illustrative example perhaps encapsulates this. A person caught up in the Operation Bugatti undercover sweep in Plymouth was described as a 'prostitute drug addict mum' by the media reporting on her court case (This is Cornwall 2009). The woman in question was reported to have been arrested for supplying three £10 bags of heroin weighing between 0.144 and 0.160 grams, to have been dependent on heroin for the preceding 15 years, and as someone who normally financed her addiction through sex work. On the occasion in question, however, the woman was sought out and approached by undercover officers who went to her home to try to arrange a drug deal. The woman accepted the opportunity to supply on two separate occasions. Although the Police and Criminal Evidence Act (1984) is clear that, in the course of their duty, an undercover officer cannot compel or 'persuade' individuals to commit an offence and that courts should reject cases that would not otherwise have been committed, undercover officers are permitted to facilitate or enable an opportunity to commit an offence by asking them to sell or buy drugs on their behalf (Bronitt 2004) and providing an 'unexceptional opportunity' to commit crime that they would have committed with another is 'perfectly acceptable' (R v Looseley [2001] UKHL 53) (as cited in College of Policing 2016, p. 56), and if an individual agrees to undercover officers' requests then the law stipulates that this is not entrapment (Brooke 1999). The law's focus on the social background of the offender is key here (Squires 2006); an addicted drug user is far less likely to be considered entrapped by a court because they are subject to opportunities and are therefore not considered 'exceptional' in the eyes of the law. Returning to the woman targeted in her home in Plymouth, her status as a known drug user provides legal protection against defining this conduct as entrapment. Undercover test purchases tend, therefore, to capture the most visible, low-level players in the drug market – buyers and users who are most often predisposed to taking these kinds of opportunities.

Police raids

This section draws on Bacon's (2016) ethnography of police detectives, drug law enforcement, and proactive investigation. The study focuses on the routine activities and occupational culture of 'drug squads', which are specialist detective units assigned to the task of tackling drug markets by utilising intelligence-led policing strategies to instigate covert operations and make cases against suspected drug dealers. Fieldwork was carried out in two police service areas between 2008 and 2010: 'Metropolis' (a borough of a city in the south of England) and 'Smallville' (a town in the north of England). In what follows, attention is given to the instrumental and symbolic functions of drug warrants from the perspective of the police. This tactic is more generally known as a 'raid'.

When the detectives were in possession of intelligence indicating that an individual or group was actively involved in drug supply, a key component of their tactical toolkit was to obtain a warrant to enter the premises where the suspect(s) resided, operated from, or stored their drugs in order to search the specified location and any persons found therein for evidence of the alleged offence. Raids were also executed to enforce arrest warrants. They could be swift, self-contained interventions or part of larger-scale covert surveillance operations or crackdowns. The overwhelming majority of raids carried out during the fieldwork period were on houses in deprived neighbourhoods with long-standing drug problems. Most took place in the early hours of the morning, when the unsuspecting target was likely to be asleep and thus unable to dispose of any contraband or incriminating items. A convoy of unmarked police cars and a tactical support van would make their way through the quiet streets and park up outside the marked address or at a predesignated spot. Police officers dressed in protective gear would then quietly assume their positions and wait for the bang of the battering ram. 'POLICE! POLICE! POLICE!' Upon entry, officers would secure the premises, detain the occupants, and then set about searching for evidence. The optimal outcome of a raid was to catch the target(s) in possession of a substantial quantity of controlled drugs and uncover evidence of conspiracy to supply or possession with intent to supply.

For the detectives, the foremost advantage of the drug warrant was that it provided them with a 'quick, cheap, and easy' method of taking out their targets and racking up arrests and seizures. Where successful, suppliers were at least temporarily removed from the market and faced criminal justice penalties and economic disruption in the form of incomplete transactions or lost resources when their drugs and ill-gotten gains were confiscated. Raids also had broader goals in that they were used as a means of disrupting distribution networks, removing sources of drugs, and inconveniencing users by making it more difficult for them to make a purchase. However, when 'backstage' (Goffman 1959) it was readily apparent that the detectives were well aware of their limitations. Warrants were described as a 'blunt instrument'. As a tactical resolution, they provided a useful tool for bagging the 'small fry' – local user-dealers of heroin and/or crack – but detracted police resources away from the bigger players. 'Smart' dealers, it was assumed, especially those operating above the retail level, were unlikely to have incriminating evidence at their home address or premises under their control and adopted risk management strategies that could only be penetrated through covert surveillance. Unsuccessful warrants and results that were not as good as expected were common causes of concern and criticism. 'Most of the time we don't come out with what we went in for'. There were days when the detectives went in for 'wholesale quantities' of heroin and left with just a few grams, others when a small amount of cannabis was all that could be salvaged, and those when nothing was found and they left empty-handed. Suspects occasionally slipped through the net because they had no fixed address and were difficult to pin down or were simply not present when the warrant was executed. These outcomes were blamed on gaps or inaccuracies in the police intelligence picture. Finally, the detectives recognised that unless they got lucky and 'struck big' a raid was not going to cause a major disruption to the larger market system or impact on levels of use, availability, and price. They knew that distribution networks are adaptable, suppliers are easily replaced, and deterrent effects are transitory. Drug warrants are not designed to change the marketplace. Their objective is to uphold the law, bring offenders to justice, and signify that something is being done.

The symbolic functions of the drug warrant tactic were to let dealers know that the police were 'onto them' and to reassure the public that they were responding to their concerns and tackling local drug problems. From a 'control signal' perspective (Innes 2014), detectives opined that forced entry warrants increase the perception and actual risk of detection for those offenders still at large and thereby deter them from engaging in drug market activity. The impression of 'the always imminent raid', Collison (1995, p. 172) notes, 'serves to sustain a symbolic influence for the squad when the lack of intelligence or resources precludes a real presence'. Some detectives wanted to be feared, recognised as a force to be reckoned with, and they aspired to be the reason why the inhabitants of the drug world had to sleep with one eye open. Others had more modest ambitions, were sceptical about the deterrent effect, and questioned whether 'the message' was actually being received as intended:

> [Drug warrants] get the other dealers all rattled up. They're sat at home wondering if they'll be next, or if the guy we've taken in is going to grass them up. The market usually goes quiet for a while because people are laying low trying to figure out what's going on.
>
> *(Detective, Smallville)*

> If I'm honest, I don't think the dealers are even half as worried about us catching up with them as we'd like to believe. We're an occupational hazard. Most of them are used to living with a heavy police presence so they're well practised at avoiding the law. Chances are they'll be a tad more cautious for a short time after a raid, but it's soon back to business as usual.
>
> *(Detective, Metropolis)*

Being a hypervisible display of power, raids are very much a 'performance' (Goffman 1959), 'ritual' (Manning 1997), or 'spectacle' (Edelman 1988), designed to demonstrate the capacity and will of the police to manage contraventions of the law and social order and send messages about who belongs within society and what behaviours will or will not be tolerated (see also Loader 1997; Loader and Mulcahy 2003; Innes 2014). These symbolic functions were particularly pronounced during National Tackling Drugs Week (Gilling 2012), when the drug squads invited journalists to accompany them on a series of highly publicised raids that were intended to raise awareness of the work being done locally to respond to local drug priorities.

News about dramatic enforcement interventions was said to 'spread like wildfire' through the community. The scene of a raid was guaranteed to attract a crowd of onlookers and endless passers-by and their interpretive accounts would be passed on through the grapevine and soon become common knowledge. These accounts then enter into the collective memory, where they 'interact and intermingle with a range of other influences upon public experiences, perceptions, and judgements about safety and security' (Innes 2014, p. 130). Detectives or tactical support officers were stationed at the entrance of the property being searched to maintain order and prevent members of the public from crossing the threshold. This vantage point enabled them to communicate with local residents and gauge their initial reactions. Subsequent reactions were occasionally fed back via informants and neighbourhood police officers, but no real effort was made to monitor the fallout. The following selection of quotations capture the various ways in which detectives perceived public reactions to drug raids:

> If it's a real scumbag you can hear the community breathe a sigh of relief when we take them away.
>
> *(Detective, Metropolis)*

> People can be genuinely shocked to find out they've been living next door to a drug dealer. It makes them all worried about what else is going on under their nose.
>
> *(Detective, Smallville)*

> In the worst affected areas the residents have mixed feelings towards drug enforcement operations. I mean, they're pleased to see that the police are doing something, but at the same time they know that arresting one or two dealers is not going to make a difference in the grand scheme of things. They've seen it all before. They know the dealers will be right back at it as soon as we're gone.
>
> *(Detective, Metropolis)*

> You'll get a few who'll come over asking questions cos they're after a bit of gossip, but most people keep their distance and let us get on with it … When we're in the rougher areas we might get a bit of lip, people telling us to stop harassing them and leave them be like. Their family and friends

> come down and start eyeballing us and giving us shit. You'll see them on their phones giving this dealer or that dealer a heads up. It can get pretty tense.
>
> *(Detective, Smallville)*

> There are people around here who hate the police more than the dealers. Hell, some of the dealers are like local celebrities in the estates. To them warrants are just another example of oppressive and discriminatory policing.
>
> *(Detective, Metropolis)*

For the most part, the detectives believed that successful raids were viewed in a positive light by law-abiding citizens and resulted in improved public confidence in the policing of drugs and enhanced satisfaction with the police. They also claimed that there was usually a slight increase in community intelligence in the immediate aftermath. That being said, it was recognised that the control signals they transmitted could also be negative in their effects. The negative effect that bothered detectives the most was that unsuccessful raids undermined their authority and made them 'look like punks'. Other undesirable consequences that can be drawn from the above quotations are that raids can increase the fear of crime, fail to have any meaningful impact on entrenched drug markets, and come across as an unfair use of power that is disproportionately directed at marginalised social groups. The police seldom considered the negative effects of raids on people who use or sell drugs.

Mirroring county lines

This section draws on ethnographic research conducted by Spicer (2021a) and considers symbolic policing specifically in relation to responses to drug market threats perceived as 'new' or 'novel'. Periodically throughout the last century, various drug market developments have been identified. Interacting with the fear, outrage, and panic regularly associated with them, these have played an important role in shaping how the wider societal 'drug problem' is understood (Reinarman and Levine 2004; Seddon 2010). One common type of market development involves unfamiliar substances emerging and becoming available. Specifically, within the United Kingdom, examples include fears around the 'arrival' of crack cocaine (Dorn et al. 1991), the heroin epidemics of the 1980s and 1990s (Pearson 1987; Seddon 2006), and the availability of novel psychoactive substances throughout the 2010s (Alexandrescu 2014). A second broad type of drug market development concerns changes to how substances are bought and sold, and the general characteristics of the 'scenes' frequented by users and dealers (Bless et al. 1995). Examples include the increased commercialised mindsets of many of those involved in supply from the latter half of the 20th century (Dorn et al. 1992), the use of violence by those involved in supply (Coomber 2015), and the adoption of the internet to facilitate illicit exchanges between buyers and sellers (Moyle et al. 2019). Aligning with the latter type, over recent years in the United Kingdom one of the most significant and high-profile drug market developments has been the so-called 'county lines' phenomena (Coomber and Moyle 2018). Involving itinerant dealing networks from major cities undertaking supply activity in more rural areas, the police have found themselves required to respond to – and be seen to respond to – this particular drug market development over a relatively short period of time. They have been urged on by other organisations such as the National Crime Agency and the Home Office, who have faced pressures to respond strategically to the identified problem too. This has then been further reinforced by the nature of the substantial levels of media and political coverage that has surrounded the topic (Spicer 2021b). Critically considering one example of how the response to this issue of county lines has played out provides valuable insight into the role of symbolism in understanding how and why drugs policing often takes the form it does, helping to further develop the theoretical framework that runs throughout this chapter.

Concentrating specifically on how the police formally organise themselves in response to drug markets, Dorn et al. (1991) noted the tendency for drugs policing to attempt to 'mirror' the illicit world. Their particular focus, following the approach that was being promoted at the time by the Broom Report (see ACPO 1985), was on how drugs policing attempted to broadly organise itself in a way that reflected the perceived hierarchical structure of the national drug market. This insight regarding the propensity for 'mirroring' arguably also has analytic value for considering drugs policing practices that operate more at the micro and meso levels and their symbolic qualities. In particular, the continued tendency for pursuing strategies and individual tactics that involve the appearance of 'matching like for like' (Dorn et al. 1991, p. 101) has resonance with the recent responses to county lines. Incorporating the concept of 'mirroring' into the framework of symbolic policing therefore provides further insight into the discrepancy between drugs policing appearances and the reality of how police officers have attempted to take action against the range of problematic components associated with this particular market form.

Illustrating this notion of 'symbolic mirroring' is one of the bespoke police tactics recently introduced in response to county lines. While often used to denote a wider phenomenon or some of the particular aspects associated with it, the original meaning of the term 'county lines' refers to the use of specific 'branded' phone lines to facilitate the supply of heroin and crack cocaine from urban hubs to more provincial locations. Considered central to the 'business model' of those engaged in this form of supply (Spicer 2019), these phone lines were identified as being a suitable target for the police. A new legal power referred to as Drug Dealing Telecommunications Restriction Orders (DTTRO 2017) was introduced, with the aim of providing police forces with the ability to apply for specific phone numbers suspected to be lying at the heart of this supply methodology to be disconnected and rendered unusable. Its introduction was promoted heavily by those in the political spheres and received significant media attention. Debating its introduction in the House of Lords, the then minister of state at the Home Office, Baroness Williams of Trafford, for example, stated:

> The mobile phone line is central to county lines activity, with some prominent lines making in excess of £5,000 per day (. . .) I hope noble Lords will approve these regulations. They will give the police a vital tool in their efforts to tackle county lines drug dealing and protect vulnerable individuals from being exploited by county lines gangs.
>
> *(Hansard 2017)*

Represented as being suitably 'bespoke' to this drug market context, its introduction was used as an attempt to reflect the apparent novel threat posed by county lines and their specific reliance on the use of branded phone numbers. The tactic was promoted as evidence of the government arming the police to fight the new migratory 'drug gang' enemies with which they were now purportedly faced (HM Government 2018). More generally, obtaining an order against an active phone line was considered a way for the police to cause more immediate 'disruption' to county lines dealers, especially where achieving prosecutions against particular individuals was found to be challenging.

In practice, however, the introduction of this high-profile power appeared to fail on both of these fronts. Instead of being an agile tactic that could be swiftly employed in response to drug market developments in their local area, the perception of many officers was that the process of applying for an order was layered with bureaucracy. As one senior detective who had been briefed on the realities of its use shortly after its announcement outlined:

> What they're suggesting is that a force sees a line that they're not happy with, they do a huge amount of work around the phone and understanding its use. They then fill out some documentation and put it up to the ROCU [Regional Organised Crime Unit], who then do the same. Then they put it up to the National Crime Agency who look at it, then maybe give it the all clear. Then it goes back to the ROCU. Then it goes back to the force, who've got to redo some of that work because it will have been a few weeks since they've put it in, and then they've got to end up going to one of three or four courts in the country that can look at it (sighs). And it's just nonsense.

In addition, while there was initial enthusiasm from some officers about the prospect of taking out one of these orders against the increasingly high-profile county lines targets they were being encouraged to pursue in their area, the ultimate realisation of what this tactic would likely achieve led to feelings of disappointment and cynicism. Causing 'disruption' to their local drug market was nothing new. Many of the officers had years of experience of achieving it in various forms by executing warrants, generating intelligence, using informants, and other traditional drugs policing approaches. Concluding that this tactic was at best just one further way of achieving this, rather than being something that might provide more significant or decisive action in the way initially promoted, left officers with little motivation to go to significant lengths to use it. In fact, it was suggested by some that if they were to use the power, it would only be done symbolically because of a desire to be 'seen' to be doing what was expected of them (Spicer 2021a).

As suggested by its apparent lack of use across the United Kingdom to date, a general apathy towards the DDTRO powers among police officers would appear to be its likely fate. By explicitly attempting to 'mirror' (Dorn et al. 1991) a particular aspect of this 'novel' drug market context, the introduction of this power could therefore be considered another particular example of 'symbolic policing' (see Spicer 2021a for further discussion). As demonstrated by the way it was introduced by politicians and others, significant efforts were made at curating an appearance that suggested it was a shiny new tactic that appropriately reflected the new and growing drug market threat, perhaps even being a breakthrough drugs policing tool with the capacity to allow officers to achieve significant success. Of course, for some it undoubtedly served some useful symbolic purposes. The 'spectacle' (Edelman 1988) constructed around its introduction produced some positive media coverage, and those in the political spheres and elsewhere were also able to cite its introduction when faced with questions about how they were responding to the high-profile area of county lines. Yet, evidence 'backstage' (Goffman 1959) from behind the drugs policing curtain suggested this was a façade. For the reality of officers on the ground, it failed to materialise into anything that would genuinely help address the drug market problem they were being faced with and told to solve.

Conclusion

By drawing on three specific examples of empirical research and advancing theory, this chapter has attempted to extend and further elaborate the idea of symbolic policing first outlined in Coomber et al. (2019). In this earlier publication, building on the conceptual work of Edelman (1985, 1988) and Innes (2004, 2014), police operations were situated as being as much about (if not more about – given the extensive difficulties of preventing drug supply in any meaningful way) being seen to be doing something about a public issue of concern rather than really doing something about it. For Edelman, action that emphasises the spectacular at the same time as promising greater security, safety, and protection of the young and innocent is often a glib diversionary act to gloss over lesser success in dealing with intractable problems. As stated above, in many areas the police have an 'impossible mandate' (Manning 1997) and are unlikely to be able to manage all issues that have come under their ambit over time. This is especially the case when it comes to the highly adaptive and evolving nature of drug markets and drug-related crime. But this does not mean that when engaged in the difficult management of difficult problems the police should not be challenged in their determination of how to frame and respond to an issue. Especially in the context of the contemporary policy zeitgeists of 'vulnerability' and 'exploitation' that currently dominate discussions regarding drug markets, it is no longer good enough to frame all criminality (e.g. drug supply) as simply 'crime' committed by 'criminals'. This can be both mistaken and also do harm, as shown by the counterproductive public health and enforcement outcomes identified in this research which are supported by numerous international studies. Drugs policing is now having to navigate a new context where those operating in drug markets can no longer simply be viewed one dimensionally as suitable targets for enforcement action. This has inevitable consequences for the signals they send out and the appearances that drugs policing attempts to cultivate.

Obviously, police work is not all about high-profile operations. The embedded dramaturgical performance of policing is embodied in all that they do (Manning 1997), from the day-to-day activities of the 'officer on the beat' up to those producing strategy. The three empirical examples provided in this chapter show these different levels of symbolic activity. Some examples (e.g. raids) are acknowledged by officers on the ground to be largely symbolic, as beyond the sweeping up of the 'low hanging fruit', outcomes are usually negligible in the difference they make to drug markets. Other, publicly debated, proffered, and actioned 'big policy' activities at ministerial level, such as those to curtail county lines, too often prove to be little more than a bureaucratic hindrance and add little to the armoury the police could call on in reality. In all of the examples provided, it is clear that in relation to drugs policing the police struggle to make serious inroads into preventing drug supply but nonetheless do employ crackdowns and raids where low-level arrests are a common thread. As noted above, the traditional framing of drug markets and suppliers as populated by 'drug dealers' of doubtful character, who commit crime and deal in harm, allows a fairly simple operational approach whereby those targeted and arrested are considered legitimate targets for enforcement and prosecution. Yet, following the child sex exploitation scandals, most famously in Rochdale and Rotherham, where vulnerable, young, exploited children were ignored by police forces and other protection services, it is clear that the police can no longer opt to frame crime, deviance, and victimhood in simplistic ways (Andell 2019; Coomber 2023). This has become most obvious in relation to county lines policing where vulnerable (mostly but not exclusively) youth are groomed or pressured into being involved in the supply of drugs such as heroin and crack cocaine to cities, towns, and rural areas across the country. In the wake of the child sex scandals, it is clear to police that many of these young people are vulnerable and exploited and while they are not 'innocent' as such, they are also not simply criminal. This is 'destructive information' (Goffman 1959) that calls into question the impression that drug policing performances typically seek to foster. It requires, and has required, not only a new framing of what drug supply is, but also a reframing of 'who' and 'what' the drug dealer is in comparison to traditional images, a recognition and process that has been taking place within the ambit of drug market research for many years (Adler 1985; Coomber 2006, 2010, 2023; Dorn et al. 1992).

Unfortunately for the police, this reorientation in response to drug market and policy developments is yet another difficult responsibility that they now have to navigate within an already messy, complex, and contingent field. However, it isn't, in our view, a problem. Rather it is an opportunity to reorient drugs policing from a relatively stark enforcement approach to a harm reduction model (Bacon and Spicer, this volume). The police in the United Kingdom no longer have the option of simply ignoring vulnerability and exploitation as they manifest within the groups they encounter and have responsibility to take action. Yet, it is important to note that this is an area where the symbolic recognition of the new context – via the setting up of local in-house units concerned with vulnerability and exploitation, and at the national level the creation of an incipient National Vulnerability Action Plan (National Police Chiefs Council 2018) – is, arguably, running ahead of practice at the coalface of policing. On the ground, vulnerable and exploited young (and older) people engaged in drug supply are still being swept up by police operations and prosecuted as criminals first and foremost. It is perhaps here where the inescapable symbolism of drugs policing can be put to better use. While inevitably parts of policing will always involve 'mirroring' the current state of the drug market as it is understood to operate, there is potential for this to go beyond superficial appearances and instead undertake the role of 'motor' (Innes 2010), whereby policing attempts to push the market to operate in less harmful ways and respond to its various actors more productively. Following Goffman's (1959) insights regarding audiences using frames to interpret signals and form impressions, the communications sent out by drugs policing could be reconfigured to align more closely with harm reduction principles. Not only could this help positively change the expectations of the public regarding what is possible and achievable for drugs policing, but it may also play an important role in developing officers' own perceptions of their functions and what they actually can and want to achieve in relation to drugs (Bacon 2022).

References

ACPO. (1985) *Final Report of the Working Party on Drugs Related Crime*. London: ACPO.

Adler, P. (1985) *Wheeling and Dealing: An Ethnography of an Upper-Level Drug Dealing and Smuggling Community*. New York: Colombia University Press.

Aitken, C., Moore, D., Higgs, P., Kelsall, J. and Kerger, M. (2002) 'The impact of a police crackdown on a street drug scene: Evidence from the street'. *International Journal of Drug Policy*. 13(3): 193–202.

Alexandrescu, L. (2014) 'Mephedrone, assassin of youth: The rhetoric of fear in contemporary drug scares'. *Crime, Media, Culture*. 10(1): 23–37.

Andell, P. (2019) *Thinking Seriously About Gangs: Towards a Critical Realist Approach*. London: Palgrave Macmillan.

Bacon, M. (2016) *Taking Care of Business: Police Detectives, Drug Law Enforcement and Proactive Investigation*. Oxford: Oxford University Press.

Bacon, M. (2022) 'Desistance from criminalisation: Police culture and new directions in drugs policing'. *Policing and Society*. 32(4): 522–539.

Bless, R., Korf, D. J. and Freeman, M. (1995) 'Open drug scenes: A cross-national comparison of concepts and urban strategies'. *European Addiction Research*. 1(3): 128–138.

Bourgois, P. and Schonberg, J. (2009) *Righteous Dopefiend*. Berkeley, CA: University of California Press.

Bourdieu, P. (1991) *Language and Symbolic Power*. Cambridge: Polity.

Bronitt, S. (2004) 'The law in undercover policing: A comparative study of entrapment and covert interviewing in Australia, Canada and Europe'. *Common Law World Review*. 33(1): 35–80.

Brooke, D. (1999) *Confessions, Illegally/Improperly Obtained Evidence and Entrapment under the Police and Criminal Evidence Act 1984*. London: University of London.

Bullock, K. (2018) '(Re)presenting "order" online: The construction of police presentational strategies on social media'. *Policing and Society*. 28(3): 345–359.

College of Policing. (2016) *Undercover Policing Guidance*. London: College of Policing.

Collison, M. (1995) *Police, Drugs and Community*. London: Free Association Press.

Coomber, R. (2006) *Pusher Myths: Resituating the Drug Dealer*. London: Free Association Books.

Coomber, R. (2010) 'Reconceptualising drug markets and drug dealers—The need for change'. *Drugs and Alcohol Today*. 10(1): 10–13.

Coomber, R. (2015) 'A tale of two cities: Understanding differences in levels of heroin/crack market-related violence'. *Criminal Justice Review*. 40(1): 7–31.

Coomber, R. (2023) 'The changing shape of illicit drug markets: Differentiation and its consequences for understanding and researching illicit drug markets'. In Ayres, T. and Ancrum, C. (eds.) *Understanding Drug Dealing and Illicit Drug Markets in the 21st Century: National and International Perspectives*. London: Routledge: 14–31.

Coomber, R. and Moyle, L. (2018) 'The changing shape of street-level heroin and crack supply in England: Commuting, holidaying and cuckooing drug dealers across "county lines"'. *British Journal of Criminology*. 58(6): 1323–1342.

Coomber, R., Moyle, L. and Mahoney, M. (2019) 'Symbolic policing: Situating targeted police operations/"crackdowns" on street-level drug markets'. *Policing and Society*. 29(1): 1–17.

Crump (2011) 'What are the police doing on Twitter? Social media, the police and the public'. *Policy and Internet*. 3(4): 1–27.

De Camargo, C. (2020) '"They wanna be us"; PCSO performances, uniforms, and struggles for acceptance'. *Policing and Society*. 30(7): 854–869.

Dorn, N., Murji, K. and South, N. (1991) 'Mirroring the market? Police reorganisation and effectiveness against drug trafficking'. In Reiner, R. and Cross, M. (eds.) *Beyond Law and Order*. London: Palgrave Macmillan: 91–106.

Dorn, N., Murji, K. and South, N. (1992) *Traffickers: Drug Markets and Law Enforcement*. London: Routledge.

Edelman, M. (1985) *The Symbolic Uses of Politics*. Urbana, IL: University of Illinois Press.

Edelman, M. (1988) *Constructing the Political Spectacle*. Chicago, IL: University of Chicago Press.

Ericson, R. (1989) 'Patrolling the facts: Secrecy and publicity in police work'. *British Journal of Sociology*. 40(2): 205–226.

Fitzgerald, J. and Threadgold, T. (2004) 'Fear of sense in the street heroin market'. *International Journal of Drug Policy*. 15(5): 407–417.

Gilling, D. (2012) 'Reasons to be cheerful? Addressing public perceptions through national tackling drugs week'. *Criminology and Criminal Justice*. 12(1): 41–60.

Goffman, E. (1959) *The Presentation of Self in Everyday Life*. London: Penguin Books.

Hansard. (2017) *Drug Dealing Telecommunications Restriction Orders Regulations*. Volume 787.

HM Government. (2018) *Serious Violence Strategy*. London: Home Office.

Human Rights Council. (2020) 'Situation of human rights in the Philippines'. *Annual Report of the United Nations High Commissioner for Human Rights and Reports of the Office of the High Commissioner and the Secretary-General*. Forty-fourth session, 15 June–3 July. Available from: https://www.ohchr.org/Documents/Countries/PH/Philippines-HRC44-AEV.pdf [Accessed 23 November 2021].

Human Rights Watch. (2020) 'Another spike in Philippines' "drug war" deaths: Latest data shows police killings rising amid Covid-19 pandemic', Sept. 28. Available from: https://www.hrw.org/news/2020/09/28/another-spike-philippines-drug-war-deaths [Accessed 23 November 2021].

Innes, M., Fielding, N. and Langham, S. (2002) *Signal Crimes and Control Signals: Towards an Evidence Based Conceptual Framework for Reassurance Policing - A Report for Surrey Police*. Guildford: University of Surrey.

Innes, M. (2004) 'Signal crimes and signal disorders: Notes on deviance as communicative action'. *British Journal of Sociology*. 55(3): 335–355.

Innes, M. (2010) 'A "mirror" and a "motor": Researching and reforming policing in an age of austerity'. *Policing: A Journal of Policy and Practice*. 4(2): 127–134.

Innes, M. (2014) *Signal Crimes: Social Reactions to Crime, Disorder and Control*. Oxford: Oxford University Press.

Lande, B. and Mangels, L. (2017) 'The value of the arrest: The symbolic economy of policing'. *European Journal of Sociology*. 58(1): 73–112.

Lindblom, C. (1959) 'The science of "muddling through"'. *Public Administration Review*. 19(2): 79–88.

Linnemann, T. (2017) 'Proof of death: Police power and the visual economies of seizure, accumulation and trophy'. *Theoretical Criminology*. 21(1): 57–77.

Loader, I. (1997) 'Policing and the social: Questions of symbolic power'. *British Journal of Sociology*. 48(1): 1–18.

Loader, I. (2016) 'In search of civic policing: Recasting the "Peelian" principles'. *Criminal Law and Philosophy*. 10(3): 427–440.

Loader, I. and Mulcahy, A. (2003) *Policing and the Condition of England*. Oxford: Oxford University Press.

Loftus, B. (2009) *Police Culture in a Changing World*. Oxford: Oxford University Press.

Maher, L. and Dixon, D. (1999) 'Policing and public health: Law enforcement and harm minimization in a street-level drug market'. *British Journal of Criminology*. 39(4): 488–512.

Manning, P. (1997) *Police Work: The Social Organization of Policing*. 2nd edn. Prospect Heights, IL: Waveland Press.

Manning, P. (2004) *The Narcs' Game: Organizational and Informational Limits on Drug Law Enforcement*. 2nd edn. Cambridge, MA: MIT Press.

Mawby, R. (2001) 'Promoting the police? The rise of police image work'. *Criminal Justice Matters*. 43(1): 44–45.

May, T. and Hough, M. (2004) 'Drug markets and distribution systems'. *Addiction Research and Theory*. 12(6): 549–563.

Moyle, L. (2019) 'Situating vulnerability and exploitation in street-level drug markets: Cuckooing, commuting, and the "county lines" drug supply model'. *Journal of Drug Issues*. 49(4): 739–755.

Moyle, L., Childs, A., Coomber, R. and Barratt, M. (2019) '#Drugsforsale: An exploration of the use of social media and encrypted messaging apps to supply and access drugs'. *International Journal of Drug Policy*. 63: 101–110.

Moyle, L. and Coomber, R. (2015) 'Earning a score: An exploration of the nature and roles of heroin and crack "user-dealers"'. *British Journal of Criminology*. 39(4): 488–512.

Moyle, L. and Coomber, R. (2016) 'Bourdieu on supply: Utilising the theory of practice to understand heroin and crack cocaine user-dealing'. *European Journal of Criminology*. 14(3): 309–328.

National Crime Agency. (2020) 'NCA and police smash thousands of criminal conspiracies after infiltration of encrypted communication platform in UK's biggest ever law enforcement operation', July 2. Available from: https://www.nationalcrimeagency.gov.uk/news/operation-venetic [Accessed 22 November 2021].

National Police Chiefs Council. (2018) *National Vulnerability Action Plan 2018–2021*, January. Available from: https://www.npcc.police.uk/documents/crime/2018/National%20Vulnerability%20Action%20Plan_18_21.pdf [Accessed 22 November 2021].

O'Neill, M. (2017) 'Police community support officers in England: A dramaturgical analysis'. *Policing and Society*. 27(1): 21–39.

Pearson, G. (1987) 'Social deprivation, unemployment and patterns of heroin use'. In Dorn, N. and South, N. (eds.) *A Land Fit for Heroin?* London: Palgrave: 62–94.

Peterborough Telegraph. (2021) 'Major police operation sees 27 arrests, drugs seized and raids in Peterborough and Whittlesey', May 27. Available from: https://www.peterboroughtoday.co.uk/news/crime/major-police-operation-sees-27-arrests-drugs-seized-and-raids-in-peterborough-and-whittlesey-3251857 [Accessed 22 November 2021].

Reinarman, C. and Levine, H. G. (2004) 'Crack in the rearview mirror: Deconstructing drug war mythology'. *Social Justice*. 31(1): 182–199.

Reiner, R. (2010) *The Politics of the Police*. 4th edn. Oxford: Oxford University Press.

Reiner, R. (2020) *Social Democratic Criminology*. London: Routledge.

Seddon, T. (2006) 'Drugs, crime and social exclusion: Social context and social theory in British drugs–crime research'. *British Journal of Criminology*. 46(4): 680–703.

Seddon, T. (2010) *A History of Drugs: Drugs and Freedom in the Liberal Age*. London: Routledge.

Sherman, L. (1990) 'Police crackdowns: Initial and residual deterrence'. *Crime and Justice*. 12: 1–48.

Spicer, J. (2019) '"That's their brand, their business": How police officers are interpreting county lines'. *Policing and Society*. 29(8): 873–886.

Spicer, J. (2021a) *Policing County Lines: Responses to Evolving Provincial Drug Markets*. London: Palgrave Macmillan.

Spicer, J. (2021b) 'Between gang talk and prohibition: The transfer of blame for county lines'. *International Journal of Drug Policy*. 87: 1–8.

Squires, D. (2006) 'The problem with entrapment'. *Oxford Journal of Legal Studies*. 26(2): 351–376.

The Independent. (2020) '45 arrests, dozens of cars and aircrafts seized in '"biggest ever"' police sting against Brazilian-European drug ring', November 28. Available from: https://www.independent.co.uk/news/brazil-europe-drug-ring-arrest-b1763175.html [Accessed 4 October 2022].

This is Cornwall. (2009) *Addict Sold Heroin to Undercover Officers*. Available from: http://www.cornwalllive.com/addict-sold-heroin-cover-officers/story-11511878-detail/story.html#CqWeC5dYAc2htRwV.99 [Accessed 23 November 2021].

Wall Street Journal. (2018) 'Bangladesh launches deadly drug crackdown as Rohingya crisis fuels smuggling'. Available from: https://www.wsj.com/articles/bangladesh-launches-deadly-drug-crackdown-as-rohingya-crisis-fuels-smuggling-1529236803 [Accessed 23 November 2021].

Windle, J., Moyle, L. and Coomber, R. (2020) '"Vulnerable" kids going country: Children and young people's involvement in county lines drug dealing'. *Youth Justice*. 20(1–2): 64–78.

Wood, E., Kerr, T., Small, W., Li, K., Marsh, D., Montaner, J. and Tyndall, M. (2004) 'Changes in public order after the opening of a medically supervised safer injecting facility for illicit injection drug users'. *Canadian Medical Association Journal*. 17(7): 731–734.

Woods, N. (2016) *Good Cop, Bad War*. London: Ebury Press.

5

POLICING CRYPTOMARKETS AND THE DIGITAL WAR ON DRUGS

James Martin, Ian Warren, and Monique Mann

Introduction

It has been more than ten years since the first large-scale cryptomarket, Silk Road, commenced operations on the dark web. Over that time, the dark web trade in illicit drugs has witnessed remarkable growth, spreading to over a dozen countries with an estimated annual turnover in the hundreds of millions of dollars (Soska and Christin 2015). The implications of this growth are profound. Drug consumers, previously limited by the availability of local suppliers, are now able to directly connect to a vast international network of drug exchange. Armed with little more than a computer, internet connection, free and readily available encryption software, and a modicum of technical proficiency, consumers can now access an unprecedented cornucopia of drugs delivered directly to the comfort of their own homes. Drug suppliers who use cryptomarkets – known colloquially as vendors – are similarly empowered to both buy and sell their products anonymously online with no physical contact with their customers, thereby reducing the likelihood of violence and arrest.

What makes the recent growth of cryptomarkets even more remarkable is that it has occurred in full view of the world's most powerful and well-resourced law enforcement agencies. In the United States (US), the ideological home of the global war on drugs, state authorities became aware of Silk Road almost as soon as it came into existence. Only a few months after the launch of Silk Road, US Senator Chuck Schumer announced to Congress the operation of a 'certifiable one-stop shop for illegal drugs that represents the most brazen attempt to peddle drugs online that we have ever seen', adding that 'it's more brazen than anything else by light years' (Ball 2013). The double emphasis of the enterprise's *brazenness* is significant. In a country with the world's highest rate of incarceration, with more than half of prisoners estimated to be imprisoned for drug offences,

DOI: 10.4324/9781003154136-6

and where tens of billions of dollars are spent annually on drug law enforcement (OMB 2020), the existence of a website selling illicit drugs freely to all and sundry was a slight that could not go unanswered. The fact that it took federal investigators nearly two and a half years to take Silk Road offline and arrest its founder Ross Ulbricht added insult to injury, exposing the limits of state power in a manner not seen since the days of Pablo Escobar or the decade-long hunt for Osama bin Laden.

What Ulbricht created was not only a powerful new vector for illicit drug exchange, but it also prompted the expansion of policing, legal, and regulatory initiatives that we collectively describe as the *digital war on drugs.* As with the conventional war on drugs, this digital iteration has seen a number of developments that challenge existing legal and law enforcement norms and expand the reach of the state into new and problematic territories. The purpose of this chapter is to analyse these developments and contextualise them within a broader understanding of the global war on drugs. The chapter first describes the new trends and old continuities between the conventional war on drugs and its digital variant, with an emphasis on policing and surveillance. Legal tactics are analysed next, followed by a discussion of some of the new forms of surveillance that state authorities are implementing to extend control over the dark web. The chapter concludes with a critical discussion emphasising why these developments, led by the US, are especially problematic by classifying dark web activity as organised criminal conspiracies that conflate a diverse and unrelated range of criminal activity with the illicit drugs trade.

Background

In 1971, US President Richard Nixon declared the contemporary war on drugs, an 'all-out offensive' against 'public enemy number one… [illicit] drug abuse'. Nixon's announcement conveyed a clear, though misleading, message that this initiative was intended to reduce drug misuse, crime, and related harms. In fact, the war on drugs was later revealed to be a cynical attempt to undermine and disrupt political opponents in the civil rights and anti-war movements, among whom illicit drug use was popular, through the use of aggressive drug law enforcement (Baum 2016). The deception at the heart of Nixon's announcement is not a mere historical footnote; it helps explain many of the problems inherent in the war on drugs, including its lack of effectiveness in reducing drug availability and drug-related crime (this was not its original intended purpose); the amplification of drug-related harms (harm towards Nixon's political opponents and their supporters was an intended outcome); as well as the spread of drug-related moral panic and entrepreneurism (political advantage through the demonisation of illicit drug users being the initial impetus for the drug war), and the resulting entrenchment of populist 'tough on drugs' policies not only in the US but also in many countries around the world (Coyne and Hall 2017).

Nixon's war on drugs, continued and expanded by subsequent administrations over decades, involved a major escalation of punitive policies aimed at disrupting illicit drug supply into and within the US. As part of this initiative, increased prison penalties for drug-related offences and increased allocation of funding to law enforcement agencies were introduced, and a new federal body, the Drug Enforcement Agency (DEA), was created with the mandate to coordinate drug law enforcement (Lynch 2012). Significantly, the war on drugs was to be fought not only domestically within the US, but was also exported internationally via political pressure leveraged by the State Department and by military intervention directed by the Pentagon (Payan 2007). Some five decades on from Nixon's original declaration, we are in a good position to not only have a clear perspective on the trends and impacts associated with the conventional global war on drugs, but also to identify the continuities with its nascent digital iteration. The following section analyses how the limited effectiveness, harm amplification, and moral panic inherent in the conventional drug war are now manifesting in the digital one.

Law enforcement interventions targeting the dark web drugs trade

Limited effectiveness

Perhaps the most striking similarity evident in both the conventional and digital drug wars is their limited effectiveness in reducing access to illicit drugs. The central aim of supply-side interventions in illicit drug markets is to disrupt supply such that the scarcity of drugs drives up their price, thereby eliminating supply entirely or reducing the amount that prospective users can afford to consume. In analysing the impact of law enforcement on drug markets in the US, several studies argue that 'modestly enforced' prohibition is the most effective means by which drug prices may be artificially boosted (Caulkins and Reuter 1998; Pollack and Reuter 2014; Strang et al. 2012).[1] Increases in the intensity of drug law enforcement beyond this point produce, at best, diminishing returns (Kuziemko and Levitt 2004) and are often short-lived as drug market participants adapt to new policing methods and tactics (May and Hough 2004; Moeller 2018). These findings indicate that the central policies of the war on drugs, namely aggressive law enforcement and expansive use of imprisonment, are of limited efficacy in raising drug prices and thereby preventing drug use, and also come with prohibitively high costs, both in terms of resource expenditure and human suffering (Strang et al. 2012).

The ineffectiveness of law enforcement in disrupting illicit drug supply is also now evident online. As outlined in the introduction, dark web drug trading continues to grow in popularity and profitability despite concerted and varied attempts on the part of law enforcement to disrupt it. In less than a decade, more than 100 cryptomarkets have come online generating a yearly revenue estimated in the hundreds of millions of dollars (EMCDDA 2018; Soska and Christin 2015). To date, the principal three tactics by which law enforcement agencies have sought to combat the dark web illicit drugs trade are takedowns of cryptomarkets, arresting vendors, and interdicting drugs in postal transit. These operations have produced similar results to supply shocks targeting the conventional illicit drugs trade; namely successes have produced only short-term benefit with little to no long-term positive effects (Décary-Hétu and Giommoni 2017; Ladegaard 2019; Soska and Christin 2015; Van Buskirk et al. 2017). Some research even points to a counterproductive effect, with high-profile dark web busts inadvertently advertising the existence of the dark web drugs trade to previously unaware drug consumers and suppliers (Ladegaard 2018). In general terms, the primary reason for this lack of effectiveness in combating the dark web drugs trade is the same as it is for the conventional drug war: market participants are highly adaptable to the interventions of law enforcement, though the specific adaptations differ according to the law enforcement tactics that are implemented.

Of the three tactics employed by law enforcement, the effects of site takedowns – the online equivalent of a raid on an open-air drug market – are the most studied. Of particular relevance is 2014's Operation Onymous, which simultaneously took down some of the largest cryptomarkets operating at the time, including Silk Road 2.0, Pandora, and Cloud 9. Multiple studies demonstrate that this largest of individual law enforcement interventions targeting cryptomarkets caused only temporary limited disruption, followed by a migration of both buyers and vendors to alternative cryptomarkets (Décary-Hétu and Giommoni 2017; Ladegaard 2019; Soska and Christin 2015; Van Buskirk et al. 2017). This adaptability on the part of cryptomarket participants, in addition to the inability of law enforcement to take down all of the cryptomarkets in operation at any given time, demonstrates the resilience of the dark web drugs trade to exogenous shocks. With more than 100 cryptomarkets coming online since the takedown of Silk Road in 2013 (Martin et al. 2019), and with popular vendors servicing different accounts simultaneously on multiple platforms (Tzanetakis 2018), dark web drug traders have demonstrated ample capacity to sidestep the effects of site takedowns and to resume operations quickly and with minimal disruption when they inevitably occur.

The effects of arresting individual vendors and postal interdiction are not as well researched. However, the limited evidence available also points to the inability of these measures to produce any long-lasting benefits. For example, studying the effect of the arrest of a popular Dutch methylene dioxymethamphetamine (MDMA) vendor, Ladegaard (2019) finds only a temporary suppressive effect among other Netherlands-based MDMA suppliers, who quickly assumed the arrested vendor's market share and resumed trading to pre-arrest levels. This finding corresponds with research regarding the effects of dealer arrests on conventional drug markets. Specifically, in circumstances of high demand and supply, arresting individual suppliers makes little long-term difference to the overall functioning of conventional drug markets. This is because there is a steady stream of new market participants ready to assume the role of supplier in the event that an existing dealer is arrested. Some studies even suggest that the combination of dealer arrests and the ready availability of new dealers has counterproductive effects on drug availability in the long term. This is because arrests enable remaining dealers to charge higher prices as compensation for increased risks, which in turn attracts new dealers seeking to profit from the higher prices now charged to consumers (Caulkins et al. 2006; May and Hough 2004).

By contrast, postal interdiction does appear to have a more sustained, though nuanced effect on the dark web drugs trade. The risk of postal interdiction is most pronounced at national borders as drug consignments make their way through customs. Décary-Hétu et al. (2016) show that most cryptomarket vendors are willing to assume this risk and are prepared to send drugs internationally. This willingness on the part of cryptomarket vendors to send drugs across national borders holds true even with respect to countries such as Australia that are generally considered to have relatively stringent border controls (Cunliffe et al. 2017). Drug buyers, on the other hand, appear to be much more circumspect, preferring vendors who are located in their own countries, and from whom they can order drugs without risking their interception at the border (Cunliffe et al. 2017; Norbutas 2018). This risk aversion on the part of customers helps to explain the prevalence of intra-regional dark web drug trading over the more limited proportion of international exchanges (Demant et al. 2018; Norbutas 2018; Tzanetakis 2018). Cunliffe et al. (2017) make the additional point that while border postal interdiction limits the amount of drug consignments purchased from foreign countries, this has the perverse effect of protecting the market share of drug distributors operating within a nation's borders.

Harm amplification

In addition to its limited effectiveness, the war on drugs is further characterised by harm amplification. Harm amplification refers to the ways in which drug law enforcement increases rather than decreases many of the harms associated with illicit drug use. This happens via a variety of different mechanisms, with three of the most pertinent described here. Firstly, due to the absence of product regulation that stems from prohibition, the potency and composition of illicit drugs vary widely. Drug consumers therefore have limited or no knowledge regarding what is in the substances they are consuming. This exposes consumers to the risk of overdose as well as poisoning due to the presence of sometimes harmful adulterants (Solimini et al. 2017). Secondly, drug consumers, suppliers, and members of the general public are exposed to systemic drug violence that results from such a profitable industry persisting with its activities outside of the control and protection of the state (Werb et al. 2011). Thirdly, drug consumers and suppliers incur both direct and indirect risks from law enforcement intervention, with the former including arrest, fines, and incarceration, and the latter including stigmatisation, loss of employment, and career disruption (Lynch 2012).

There is strong evidence to suggest that drug users and suppliers are increasingly turning to the dark web to escape the harms now entrenched in conventional drug markets by the war on drugs. For example, drug consumers who use cryptomarkets cite the availability of higher quality and less adulterated drugs as one of the primary reasons to source drugs online (Barratt et al. 2016). The absence of violence is another major attraction reported by cryptomarket users (Barratt et al. 2016) as well as vendors (Martin et al. 2020). Consumers and vendors also report a sense of relative safety from law enforcement when acquiring drugs via cryptomarkets compared to other, offline sources (Barratt et al. 2016; Martin et al. 2020). It is important to note that not all of these perceptions have been empirically tested, and whether or to what extent cryptomarkets offer a safer site of drug exchange remains an open question. Also worth noting is that using cryptomarkets is clearly not without risk. Fatal drug overdoses have occurred following the consumption of drugs purchased online; there have been numerous arrests of suppliers and consumers using cryptomarkets; and while violence is not encountered on cryptomarkets, other threats, such as doxxing and scams, remain prevalent. Nonetheless, the perception, if not the reality, that prohibition-related risks are lower on drug cryptomarkets appears to be a major factor driving their current growth.

Dark web drugs: the latest evolution of a moral panic

Given the ineffectiveness and harm amplification associated with the war on drugs, one may question how such a set of policies has remained in place for so long, let alone how state authorities are able to justify its present expansion into the digital realm. One possible answer to these questions is that state authorities, and law enforcement agencies in particular, maintain support for both the conventional and digital drug wars by misleading the general public about the dangers of illicit drugs, and the people who both use and supply them. Examples of misleading narratives about the dangers supposedly inherent in illicit drugs abound in both the pre-drug war and contemporary periods. These range from the 'reefer madness' period in the 1930s, when cannabis use was linked to insanity, 'Satanic' jazz music, and the sexual promiscuity of white women with 'Negroes, entertainers and any others' (Heidt and Wheeldon 2021) to the 2005 'Faces of Meth' campaign, when before and after mug shots of 'meth heads' were displayed in order to publicly demonstrate 'how disgusting meth, and all other illegal drugs can make your mouth and teeth' (Linnemann and Wall 2013, p. 319). Consistent among these narratives is the notion that illicit drug use leads inevitably to physical and moral decay. The tethering of domestic and international drug trafficking with organised crime serves a similar emotive function that justifies a raft of contentious international and domestic law enforcement measures as part of the war on drugs (Andreas and Nadelmann

2006). These narratives not only intentionally exaggerate the harms associated with illicit drug use, but they also create moral panic among the public who, once misinformed about the nature and magnitude of the risk posed by illicit drug use and supply, are prepared to tolerate increasingly invasive law enforcement intervention to mitigate an overinflated 'threat'. This issue has been common in Australia, and internationally, in the incremental tightening of criminal legislation, law enforcement, and surveillance of many migrant groups (e.g. successive campaigns targeted at 'outsiders' such as Italian, Chinese, Vietnamese, and Eastern European migrants) or other subcultures commonly linked to illicit drug trafficking, including outlaw motorcycle gangs (Katz 2011; Mann 2020). While the target groups or sources of moral panic change over time, the same moral panic processes occur again and again.

We now see similar attempts to create a moral panic in law enforcement discussion of the dark web drugs trade. This is done by conflating the use of cryptomarkets to acquire illicit drugs with other more dangerous law breaking also facilitated by the dark web, such as terrorist financing or the dissemination of child exploitation material (CEM). For example, a recent statement from the Australian Federal Police (AFP) describes the dark web as 'a commerce underbelly used by child sex offenders, organised crime syndicates and those who sought to harm law abiding citizens' (AFP 2021). While it is true that child sex offenders do use the dark web to disseminate illegal material, missing from these descriptions is any disclaimer that the cryptomarkets used for the trading of illicit drugs strictly and uniformly enforce prohibitions on CEM, as well as many other unambiguously harmful goods and services (Martin et al. 2019). This includes bans on 'assassination services', which are also falsely implied by law enforcement to be widespread on the dark web, despite no verified cases of their use occurring anywhere in the world, apart from by scammers and undercover law enforcement agents (Martin et al. 2019).

Perhaps the most well-known accusation of 'hitmen for hire' associated with the dark web concerns Silk Road administrator, Ross Ulbricht. In the original indictment against Ulbricht, US authorities alleged that he ordered multiple 'hits' against a number of individuals, the first of which was an act of revenge against a co-conspirator and Silk Road moderator for stealing some $350,000 dollars from the site (USA v. Ulbricht 2014, p. 26). None of these alleged murders was carried out and charges were not pursued. The reason for this, it was later revealed, was that the individual who had stolen money from the site and the supposed hitman were undercover US law enforcement agents (Jeong 2015). Regardless of the fact that the charges were not pursued, and that the two US Secret Service agents involved were subsequently jailed for corruption relating to their theft from Ulbricht, the damage was done. The myth of hitmen for hire on the dark web was further popularised and Ulbricht was condemned in court by the prosecution, and in the news media, for being no different from any other 'traditional drug dealer on the street who uses violence to protect his corner' (USA v. Ulbricht 2014, p. 26).

Overly inflated rhetoric regarding the dangers of the dark web drugs trade has also been used explicitly to justify expanded law enforcement powers. When discussing the introduction of a new suite of online surveillance powers (discussed further below), the former Australian Home Affairs Minister Peter Dutton publicly dismissed concerns of state overreach, claiming that

> if you're a paedophile you should be worried about these powers, if you're a terrorist you should be worried about these powers. If you're committing a serious offence in relation to the trafficking of drugs – of ice for example, that's being peddled to children – you should be worried about these power.
>
> *(McCulloch 2020)*

With this example, we see both the conflation of different and unrelated threats – terrorism, child sexual abuse, and illicit drug trading – alongside more familiar and also misleading tropes about drug suppliers selling drugs to children. This is despite there being significant barriers to entry that make cryptomarket purchasing difficult (though not impossible) for children (Barratt and Aldridge 2016). There is also no evidence that cryptomarket vendors specifically target children for drug sales. Indeed, as is the case with the offline drugs trade, children typically make poor targets for illicit drug sales if for no other reason than their levels of disposable income are low and sales to children attract additional risk which drug suppliers tend to avoid when possible (Coomber 2010).

General US legal and investigative strategies to break criminal conspiracies

Many forms of transnational dark web policing activity have historically been driven by US laws that empower law enforcement agencies to engage in extraterritorial surveillance outside of the sovereign jurisdiction of the US. As with the transnational drug trade, these measures pre-date the online era but continue to inform developments in policing the dark web by US authorities acting alone or in cooperation with select international partners. Central to these processes is the role of law as symbolic in the politicisation and subsequent criminalisation of organised crime that reflects the expressive function of state power (Mann 2020, p. 80). This supports expanded legal responses to moral panics surrounding drug distribution based on either real or imagined threats of its nature and extent. While our primary focus is on recent developments, it is important to recognise two main historical precedents for the expansion of contemporary dark web policing methods. These are the use of legislative responses under the Racketeer Influenced and Corrupt Organisations (RICO) and Continuing Criminal Enterprise (CCE) acts, and the pursuit of charges associated with criminal conspiracies (see Mann and Warren 2018). Both of these developments are important for endorsing extraterritorial policing by framing transnational online crime as organised crime, which in turn provides the justification for various expansive forms of transnational electronic surveillance of the dark web that are invoked today.

The expansion of the RICO legislation to encompass extraterritorial activity is clearly designed to protect US commercial and business interests in the online era. This is considered a viable enhancement of US investigative jurisdiction because regulatory processes 'that emphasize physical location' are commonly considered to 'encourage criminals to strike America's citizens and economy with impunity from beyond its physical borders' even though they might also lead to 'overzealous charging' for the same course of conduct (Mann and Warren 2018, p. 248; Mark 2013; Otey 2015, p. 63). Similarly, the CCE Act, commonly referred to as the 'kingpin' statute, carries penalties for the distribution of any illicit substances that can lead to 20 years to life imprisonment for a first or subsequent offence if the total value of the controlled substances is proved to be $2 million dollars or more (see Yeh 2012, pp. 8–9).

The CCE Act was crucial in the case against Silk Road administrator Ross Ulbricht, even though the indictment failed to allege that Ulbricht was the manager of the site or that he held the role as upper management of a drug-trafficking organisation, and a continuing series of predicate offences with sufficient detail (see USA v. Ulbricht 2014, pp. 13–21). Ulbricht's case was complicated by the introduction of several additional charges of 'intentionally access[ing] computers without authorization', which were considered part of a conspiracy to contravene the Computer Fraud and Abuse Act that involved 'making certain software available to purchasers', even though there was no proof that his knowledge or intention to commit these offences encapsulated the conduct of vendors and users of Silk Road (USA v. Ulbricht 2014, p. 22). The result of these prosecution tactics is that by identifying Ulbricht as the centre of the conspiracy, he become responsible for engineering the conduct of all people who used Silk Road for criminal purposes both within and *outside* the US, even if it was technically impossible for him to have established direct relationships with most of the vendors and buyers using the cryptomarket. Although it was technically impossible for US authorities to prove that each co-conspirator knew their specific 'relation to each other and to Ulbricht' given the anonymous nature of the encrypted transactions facilitated through Silk Road (Mann and Warren 2018, p. 249), Ulbricht's conviction was justified because he was considered to be at the centre of the conspiracy due to his presumed role as site manager. Therefore, he was legally deemed to be the coordinator of the illicit conduct of others.

A similar logic frames the cases involving several other international 'fugitives' wanted in the US for hosting online platforms that have led to large-scale criminal copyright violations (Boister 2017; Palmer and Warren 2013). These range from early cases involving the online distribution of computer programs resulting from the hacking of product keys on CD ROMs (Griffiths v. USA 2004), to the administrators of dark web sites that host CEM (Russell 2017). The methodologies underpinning these investigations are simple and in line with the conspiracy provisions fostered under the RICO and the CCE acts. However, their status as investigative success stories must also be tempered by the view that they stretch accepted boundaries of existing laws (c.f. Urbas 2006). In general, expanded investigative provisions result from a moral crusade against all forms of transnational crime that is considered organised by nature (see Mann 2020). The demonisation of hidden online conduct under an organised crime framework is magnified by the rhetoric of the international war on drugs that has long been driven by US political, legal, and commercial interests (Andreas and Nadelmann 2006). The legislative expansion into the extraterritorial domain enhances US law enforcement power and the willingness to identify those considered to be at the centre of transnational conspiracies. This then requires enhanced transnational police cooperation and extraterritorial surveillance power to access and intercept communications between suspects for evidentiary purposes (Warren et al. 2020). The ultimate goal is to ensure that offenders are brought to trial in the US, regardless of their geographic locations at the time any conspiracies or actual offending were detected by US enforcement agencies (see Mann et al. 2018).

Several other processes work in tandem with these legislative developments. For example, the seizure and operation of clandestine sites as honeypots that identify users who log in while not suspecting that they are being operated by law enforcement agencies have long raised concern about potential entrapment and the ethical conduct of police (Walden and Flannagan 2003). More recently, as we discuss below, the honeypot tactic has been used by Dutch police to identify people engaged in illicit drug transactions through the Hansa cryptomarket (Greenberg 2018) and the US Federal Bureau of Investigation (FBI) in Operation Pacifier after a takedown of the Playpen dark web site (Russell 2017; Weidenhouse 2017). The global reach of operating honeypot sites that are seized and then subsequently operated by law enforcement agencies represents a form of 'lawful illegality', where police intentionally stretch the jurisdictional reach of their surveillance activities (Austin 2015; Warren et al. 2020). Lawful illegality becomes extremely problematic when judges must rely on the technical expertise of highly specialist police investigators, which can result in favouring moral arguments for the expansion of police power. US experience indicates that these procedures intentionally exploit geographic anomalies in warrant procedures to extend the admissibility of evidence against any person in the world who logged into a honeypot site operated by law enforcement agents, and statutes were later amended to allow for this (in particular Rule 41 of Criminal Procedure in the US, see Warren et al. 2020).

The combination of analogue and digital measures is built on an incremental expansion of US extraterritorial investigative power to detect and prevent organised criminal activity more broadly, to the extent that any dark web activity is now equated with organised crime and transnational conspiracies that affect US interests. By eroding legal constraints on investigative jurisdiction that were conventionally based on geography or physical territory, current procedures aim to identify any user of the dark web regardless of their geographic location within the US (Russell 2017; Warren et al. 2020), or internationally (Warren 2015). This knowledge would otherwise remain unknown due to the use of geolocation masking technologies such as virtual private networks (VPNs) and The Onion Router (Tor). By extension, the process of intelligence sharing has now become the norm to build prosecutions by loosening the standards of admissibility in court that were historically constrained by the criminal law. As such, complex investigations into any dark web activity build on the incremental expansion of procedures for dismantling 'conspiracies' into any aspect of digital criminality, including various forms of surface web activity such as the intentional violation of copyright laws through unlawful file sharing.

The ultimate aim of these processes is to attribute responsibility to a leading manager or 'kingpin' who is deemed to have knowledge of all illicit communications that form the basis of the broader conspiracy. This is so even if the kingpin's actual intention or knowledge of the extent of the illegality occurring through dark web platforms they have created or managed is unattainable. Both the Silk Road prosecution against Ulbricht, and the intended prosecution of Alexandre Cazes for his alleged role in leading activity in the cryptomarket AlphaBay (before his suicide in a Thai prison pending extradition to the US), were characterised by these features. In each case, the nature of the illicit goods and services traded in the cryptomarket made little difference to investigators, as 'illicit drugs, financial data, stolen credit cards, and other illegal merchandise' are consolidated to define dark web activity in any location, or among a specific community of users, as suspicious and unlawful (Easttom 2018, p. 29). Using a combination of domestic and foreign intelligence to construct a case that suggests a widespread and systematic conspiracy, the aim is to take down a suspect dark web site, and in some instances to run it as a honeypot to identify as many suppliers and site administrators as possible. These people are then redefined as co-conspirators to make the case against the kingpin (Mann and Warren 2018). Incremental changes to US criminal procedural law appear to reflect a pre-existing 'norm of cooperation' that fosters transnational information sharing about kingpins and co-conspirators, because there appear to be few concerns from foreign governments about the routine use of foreign searches to sustain criminal prosecutions (Kerr and Murphy 2017, p. 65). Moreover, it is generally considered that the adoption of US legal and investigative standards in this field will ultimately protect the authorities and law-abiding members of the public in foreign jurisdictions (Daskal 2019). This is so even if these mechanisms can be viewed as a form of lawful illegality that ratifies intentional police attempts to flout existing jurisdictional and due process protections (Austin 2015; Warren et al. 2020), by operating honeypot sites that potentially entrap suspects regardless of their geographic locations or ultimate intention in using drug cryptomarkets.

Expansion of surveillance powers and capabilities targeting the dark web

Commensurate with the trends outlined above, a raft of new legislative measures in various jurisdictions has been explicitly designed to enhance the powers and ability of law enforcement and intelligence agencies to undertake surveillance and investigations on the dark web. In this section, we focus on recent attempts by the Australian government to enhance law enforcement's ability to access encrypted communications, and then consider powers to conduct computer network operations (CNOs), also known as network investigative techniques (NITs) (Molnar et al. 2017). These powers are significant and highly contentious, given numerous concerns regarding Australia's approach to covert police investigations on the dark web (Bleakley 2019). Enhanced CNO powers represent an explicit attempt to shine 'light' on the 'dark' web (Kerr and Murphy 2017) and also have extraterritorial implications insofar as law enforcement do not have the capacity to know the location of target computers and suspects before the powers are exercised due to the use of technologies that mask geolocation, as described above. Such sweeping global and extraterritorial investigative powers raise concerns for due process and the limits of state jurisdiction, while extending an already extensive suite of powers that law enforcement agencies have to undertake the surveillance of electronic communications and online activity. This includes communications that are concealed through technological and anonymising means such as encryption and decentralisation, which are used for cryptocurrencies. These developments reflect international trends, while mirroring established US procedures in relation to expanding surveillance powers for dark web policing. However, Australia is the only Western democracy that lacks an enforceable human rights framework at the federal level, in contrast to the constitutional rights protections in the US. It is therefore important to document these developments as the due process protections or constraints on the extraterritorial surveillance of the dark web or its users that apply in other jurisdictions might be irrelevant to those conducted under current and proposed Australian reforms (Mann et al. 2018).

Accessing, undermining, or backdooring encrypted communications

A long history of 'cryptowars' extends back to the 1990s and there have been many attempts by governments and law enforcement agencies around the world to access encrypted forms of communication (Koops and Kosta 2018). Numerous attempts have been made to undermine encryption or access encrypted forms of communication through legal and technical means across most Western jurisdictions, and Five Eyes countries in particular have shown great enthusiasm in introducing new powers for law enforcement to do so (see Mann et al. [2020] for a review of legal approaches in Five Eyes countries). In Australia, the Telecommunications and Other Legislation Amendment (Assistance and Access)

Act 2018 (Cth) (herein Assistance and Access Act) was introduced at the end of 2018 and adopts a slightly different approach to those adopted by other Five Eyes governments such as the US, the United Kingdom, Canada, and New Zealand (see Mann et al. 2020). This law introduces a suite of powers that allows law enforcement agencies to request designated communications providers (DCPs), very broadly defined, to carry out a range of 'acts or things' via a graded series of technical assistance requests (TARs), technical assistance notices (TANs), or technical capability notices (TCNs) (Mann et al. 2020). TARs are voluntary requests issued to DCPs, which escalate to compulsory notices in the event of non-compliance with initial requests. TCNs differ and are designed to ensure that DCPs are *capable* of providing assistance, which may involve the creation of new ways to provide assistance to law enforcement in accessing communications.

The rationale supporting the introduction of the Assistance and Access Act was that 'over 90% of telecommunications information being lawfully intercepted by the Australian Federal Police now uses some form of encryption' and the

> increasing use of encryption has significantly degraded law enforcement and intelligence agencies' ability to access communications and collect intelligence, conduct investigations into organised crime, terrorism, smuggling, sexual exploitation of children and other crimes, and detect intrusions into Australian computer networks.
>
> *(The Parliament of the Commonwealth of Australia 2018, p. 2)*

Significantly, this law applies extraterritorially, as these powers can be used by Australian law enforcement to provide assistance to overseas law enforcement agencies to enforce foreign laws and also attempt to regulate transnational DCPs. The DCP draws in a wide range of Australian and offshore entities including carriers, carriage service providers, intermediaries, and any provider of an electronic service or software for any users in Australia (Ford and Mann 2019; Mann et al. 2020). This may, for example, also apply to providers of virtual private networks that are used to conceal geolocation. A very significant and recent (June 2021) case of law enforcement's possible use of the Assistance and Access Act relates to Operation Ironside in which law enforcement created their own encrypted network via an app known as ANOM installed onto specialised devices provided to suspected offenders. ANOM had a built-in weakness or backdoor so law enforcement could surveil users of ANOM in real time. The Australian Federal Police commissioner stated at the press release concerning Operation Ironside that the assistance and access powers were used as part of the operation; however, at the time of writing, warrants supporting the exercise of law enforcement powers are not publicly available, and it should also be noted that Operation Ironside commenced before the Assistance and Access Act was passed as law (Prime Minister of Australia 2021). Given this, Operation Ironside raises many significant questions about the legitimate use of surveillance powers, and also the international exchange and sharing of information with foreign powers, in particular the US FBI.

Computer network operations to hack the dark web

Governments and law enforcement agencies around the world have also shown enthusiasm for remote access or lawful hacking powers to infiltrate, surveil, and actively disrupt dark web activities through CNOs or NITs. The Surveillance Legislation Amendment (Identify and Disrupt) Act (Cth), herein Identify and Disrupt Act, enables law enforcement agencies to disrupt, surveil, and take over dark web networks. These powers are closely related to amendments to Rule 41 of Criminal Procedure introduced in the US at the end of 2016, which enable US law enforcement agencies such as the FBI to conduct remote hacking of target computers that may be located outside the jurisdiction where the warrant was issued (as discussed above, see Warren et al. 2020). The use of remote hacking into Hansa (Operation GraveSac) and AlphaBay (Operation Bayonet) by the FBI, the DEA, and Dutch police was authorised by a Dutch judicial authority. According to Europol (2017), this warrant involved:

> taking covert control of Hansa under Dutch judicial authority... which allowed Dutch police to monitor the activity of users without their knowledge, and then shutting down AlphaBay during the same period. It meant the Dutch police could identify and disrupt the regular criminal activity on Hansa but then also sweep up all those new users displaced from AlphaBay who were looking for a new trading platform.

These laws are considered necessary because it is believed that existing law enforcement surveillance powers are 'not suitably adapted to identifying and disrupting targets where those targets are actively seeking to obscure their identity and the scope of their activities' (The Parliament of the Commonwealth of Australia 2020, p. 2). The Identify and Disrupt Act enables Australian law enforcement agencies to 'collect intelligence, conduct investigations, disrupt and prosecute the most serious of crimes, including child abuse and exploitation, terrorism, *the sale of illicit drugs*, human trafficking, identity theft and fraud, assassinations, and the distribution of weapons' (The Parliament of the Commonwealth of Australia 2020, p. 2, emphasis added). Three new powers are now conferred on the Australian Federal Police and the Australian Criminal Intelligence Commission (ACIC), with enforcement assistance from the Australian Signals Directorate (ASD). These powers are

1. data disruption warrants that will enable the disruption of data 'by modifying, adding, copying or deleting in order to frustrate the commission of serious offences online'

2. network activity warrants that provide for the collection of 'intelligence on serious criminal activity being conducted by criminal networks', and
3. account takeover warrants that provide 'the ability to take control of a person's online account for the purposes of gathering evidence to further a criminal investigation'. (Parliament of the Commonwealth of Australia 2020, pp. 2–3).

The Department of Home Affairs (2020) explains that these powers are required due to the obstacles of 'attributing criminal activity to particular individuals, organisations, premises or devices, especially on the dark web'. The explanatory memorandum (The Parliament of the Commonwealth of Australia 2020, p. 2) outlines the rationale supporting the introduction of the new powers, because 'cyber-enabled serious and organised crime, often enabled by the dark web and other anonymising technologies, such as bespoke encrypted devices for criminal use, present a direct challenge to community safety and the rule of law' and 'on the dark web criminals carry out their activities with a lower risk of identification and apprehension'. Like the assistance and access powers described above, it is foreseeable that these laws will have extraterritorial impact. The Australian provisions are particularly susceptible to unconstrained extraterritorial reach, because anonymising and geolocation masking technologies such as The Onion Router or VPNs are being used to conceal the identities and geographic locations of target users, meaning law enforcement agencies do not know whether the target computer is located within their lawful jurisdiction prior to the powers being exercised.

Equally problematic is that many forms of extraterritorial dark web surveillance are deemed necessary to combat a range of criminal threats online, with targets conflated as 'the enemy', who are engaged in various activities for commercial or violent benefit, including drug and arms trafficking, the sharing of CEM, and, as aptly demonstrated in the Silk Road takedown, even unproven claims of contract killings. Equally, such discourses are used to provide initial or ex-post justifications for various forms of extraordinary dark web surveillance to identify people and activities considered beyond the investigative reach of law enforcement agencies acting with the best moral or legal intentions (Andreas and Nadelmann 2006; Blakesley and Stigall 2004; Kerr and Murphy 2017). However, there are a range of due process impacts of extraterritorial law enforcement surveillance and the very real risk that actual prosecutions that reach court will be jeopardised (see Warren et al. 2020). Expanded transnational surveillance also comes with significant consequences for the privacy and civil liberties of individuals around the world.

Conclusion

This discussion emphasises that the digital war on drugs is the contemporary extension of a vast legal and law enforcement apparatus developed by the US and exported globally over the past half century. It extends from Nixon's original war on drugs that both built and extended from previous anti-drug purges by introducing a labyrinth of technical laws, procedures, and enforcement tactics that raise numerous concerns about due process rights, while conferring enormous powers on police to 'bust' domestic and transnational conspiracies. There are discursive, ideological, and instrumental aspects to these processes (Dixon 1997, p. 291) that emphasise the imperatives to take down not just methods of illicit drug distribution through cryptomarkets, but also the 'kingpins' who are deemed by law enforcement to be behind their operation. This is achieved through a philosophy of enforcement supported by RICO and CCE legislation, and a prosecutorial approach that favours laying conspiracy charges with low evidentiary thresholds for collective organised criminal activity that extend extraterritorially. These approaches expand into the digital domain, supported by new online surveillance powers that fortify these investigative philosophies.

Of particular importance is how more intrusive surveillance laws validate what appears to be the willingness to use clandestine tactics, such as the operation of dark web sites as honeypots after they have been seized, which entrap many unsuspecting users who provide the basis for prosecuting the kingpin. Numerous examples we raise in this chapter, including Silk Road, AlphaBay, and Hansa, have followed this approach (see Mann and Warren 2018). However, the enforcement successes in these cases are based on questionable legal tactics, or in Austin's (2015) terms a process of 'lawful illegality', where the police test the waters by invoking contentious surveillance technologies that subsequently become validated under legislation endorsing their extraterritorial scope because of their success in achieving significant 'busts' of cryptomarket administrators or kingpins. These legal approaches also become accepted in judicial decisions examining the extraterritorial reach of warrants supporting CNOs or NITs (Warren et al. 2020), and, as our Australian examples show, provide a form of transnational regulatory arbitrage when sanctioned under law (Mann et al. 2020). As with the Nixon reforms that invoked drug laws to eliminate political opponents, these processes form part of an incremental expansion of national police authority into a transnational surveillance state based on the powers of some jurisdictions that shape and facilitate enforcement activity in other jurisdictions. This is possible through more permissive extraterritorial police powers to instigate prosecutions of dark web kingpins that are sustained by the contentious identification of more and more co-conspirators regardless of their geographic locations (Ghappour 2017). The capacity to entrap suspects through myriad extraterritorial surveillance processes within the dark web can also fuel other questionable law enforcement activities that are subject to limited scrutiny or accountability (Bleakley 2019) due to their covert and transnational character (Bowling and Sheptycki 2015).

These processes have strong popular appeal due to the moral panic associated with dark web criminality, which is politically exploited by tethering illicit drug distribution to claims of its links to organised crime, the dissemination of child exploitation material and related forms of harm against children, terrorism, contract killing, and other insidious behaviours linked to the dark web. Hence, the conflation of all dark web activity as *dark*, evil, and requiring visibility, becomes the political basis for expanded laws to counter moral anxieties about technological processes of communication that many people do not engage with or know about. As with previous expansions of criminal and policing laws, these moral imperatives overshadow consideration of the self-imposed constraints on drug cryptomarket activity that increasingly appear to have a range of positive health, safety, and economic effects for consenting drug sellers and consumers. Regrettably, the moral panic surrounding illegality in drug cryptomarkets renders these benefits difficult to counter in the political and enforcement sphere. This raises the inevitable point that the digital war on drugs is simply a logical extension of its historical predecessor, which offers little hope of its value in addressing any actual individual or social harms associated with illicit drug consumption and distribution.

Note

1 An important limitation of these studies is that they only analyse the comparative effectiveness of different supply side measures rather than alternative strategies for reducing drug harms. Studies that examine alternative strategies point to the effectiveness of demand reduction (Rydell and Everingham 1994) and legalisation with taxation (Murphy and Grossman 2006) as more effective in reducing drug-related crime and harm than supply-side interventions.

References

Andreas, P. and Nadelmann, E. (2006) *Policing the Globe: Criminalization and Crime Control in International Relations*. New York: Oxford University Press.

Austin, L. (2015) 'Lawful illegality: What Snowden has taught US about the legal infrastructure of the surveillance state'. In Geist, M. (ed.) *Law, Privacy and Surveillance in Canada in the Post-Snowden Era*. Ottawa: University of Ottawa Press: 103–125.

Australian Federal Police. (2021) 'AFP executes search warrants in Queensland after the takedown of the world's largest illegal dark web marketplace'. Available from: https://www.afp.gov.au/news-media/media-releases/afp-executes-search-warrants-queensland-after-takedown-worlds-largest [Accessed 14 April 2021].

Ball, J. (2013) 'Silk Road: The online drug marketplace that officials seem powerless to stop'. *The Guardian*. Available from: https://www.theguardian.com/world/2013/mar/22/silk-road-online-drug-marketplace [Accessed 14 April 2021].

Barratt, M. and Aldridge, J. (2016) 'Everything you always wanted to know about drug cryptomarkets* (* but were afraid to ask)'. *International Journal of Drug Policy*. 100(35): 1–6.

Baum, D. (2016) 'Legalize it all'. *Harper's Magazine*. Available from: https://harpers.org/archive/2016/04/legalize-it-all/ [Accessed 14 April 2021].

Blakesley, C. and Stigall, D. (2004) 'Wings for talons: The case for the extraterritorial jurisdiction over sexual exploitation of children through cyberspace'. *Wayne Law Review*. 50(1): 109–159.

Becker, G., Murphy, K. and Grossman, M. (2006) 'The market for illegal goods: The case of drugs'. *Journal of Political Economy*. 114(1): 38-60.

Bleakley, P. (2019) 'Watching the watchers: Taskforce Argos and the evidentiary issues involved with infiltrating dark web child exploitation networks'. *The Police Journal*. 92(3): 221–236.

Boister, N. (2017) 'Law enforcement cooperation between New Zealand and the United States: Serving the internet "pirate" Kim Dotcom up on silver platter?' In Hufnagel, S. and McCartney, C. (eds.) *Trust in International Police and Justice Cooperation*. Oxford: Hart Publishing: 193–220.

Bowling, B. and Sheptycki, J. (2015) 'Global policing and transnational rule with law'. *Transnational Legal Theory*. 6(1): 141–173.

Caulkins, J. and Reuter, P. (1998) 'What price data tell us about drug markets'. *Journal of Drug Issues*. 28(3): 593–612.

Caulkins, J., Reuter, P. and Taylor, L. (2006) 'Can supply restrictions lower price? Violence, drug dealing and positional advantage'. *The BE Journal of Economic Analysis and Policy*. 5(1): 1–20.

Coomber, R. (2010) 'Reconceptualising drug markets and drug dealers – The need for change'. *Drugs and Alcohol Today*. 10(1): 10–13.

Coyne, C. and Hall, A. (2017) *Four Decades and Counting: The Continued Failure of the War on Drugs*. Washington, DC: Cato Institute Policy Analysis.

Cunliffe, J., Martin, J., Décary-Hétu, D. and Aldridge, J. (2017) 'An island apart? Risks and prices in the Australian cryptomarket drug trade'. *International Journal of Drug Policy*. 50: 64–73.

Daskal, J. (2019) 'Privacy and security across borders'. *The Yale Jaw Journal Forum*. 128: 1029–1051.

Décary-Hétu, D. and Giommoni, L. (2017) 'Do police crackdowns disrupt drug cryptomarkets? A longitudinal analysis of the effects of operation onymous'. *Crime, Law and Social Change*. 67(1): 55–75.

Décary-Hétu, D., Paquet-Clouston, M. and Aldridge, J. (2016) 'Going international? Risk taking by cryptomarket drug vendors'. *International Journal of Drug Policy*. 35: 69–76.

Demant, J., Munksgaard, R., Décary-Hétu, D. and Aldridge, J. (2018) 'Going local on a global platform: A critical analysis of the transformative potential of cryptomarkets for organized illicit drug crime'. *International Criminal Justice Review*. 28(3): 255–274.

Department of Home Affairs. (2020) *Surveillance Legislation Amendment (Identify and Disrupt) Bill 2020*. Available from: https://www.homeaffairs.gov.au/about-us/our-portfolios/national-security/lawful-access-telecommunications/surveillance-legislation-amendment-identify-and-disrupt-bill-2020 [Accessed 29 November 2021].

Dixon, D. (1997) *Law in Policing: Legal Regulation and Police Practices*. Oxford: Clarendon Press.

Easttom, C. (2018) 'Conducting investigations on the dark web'. *Journal of Information Warfare*. 17(4): 26–37.

European Monitoring Centre for Drugs and Drug Addiction. (2018) *Darknet Markets Ecosystem - Lifetimes and Reasons for Closure of Over 100 Global Darknet Markets*. EMCDDA Rapid Communication. Luxembourg: Publications Office of the European Union.

Europol. (2017) 'Massive blow to criminal dark web activities after globally coordinated operation'. Available from: https://www.europol.europa.eu/newsroom/news/massive-blow-to-criminal-dark-web-activities-after-globally-coordinated-operation [Accessed 29 November 2021].

Ford, D. and Mann, M. (2019) *International Implications of the Telecommunications and Other Legislation Amendment (Assistance and Access) Act 2018*. Australian Privacy Foundation. Available from: https://privacy.org.au/wp-content/uploads/2019/06/APF_AAAct_FINAL_040619.pdf [Accessed 29 November 2021].

Ghappour, A. (2017) 'Searching places unknown: Law enforcement jurisdiction on the dark web'. *Stanford Law Review*. 69(4): 1075–1136.

Greenberg, A. (2018) 'Operation Bayonet: Inside the sting that hijacked an entire dark web drug market. *Wired*. Available from: https://www.wired.com/story/hansa-dutch-police-sting-operation/ [Accessed 29 November 2021].

Heidt, J. and Wheeldon, J. (2021) 'Data, damn lies, and cannabis policy: Reefer Madness and the methodological crimes of the new prohibitionists' *Critical Criminology*. https://doi.org/10.1007/s10612-020-09548-8.

Jeong, S. (2015) 'Could the crimes of two corrupt agents free Ross Ulbricht?' *Forbes Magazine*. Available from: https://www.forbes.com/sites/sarahjeong/2015/04/17/could-the-crimes-of-two-corrupt-agents-free-ross-ulbricht/ [Accessed 14 April 2021].

Katz, K. (2011) 'The enemy within: The outlaw motorcycle gang moral panic'. *American Journal of Criminal Justice*. 36(3): 231–249.

Kerr, O. and Murphy, S. (2017) 'Government hacking to light the dark web: What risks to international relations and international law?' *Stanford Law Review Online*. 70(1): 58–69.

Koops, B.-J. and Kosta, E. (2018) 'Looking for some light through the lens of "Cryptowar" history: Policy options for law enforcement authorities against "going dark"'. *Computer Law and Security Review*. 34(4): 890–900.

Kuziemko, I. and Levitt, S. D. (2004) 'An empirical analysis of imprisoning drug offenders'. *Journal of Public Economics*. 88(9–10): 2043–2066.

Ladegaard, I. (2018) 'We know where you are, what you are doing and we will catch you: Testing deterrence theory in digital drug markets'. *British Journal of Criminology*. 58(2): 414–433.

Ladegaard, I. (2019) 'Crime displacement in digital drug markets'. *International Journal of Drug Policy*. 63: 113–121.

Linneman, T. and Wall, T. (2013) '"This is your face on meth": The punitive spectacle of "white trash" in the rural war on drugs'. *Theoretical Criminology*. 17(3): 315–334.

Lynch, M. (2012) 'Theorizing the role of the "war on drugs" in US punishment'. *Theoretical Criminology*. 16(2): 175–199.

Mann, M. (2020) *Policing and Politicising Organised Crime*. London: Routledge.

Mann, M. and Warren, I. (2018) 'The digital and legal divide: Silk Road, transnational online policing and southern criminology'. In Carrington, K., Hogg, R., Scott, J. and Sozzo, M. (eds.) *Palgrave Handbook of Criminology and the Global South*. London: Palgrave Macmillan: 245–260.

Mann, M., Warren, I. and Kennedy, S. (2018) 'The legal geographies of transnational cyber-prosecutions: Extradition, human rights and forum shifting'. *Global Crime*. 19(2): 107–124.

Mann, M., Daly, A., Wilson, M. and Suzor, N. (2018) 'The limits of (digital) constitutionalism: Exploring the privacy-security (im)balance in Australia'. *International Communication Gazette*. 80(4): 369–384.

Mann, M., Daly, A. and Molnar, A. (2020) 'Regulatory arbitrage and transnational surveillance: Australia's extraterritorial assistance to access encrypted communications'. *Internet Policy Review*. 9(3): 1–20.

Mark, G. (2013) 'RICO's extraterritoriality'. *American Business Law Journal*. 50(3): 543–608.

Martin, J., Cunliffe, J. and Munksgaard, R. (2019) *Cryptomarkets: A Research Companion*. Bingley: Emerald Group Publishing.

Martin, J., Munksgaard, R., Coomber, R., Demant, J. and Barratt, M. (2020) 'Selling drugs on darkweb cryptomarkets: Differentiated pathways, risks and rewards'. *British Journal of Criminology*. 60(3): 559–578.

May, T. and Hough, M. (2004) 'Drug markets and distribution systems'. *Addiction Research and Theory*. 12(6): 549–563.

McCulloch, D. (2020) 'Cyber spies to help catch dark web lurkers'. *Australian Associated Press*. Available from: https://www.aap.com.au/cyber-spies-to-help-catch-dark-web-lurkers/ [Accessed 14 April 2021].

Moeller, K. (2018) 'Drug market criminology: Combining economic and criminological research on illicit drug markets'. *International Criminal Justice Review*. 28(3): 191–205.

Molnar, A., Parsons, C. and Zouave, E. (2017) 'Computer network operations and 'rule-with-law' in Australia'. *Internet Policy Review*. 6(1): 1–15.

Norbutas, L. (2018) 'Offline constraints in online drug marketplaces: An exploratory analysis of a cryptomarket trade network'. *International Journal of Drug Policy*. 56: 92–100.

Office of Management and Budget (OMB). (2020) *Budget of the US Government*. Washington, DC: US Government Publishing Office.

Otey, M. (2015) 'Why RICO's extraterritorial reach is properly coextensive with the reach of its predicates'. *Journal of International Business and Law*. 14(1): 33–65.

Palmer, D. and Warren, I. (2013) 'Global policing and the case of Kim Dotcom'. *International Journal for Crime, Justice and Social Democracy*. 2(3): 105–119.

Payan, T. (2007) *Cops, soldiers, and diplomats: Explaining agency behavior in the war on drugs*. Lanham, MD: Lexington Books.

Pollack, H. and Reuter, P. (2014) 'Does tougher enforcement make drugs more expensive?' *Addiction*. 109(12): 1959–1966.

Prime Minister of Australia. (2021). *Press Release Concerning Operation Ironside*. Available from: https://www.pm.gov.au/media/press-conference-sydney-cpo-nsw [Accessed 29 November 2021].

Russell, Z. (2017) 'First they came for the child pornographers: The FBI's international search warrant to hack the dark web'. *St Mary's Law Journal*. 49(1): 269–315.

Rydell, C. and Everingham, S. (1994) *Controlling Cocaine. Supply Versus Demand Programs*. Santa Monica, CA: Rand Corporation.

Solimini, R., Rotolo, M., Pellegrini, M., Minutillo, A., Pacifici, R., Busardò, P. F. and Zaami, S. (2017) 'Adulteration practices of psychoactive illicit drugs: An updated review'. *Current Pharmaceutical Biotechnology*. 18(7): 524–530.

Soska, K. and Christin, N. (2015). 'Measuring the longitudinal evolution of the online anonymous marketplace ecosystem'. In *Proceedings of the 24th USENIX Conference on Security Symposium*: 33–48. Washington D.C.

Strang, J., Babor, T., Caulkins, J., Fischer, B., Foxcroft, D. and Humphreys, K. (2012) 'Drug policy and the public good: Evidence for effective interventions. *The Lancet*. 379(9810): 71–83.

The Parliament of the Commonwealth of Australia. (2018). *Explanatory Memoranda of the Telecommunications and Other Legislation Amendment (Assistance and Access) Bill 2018*. Available from: https://parlinfo.aph.gov.au/parlInfo/download/legislation/ems/r6195_ems_1139bfde-17f3-4538-b2b2-5875f5881239/upload_pdf/685255.pdf;fileType=application%2Fpdf [Accessed 29 November 2021].

The Parliament of the Commonwealth of Australia. (2020). *Explanatory Memoranda of the Surveillance Legislation Amendment (Identify and Disrupt) Bill 2020*. Available from: https://parlinfo.aph.gov.au/parlInfo/download/legislation/ems/r6623_ems_cdf486bc-4c7c-475f-89cb-78af48798af8/upload_pdf/JC000627.pdf;fileType=application%2Fpdf [Accessed 29 November 2021].

Tzanetakis, M. (2018) 'Comparing cryptomarkets for drugs: A characterisation of sellers and buyers over time'. *International Journal of Drug Policy*. 56: 176–186.

United States of America v Griffiths [2004] FCA 879 (7 July 2004).

United States of America v. Ulbricht (2014) (Electronically filed memorandum of law in support of the defendant Ross Ulbricht's pre-trial motions challenging the face of the indictment). Available at https://www.wired.com/wp-content/uploads/2014/04/Ulbricht3.pdf. [Accessed 29 November 2021].

Urbas, G. (2006) 'Cross-national investigation and prosecution of intellectual property crimes: The example of "operation Buccaneer"'. *Crime, Law and Social Change*. 46(4/5): 207–221.

Van Buskirk, J., Bruno, R., Dobbins, T., Breen, C., Burns, L., Naicker, S. and Roxburgh, A. (2017) 'The recovery of online drug markets following law enforcement and other disruptions'. *Drug and Alcohol Dependence*. 173: 159–162.

Walden, I. and Flanagan, A. (2003) 'Honeypots: A sticky legal landscape?' *Rutgers Computer and Technology Law Journal*. 29(2): 317–370.

Warren, I. (2015) 'Surveillance, criminal law and sovereignty'. *Surveillance and Society*. 13(2): 300–305.

Warren, I., Mann, M. and Molnar, A. (2020) 'Lawful illegality: Authorizing extraterritorial police surveillance'. *Surveillance and Society*. 18(3): 357–369.

Weidenhouse, K. (2017) 'Playpen, the NIT, and Rule 41(b): Electronic searches for those who do not wish to be found'. *Journal of Business and Technology Law*. 13(1): 143–169.

Werb, D., Rowell, G., Guyatt, G., Kerr, T., Montaner, J. and Wood, E. (2011) 'Effect of drug law enforcement on drug market violence: A systematic review'. *International Journal of Drug Policy*. 22(2): 87–94.

Yeh, B. (2012) *Drug Offenses: Maximum Fines and Terms of Imprisonment for Violation of the Federal Controlled Substances Act and Related Laws*. Washington, DC: Congressional Research Service. Available from: https://www.everycrsreport.com/files/20121213_RL30722_c4b7ba4df9a8901c227c979d19fd6e0b9bc8249f.pdf. [Accessed 29 November 2021].

6

POLICING DRUGS IN THE CARIBBEAN

Matthew Louis Bishop and Dylan Kerrigan

Introduction

In mid-2010, Jamaica experienced an unprecedented crisis when the people of Tivoli Gardens, a poor Kingston 'garrison' community, resisted government efforts to extradite a notorious cocaine trafficker and local 'Don' (gang boss), Christopher 'Dudus' Coke. In the ensuing stand-off between armed residents and state forces, dozens of people lost their lives (at least 73 civilians and 4 members of the security services). The trigger for the violence was the long-awaited decision to sign Coke's extradition papers: Tivoli also happened to be in the Kingston West constituency of erstwhile Jamaica Labour Party (JLP) Prime Minister Bruce Golding. He was faced with the troubling dilemma of whether to offer political protection to a dominant gangster who represented the de facto force of order within the garrison, with whom his own influence was unavoidably symbiotically connected, and whose fall would lead to a new power vacuum, or to hand him over to the United States to stem the continued bleeding of diplomatic capital. Ultimately, the pressure for the latter became overwhelming. In 2014, while the inquest over the 'Dudus Affair' continued to dominate Jamaica's public conversation, a young, middle-class man called Mario Deane was arrested by police in Montego Bay with a single 'spliff' (cannabis cigarette) and placed in a cell over the weekend. He never emerged, having been beaten to death by other prisoners. The outrage this incident provoked was immediate and profound: by 2015, the People's National Party (PNP) government had amended the Dangerous Drugs Act, effectively decriminalising the possession of recreational cannabis and creating the legal foundations for the introduction of a medical industry.

These two disparate processes, from a single Caribbean country, emphasise the messy, complicated, and contradictory experiences of drugs and their

DOI: 10.4324/9781003154136-7

policing in this part of the world. The region neither produces nor consumes illicit narcotics in great quantities, yet frequently experiences violent spillovers from trafficking and retains highly punitive – even anachronistic – legal, judicial, and penal regimes. Most islands are culturally conservative with very low prevalence rates for substances such as cocaine or heroin and similarly low consumption of licit substances, especially tobacco. In much of the region, though, cannabis is widely cultivated and consumed – it is central to Rastafari identity, especially – to the extent that it is not viewed as 'a narcotic' by many and, in many places, is rapidly being decriminalised anyway. Of course, the binary distinctions we draw between different substances – licit/illicit, narcotic/medicine, harder/softer – are themselves imbued with enduring relations of power and constructions of reason that serve particular vested interests (see Seddon 2016). For the Caribbean, these experiences are profoundly colonial: not only did the global norms and architectures which underpinned prohibition by crystallising those binaries emerge before the region's territories became independent states, taking little heed of their cultural mores or social contexts, but also the policing of drugs itself within those societies reflected particular enduring relations of coloniality inherited from a deeply exclusionary political order that was constructed entirely to facilitate extractive interests.

The development of policing, then, cannot be disconnected from this wider colonial experience and the patterns of order (and disorder) that it reproduced over time. Understanding this heritage is crucial to grasp both change – or the lack of it – throughout the region's modern history, and the operation of what are often deeply exclusionary forms of policing today. Indeed, the very creation of policing systems was not about protecting a broad-based citizenry, but rather perpetuating the oppression of enslaved peoples by a dominant minority. Caribbean criminologists, such as Joan Mars (2002) in Guyana and Kerron King (2009) in Trinidad and Tobago, among others (e.g. Deosaran 2017; Johnson et al. 2014; Trotman 1986), have written about how the establishment of policing in the Caribbean plantation societies was connected to power relations and fundamentally about 'maintaining social control under the slave system' (King 2009, p. 8). Community policing was never part of the equation and instead paramilitary policing was the norm (Danns 1982; Harriot 2000; Johnson 1991). Speaking about the institution of policing in the region, Johnson et al. (2014, p. 956) make a similar observation: 'The style of policing that is common in Caribbean nations like Trinidad and Tobago which treat[s] the policed like subjects rather than citizens is rooted in the region's tumultuous colonial history'.

The extant and evolving political economy of drug prohibition threatens to reproduce familiar neo-colonial patterns. On the one hand, as a major transhipment point for Andean cocaine heading to North America and Europe, it has long found itself at the sharpest end of the frontline of the 'war on drugs', paying massive residual costs in terms of violence and insecurity that enrich a small elite of untouchable traffickers and corrupted politicians, while also increasing the militarisation of state agencies and community violence. On the other hand, this is unlikely to abate any time soon even as some parts of the world move towards more humane and intelligent forms of drug policy based on harm reduction principles. Cocaine flows will not plausibly be subject to any decriminalising – let alone legalising – agenda in the near future, reinforcing their residual trades in weapons, ammunition, and people. Moreover, despite the gradual shifts in rhetoric, discourse, and policy regarding the policing of drugs, the difficulties faced by many Caribbean states in moving decisively towards approaches based on harm reduction principles appear almost insurmountable. Although much of the region has now decriminalised cannabis or signalled an intention to do so, there remains a long way to go before this translates into the wholesale recasting of drastically under-resourced yet increasingly militarised policing systems, predicated on the most punitive forms of enforcement and carceral policies. Indeed, the enduring violence associated with trafficking and the institutionalisation of gang activity in many places only reinforce these tendencies.

The chapter explores the distinctive nature of the 'drug problem' in the Caribbean in three sections. First, we discuss how the barriers that exist fundamentally reflect both enduring legacies of colonial brutality in which policing systems were established to maintain order in deeply racially stratified societies and a post-independence settlement that coincided with intense anti-drug surveillance led by the United States. Second, we explain the changing geopolitical context since the dawn of independence, showing how Caribbean policing systems have evolved in tandem with US-driven security interventions, entrenching structural dynamics which inhibit them from either emulating legal shifts elsewhere or developing more humane criminal justice systems. Third, we examine how the securitising, militarising, and privatising of 'hard' interventions on the basis of imported policing models that sit uneasily with local culture, in tandem with deteriorating public infrastructure for 'soft' policy geared towards social transformation, have exacerbated this picture, leading to sustained antagonism between the police and marginalised populations. Finally, we conclude by reflecting on the wider implications of our broader argument.

Colonial legacies

All Caribbean societies fundamentally reflect their colonial inheritance. More than any other region on earth, the effect of the totalitarian plantation system – in which pre-existing society was largely wiped out, with a new one grafted onto a tabula rasa (Lewis 1968) – meant that the entire legal, social, and political order was subordinated to satisfying extractive interests. Whole islands served no other purpose than to generate wealth for plantocrats via the system of sugar slavery, which in turn produced peculiar structures of race, class, and gender stratification (James 1938). These have endured to the present day, shaping political systems (Bishop et al. 2020), patterns of economic accumulation (Marshall 2002), and social relations typified by distinctly raced, classed, and gendered forms of domination and subordination (Thompson 2021). In short, the Caribbean's challenges are largely rooted in its colonial legacy, and the problematic forms of post-colonial sovereignty and citizenship that have endured (Watson 2015). Central to our purposes here is how these have shaped the drug economy, in terms of who controls it, where the boundaries – both formal and informal – between the licit and illicit are defined and policed, and how the police and other state forces carry out their functions.

At its most basic, policing in much of the region emerged to ensure order within a plantation society where essentially every aspect of social and political life was subordinated to this most peculiar of economic systems. As Mars (2002, p. 83) noted in her historical account, 'the model of organized policing that was eventually implemented in colonial Guyana [and, by implication, elsewhere] differed greatly from that of the home country of the European colonists who established permanent settlement in the colonies'. She discusses the role of slave patrols to 'protect the continuity of the labour supply that was constantly being threatened by the practice of slaves regularly escaping into the interior, where they would set up their bush settlements' (2002, p. 67). She also mentioned that the policing of slaves was implemented to ensure that any resistance by the enslaved through riots and rebellion could be quelled. Taken together, this is evidence of how planters and colonial elites enforced their control over the society and maintained the flow of labour for the riches they received via the plantation economy. These are two factors influencing the establishment and early development of policing throughout the region where sugar production and slavery dominated entire territories.

King (2009, p. 8) adds another lens to this historical account when he critiques Mars' analysis of policing for her subdivision between policing during slavery and afterwards:

> To argue that the slaves were policed, apprehended and convicted of crime, as Mars tried to prove, would be to assume that the slaves were persons guilty of a crime or could be interpreted as such. In reality, the slaves of Guyana and any state for that matter were not criminals but victims; therefore a victim cannot in the true sense of the word be policed. Mars wrongly suggested this when she defined the slavery period of policing as 'policing the powerless'. A people who are enslaved cannot be policed for slave revolts, uprising or rebellion because they are simply responding to the crimes of the Slave Masters. It is somewhat absurd to think that victims who resist domination are described as being policed.

The point is an important one for Caribbean-centric accounts of policing. King's central contention is that the enslaved were not 'punished but they were victimized' and, by the same token, they were not 'policed, they were hunted' (2009, p. 12). He also explains that this is an important distinction rarely reflected in how the story of colonial policing in the region is told. More broadly, though, such historical accounts of the emergence of colonial policing offer three key insights about the process applicable for much of the wider region. Firstly, there is an instinctive emphasis on control and coercion rather than service and protection as the primary function of policing. Secondly, appalling police behaviour, no matter how reprehensible, is constantly legitimised by the executive and judiciary. Thirdly, policing is characterised by an indiscriminate resort to violence and the use of deadly force deployed as a means of social control, especially crowd control.

Caribbean sociologists and criminologists such as Danns (1982) have long emphasised and illustrated the continuities between how the police and other aspects of Caribbean criminal justice systems established during the injustices of the colonial period extended into independence and the neo-colonial era (see also Kerrigan 2021). Some also note the lack of trust in authorities such as the police and courts that is a symptom of such legacies (Johnson et al. 2014). For example, writing at the turn of the millennium about paramilitarism in the Jamaica Constabulary Force (JCF), Anthony Harriot (2000, p. 72) explained that the origins of the relationship were to be found in 'the structures of power, originating in the colonial period, that treat the policed like subjects rather than citizens'. He notes that the tactics of paramilitarism do not betray an interest in actually solving social problems or treating the inequalities and lack of resources at the root of much crime in the Caribbean. This is similar to academic criticisms made about the increased securitisation and militarisation discourse adopted by the police in Trinidad (Johnson et al. 2014; Kerrigan 2018). For example, Mastrofski and Lum (2008, p. 486) argue that the scale of paramilitarism in the Trinidad and Tobago Police Service (TTPS) derives directly from a British colonial inheritance in which such approaches were not simply tolerated, but rather entirely integral to the mode of policing:

> The police were a paramilitary organization, headed by military officers (some of whom had served in other British colonies) who envisioned their organization's role as repression of a rebellious public that threatened the island's elite – done under the guise of maintaining law and order.

There were, moreover, good reasons for the small, usually white, and often ethnically exclusive Creole plantocratic caste that dominated many Caribbean societies to fear destabilisation from below. From the uprisings and rebellions that marked agitation on plantations themselves during the dying days of slavery in the early 19th century, to the widespread labour riots that marked the waning of the colonial period after a hundred years of post-emancipation developmental neglect in the early 20th century, the social order was marked by tension. Yet, rather than a fundamental improvement, independence for many Caribbean nations saw the re-intensification of enduring structural inequalities and class hierarchies (Bishop 2013). The 1970s witnessed a sustained collapse in the region's terms of trade in tandem with wider declines in commodity prices, feeding into pronounced social and political crises throughout the 1980s and early 1990s. This coincided with the failure of radical political experiments – Manley's socialism in Jamaica, revolution in Grenada, a short-lived Islamist coup in Trinidad, and the Burnham dictatorship in Guyana (Payne 1976; Thorndike 1993) – all of which ultimately foundered against pronounced US opposition, destabilisation, and intervention, as well as internal opposition and middle-class out-migration. However, it was during this period, as the region struggled with economic turmoil, that flows of cocaine were re-routed through it, alongside the ongoing decline of the Colombian cartels (Hobson 2014; Miller and Hendricks 2007; Stambøl 2015). This, in turn, invited renewed US pressure, albeit no longer of an anti-communist flavour, but rather focused on the perceived security challenges generated by the drug trade. This occurred in a distinctly 'episodic' fashion (Bernal 2015, p. 76), as the Caribbean only ever enjoys a sporadically peripheral place within Washington's benignly neglectful strategic thinking. Yet, US surveillance became so pervasive at this point that some even spoke seriously about the threat of 're-colonization' as Reagan's Caribbean Basin Initiative (CBI) gave way to the 'Shiprider' agreements which effectively gave US anti-drug bodies the right to exercise monitoring power inside the boundaries of Caribbean states (Watson 2003).

Central to the US anti-drug agenda was a distinctly racialised set of assumptions deriving from its own historical experience. As controversial revelations by the journalist Dan Baum (2016) demonstrated, the prosecution of the 'war on drugs' by the Nixon administration in the early 1970s had been a pretext to facilitate the stigmatisation and harassment of minority groups. Nixon adviser, Richard Ehrlichman, told Baum in 1994 that, 'by getting the public to associate the hippies with marijuana and blacks with heroin, and then criminalizing both heavily, we could disrupt those communities'. In truth, though, this followed a similar pattern to American prohibition since its very earliest days. From the very establishment of the Federal Bureau of Narcotics (FBN) under Harry Anslinger, prohibition was geared towards – and drew sustenance from – stoking fear and waging alarmist campaigns against minorities, with cocaine associated with African Americans, opium with Chinese Americans, and 'marihuana' (the name chosen specifically because of its Spanish connotations) with Mexicans (Hari 2015). The painful irony was that, in many cases, poor minorities could not afford these substances: in the southern United States, where black Americans did not have the means to see doctors and were generally banned from soda fountains, opium was overwhelmingly prescribed to wealthy white housewives, and cocaine was consumed by middle-class whites in their drinks (Cohen 2006).

The broader point is that US power and its dysfunctional racial politics were central to prohibition, both domestically and internationally: as Ethan Nadelmann (1990, p. 511) notes, in the post-war era, 'the global drug enforcement regime reflected the desire and capacity of the United States to impose its drug-related norms on the rest of the world'. However, these norms were grounded in racialised – even neo-colonial – assumptions about that world. As it exported, often brutally, the drug war throughout the Americas, local knowledge and customs regarding different substances – coca in the Andes, cannabis in the Caribbean – were disregarded and intensified prohibition imposed punitive carceral costs on cultivators and consumers who were often among the most marginalised peoples in their societies. Moreover, the gradual establishment of Drug Enforcement Agency (DEA) offices in dozens of countries around the world – including teams of officers in many US embassies throughout Latin America and the Caribbean – alongside the aggressive expansion of prohibitionist agendas by the FBN, rendered some countries effectively client states of US anti-drug interests. In Jamaica, for example, when an earlier attempt was made to decriminalise cannabis, at the behest of an exhaustive process of consultation across society by the National Commission on Ganja (2001) led by the late Professor Barry Chevannes, the United States essentially threatened to cut aid and put heavy pressure on the government to 'shelve the report' (Klein 2016, p. 2).

In the Caribbean itself, the post-colonial inheritance led not only to deeply class and race-stratified societies, but also starkly divided patterns of geographic settlement. In Kingston, the affluent 'uptown' neighbourhoods beyond 'New Kingston' tended to be occupied by the lighter-skinned middle classes and often-white (i.e. descendants of plantocrats) upper-class businesspeople, whereas the 'downtown' districts south of Halfway Tree – of which Trenchtown is probably the most infamous – tended to be populated with the proletarian poor, black masses. The former are sites of affluence and, sometimes, excess; the latter are frequently associated with violence and drugs. Yet, it is in the rarefied uptown neighbourhoods where the financiers of the drug trade might be found, and the gangs that blight downtown are a reflection of sustained development failures, entrenched poverty, and state absence (Thomas 2016, 2019). A similar story might be told of Trinidad's capital, Port of Spain (POS). After slavery, inward migration of indentured Indian labourers saw some Afro-Trinidadians leave the plantations in the rural south and move to the outskirts of the capital in the north-west. Today, the country's major violence hotspots are the east POS districts of Beetham, Laventille, and Sea Lots. Gang violence is endemic, yet is actually disconnected from the drug trade itself, most of which takes place at sea and is financed by wealthy elites who tend not to be Afro-Trinidadian (Baird et al. 2021).

In sum, policing and other aspects of Caribbean criminal justice systems such as prisons (Anderson et al. 2020) and courts profoundly reflect colonially constituted hierarchies of race, class, and gender (Kerrigan et al. 2019; Lazarus-Black 2001; Robinson and Bulkan 2017). We see this in police culture and tactics such as paramilitarism. We see it in terms of who the police target and perceive as criminals, which, across the Caribbean, is grounded in enduring transhistorical class and race hierarchies. This is evident in the most prosaic realities, such as the staggering disparity in the policing of white-collar crimes vs street-level crimes (Kerrigan and Sookoo 2013). We also see it in the power relations between the sovereign states that comprise the Caribbean region and American hegemony around anti-drug initiatives which replay the same colonial violence against local

Caribbean communities, that, to borrow Kerron King's (2009) analogy, are due to the consumption economy of North American and European populations and their insatiable demand for drugs, with Caribbean peoples their structural victims, as much as anything else.

Geopolitical shifts

It is not an overstatement to say that, aside from some exceptions – e.g. the various crises in Haiti or the normalisation of US–Cuba relations – narcotics interdiction and the perceived security threats associated with it have become the almost sole focus of the US posture towards the region. The irony, though, is that the Caribbean has borne the brunt of violence – murder rates almost everywhere have grown precipitously, especially so in major transhipment points such as Jamaica and Trinidad – despite relatively little cocaine being consumed locally (UNODC 2019). Comparatively few people are actually directly involved in the drug trade, but the floods of weapons that have accompanied cocaine cargos over the years catalysed ever more violent gang activities as those entities fought for prominence in marginalised communities (Baird et al. 2021). By the 2000s, and especially after 9/11, all US policy towards the wider region came to be framed by the new securitisation paradigm, with the wars on drugs and terror feeding off of each other in ever darker ways (Tate 2015). This led to an even greater intensification of the focus on drugs and organised crime. However, another irony was that the narrowing of Washington's agenda towards the region, to the extent that almost all diplomatic activity became framed through the twin prism of the wars on drugs and terror, also coincided with a sharp diminution in resources as American aid, personnel, and security infrastructure were increasingly redirected to Iraq and Afghanistan (in turn helping the booming drugs and weapons trades to continue to flourish).

The most contentious example – in the Jamaican case, at least – was the US attempt to extradite Dudus in 2009. This episode has been much picked over (Edmonds 2016; Haughton 2014; Lewis 2012; Meikle and Jaffe 2015), so it does not really concern us here, other than to make the point that, in contrast to the conclusion that is usually drawn – i.e. that it illustrates how relatively powerless Jamaica is vis-à-vis the United States – it potentially reveals something rather different. It actually shows just how deeply embedded criminal activity had become (and remains) within the state apparatuses of Caribbean countries, to the extent that it should not be considered an aberration, but rather a constitutive element of the prevailing political-economic – and, as Rivke Jaffe (2012) suggests, aesthetic – settlement. Indeed, what is most shocking about the Dudus Affair is that, aside from episodic periods of pressure being applied, the combination of Washington's benign developmental neglect with the assertive pursuit of its broader prohibitionist agenda has inadvertently facilitated the institutionalisation of criminal networks in the region while reinforcing a political economy of drug trafficking in which sustained demand for cocaine by North

American consumers displaces violence and insecurity to the small Caribbean countries least able to bear them. These spaces, where drugs transact and tranship, facilitate processes that have been abandoned to black markets necessarily controlled by gangsters whose only means of enforcing contracts is by bribery and violence.

As others have pointed out, US interventionism in the Caribbean for security purposes is nothing new (Agozino et al. 2009). As such, understanding the region's policing systems necessitates recognising the influence of US interests and how these shaped both the architecture and practices of policing and security after the departure of former European colonisers. First, the structural adjustment policies of the 1980s devastated living standards and increased inequality, with a litany of consequences for recorded crime levels, including social fragmentation across, especially, increasingly ghettoised urban areas and the removal of social safety nets. For Agozino et al. (2009, p. 289), 'The emergence of illicit and semi-licit markets in a range of commodities – including drugs, guns, financial services, endangered species, illegal timber and fish and human labour – were part and parcel of this trend'. Over time, the increased incorporation of Caribbean territories as crucial nodes within hemispheric trafficking networks has led to a flood of weapons, especially, and these have, in turn, fundamentally shifted the opportunity structures for criminal accumulation and, over time, helped to embed ever more intense violence practices and gang cultures (see Baird et al. 2021).

In fact, by the turn of the millennium, crime levels, especially homicides and other acts of interpersonal violence, were causing great alarm. This led to the development of increasingly internationalised, privatised, and militarised policing initiatives to combat increases in drug trafficking (see Bowling 2010). These initiatives pooled 'the resources of local island domestic enforcement' while also often being 'completely underwritten with foreign police assistance' (Agozino et al. 2009, p. 296). They would also require substantial inputs from metropolitan police forces and their personnel, such that a range of regional bodies – e.g. the Regional Security System, the Association of Caribbean Commissioners of Police, and the Caribbean Customs Law Enforcement Council – were shaped and funded by external powers. In some cases, senior police officers were even recruited from metropolitan countries to serve among the top brass in highly sensitive positions: in Trinidad and Tobago, for example, for two short and difficult years in which they met stiff resistance amid an explosion in gang-related murders, Canadians Dwayne Gibbs and Jack Ewatski served as commissioner and deputy commissioner of the TTPS. On one level, all of this is uncontroversial: policing systems globally have become internationalised in tandem with the challenges they face moving in an increasingly borderless fashion (Bowling 2010). At the same time, though, the nature of the training received by local police forces, the methods deployed to solve what are, at root, deep-seated social problems, and the prioritisation of prohibitionist assumptions about the drug war – which in turn have driven increasingly problematic militarised approaches to it – demonstrate the pitfalls and problems of a US posture towards regional policing needs, culture, and outcomes.

A striking example is given by Agozino et al. (2009). They note that 'Operation Kingfish' began in 2004 and was a multinational initiative to 'take out' regional 'drug kingpins' in the cocaine trade. Approximately 12 metric tons of cocaine with a street value estimated at $5 billion and weapons were seized and 51 arrests made. Further seizures were made in 2005 and 2006. The operation involved deploying 'specially vetted persons from the Jamaica Constabulary Force, the Caribbean police intelligence community – largely Special Branch – Military Intelligence and a variety of internationally seconded officers' (Agozino et al. 2009, p. 296). It was intelligence-led policing and went after 12 different Jamaican gangs, escalating state violence and ultimately generating power vacuums in poorer communities poorly equipped to cope with disruption of the authority structures under which they live. However, when measured in terms of reducing the actual supply of cocaine through the Caribbean or the levels of violence, it failed: murder rates actually increased as Kingfish proceeded, not least because the operation also incited increased violence between rival groups. This chimes with evidence from Latin America where militarised confrontations between the state and traffickers simply raise the temperature, inciting ever more brazen acts of violence on the part of the latter as they assertively defend their control of the markets bequeathed to them by the prohibition of narcotics (see Lessing 2017). This, in turn, can paradoxically weaken, rather than strengthen, the state monopoly of violence and render people in poorer communities less, rather than more, secure. Consequently, it is not difficult to understand why so many people defer to the authority structures of gangs in the urban margins of Kingston or Port of Spain rather than formal state forces (Jaffe 2013; Pawelz 2018).

A general problem is that large-scale interventions – quite apart from the damage they can do to an already fractured social fabric – rarely, if ever, target the powerful actors financing the drug trade, but zero in on 'big fish' like Dudus and gang bosses in poorer communities who do the overt 'dirty work' associated with trafficking. This process has a distinctly raced and classed logic underpinning it: those who are caught in the dragnet of anti-drug policing are overwhelmingly black and from marginalised places, even if they have risen to become very powerful leaders of those communities. Evidence of who, exactly, the financiers behind the trade might be is difficult to come by, for obvious reasons. But, anecdotally, they are frequently believed to be powerful members of the merchant classes who live far from the violence-scarred urban districts. This, in turn, reflects broader patterns of exclusionary state-building and settlement that derive directly from the region's plantation heritage. Of course, if one believes that drug interdiction matters, then perhaps disrupting supply lines is a good thing. However, supply is unlikely to abate as long as demand remains, so all that these initiatives did on the ground was to continually destabilise poor communities as development resources were never ploughed in because structurally adjusted Caribbean governments could not afford them (while largely failing to stem supply). In fact, the damage to many islands has been significant: as drug trafficking declined relatively throughout the 2010s due to the re-routing of cocaine via West Africa and Mexico, homicidal violence did not decrease. Rather, once it had become institutionalised as a core means of resolving conflict in a context of fraying social capital, the continued availability of firearms has ensured that murders have stubbornly persisted at a terrifyingly high level.

In sum, the institutionalisation of American mores around policing and the perceived centrality of 'the drug problem' to wider security concerns have relentlessly shaped the geopolitical context. In general, this has inhibited Caribbean countries from developing more humane criminal justice systems. In fact, quite the contrary: a marked lack of resources alongside rapidly rising violent crime has led to logjams in many judicial systems and appalling conditions in prisons. These include, for example, in Guyana:

> Gross overcrowding which is inimical to rehabilitation and reintegration in society; Inadequate security personnel, arrangements and equipment – i.e. insufficient monitoring and warning mechanisms in the prisons; Inhumane conditions in the prisons that both staff and prisoners have to endure; Multiple violations of prisoners' human rights; Insufficient alternatives to incarceration offered by the criminal justice system.
>
> *(Ifill 2019)*

A lack of funding for prison services in the region means, more generally, that carceral spaces have problems providing inmates with critical items for their daily life, such as clothing, sheets, food, water, soap, toilet paper, and guaranteed access to health care (UNDP 2012; UNST 2016, p. 9). The food and often-brackish water are frequently unhygienic, causing skin lesions and health problems. Toilet facilities are minimal. Overcrowding, where cells designed for 6 men might house 14, means that men are forced to share rotten foam mattresses, sleep on floors, or if they can, make a hammock in the ceiling from a sheet (Sarsfield and Bergman 2017, 2016; UNST 2016). Many prisons in the anglophone Caribbean are also physical structures built by the British or are located on former plantations, bringing home the legacies and continuities of places defined and scarred by enslavement once more. Human rights organisations also report physical violence by guards, such as corporal punishment and emplacement in dark cells, alongside other forms of punishment that are prohibited under international regulations, such as repeated solitary confinement, reduction of diet, or 'close confinement' continually utilised as standard methods of discipline in Caribbean prisons (Sarsfield and Bergman 2017). When the COVID-19 pandemic wound its way towards the region in early 2020, harrowing scenes of terrified inmates in overcrowded, unsanitary penal buildings, flooded social media (Kissoon 2020).

The only partial exception to this unremittingly bleak picture is the tentative shift towards cannabis legalisation – or, at least, decriminalisation – in some parts of the region. This, again, derives from a different geopolitical reordering process, i.e. the fact that those states (including some US states) with the legal or physical space to resist federal anti-drug law, have moved towards radical experiments in changing the status of cannabis. In fact, it is no surprise that the first movers on this were western US states (Colorado, Washington, Oregon), which in turn changed the geopolitical calculation and allowed, first, Uruguay (one of the most geographically distant countries from the United States and small enough to fly under the radar) and then Canada (a powerful country that can resist US influence) to move furthest. In the Caribbean, Jamaica has been the pioneer: in contrast to its experience in the early 2000s, it now enjoys the policy space to engender meaningful reform, as the United States no longer has the capacity to prevent other states from decriminalising the plant (although recreational legalisation, even despite the United States having sanctioned this domestically, remains a grey area since legalisers technically find themselves in breach of the international conventions). In tandem with a handful of Latin American countries, Jamaica pushed for a UN General Assembly Special Session (UNGASS) in 2016, advocating the idea that greater flexibility was required in the drug treaties to facilitate the distinctive needs of different societies. This ultimately failed in the short term (see Bishop 2016), but it initiated a debate that is ongoing at the global level and, in 2020, the UN Commission on Narcotic Drugs (CND) finally acceded to the limited – but nonetheless symbolically important – partial reclassification of cannabis (from Schedule IV of the 1961 Convention to Schedule I) meaning that its medical use could be researched and recognised.

Jamaica's domestic reforms have been a watershed. The Dangerous Drugs Amendment Act (DDA) of 2015 saw the establishment of a medical cannabis industry and possession of small amounts for recreational consumption decriminalised. The country did not move to full legalisation, because – unlike Uruguay and Canada – it is, for historical and geopolitical reasons, directly in the US sphere of influence, cannabis remains both federally and globally prohibited, and the State Department, which is still populated with people who built careers as drug warriors, is an omnipresent feature of the country's international diplomacy. Put differently: despite the US tolerating recreational legalisation among many of its own states, Jamaican reformers were unwilling to take the risk of a backlash. The Obama administration actually faced a thorny problem: partial domestic legalisation placed the United States outside of the very conventions it had imposed on the world since the 1960s; therefore, in 2014, William Brownfield, assistant secretary at the Bureau of Narcotics at the State Department, called for 'flexibility' within the treaties. This fudge both opened the space for policy experimentation within countries such as Jamaica and Uruguay, and paved the way for their diplomacy in the run-up to UNGASS.

For Jamaica's pro-decriminalisation politicians and activists, the DDA reforms were not about cannabis per se. In fact, they were about repairing painful historical legacies of marginalisation on the part of Rastafari communities and those in the inner cities who have been repeatedly brutalised by the police, with possession of small amounts of cannabis a pretext for arrest. The Act protected them in at least three ways. First, possession itself was decriminalised: it became a 'ticketable' offence rather than a criminal one, but the government chose never to print the tickets, meaning that they could never be issued. Second, the sacramental importance of the plant for Rastafari communion was embedded in the law: this reflected Jamaica's wider international diplomatic efforts where, alongside countries such as Bolivia (and coca), it argued that there was no reason why the rights of religious expression laid out in the Universal Declaration of Human Rights, or, indeed, those embedded in the various treaties pertaining to development, should be automatically subordinated to the UN drug treaties with which they were evidently in tension (see Schleifer et al. 2015). Third, the reforms dramatically reduced pressure on the criminal justice system: arrests of young men dropped by around 90 per cent and the government essentially expunged all prior drug possession convictions. This was crucial, not least since those very convictions hampered people in accessing work or opportunities abroad, including US visas. Since then, a number of Caribbean countries – among them Trinidad and Tobago, Antigua-Barbuda, St Vincent and the Grenadines, and St Kitts and Nevis – have decriminalised, and the Caribbean community convened a commission which reported on the prospects for developing a regional approach to shifts in law and policy governing cannabis (Caribbean Community Secretariat 2018).

Between securitisation and privatisation

Unfortunately, very real improvements in the ways in which cannabis is policed in many parts of the region are exceptional, i.e. this particular substance has largely been hived off to be managed in its own ways, with the wider panorama of punitive, increasingly securitised, militarised, and privatised policing continuing largely untroubled. In many respects – as we suggested earlier – this actually has very little to do with drugs, or the value accruing to those who benefit most from the drug trade. Rather, it is about policing poor, often gang-afflicted communities where drugs (mostly cannabis and a limited amount of crack cocaine serving the small market for impoverished addicts) are certainly present, but have relatively little effect on patterns of wider crime and violence. Put differently: while gangs, of course, control the drug markets that exist, and the most sophisticated may perform critical functions at different stages of drug trafficking – usually providing muscle where transiting occurs – small local drug markets are neither the central item in their criminal portfolio nor the main driver of contestation between gangs. In fact, in most cases, gangs perform a crucial mediating function between politicians and poor communities, providing order – albeit a particularly Hobbesian form of it (Arias 2018) – and distributing state largesse in the form of government contracts. It is this which generally explains rising violence, with drugs historically being the simple pretext for police crackdowns.

As Watson and Morgan (2020) recently discussed of Trinidad and Tobago, and others such as Seepersad and Williams (2012) have pointed out, the inherently punitive, rather than preventative, character of local law enforcement necessarily breeds failure. In Jamaica, amid high crime rates over the last three decades, the main government strategy has been to fight fire with fire and introduce a number of measures that can be described as punitive policing, with little success in terms of the state objective of reducing the homicide rate over a sustained period of time. These include the introduction of specialised police units to tackle violent crimes and special security zones called 'zones of special operations (ZOSOs)', partnerships with UK and US police forces, and the purchase of militarised police equipment, states of emergency, and many different types of legislation (which regularly conflict with citizens' constitutional rights). Some of these measures may impact violent crime levels in the short term, but with time, the levels simply rise again. They also create breakdowns with the communities that they are intended to help and increase their marginalisation, leading to distrust and poor relations with the police. It is also true in Jamaica that between 1990 and 2000, the police shot dead more than 1,400 people without clear reason (Amnesty International 2001). This punitive approach, which continues today across the regions as illustrated in the Caribbean's own Black Lives Matter anti-police protests in 2020 (Reyes and Gahman 2020), can never achieve and is clearly not designed to achieve a 'positive peace'.

In many Caribbean states, the discourse of securitisation has also become an important element in national security frameworks. In the context of policing, securitisation theory is a weaponised solution to social problems. Securitisation theory can be understood in two key ways. One as an illocutionary speech act (Oren and Solomon 2015, p. 313). This is the process by which governments identify a criminal problem and teach their citizens what to fear and consider a threat. The state will then identify an emergency solution to this issue (state violence) and attack the 'problem' (usually the lives of certain citizens) with militarised force (Holbraad and Pedersen 2012, p. 166). But securitisation is again about a 'negative peace'. In weaponised solutions to social problems there are no considerations of inequalities, racism, structural poverty, and many other cumulative factors in the growth of criminal problems. The consequences of militarised force as the 'solution' to social problems do not provide security, rather they worsen citizen vulnerability to insecurity (Balzaq 2011, p. 3).

Policing is also becoming increasingly privatised. A decade ago, Rita Abrahamsen and Michael Williams (2011, p. 1) noted how, 'in almost every society across the globe, private security has become a pervasive part of everyday life, and in many countries private security personnel now outnumber their public counterparts by a considerable margin'. In the Caribbean, this process has intensified for two reasons. On the one hand, the violence panorama – at least in terms of homicides – has become much more acute, so much so that the United Nations Development Programme (UNDP) was moved just a few years ago to publish a series of Caribbean human development reports, which focused directly on the question of the relationship between development in the region and citizen security (UNDP 2012, 2016). One outcome of this sense of fear and insecurity among the population has been the generalised proliferation of private security firms. In recent decades, there has been both an increasing demand for, and a phenomenal increase in, the numbers of such companies in the Caribbean (Anyanwu 2012). Throughout the region, private security firms, which often have officers in greater number than formal state security agencies, now provide a range of services that increasingly stray close to 'core' policing functions and, in some cases, have even usurped them (see Bishop and Montoute 2017; Bishop et al. 2013).

On the other hand, this is deeply problematic: it intrinsically betrays the implied Hobbesian social contract in which the state is fundamentally the provider of, and enjoys a monopoly over, the legitimate use of violence. However, Caribbean societies – especially today – exist far from this theoretical ideal: as we have discussed, their police forces were created as mechanisms of colonial exploitation and are marked by both arbitrariness and an inability to enforce that social contract in many parts of their territories which are frequently engulfed in violence. Private security companies are, in many cases, better resourced, more technologically advanced, and capable of supporting police operations with capacities that do not exist within the public service (Bishop and Montoute 2017). Moreover, in more well-to-do districts, they are often viewed as a necessary evil to ensure the protection of property in contexts of elevated crime (and fear of it). However, this illustrates the wider challenge. Many Caribbean societies are, today, deeply insecure. The state is unable to assuage this insecurity and often contributes to it, so, while poorer people derive their private forces such as Dons and their gangs, wealthier people derive theirs from private security companies.

Conclusion

This is an inherently troubling picture: when societies devote greater resources to providing security rather than generating wealth and social capital, it tells us something extremely worrying. In the case of many Caribbean countries, a sustained development crisis that began in the colonial era, when entirely new plantation societies were grafted onto whole islands and oriented to serve the purposes of extractive capital, has continued into the present era via the neglect of the late colonial period, the successive crises of the late 20th century, and, today, a seemingly intractable violence panorama. The story of drugs and their policing only intersects tangentially with this story: the region has unquestionably been, at times, a crucial transhipment point for Andean cocaine transiting north, and this has brought with it weapons and the attention of powerful actors. But the wider problem of 'drug-related' violence that occupies the minds of many policymakers is, in our view, misdiagnosed. The challenge facing the region is, at once, a development challenge: it is rooted in exclusionary state–society settlements; a legal, judicial, and penal order that is at once excessively punitive and focused on the wrong things; a commitment to prohibition that does not respect the local cultural scene when it comes to substances like cannabis; and the enduring dominance of interventionist models that still seek to extract capital rather than build it. Until some of these persistent problems inherited from the past are honestly examined and dealt with in ways that heal a painfully fractured set of societies, the neo-colonial models of policing that keep failing to deal with a landscape in which drugs and violence are not connected in the simplistic ways that they are generally perceived to be, we are likely to remain in the same problematic loop.

References

Agozino, B., Bowling, B., Ward, E. and St Bernard, G. (2009) 'Guns, crime and social order in the West Indies'. *Criminology and Criminal Justice*. 9(3): 287–305.

Amnesty International. (2001) *Jamaica: Killings and Violence by Police: How Many More Victims?* April 9 2001: AMR: 38/003/2001.

Anderson, C., Ifill, M., Adams, E. and Moss, K. (2020) 'Guyana's prisons: Colonial histories of post-colonial challenges'. *Howard Journal of Crime and Justice*. 59(3): 335–349.

Anyanwu, D. (2012) 'The state of private security companies in Trinidad and Tobago: Towards the development of a governance system'. *African Journal of Criminology and Justice Studies*. 6(1–2): 45–66.

Arias, E. (2018) *Criminal Enterprises and Governance in Latin America and the Caribbean*. Cambridge: CUP.

Baird, A., Bishop, M. and Kerrigan, D. (2021) '"Breaking bad"? Gangs, masculinities, and murder in Trinidad'. *International Feminist Journal of Politics*. https://doi.org/10.1080/14616742.2021.1931395.

Balzaq, T. (ed.) (2011) *Securitisation Theory: How Security Problems Emerge and Dissolve*. London: Routledge.

Baum, D. (2016) 'Legalize it all'. *Harper's Magazine*. Available from: https://harpers.org/archive/2016/04/legalize-it-all/ [Accessed 21 October 2021].

Bernal, R. (2015) *The Influence of Small States on Superpowers: Jamaica and U.S. Foreign Policy*. Lanham, MD: Lexington Books.

Bishop, M. (2013) *The Political Economy of Caribbean Development*. London: Palgrave.

Bishop, M., Epps, K., Hill, S., Mountoute, A. and Siebert, J. (2013) *Private security companies in the Caribbean: Case studies of St Lucia, Trinidad and Tobago, and Jamaica*. St Augustine, Trinidad and Waterloo, ON: UWI Institute of International Relations and Project Ploughshares.

Bishop, M. (2016) 'Negotiating flexibility at UNGASS 2016: Solving the "world drug problem"?' *SPERI Global Political Economy Brief No. 5*. Available from: http://speri.dept.shef.ac.uk/wp-content/uploads/2016/11/Global-Brief-5-Negotiating-Flexibility-at-UNGASS-2016-Solving-the-World-Drug-Problem.pdf.

Bishop, M. and Montoute, A. (2017) 'Private security in the Caribbean'. In Izarali, M. (ed.) *Crime, Violence and Security in the Caribbean*. New York: Routledge: 200–219.

Bishop, M., Corbett, J. and Veenendaal, W. (2020) 'Labor movements and party system development: Why does the Caribbean have stable two-party systems, but the Pacific does not?' *World Development*. 126: 1–12.

Bowling, B. (2010) *Policing the Caribbean: Transnational Security Cooperation in Practice*. Oxford: OUP.

Caribbean Community Secretariat. (2018) *Report of the CARICOM Regional Commission on Marijuana 2018*. Guyana: Georgetown. Available from: https://caricom.org/final-report-report-of-the-caricom-regional-commission-on-marijuana/ [Accessed 22 October 2021].

Cohen, M. (2006) 'Jim Crow's drug war: Race, Coca Cola, and the southern origins of drug prohibition'. *Southern Cultures*. 12(3): 55–79.

Danns, G. (1982) *Domination and Power in Guyana: A Study of the Police in a Third World Context*. New Brunswick: Transaction Publishers.

Deosaran, R. (2017) 'Foreword'. In Izarali, M. (ed.) *Crime, Violence and Security in the Caribbean*. New York: Routledge: xiii–xviii.

Edmonds, K. (2016) 'Guns, gangs and garrison communities in the politics of Jamaica'. *Race and Class*. 57(4): 54–74.

Hari, J. (2015) *Chasing the Scream: The First and Last Days of the War on Drugs*. London: Bloomsbury.

Harriot, A. (2000) *Police and Crime Control in Jamaica: Problems of Reforming Ex-Colonial Constabularies*. Mona, Jamaica: University of the West Indies Press.

Haughton, S. (2014) 'The 2009 Jamaica-USA extradition affair: A 'securitized' response to Jamaica's drug problem'. *Caribbean Journal of International Relations & Diplomacy*. 2(3): 15–41.

Hobson, C. (2014) 'Privatising the war on drugs'. *Third World Quarterly*. 35(8): 1441–1456.

Holbraad, M. and Pedersen, M. (2012) 'Revolutionary securitisation: An anthropological extension of securitisation theory'. *International Theory*. 4(2): 165–197.

Ifill, M. (2019) 'Understanding the challenges facing the Guyana Prison Service'. *MNS Disorders in Guyana's Jails 1825 to the Present Day*. Avaiable from: https://mnsguyana.le.ac.uk/2019/11/04/understanding-the-challenges-facing-the-guyana-prison-service/.

Jaffe, R. (2012) 'The popular culture of illegality: Crime and the politics of aesthetics in urban Jamaica'. *Anthropological Quarterly*. 85(1): 79–102.

Jaffe, R. (2013) 'The hybrid state: Crime and citizenship in urban Jamaica'. *American Ethnologist*. 40(4): 734–748.

Johnson, D., Maguire, E. and Kuhns, J. (2014) 'Public perceptions of the legitimacy of the law and legal authorities: Evidence from the Caribbean'. *Law and Society Review*. 48(4): 947–978.

Johnson, H. (1991) 'Patterns of policing in the post-emancipation British Caribbean, 1835–95'. In Killingray, D. and Anderson, D. (eds.) *Policing the Empire: Government, Authority and Colonial Control, 1830–1940*. Manchester: Manchester University Press: 71–91.

James, C. (1938) *The Black Jacobins*. London: Secker and Warburg.

Kerrigan, D. (2018) 'Language-in-use living under militarisation and insecurity: How securitisation discourse wounds Trinidad'. *The Journal of Latin American and Caribbean Anthropology*. 23(3): 416–436.

Kerrigan, D. (2021) 'Exploring alienation, bias and coloniality in twenty-first-centuary magistrates' courts of Trinidad and Tobago.' In Rodríguez, E. and Reddock, R. (eds.) *Decolonial Perspectives on Entangled Inequalities: Europe and the Caribbean*. London: Anthem Press: 131–153.

Kerrigan, D. and Sookoo, N. (2013) 'White collar crime in Trinidad'. In Seepersad, R. and Bissessar, A. (eds.) *Gangs in the Caribbean*. London: Cambridge Scholars: 149–174.

Kerrigan, D., Jamadar, P., Elahie, E. and Sinanan, T. (2019) 'Securing equality for all – The evidence and recommendations'. In Matthews, J. and Amoah, J. (eds.) *Caribbean*

Judicial Dialogue: Equality for All in the Administration of Justice. Mona, Jamaica: Faculty of Law, University of the West Indies: 61–98.

King, K. (2009) 'Policing your brother as the other: An analysis of policing in Trinidad and Tobago "measuring paramilitarism"'. Paper presented at the Tenth Annual Conference Navigating Risks and Building Resilience in Small States, Sir Arthur Lewis Institute of Social & Economic Studies (SALISES), Cave Hill Campus, Barbados, March 25–27, 2009.

Kissoon, C. (2020) 'Prisoners attempt breakout during COVID-19 riot'. *Trinidad Express*. Available from: https://trinidadexpress.com/newsextra/prisoners-attempt-breakout-during-covid-19-riot/article_45beeb2c-688f-11ea-ad97-23afb13212b1.html.

Klein, A. (2016) *Ganja in the English-speaking Caribbean: From Security Threat to Development Opportunity*. Swansea: Global Drug Policy Observatory.

Lazarus-Black, M. (2001) 'Law and the pragmatics of inclusion: Governing domestic violence in Trinidad and Tobago'. *American Ethnologist*. 28(2): 388–416.

Lessing, B. (2017) *Making Peace in Drug Wars: Crackdowns and Cartels in Latin America*. Cambridge: CUP.

Lewis, G. (1968) *The Growth of the Modern West Indies*. New York: Monthly Review Press.

Lewis, R. (2012) 'Party politics in Jamaica and the extradition of Christopher "Dudus" Coke'. *The Global South*. 6(1): 38–54.

Mars, J. (2002) *Deadly Force, Colonialism, and the Rule of Law: Police Violence in Guyana*. Westport, CT: Davis & Elikins College, Praeger.

Marshall, D. (2002) 'At whose service? Caribbean state posture, merchant capital and the export services option'. *Third World Quarterly*. 23(4): 725–751.

Mastrofski, S. and Lum, C. (2008) 'Meeting the challenges of police governance in Trinidad and Tobago'. *Policing*. 2(4): 481–496.

Meikle, T. and Jaffe, R. (2015) ''Police as the new don'? An assessment of post-Dudus policing strategies in Jamaica'. *Caribbean Journal of Criminology*. 1(2): 75–100.

Miller, J. and Hendricks, N. (2007) 'Applying the problem-solving model to a developing world context: The case of murder in Trinidad and Tobago'. *Crime Prevention and Community Safety*. 9(4): 275–290.

Nadelmann, E. (1990) 'Global prohibition regimes: The evolution of norms in international society'. *International Organization*. 44(4): 479–526.

National Commission on Ganja. (2001) *A Report to Rt. Hon. PJ Patterson, QC, MP, Prime Minister of Jamaica*. Jamaica: Kingston. August 7. Available from: https://www.cannabis-med.org/science/Jamaica.htm.

Oren, I. and Solomon, T. (2015) 'WMD, WMD, WMD: Securitisation through ritualized incantation of ambiguous phrases'. *Review of International Studies*. 41(2): 313–336.

Payne, A. (1976) 'From Michael with love: The nature of socialism in Jamaica'. *Journal of Commonwealth and Comparative Politics*. 14(1): 82–100.

Pawelz, J. (2018) 'Hobsbawm in Trinidad: Understanding contemporary modalities of urban violence'. *Conflict, Security and Development*. 18(5): 409–432.

Reyes, J.-R. and Gahman, L. (2020) 'Violence in the time of COVID: Dispatches from the Caribbean'. *Discover Society*. Available from: https://discoversociety.org/2020/08/03/violence-in-the-time-of-covid-dispatches-from-the-caribbean/ [Accessed 16 August 2020].

Robinson, T. and Bulkan, A. (2017) 'Enduring sexed and gendered criminal laws in the anglophone Caribbean'. *Caribbean Review of Gender Studies*. 11: 219–240.

Sarsfield, R. and Bergman, M. (2016) *Study of Inmates in the Bahamas*. Buenos Aires: Center for Latin American Studies on Crime and Violence, UNTREF, Inter-American Development Bank.

Sarsfield, R. and Bergman, M. (2017) *Study of Inmates in Guyana*. Buenos Aires: Center for Latin American Studies on Crime and Violence, UNTREF, Inter-American Development Bank.

Schleifer, R., Sagredo, J. and Avafia, T. (2015) *Addressing the Development Dimensions of Drug Policy*. New York: United Nations Development Programme.

Seddon, T. (2016) 'Inventing drugs: A genealogy of a regulatory concept'. *Journal of Law and in Society*. 43(3): 393–415.

Seepersad, R. and Williams, D. (2012) *A Report on Citizen Security: Human Development and the Shift to better Citizen Security*. Port of Spain, Trinidad: United Nations Development Programme.

Stambøl, E. (2015) 'Governing cocaine supply and organized crime from Latin America and the Caribbean: The changing security logics in European Union external policy'. *European Journal on Criminal Policy and Research*. 22(1): 1–18.

Tate, W. (2015) *Drugs, Thugs and Diplomats: US Policymaking in Colombia*. Stanford, CA: Stanford University Press.

Thomas, D. (2016) *Exceptional Violence: Embodied Citizenship in Transnational Jamaica*. Durham, NC: Duke University Press.

Thomas, D. (2019) *Political Life in the Wake of the Plantation: Sovereignty, Witnessing, Repair*. Durham, NC: Duke University Press.

Thompson, M. (2021) 'Cultivating "new" gendered food producers: Intersections of power and identity in the postcolonial nation of Trinidad'. *Review of International Political Economy*. 28(1): 177–203.

Thorndike, T. (1993) 'Revolution, democracy, and regional integration in the Eastern Caribbean'. In Payne, A. and Sutton, P. (eds.) *Modern Caribbean Politics*. Baltimore, MD: The Johns Hopkins University Press: 147–175.

Trotman, D. (1986) *Crime in Trinidad: Conflict and Control in a Plantation Society, 1838–1900*. Knoxville, TN: University of Tennessee Press.

UNDP (2012) *Caribbean Human Development Report 2012: UNDP Citizen Security Survey 2010: Summary of Findings*. New York: United Nations Development Programme.

UNDP (2016) *Caribbean Human Development Report*. Bridgetown, Barbados: United Nations Development Programme' (UNDP).

UNODC (2019) *World Drug Report 2019*. Vienna: UN Office on Drugs and Crime.

UNST (2016) *Antigua and Barbuda UPR: Joint Submission from the United Nations Subregional Team for Barbados and the OECS*. Available from: https://www.upr-info.org/sites/default/files/document/antigua_and_barbuda/session_25_-_may_2016/unst_barbadosoecs_upr25_atg_e_main.pdf.

Watson, D. and Morgan, P. (2020) '"Criminals, Taliban, terrorists, murderers": Community perceptions of police in a crime hotspot in Trinidad'. *Caribbean Quarterly*. 66(2): 281–300.

Watson, H. (2003) 'The "Shiprider" solution and post-cold war imperialism: Beyond ontologies of state sovereignty in the Caribbean'. In Marshall, D. and Barrow-Gilesm, C. (eds.) *Living at the Borderlines: Issues in Caribbean Sovereignty and Development*. Kingston: Ian Randle: 226–274.

Watson, H. (ed.) (2015) *Globalization, Sovereignty and Citizenship in the Caribbean*. New York: Routledge.

7

POLICING OF DRUGS IN SCOTLAND

Moving beyond the stalemate to redesigning the chess board

Maria Fotopoulou and Elizabeth Aston

Introduction

At the time of writing, Scotland is in the midst of a drug crisis, holding the position of various tragic 'first' places. The number of drug-related deaths in Scotland increased by 6% between 2018 and 2019 and then by a further 5% in 2020, when it reached the largest number since records began in 1996 and more than double the number recorded a decade ago. In 2019, Scotland's drug death rate was higher than those reported for all the EU countries, and was approximately three and a half times that of the United Kingdom as a whole (National Records of Scotland 2020). In 2015, in Greater Glasgow and Clyde, an HIV outbreak identified among people who inject drugs was the largest such incident in the United Kingdom for 30 years (McAuley et al. 2019). In terms of policing the drug problem, the proportion of searches conducted on the basis of drugs is very high, at 81% in 2020 (Police Scotland 2021a), and has been at a similar rate (77–82%) for the last few years. The vast majority of recorded drug crimes (86%) are for possession (Scottish Government 2020a). Scotland continues to have one of the highest rates of imprisonment in Europe (SCCJR 2019), partly attributed to a greater number of those convicted for drug-related offences (Tombs and Piacentini 2012). The use of very short sentences, serially served and largely driven by convictions where drug and alcohol are implicated, is so common in Scotland that they have been given their own name: 'doing life by instalments' (Armstrong and Weaver 2013, p. 302).

The policing of drugs in Scotland is currently taking place within a context where policies and practices to address the drug problem and to minimise negative health, social, and legal impacts associated with drug use seem to thus far be ineffective, or even unintentionally harmful. However, it is exactly because of this context that a focus on harm reduction policing[1] is even more urgent.

DOI: 10.4324/9781003154136-8

The policy context in Scotland should – in theory – be conducive to fostering a progressive approach. Firstly, the drugs portfolio of the Scottish government moved from justice to the population health directorate more than a decade ago and the 2018 drugs strategy (Scottish Government 2018) recognises that problem drug use is a public health issue and plans to focus on a human rights-based approach. Secondly, the purpose of policing (enshrined in legislation since 2012) includes improving well-being and safety, and Police Scotland's new drug strategy (launched in 2020) aims to reduce harm and develop a public health approach. However, there is a gap between policy and practice and we also need to be cognisant of the salience of drug legislation, which sits at a UK level.

In this chapter, we aim to elucidate premises and developments that make up the current context within which drugs are policed in Scotland, starting with the relevant macro and micro policy environment. Our discussion is guided by the concept of the 'risk environment', a framework that promotes an 'understanding of how environmental conditions, and different risk environments, shape the introduction (or not) of harm reduction policies and responses as well as their implementation and impact' (Rhodes 2002, p. 87). We move on to describe current policing practices towards Scotland's drug problem and discuss their tangible effects for people who use drugs. We finish by laying out our suggestions for the future. By following this trajectory, we aim to highlight what we see as the characteristics of the stalemate in the policing of the drug problem and sketch out an alternative future where harm reduction is firmly recognised as a basic human right for people who use drugs, their communities, and ultimately for Scotland as a whole.

Regulating the drug problem: macro-level policy

For the vast majority of jurisdictions and within the context of prohibitionist approaches, the world's drug problem has been effectively constructed as a criminal justice rather than a health issue. However, the construction of social problems delineates the repertoire of responses societies choose to adopt towards them. Essentially, as Bacchi suggests, policy responses to social problems is not the 'government's best effort to *solve* "problems"; rather, policies *produce* "problems" with particular meanings that affect what gets done or not done, and how people live their lives' (Bacchi 2012, p. 22). As such, the way the drug problem has been historically constructed – and continues to be constructed – is not inconsequential; its construction enables or even dictates the approach taken to 'tackle' it, with its intended or unintended consequences.

Despite over 20 years of devolution, the drug problem in Scotland is still largely governed by the 1971 Misuse of Drugs Act (MDA); the overarching piece of legislation that regulates the production, supply, and possession of controlled drugs in the United Kingdom, and underpins successive UK governments' criminal justice approach to drugs. However, drug policy and legislation not only impact on people's lives where contact with the criminal justice system

(CJS) is concerned. Policy and legislation shape the practice responses we put in place and restrict our imagination in terms of alternative ways of acting; they define the context within which harm reduction interventions are introduced and delivered. In this way, policy and legislation constitute one of the factors shaping the environment within which people consume substances, intentionally or unintentionally adding or taking away from the risk associated with drug use (Rhodes 2002). Simultaneously, they dictate the ways such environments are policed. In this respect, the 1971 MDA creates enabling conditions for the introduction and delivery of public health interventions or, in some cases, impedes their establishment.

The way the MDA has contributed to the creation of a risk environment for people who use drugs in the United Kingdom, including Scotland, is exemplified in the fate of safe consumption rooms which, at the time of writing, are non-existent in the four nations. This is despite the continually increasing numbers of drug-related deaths (National Records of Scotland 2020), the aftermath of a HIV outbreak in Glasgow (McAuley et al. 2019), a wealth of evidence on the effectiveness of safe consumption rooms as a drug death prevention intervention (EMCDDA 2018), and recommendations by the Advisory Council on the Misuse of Drugs (ACMD 2016) for their establishment. This was also despite calls from the Glasgow City Health and Social Care Partnership, who wrote to the Lord Advocate of Scotland in 2016 requesting him 'to issue a letter of comfort'. This document would contain a guarantee that the facility's operation would not be legally challenged or the subject of prosecution, despite the technically illegal activity that would be conducted inside (Scottish Affairs Committee 2019). In November 2017, the Lord Advocate declined this call. When giving evidence to the Scottish Affairs Committee two years later, he justified this decision:

> the basic point is a recognition that, for such a facility to operate effectively, you need an appropriate legislative framework that establishes an appropriate system for licensing and oversight, addresses the scope of exemptions from the criminal law, and deals with issues of civil liability. There must also be a recognition that legislation resolves the policy issues in a democratically accountable way. I simply cannot create that kind of regime through a letter of comfort.[2]
>
> *(Wolfe 2019)*

Efforts to introduce safe consumption rooms in Scotland in 2017–2018 met the same fate. The freedom of information request (FOI/19/01755) communication between Aileen Campbell (MSP), the then Scottish government minister for public health and sport and the UK government minister for crime, safeguarding, and vulnerability, clearly shows the stalemate and also makes clear that drug control remains the responsibility of the UK government and that there are no plans to devolve this 'important responsibility'. As Victoria Atkins (MP) states:

> There is no legal framework for the provision of Drug Consumption Rooms in the UK and we have no plans to introduce them. A range of offences is likely to be committed in the operation of drug consumption rooms. It is for local police forces to enforce the law in such circumstances and, as with other offences of this type, we would expect them to do so.
>
> *(FOI/19/01755)*

Unlike UK-wide drug laws, devolved administrations, including Scotland, publish their own drug strategies. Reviewing the progress of the Scottish government since the 'Road to Recovery' strategy of 2008, Audit Scotland (2019) paints a bleak picture, but does identify the implementation of certain drug harm reduction strategies (such as the supply of naloxone, the provision of sterile injecting equipment, and opioid substitution therapy) as 'paving the way to longer-term improvement' (Audit Scotland 2019, p. 6). However, they note that despite additional investment in drug and alcohol services, the 'cost effectiveness and value for money of the investment made over the last ten years had not been set out' (Audit Scotland 2019, p. 6). The Scottish government (2018) drug strategy 'Rights, Respect and Recovery' recognises problem drug use as a public health issue and aims to focus on a holistic, human rights-based approach to reducing avoidable deaths related to problem drug use. It highlights, for example, prevention and early intervention, delivering in partnership, and a public health approach to justice. The intended outcome related to the latter involves diverting vulnerable people from the justice system wherever possible and fully supporting those within justice settings. In order to achieve this, commitments made by the Scottish government include ensuring 'that people who come into contact with justice agencies are provided with the right support from appropriate services' and setting up a group to advise on the contribution and limitations of the MDA to health outcomes in Scotland. While the intended outcome is to *divert vulnerable people from the justice system*, in contrast the strategy also commits to 'support the work of Police Scotland, to ensure that those groups involved in *drug dealing or distribution* are being effectively targeted for *prosecution*' (emphasis added). Here, the focus is on the police role in aiming to control the supply of drugs, as set out in the Serious and Organised Crime strategy (2015).

It is in this context that the Drug Deaths Taskforce (DDTF) was established in 2019, to take an evidence-based approach to identifying key areas of action required by partners to address the challenge of reducing drug-related deaths in Scotland. Although it is acknowledged that the response must be multifaceted, some of the six identified areas of action of particular relevance to our discussion include the targeted distribution of naloxone, optimising public health surveillance, and supporting those in the justice system. For example, Police Scotland have recently initiated a DDTF-funded 'test of change' where police in three 'test-bed' areas are being trained and have the opportunity to carry naloxone. Secondly, the DDTF recently funded a project to pull together the evidence base to prepare for the implementation of drug-checking services in Scotland.

Thirdly, various DDTF-funded projects support people in contact with the justice system; for example, Wayfinders in East Dunbartonshire places peer navigators within the justice system to support people who have problems with drug use. Furthermore, the DDTF Criminal Justice and Law group reported on visits they undertook to explore how operational practice could be altered to support better health outcomes for people who use drugs.

Leeway afforded by meso- and micro-level policy and policing practices

International and national drug laws and strategies certainly shape the contexts within which drugs are consumed and people who use drugs are policed. However, policies and practices at a lower level, such as at the organisational level of police forces – in various parts of the world – have hugely impacted this intersection of public health and policing. For example, directly linking their findings to this conceptualisation of a risk environment, Miller and colleagues (2008) spoke about how street-level policing practices in Mexico influence injecting drug users' willingness to carry injecting equipment, despite syringe possession not being a crime. Similarly, in an Australian context, Maher and Dixon (1999) discussed how what can be considered a success of 'policing practices', such as the successful crackdown of drug markets, can essentially have negative consequences for public health.

However, changes to policing practices with the stated aim of promoting public health approaches to the drug problem have also been noted. Indeed, historically, the police have played a pivotal role in the introduction of, for example, safe consumption rooms; in the Netherlands, the majority of the facilities seem to have originated from initiatives by residents and police, with the support of local authorities, with the shared aim being the reduction of public nuisance (Hedrich 2004). When needle syringe programmes (NSPs) were first introduced in England and Wales, the Metropolitan Police Service (MPS), London, issued a Police Order in June 1988 stating that it was service policy that people who inject drugs should not be arrested for carrying injecting equipment in a public place – as would be the case under the provisions of Section 139 of the Criminal Justice Act 1988 (Monaghan and Bewley-Taylor 2013). In an attempt to strike a balance between law enforcement and public health, the commissioner of New South Wales Police discouraged police officers from making unwarranted patrols in the vicinity of needle and syringe exchange programmes, acknowledging that a heavy police presence acts as a barrier to accessing services (Monaghan and Bewley-Taylor 2013). More recently, in Canada, the Vancouver Police Department developed and implemented an organisation-wide policy which endorsed harm reduction strategies for people who inject drugs, to promote safe, open, and ready access to harm reduction interventions in the area (Lansberg et al. 2016). In this same jurisdiction, the local police department supported the establishment of a pilot safe consumption room and subsequently introduced a strategy of actively promoting its use by people who injected in public through police referrals to the service (DeBeck et al. 2008).

It becomes evident then, that meso- and micro-level policy, and the way this shapes policing practice, can have direct implications for the effectiveness of public health interventions. Depending on the way organisational policies shape local environments, members of the police working at street level can actively promote harm reduction principles or indeed diminish people's access to health services and safer use of drugs. As such, policing practices can lead to change or contribute to structural violence (Sarang et al. 2010).

Can there be such leeway in Scotland?

Policing in Scotland has undergone significant change over the last decade, with the formation of Police Scotland in 2013 bringing together the eight legacy police forces and intensifying the politicisation of policing. The legislative basis for the new single police service also enshrined a new purpose of policing: 'to improve the safety and wellbeing of persons, localities and communities' (Police and Fire Reform (Scotland) Act 2012, Section 32). The Act states that this must be achieved by working in a manner which is 'accessible to and engaged with communities'; 'promotes measures which prevent crime, harm and disorder'; and involves 'working in collaboration with others'. Although there may be potential perceived tensions within aspects of the purpose of policing, e.g. between securing both the safety of communities and the well-being of people (including people who use drugs), this legislation clearly provides a mandate for police to work in partnership to improve well-being and prevent harm, which goes far beyond a narrow crime fighting purpose with enforcement-based solutions focused on bringing offenders to justice. The Act provides a strong basis for police in Scotland to focus efforts on harm reduction, particularly when it comes to dealing with people who use drugs, by engaging communities and working collaboratively to adopt a public health approach to policing.

In 2020, Police Scotland launched their first drugs strategy (Ritchie 2020), which aims to adopt a whole systems approach with partners to reduce the harm caused by the supply and consumption of drugs through an integrated prevention and enforcement approach. This involves working to reduce drugs deaths and prevent harm by developing new approaches with partners to support the activity of the DDTF under the Scottish government's drugs strategy. The strategy also aims to adopt a public health approach to the policing of drugs and prioritises prevention, alongside enforcement. The activity of the drug strategy board is supported by a substance harm prevention sub-group, with the enforcement activity driven in parallel by serious and organised crime structures. While this is not unproblematic and there are obvious tensions between enforcement and prevention, given, for example, the potential unintended consequences where enforcement may exacerbate harm for people who use drugs, it is worth noting that at least the strategy purports to focus on targeting enforcement towards suppliers posing the greatest threat. Indeed, Stevens (2013) highlights the potential effectiveness of targeting drug dealers who are causing the highest levels of harm with 'pulling-levers' approaches, e.g. diversion into treatment, as an example of applying harm reduction principles to policing.

During the deliberations of the Scottish Affairs Committee on problem drug use in Scotland, suggestions were made to sketch out a way for safe consumption rooms to be introduced and safely operate in the country. Such suggestions included the establishment of an agreement between safe consumption rooms – where these were to be introduced – and the local police not to pursue drug-related offences within the facility (Scottish Affairs Committee 2019), echoing ways of working highlighted in other countries and discussed above. This was indeed viewed positively by some, with Assistant Chief Constable Steve Johnson of Police Scotland noting that 'if the proposed facility was "legitimate", Police Scotland would work with the NHS and other stakeholders to support it' (Scottish Affairs Committee 2019, p. 272).

However, it was also noted that such arrangements, operating in parallel but also in contravention of the current legislative context, may not be tenable; a concern that was also put forth by police force representatives. Such concerns were aptly explained by Assistant Chief Constable Johnson:

> From an officer perspective, if you are an officer and you are walking the streets of Glasgow where that facility is and you stop someone who is on their way [there] in possession of those drugs, there is a hefty dose of the 'woulda, coulda, shoulda' squad. If the person does not then go to the safe facility […] but takes themselves down by the side of the Clyde and injects and falls in the river and dies, the 'woulda, coulda, shoulda' would be 'what are the police doing? You had a power; you did not exercise it'. That person should have been in a custody facility, put in front of the sheriff, from the sheriff to the court […] That is a harsh reality faced.
>
> *(Scottish Affairs Committee 2019, p. 274)*

It needs to be recognised that the ambiguity characterising the spaces created by micro-level policies threatens the viability of the approaches taken within them. Perhaps an illustrative example of this comes from the case of Peter Krykant, a drug activist operating a mobile safe consumption room in Glasgow, in the face of legislation that prohibits its existence. Disillusioned by the inaction of both the UK and Scottish governments amidst the context of rising drug-related death and the recent HIV outbreak in Glasgow, Krykant decided to deliver the service himself. Despite the facility providing a much-needed service and receiving positive international media attention, his efforts have not always been received favourably. After months of operating the van, on 23 October 2020 he was charged for obstructing police officers carrying out their duties in respect of the Misuse of Drugs Act 1971 on Parnie Street, Glasgow. Essentially, he was charged with obstructing police who sought to search his van. He was not arrested, but police officers submitted a report to the prosecutor fiscal. Krykant did not eventually face court action and James Wolffe, Scotland's Lord Advocate, applied discretion and the charges were dropped (The Guardian, 2020). However, the case is indicative of how the lack of a clearly defined legislative context can hinder public health approaches that operate in grey zones of tolerance which are as easily taken away as they are afforded by policing practices.

The public health approach to policing is currently developing in Scotland and is being guided by Police Scotland's drug strategy board. However, innovations of relevance to drugs which are being implemented thus far are, perhaps understandably, operating within the legislative parameters, rather than at their boundaries. Although calls for police in Scotland to carry naloxone go back much further (McAuley and Aston 2018), through recent work with the DDTF, Police Scotland commenced a pilot project in 2021, where police in three 'test-bed' areas are being trained and can then volunteer to carry naloxone (Police Scotland 2021b). Currently, the pilot is being independently evaluated by a team at Edinburgh Napier and Glasgow Caledonian universities. In the run up to this 'test of change', Police Scotland worked with various partners, through a Naloxone Delivery Steering Group, to iron out various issues and prepare for training and implementation. Indications suggest that the response from officers has generally been positive, despite fervent opposition from the Scottish Police Federation whose concerns appear to centre on the expansion of the police role into health. Police Scotland officers had already encountered people experiencing overdose and administered naloxone while awaiting ambulance response on 12 occasions by May (Rae 2021) and 37 occasions by August (Livadeas 2021).

We will now turn our attention to the ways people who use drugs are currently policed in Scotland and highlight the consequences of such policing practices for people who use drugs, their families, and communities.

Policing practices, police disposals, and their aftermath in Scotland

Stop and search practices

Stop and search is a police power where public safety needs must be balanced with individual human rights. Although people who use drugs are also subject to more 'informal' policing encounters (related to 'communicative surveillance' and 'intelligence gathering' (Lister et al. 2008)), stop and search is one of the main formal ways, along with formal warnings and arrests, in which people who use drugs are policed and come into contact with the CJS. In the United Kingdom and beyond, the most common ground for stopping and searching people is on suspicion of the possession of drugs (Shiner et al. 2018). The most recent statistics in Scotland (Police Scotland 2021a) show a figure of 81% in 2020. Searches on drugs grounds raise particular questions regarding human rights (e.g. rights to privacy, health, and non-discrimination (INPUD 2015)). At the same time, the effectiveness of this police power in protecting the public has long been called into question and its purported crime reduction impact has not been backed up by evidence (Tirattelli et al. 2018). In contrast, we do know that repeated use of enforcement-based policing, including stop and search, has a negative impact on police-community relations (Hail et al. 2018). Tirattelli et al. (2018) conclude that stop and search is used as a tool of social control, and concerns have also repeatedly been raised about ethnic disproportionality and associated negative outcomes (Shiner et al. 2018).

Furthermore, when it comes to drugs we also need to consider the impact of stop and search on effectiveness in a broader sense, on access to harm reduction services and the right to a high standard of health. As discussed above, perceived levels of police enforcement impact on the willingness of people who use drugs to access harm reduction services and carry materials such as clean syringes and take-home naloxone, which users may fear will be perceived as drug paraphernalia and thereby grounds for being taken to a police station for a more intrusive search (McAuley and Aston 2018). This is in keeping with Sarang et al.'s (2010) findings that policing strategies are critical to creating environments which may increase risk and undermine harm reduction for people who inject drugs.

For quite some time, the legislative basis for stopping, searching, and detaining someone without arrest in Scotland lay in the Criminal Justice Scotland Act 1980, the Criminal Justice Procedure Act 1995, and the MDA 1971. Prior to 2014, stop and search in Scotland had not been subject to the same scrutiny or academic attention as England and Wales (Aston et al. 2019). Murray (2014) shed light on the rate of stop and search in 2010 being far higher than that of England and Wales, and the overwhelming reliance (70%) on 'consensual' or non-statutory search. A period of intense media and political attention, research (e.g. O'Neill et al. 2015), and scrutiny (HMICS 2015), including the establishment of an Independent Advisory Group on Stop and Search (Scott 2015), led to fundamental legislative and policy changes to this police practice. These were introduced in the Criminal Justice Scotland Act 2016, including the abolishment of the controversial practice of 'non-statutory' search (which were mostly for alcohol and drugs). Available data on stop and search may reflect these changes: there were 640,699 recorded instances of stop and search, a figure which decreased dramatically to a low of 29,768 in 2017–2018. The volume has been sitting at around 30,000–40,000 since, and in 2019–2020 the recorded figure was 41,167 (HMICS 2020).

With the requirement of a statutory basis for searches, and the associated dramatic reduction in the volume of stop and search, the rate of 'positive searches'[3] where an item was found increased with a more targeted approach (Scott 2019a). At the point when consensual searches were used, the rate of finding an item during searches conducted on drugs grounds was only 12% (in 2013–2014, HMICS 2015). The 'positive rate' for drugs searches has been higher at around 36–39% in recent years (36% in 2020, Police Scotland 2021a), which suggests that as the volume of searches has reduced, and is based on legislative grounds, the chances of finding drugs has increased. Nonetheless, it is worth highlighting that this means that the vast majority of times that the power of search is used on people, drugs are not found. Of the 11,162 searches where drugs were found between April and December 2020, the vast majority (61%) were Class B drugs, with 20% being Class A and 19% Class C (Police Scotland 2021a).

Despite improvements to the stop and search records and database and the increased transparency with making data publicly available, unfortunately it is not possible for the police to match nominal data in order to make data on multiple searches of individuals public. We know that of the 33,452 searches recorded in Scotland between April and December 2020, 4,413 individuals were searched two or more times (Police Scotland 2021a), but we do not have more information about how many times people have been repeatedly searched, which may have shed some light on the ways people who use drugs are policed. At the same time, and despite the recent changes in stop and search practices, the proportion of searches on drugs grounds is now higher. The figures are not comparable as the legislative context has changed dramatically and the recording practices and accuracy of the data pre-2017 were highly questionable. However, based on 2013–2014 figures, the recorded reason for searches was drugs in 44% of searches and another 31% (mainly consensual) were for alcohol (HMICS 2015). Since the legislative changes, the proportion of searches on drugs grounds has been around 77–82%: 81% of searches were on drugs grounds in 2020 (Police Scotland 2021a), 77.5% in 2019–2020 (Police Scotland 2020a), 78% in 2018–2019 (Police Scotland 2019), and 82.6% in 2017–2018 (Police Scotland 2018). Shiner et al. (2018) found that the proportion of searches in England and Wales on drugs grounds had increased from a half in 2010–2011 to two-thirds in 2016–2017.

Considering the attention given to stop and search in Scotland in recent years and the high proportion of searches on the basis of drugs grounds, surprisingly little attention has been paid in the various scrutiny documents to the policing of drugs or people who use drugs. The 12-month review of the code of practice (McVie 2019) did acknowledge that strip searches were overwhelmingly conducted for drugs (69%); 1 in 20 searches involved a strip search, with 66% of them conducted inside a police station rather than in public view. Women were more likely to be subject to a strip search than men, but with lower detection rates for women (42% compared to 50% for men). The report concluded that the introduction of a code of practice for stop and search was successful in achieving a higher standard of evidence based on reasonable suspicion, more 'positive' rates (finding an illicit item), and improved proportionality in terms of searches by sex, age group, and ethnic identity. However, concerns were also raised regarding the greater use of strip searches for women and lower positive outcomes for searches involving young people.

Statistics from the Scottish Police Authority (SPA) Forensic Services on the volume of drug analysis cases (12,600 in 2019), a 33% three-year demand increase in referrals from Police Scotland, and the fact that 82% of the cases in 2019 were for possession (SPA 2020) does not suggest that there has been a reduction in the policing of drugs commensurate with the reduction in the volume of stop and search. Preliminary analysis of drug-related stop and search during COVID-19 suggests there was a localised increase in certain parts of Glasgow during spring 2020. The analysis of data by the Independent Advisory Group on temporary police powers related to COVID-19 suggests that most people receiving a fixed penalty notice for breaching COVID-19 restrictions had a prior criminal history (McVie 2021). However, there has been virtually no discussion regarding the policing of people who use drugs in this context where two public health emergencies, a pandemic and a drug-related death epidemic, collide. Recently, concerns have also been raised in the media (McGivern 2021) regarding reports of searches of people who use drugs in Glasgow near harm reduction facilities. Yet, the strategic aim is to adopt a public health approach to the policing of drugs at both a local level in Glasgow (Police Scotland 2020b) and a national level in Police Scotland's drug strategy (Ritchie 2020).

Police recorded warnings

Police in Scotland can deal with people accused of a crime in a variety of other direct ways. Of particular interest to the ways that drugs are policed in Scotland is the measure of recorded police warnings (RPWs), which was introduced in Scotland in 2016 to deal with a wider range of low-level offences, including the possession of drugs. This is focused on the possession of cannabis, although there have been calls to extend it to other substances too (Scottish Affairs Committee 2019). RPWs can take the form of a warning issued on the spot or a notice issued retrospectively. RPWs replaced the former practice of formal adult warnings; however, they can also be issued to people over the age of 16. RPWs do not constitute a finding of guilt but can be taken into account if the person comes to further notice of the police within a period of two years from the initial warning. The scheme aims to 'have a positive impact on individuals by not criminalising them, minimising police bureaucracy and maximising operational officers' time' (Police Scotland 2020c, p. 4). We need to clarify here that RPWs do not constitute a measure of full decriminalisation, as the measure can be – and is – delivered in the current legislative context.

In the year following its introduction, this alternative to prosecution measure became the most used police disposal with 19,678 issued in 2016–2017 (Scottish Government 2020b). Although there was a small decrease in their use the following year (17,332 in 2017–2018), in 2018–2019 RPWs were the most used police disposal, making up 61% of police disposals – or 22,070 RPWs (Scottish Government 2020b). Unfortunately, official publications have not always contained a breakdown of the different offences for which RPWs have been issued in Scotland but we do know that 77% of RPWs were issued in 2017–2018 for offences that fall into the 'Other' category (Scottish Government 2019a). The latest figures available, however, are quite informative in regard to the dominance of drug-related offences among RPWs; in 2018–2019 drug offences were the most common reason for their disposal (29%) (Scottish Government 2020b).

Diversion from prosecution in Scotland

The policing practices discussed above can be viewed in the context of diversion from prosecution schemes. Across the United Kingdom, diversion schemes are mainly police-led initiatives that involve diverting people caught committing minor offences from the CJS. Diversion schemes for drug-related offences are usually applied in cases of possession for personal use or – in fewer cases – to supply or cultivation offences that are deemed to be minor. For example, Durham Constabulary's Checkpoint is a deferred prosecution scheme whereas Thames Valley Police's Drug Diversion Scheme provides direct access to drug services without admission of guilt and can be used for possession (but not supply) of any category of drug (see Spyt and Kew, this volume). Scotland has implemented diversion from prosecution schemes since the 1980s, with the stated aim of providing support targeting the underlying causes of offending, such as substance use (Scottish Government 2021). Diversion schemes were rolled out nationally in 2000 and have targeted primarily people who use drugs, as well as young people and women.

At the UK level, such police-led schemes usually involve police offering referral to treatment and support services as an alternative to arrest, prosecution, or formal caution. However, in Scotland diversion works rather differently, potentially reflecting the different relationship between the police and prosecutors in Scotland in comparison to the rest of the United Kingdom (Price et al. 2021). As Price and colleagues (2021, p. 119) note:

> Police officers in Scotland have a statutory duty to report all offenses to Scotland's Crown Office and Procurator Fiscal Service (COPFS) who determine who will be prosecuted and who will not, based on an assessment of all of the facts and circumstances of each individual case.

This is reflected in the most recent National Guidelines on Diversion from Prosecution in Scotland, where the Scottish diversion process is clearly defined as a process by which the 'Crown Office and Procurator Fiscal Service (COPFS) are able to refer a case to social work – and their partners' (Community Justice Scotland 2020, p. 3). Essentially, the approach involves instances where prosecution may be waived or a decision on prosecution deferred pending successful completion of the social work scheme (Scottish Government 2020c).

Within the most recent National Guidelines on Diversion from Prosecution in Scotland, diversion is described as a three-stage process, with the police only involved in the first, initial phase (Community Justice Scotland 2020). According to the guidelines, the role of the police is vital as they constitute the starting point for diversion processes to be potentially adopted; however, this role is limited to appraising and recording antecedent information about the incident and person involved, in the relevant section of the form to be submitted to COPFS. Vital as this may be as a starting point, it is exactly that – a point of initiation of a process rather than a distinct police-led initiative. In addition, diversion in

Scotland is also understood as a scheme which can be offered post-conviction in court, in which case it is essentially diversion from custodial sentences rather than diversion from police custody.

Acknowledging the specific features that Scottish diversion schemes take, we highlight recent and historical figures of all diversion cases in the country. We note here that diversion schemes in Scotland have historically been offered to small numbers of people, especially when compared to other fiscal disposals (Scottish Government 2021). Latest figures highlight an 8% increase in the number of diversion from prosecution cases commenced in 2019–2020 in comparison to 2018–2019 (Scottish Government 2021) (Table 7.1).

It needs to be noted here that the breakdown of types of offences for cases where diversion is offered is not available in criminal justice social work publications. However, as Price and colleagues note through a personal communication, in 2018–2019 internal statistics from the Crown Office showed that within that period '790 diversions where offered in cases where drug possession was reported alongside other offense types' (Price et al. 2021, p. 119). A further note needs to be made on the predominance of cases involving young people (aged 16–20) within diversion offers; according to the latest available figures for 2019–2020, 50% of cases where diversion was offered involved young people, clearly showing the previously stated focus of the scheme on this population group.

Police-led initiatives to divert people from the criminal justice system

The Positive Outcomes Project (POP) is a unique project developed by a joint DDTF proposal between Police Scotland and the Glasgow Health and Social Care Partnership (GHSCP), and currently involves a partnership with the charity Aid and Abet, who provide input from people with lived experience. The project predominantly supports men who are engaged in what is termed 'chaotic' substance use and have been involved in persistent offending. Within the context of the project, police officers, addiction workers, and a recovery coordinator with lived experience, coordinate with the aim of helping people stabilise their problematic use and reduce reoffending. Peer mentors with lived experience are based in police custody suites in Glasgow with the aim being to support people with addictions and offending behaviour by providing support and access to services, with a focus on Glasgow Housing First services. However, as this initiative

TABLE 7.1 Diversion from prosecution cases in Scotland.

Diversion from prosecution	*2013–2014*	*2014–2015*	*2015–2016*	*2016–2017*	*2017–2018*	*2018–2019*	*2019–2020*
Cases commenced	1,710	1,869	1,859	2,006	1,725	1,849	1,990
Individuals	1,657	1,812	1,787	1,960	1,686	1,789	1,927
Cases successfully completed	1,374	1,355	1,330	1,578	1,367	1,416	1,578

Source: Scottish Government (2021) Criminal Justice Social Work Statistics: 2019 to 2020.

occurs during the booking process in a police custody suite it should be noted that it occurs after arrest, rather than fully diverting people who use drugs from the CJS (as per the Thames Valley Police, see Spyt et al. 2019).

A recent Social Return on Investment Study evaluating POP highlighted the cost-effectiveness and social value of the approach; focusing on a one-year period, the study suggested a social return of £4.50 for every £1 invested, while the corresponding figure rose to £7.50 when focusing on a two-year period (Scott 2019b). Participating service users spoke of reductions in substance use, making better-informed decisions about using substances, and thinking about their actions before reoffending (Scott 2019b). Although based on a small sample, such qualitative findings are promising and clearly highlight the role of police officers in effectively supporting vulnerable people who face problems with substance use. A similar project has been introduced in Edinburgh (VOW Project); again a Police Scotland–led initiative in partnership with Aid and Abet, with the aim of reducing offending and harm to people in Edinburgh. VOW works to empower young people (aged 16 and over, resident in Edinburgh) involved with the CJS and deemed to be at significant risk of experiencing drug-related harm. A recent evaluation of VOW has also highlighting promising results in relation to desistance (O'Rourke and Buchan 2019).

Arrests and criminal proceedings

In Scotland, drug-related crime is recorded under the category 'other crimes'. Specifically, according to the classification of crimes and offences, the category 'other crimes' includes 'Production, manufacture or cultivation of drugs; possession and supply of controlled drugs; related money laundering offences and finally bringing drugs into prison' (Scottish Government 2020a).

Throughout the past decade, drug crimes have remained the biggest contributor to overall figures of recorded 'other' crime, despite a 12% decrease from 2009–2010 to 2018–2019 (Scottish Government 2019b). However, recent figures suggest a reversal of this downward trend with an 8% increase from 32,399 in 2017–2018 to 34,831 in 2018–2019, when drug crimes made up 56% of 'other crimes' (Scottish Government 2019b). It should also be noted that this upward trend was observed throughout Scotland with the majority of local authorities (25/32) reporting increasing figures (Scottish Government 2019b). A reason initially put forward for this increase relates to an amendment to the Misuse of Drugs Act 1971, which extended the list of Class C controlled substances with the addition of etizolam (a type of benzodiazepine). However, this noted increase had also been discussed as potentially caused by operational decisions given that a majority of the crimes related to drug possession – by far the biggest category of recorded drug crime – were identified during police patrols and warrant-based searches (Scottish Government 2019b). The very latest figures for drug crimes confirm its dominance among 'other crimes' recorded in Scotland as it made up 55% of this category in 2019–2020 (Scottish Government 2020a), with the vast majority of these (86%) referring to drug possession charges (Scottish Government 2020a). However, we also need to note here that for this last year of reporting, the introduction of new drug driving laws in Scotland – where police now have powers to test drivers suspected of drug use – may have impacted these figures.

On a global level, the predominance of possession charges among global data on drug offences has been noted previously. Latest data available at EU level also suggest that the vast majority of drug offences involve possession charges (79% of offences in 2017 – the latest year of analysis), and the majority of those (75%) involve cannabis (EMCDDA 2019). The latest available data at the UK level, as reported by the UK Reitox Focal Point to the EMCDDA, resonate with a rather imbalanced picture; in 2015/2016 approximately 107,000 court convictions and police cautions for drug offences were reported in England, Wales, Scotland, and Northern Ireland of which 63% (67,490) related to the possession of drugs (UK Focal Point on Drugs 2019).

This picture is also reflected in Scotland where the majority of seizures of controlled substances in recent years is estimated to involve seizures for drug possession crimes, where quantities are small enough to be considered for personal use rather than crimes of supply. As shown in the Table 7.2, the number of seizures from crimes relating to drug possession has consistently outnumbered those relating to crimes of possession with intent to supply (Scottish Government 2019b).

Latest available data from a review undertaken each year on a subsample of 400 cases involving drug possession charges, clearly highlight the predominance of cannabis. In 2018–2019, cannabis was the most commonly seized drug by a considerable margin (51%), which in absolute numbers translated into 15,200 crimes of cannabis possession (Scottish Government 2020a).

Such figures raise questions about the best use of police and forensics resources and time. Should police enforcement efforts be focused on types of crime (i.e. possession) where the quantity of drugs seized is small enough to be considered for personal use? Evidence from Portugal where de jure decriminalisation of drug possession has been implemented since 2001, highlights that a significant number of possession cases were diverted from the CJS while charges for trafficking

TABLE 7.2 Recorded drug possession crimes in Scotland.

Crime category	*2009–2010*	*2010–2011*	*2011–2012*	*2012–2013*	*2013–2014*	*2014–2015*	*2015–2016*	*2016–2017*	*2017–2018*	*2018–2019*
Possession with intent to supply	9,131	6,144	5,423	3,861	3,594	3,700	3,976	3,531	3,877	3,973
Possession of drugs	29,179	26,960	28,326	29,150	30,451	31,632	29,929	27,766	27,171	29,843

Source: Scottish Government (2019b).

increased by 11% when comparing the four years prior to decriminalisation with the four years subsequent to it (Hughes and Stevens 2007). As the authors note, this latter figure 'may reflect the increased focus on trafficking by the police, or an increase in the occurrence of trafficking in and through Portugal, or a combination of the two factors' (Hughes and Stevens 2007, p. 4). Although an in-depth analysis of the policy change in Portugal is beyond the scope of this chapter, such figures necessitate reflection in the context of the statistics quoted above for Scotland.

Cases proceeded to court, convictions, and people sentenced to custody

Policing practices are a gateway to contact with and entry into the CJS. Although not the main focus of this chapter, we conclude this section by providing data on the number of people whose cases do proceed to court.

Latest figures on criminal proceedings in Scotland highlight that 5,655 individuals were proceeded against in court for drug-related offences, with a charge proven in the vast majority (4,997) of cases (Scottish Government 2020b). According to a freedom of information request to the Scottish government (FOI reference: FOI/18/02863), the number of people sentenced to custody for drug-related crimes from 2007–2008 to 2016–2017 (where these were the main crime) is subject to fluctuations, although an increasing trend can be observed for the final year that the FOI focused on. In contrast to recorded crime data, the number of people who are sentenced to custody because of supply and possession with intent to supply offences, have outnumbered those who have received a custodial sentence for the possession of drugs.

However, the number of people who are imprisoned for mere possession charges is by no means negligible, especially if we consider the impact of such an experience on people's lives. A detailed discussion of the effects of imprisonment is beyond the scope of the present discussion. However, we cannot but mention here that self-inflicted deaths are over six times more likely in prison than in the general population (Prison Reform Trust 2019), while for people who use drugs, experience of incarceration has been shown to be a risk factor increasing vulnerability to Hep C (Larney et al. 2013) and HIV infection (EMCDDA 2012). People with lived experience of prison experience a myriad of problems upon release including, but not limited to, loss of accommodation, diminished education and employment opportunities, and stigmatisation. Far-reaching consequences on family life and relationships that can include loss of custody of children are also well documented in the literature (EMCDDA 2017). Parental imprisonment has also been discussed in the context of adverse childhood experiences (ACEs), with children of incarcerated parents exposed to nearly five times as many other ACEs as their counterparts without incarcerated parents (Turney 2018). Experience of imprisonment in no way translates automatically into stopping drug use. This is aptly demonstrated in the most recent Scottish prisoner survey where 39% said that they had used illegal drugs in prison at some point, a figure which has remained the same since 2015 (SPC 2020). Finally, for people who use drugs, release from prison has been consistently highlighted as an overdose risk factor (EMCDDA 2017).

An alternative future for policing of drugs in Scotland: demanding the impossible?

In writing this chapter, we were guided by the concept of the risk environment (Rhodes 2002) to analyse how drug policy, organisational-level policies, and policing practices shape the context within which people who use drugs live and operate. While the *language* of the policy context signals a progressive approach, there is a gap between policy and practice. We highlighted that despite devolution, Scotland is constrained in its response to its drug problem by UK-level legislation – the 1971 Drugs Act – which has been criticised over

> the lack of effectiveness… in drawing the right balance between the dangers associated with each type of drug, in deterring drug use and in providing a fair, balanced and proportionate response to drug use by different (particularly ethnic) groups in society.
>
> *(Reuter and Stevens 2007, p. 50)*

As we have shown, the proportion of searches conducted on the basis of drugs is very high in Scotland, yet Stevens (2013) calls for a reduction in expensive and potentially counterproductive approaches such as large-scale stop and search. The majority of drugs found were Class B and the vast majority of drug analysis cases referred to SPA Forensic Services in 2019 were for possession. This suggests that a different approach will need to be taken if, as per the police drugs strategy, enforcement is to be targeted towards suppliers posing the greatest threat. We discussed how Scottish government initiatives (e.g. the National Naloxone Programme) and Police Scotland organisational-level policies are being implemented with the aim of reducing harm resulting from involvement with drugs. In this respect and in relation to Scotland, we agree with Bacon (2022) that on a global scale, and despite the continuous focus on supply and demand reduction, drug law enforcement policies and practices are characterised by a greater focus on harm reduction. Although these are positive moves forward, clearly in order to bring significant changes to the policing of people who use drugs there is a need for fundamental shifts in the 'field', including legislation.

That said, real change in police practice and culture will also require effective leadership and a strong commitment to organisational justice (Aston et al. 2019). Furthermore, as Bacon (2016) argues, clear definitions, guidelines, and training are needed to focus policing practice on how to target harms. We highlighted the usefulness of these suggestions in examples from countries where decisive action and strong messages from leadership have allowed the police to begin to push the boundaries and practice 'outside the lines' of current restrictive policies, with the aim of protecting the health and well-being of people who consume drugs. Although we note the existence of police-led initiatives (e.g. POP and VOW), we would like to see diversion from the criminal justice system at the earliest possible point. We also note reticence in taking more resolute steps that would enable the introduction of life-saving interventions such as safe consumption rooms in Scotland. We thus call for clearer, stronger messages from police leaders and partners in Scotland to pave the way for harm reduction to be firmly recognised as a basic human right and open up possibilities for policing practice that upholds and protects this right. Some of this is now evident in the Drug Law Reform Report (DDTF 2021), which makes recommendations for change.

As things stand, we are in a stalemate, with some possibility for action which may well be negated by the wider context within which it occurs – a context created by the criminalisation of the possession of illicit drugs. We thus call for further consideration to be given to ameliorating the harms resulting from the policies that govern the drug problem in the United Kingdom. Furthermore, in this field, advocacy groups, activists, recovery communities, and others with lived or living experience of drug use may have a central role, as will public engagement and political will. What we ultimately propose is to go back to the drawing board to change the limits of what can be done. There is very little doubt that the punitive approach that has been implemented towards the drug problem – globally, as well as in the United Kingdom – has failed to address the problem; if anything it has created more harm. In acknowledgement of this, across the globe jurisdictions are decriminalising drug use (Eastwood et al. 2016). The evidence base on positive outcomes of alternatives to criminalisation approaches in relation to the harm caused by criminal convictions, to rates of recidivism and drug-related health harm is growing (Stevens et al. 2022). What is thus needed for Scotland is the political courage to acknowledge the stalemate produced by heavily prohibitionist policies and the will to redesign the chessboard that is the policy landscape. In doing so, Scotland would move towards ensuring effective support for people who use drugs, respect of their human rights, and the promotion of social justice for them, their families, and their communities. If the rules are not working, it is time to change them. As the ancient Roman statesman Cicero famously said: 'The Welfare of the people is the ultimate law' – it is high time Scotland listened.

Notes

1 We identify harm reduction policing as a set of policies and practices that engage 'communities in a manner that builds trust, addresses the needs of individuals using drugs, and reduces adverse effects of drugs and drug enforcement' (Krupanski 2018, p.4)
2 We should note here that in May 2021, the Scottish Lord Advocate announced his resignation, prompting some to hope for a reconsideration of the issue (Powell 2021).
3 A positive stop and search is when an item is recovered where possession implies criminality on the part of the person being searched or where an item has been recovered which is potentially harmful.

References

ACMD. (2016) *Reducing Opioid-Related Deaths in the UK*. London: Home Office.

Armstrong, S. and Weaver, B. (2013) 'Persistent punishment: User views of short prison sentences'. *Howard Journal of Criminal Justice*. 52(3): 285–305.

Aston, E., Murray, K. and O'Neill, M. (2019) 'Achieving cultural change through organizational justice: The case of stop and search in Scotland'. *Criminology and Criminal Justice*. 21(1): 40–56.

Audit Scotland. (2019) *Drug and Alcohol Services: An Update*. Available from: https://www.audit-scotland.gov.uk/uploads/docs/report/2019/briefing_190521_drugs_alcohol.pdf.

Bacchi, C. (2012) 'Strategic interventions and ontological politics: Research as political practice'. In Bletsas, A. and Beasley, C. (eds.) *Engaging with Carol Bacchi: Strategic Interventions and Exchanges*. Adelaide: University of Adelaide Press: 141–156.

Bacon, M. (2016) 'Maintaining order in the drug game: Applying harm reduction principles to drug detective work'. *Police Practice and Research*. 17(4): 306–316.

Bacon, M. (2022) 'Desistance from criminalisation: Police culture and new directions in drugs policing'. *Policing and Society*. 32(4): 522–539.

Community Justice Scotland. (2020) *Diversion from Prosecution Guidance*. Available from: https://communityjustice.scot/wp-content/uploads/2020/06/Diversion-from-Prosecution-Guidance-Version-4.0-FINAL-VERSION-April-2020.pdf [Accessed 19 May 2021].

DeBeck, K., Wood, E., Zhang, R., Tyndall, M., Montaner, J. and Kerr, T. (2008) 'Police and public health partnerships: Evidence from the evaluation of Vancouver's supervised injection facility'. *Substance Abuse Treatment, Prevention, and Policy*. 3(1): 1–5.

Drug Deaths Taskforce. (2021) *Report on Drug Law Reform*. Available from: https://drugdeathstaskforce.scot/media/1248/drug-law-reform-report-sept-6th-21.pdf.

EMCDDA. (2012) *Prisons and Drugs in Europe: The Problem and Responses*. Lisbon: European Monitoring Centre for Drugs and Drug Addiction.

EMCDDA. (2017) *Health and Social Responses to Drug Problems: A European Guide*. Lisbon: European Monitoring Centre for Drugs and Drug Addiction.

EMCDDA. (2018) *Drug Consumption Rooms: An Overview of Provision and Evidence*. Lisbon: European Monitoring Centre for Drugs and Drug Addiction.

EMCDDA. (2019) *European Drug Report: Trends and Developments*. Lisbon: European Monitoring Centre for Drugs and Drug Addiction.

Eastwood, N., Fox, E. and Rosmarin, A. (2016) *A Quiet Revolution: Drug Decriminalisation Across the Globe*. London: Release.

FOI/18/02863. Number of People Sentenced to Custody for Drug Possession: FOI Release. Available from: https://www.gov.scot/publications/foi-18-02863/ [Accessed 20 May 2021].

FOI/19/01755. Safer Drug Consumption Room Correspondence with UK Home Office: FOI Release. Available from: https://www.gov.scot/publications/foi-19-01755/ [Accessed 20 May 2021].

Hedrich, D. (2004) *European Report on Drug Consumption Rooms*. Lisbon: European Monitoring Centre for Drugs and Drug Addiction.

Hail, Y., Aston, L. and O'Neill, M. (2018) *Review of Evidence: What Effect Do Enforcement-orientated and Engagement-orientated Methods of Visible Policing Have on Public Confidence?* Scottish Institute for Policing Research. Available from: http://www.sipr.ac.uk/Plugin/Publications/assets/files/Review_methods_of_visible_policing_and_public_confidence_Hail_%20Aston_%20O'Neill.pdf.

HM Inspectorate of Constabulary Scotland. (2015) *Audit and Assurance Review of Stop and Search: Phase 1*. Edinburgh: HMICS.

HMICS. (2020) 'European cooperation in science and technology action on police stops - Online event 24 November 2020'. Available from: https://polstops.eu/wp-content/uploads/2020/11/HMICS-Submission-European-Cooperation-in-Science-and-Technology-Action-on-Police-Stops-Online-Event-24-November-2020-v2.pdf.

Hughes, C. and Stevens, A. (2007) *The Effects of Decriminalization of Drug Use in Portugal*. Oxford: Beckley Foundation.

INPUD. (2015) *The Human Rights of and Demands from People Who Use drug*. London: International Network of People Who Use Drugs.

Krupanski, M. (2018) *Policing and Harm Reduction*. New York: Open Society Foundations.

Landsberg, A., Kerr, T., Milloy, M.-J., Dong, H., Nguyen, P., Wood, E. and Hayashi, K. (2016) 'Declining trends in exposures to harmful policing among people who inject drugs in Vancouver, Canada'. *Journal of the International AIDS Society*. 19: 20729.

Larney, S., Kopinski, H., Beckwith, C., Zaller, N., Jarlais, D., Hagan, H., Rich, J., van den Bergh, B. and Degenhardt, L. (2013) 'Incidence and prevalence of hepatitis C in prisons and other closed settings: Results of a systematic review and meta-analysis'. *Hepatology*. 58(4): 1215–1224.

Lister, S., Seddon, T., Wincup, E., Barrett, S. and Traynor, P. (2008) *Street Policing of Problem Drug Users*. York: Joseph Rowntree Foundation.

Livadeas, C. (2021) 'National trial of naloxone in Scotland is saving lives, says force'. *Police Oracle*. Available from: https://www.policeoracle.com/news/police_equipment_news/2021/Aug/31/national-trial-of-naloxone-in-scotland-is-saving-lives--says-force_107793.html/news.

McAuley, A. and Aston, L. (2018) 'Fear of police stop and search can deter opioid users from carrying anti-overdose kits'. *The Conversation*. Available from: https://theconversation.com/fear-of-police-stop-and-search-can-deter-opioid-users-from-carrying-anti-overdose-kits-102955.

McAuley, A., Palmateer, N., Goldberg, D., Trayner, K., Shepherd, S., Gunson, R., Metcalfe, R., Milosevic, C., Taylor, A., Munro, A. and Hutchinson, S. (2019) 'Re-emergence of HIV related to injecting drug use despite a comprehensive harm reduction environment: A cross-sectional analysis'. *The Lancet HIV*. 6(5): e315–e324.

McGivern (2021) 'Scots drugs campaigners fury at "stop and search" crackdown'. *Daily Record*. Available from: https://www.dailyrecord.co.uk/news/scottish-news/stop-search-crackdown-enrages-drugs-23814663.amp?utm_source=twitter.com&utm_medium=social&utm_campaign=sharebar&__twitter_impression=true.

McVie, S. (2019) *Twelve Month Review of the Code of Practice for Stop and Search in Scotland: Quantitative Report*. Edinburgh: Scottish Government.

McVie, S. (2021) 'Second data report on police use of fixed penalty notices under the coronavirus regulations in Scotland'. In Scott, J. (ed.) *Seventh Report of the Independent Advisory Group on Police Use of Temporary Powers Related to the Coronavirus Crisis*. Available from: https://www.spa.police.uk/spa-media/2gyl4ysl/rep-b-20210222-item-6-iag.pdf

Maher, L. and Dixon, D. (1999) 'Policing and public health: Law enforcement and harm minimization in a street-level drug market'. *British Journal of Criminology*. 39(4): 488–512.

Miller, C., Firestone, M., Ramos, R., Burris, S., Ramos, M., Case, P., Brouwer, K., Fraga, M. and Strathdee, S. (2008) 'Injecting drug users' experiences of policing practices in two Mexican–US border cities: Public health perspectives'. *International Journal of Drug Policy*. 19(4): 324–331.

Monaghan, G. and Bewley-Taylor, D. (2013) *Police Support for Harm Reduction Policies and Practices Towards People Who Inject Drugs*. London: International Drug Policy Consortium.

Murray, K. (2014) *Stop and Search in Scotland: An Evaluation of Police Practice*. Scottish Centre for Crime & Justice Research. Available from: http://www.sccjr.ac.uk/wp-content/uploads/2014/01/Stop_and_Search_in_Scotland1.pdf.

National Records of Scotland. (2020) *Drug-Related Deaths in Scotland in 2019*. Edinburgh: NRS.

O'Neill, M., Aston, L. and Krause, A. (2015) *The Fife Division (Police Scotland) Stop and Search Pilot Evaluation: Findings and Recommendations*. Scottish Institute for Policing Research. Available from: http://www.sipr.ac.uk/Plugin/Publications/assets/files/Stop_and_Search_Pilot_Evaluation_Report.pdf.

O'Rourke, S. and Buchan, G. (2019) 'Edinburgh's VOW project with aid & abet'. In *The Fifth International Conference on Law Enforcement and Public Health*, Edinburgh, Scotland, 21–23 October. Available from: https://leph2019edinburgh.com/wp-content/uploads/2019/11/5.orourke-and-buchan-leph-conference-slides.pdf.

Police Scotland. (2018) *Management Information National Stop and Search Database: Quarterly Report – April–March 2017/18*. Police Scotland Analysis and Performance Unit.

Police Scotland. (2019) *Management Information National Stop and Search Database: Quarterly Report – April–March 2018/19*. Police Scotland Analysis and Performance Unit.

Police Scotland. (2020a) *Management Information National Stop and Search Database: Quarterly Report – April–December 2019/20*. Police Scotland Analysis and Performance Unit.

Police Scotland. (2020b). *Greater Glasgow Division Launch Drugs Strategy*. Available from: https://www.scotland.police.uk/what-s-happening/news/2020/february/greater-glasgow-division-launch-drugs-strategy/.

Police Scotland. (2020c) *Direct Measures Standard Operating Procedure*. Police Scotland Criminal Justice Services Division.

Police Scotland. (2021a) *'Management Information National Stop and Search Database: Quarterly Report – April–December 2019/20*. Police Scotland Analysis and Performance Unit.

Police Scotland. (2021b) *Management Information National Stop and Search Database: Quarterly Report – April–December 2020/21*. Police Scotland Analysis and Performance Unit.

Powell, M. (2021). Twitter. https://twitter.com/MartinTransform/status/1396558565066825728.

Price, T., Parkes, T. and Malloch, M. (2021) '"Discursive struggles" between criminal justice sanctions and health interventions for people who use drugs: A qualitative exploration of diversion policy and practice in Scotland'. *Drugs: Education, Prevention and Policy*. 28(2): 118–126.

Prison Reform Trust. (2019) *Bromley Briefings Prison Factfile Winter 2019*. London: Prison Reform Trust.

Rae, S. (2021) 'Long read: Dundee police trial carrying naloxone in hope of battling city's drug death epidemic'. *Evening Telegraph*. Available from: https://www.eveningtelegraph.co.uk/fp/long-read-dundee-police-trial-carrying-naloxone-in-hope-of-battling-citys-drug-death-epidemic/.

Rhodes, T. (2002) 'The "risk environment": A framework for understanding and reducing drug-related harm'. *International Journal of Drug Policy*. 13(2): 85–94.

Ritchie, ACC Gary (2020) 'Police Scotland: Plans and approach to the drug problem'. *Presentation at SIPR/DRNS Approaches to Policing of Drugs Event*. Available from: http://sipr.ac.uk/events/joint-drns-sipr-event-approaches-to-policing-of-drugs.

Reuter, P. and Stevens, A. (2007) *An Analysis of UK Drug Policy*. London: UKDPC.

Sarang, A., Rhodes, T., Sheon, N. and Page, K. (2010) 'Policing drug users in Russia: Risk, fear, and structural violence'. *Substance Use and Misuse*. 45(6): 813–864.

Scott, J. (2015) *The Report of the Advisory Group on Stop and Search*. Edinburgh: Scottish Government.

Scott, J. (2019a) *Twelve Month Review of the Code of Practice for Stop and Search in Scotland by the Independent Advisory Group on Stop and Search*. Edinburgh: Scottish Government.

Scott, S. (2019b) *The Social Return on Investment (SROI) Study of the Positive Outcomes Project (POP)*. Community Justice Scotland. Available from: https://www.glasgowcpp.org.uk/CHttpHandler.ashx?id=49212&p=0 [Accessed 7 May 2021].

Scottish Affairs Committee. (2019) *Problem Drug Use in Scotland*. London: House of Commons.

Scottish Centre for Crime and Justice Research. (2019). *Scotland's Prison Population*. Available from: https://www.sccjr.ac.uk/wp-content/uploads/2019/10/7-Scotlands-prison-population.pdf [Accessed 19 May 2021].

Scottish Government. (2018) *Rights, Respect and Recovery: Scotland's Strategy to Improve Health by Preventing and Reducing Alcohol and Drug Use, Harm and Related Deaths*. Edinburgh: Scottish Government.

Scottish Government. (2019a) *Criminal Proceedings in Scotland 2017–2018*. Edinburgh: Scottish Government.

Scottish Government. (2019b) *Recorded Crime in Scotland 2018–2019*. Edinburgh: Scottish Government.

Scottish Government. (2020a) *Recorded Crime in Scotland 2019–2020*. Edinburgh: Scottish Government.

Scottish Government. (2020b) *Criminal Proceedings in Scotland 2018–2019*. Edinburgh: Scottish Government.

Scottish Government. (2020c) *Criminal Justice Social Work Statistics in Scotland 2018–2019*. Edinburgh: Scottish Government.

Scottish Government. (2021) *Criminal Justice Social Work Statistics: 2019 to 2020*. Edinburgh: Scottish Government.

Scottish Police Authority. (2020) *Forensic Services Committee Drug Analysis*, 3rd February 2020. Available from: https://www.spa.police.uk/spa-media/gmkmqb3n/repc202801-item-9-drug-analysis.pdf.

Shiner, M., Carre, Z., Delsol, R. and Eastwood, N. (2018) *The Colour of Injustice: 'Race', Drugs and Law Enforcement in England and Wales*. London: StopWatch.

Spyt, W., Barnham, L. and Kew, J. (2019) 'Diversion: Going soft on drugs?' *Thames Valley Police Journal*. 4: 44–58.

Stevens, A. (2013) *Modernising Drug Law Enforcement: Applying Harm Reduction Principles to the Policing of Retail Drug Markets*. London: International Drug Policy Consortium.

Stevens, A., Hughes, C., Hulme, S. and Cassidy, R. (2022) 'Depenalization, diversion and decriminalization: A realist review and programme theory of alternatives to criminalization for simple drug possession'. *European Journal of Criminology*. 19(1): 29–54.

The Guardian. (2020) 'Operator of Glasgow safe drug-use van charged at service'. Available from: https://www.theguardian.com/society/2020/oct/24/operator-of-glasgow-safe-drug-use-van-peter-krykant-arrested-and-charged [Accessed 18 August 2021].

Tiratelli, M., Quinton, P. and Bradford, B. (2018) 'Does stop and search deter crime? Evidence from ten years of London-wide data'. *British Journal of Criminology*. 58(5): 1212–1231.

Tombs, J. and Piacentini, L. (2012) 'Prisons and imprisonment in Scotland'. In Croall, H., Mooney, G. and Munro, M. (eds.) *Criminal Justice in Scotland*. Cullompton: Willan: 238–260.

Turney, K. (2018) 'Adverse childhood experiences among children of incarcerated parents'. *Children and Youth Services Review*. 89: 218–225.

UK Focal Point on Drugs. (2019) *United Kingdom Country Drug Report 2019*. Lisbon: EMCDDA.

Wolfe, J. (2019) 'Scottish affairs committee oral evidence 9/7/19'. Available from: http://data.parliament.uk/WrittenEvidence/CommitteeEvidence.svc/EvidenceDocument/Scottish%20Affairs/Problem%20drug%20use%20in%20Scotland/Oral/103661.html [Accessed 20 May 2021].

8

TREADING THE PATHS OF DRUG DIVERSION

Wojciech Spyt and Jason Kew

Introduction

Enforcement of drug prohibition in the United Kingdom is a central tenet in government policy to contain and prevent drug misuse. However, over the last decade, there has been a comparative shift towards the treatment of people found in possession of drugs, and away from criminalisation through traditional criminal justice routes. The implementation of drug diversion as a policy has been observed in several parts of the world, in conjunction with, or in lieu of, penalising those found in possession of drugs (Stevens et al. 2022). If drug addiction is viewed through the lens of public health, as is generally the case for tobacco and alcohol (Berridge 2013; Mold 2018), then addressing the addiction through behavioural strategies (Heather 2006; Herman and Sofuoglu 2010) becomes a natural policy option for dealing with illicit drug use (Lindquist-Grantz et al. 2021).

Within England and Wales, this policy change has most recently been led by four separate regional police forces. The emphasis in the policies enacted allows the opportunity for individuals to avoid the stigma of gaining a criminal record, while at the same time offering incentives to attend drug diversion programmes and treatment. Three of these approaches constitute deferred prosecution schemes put in place by Avon and Somerset (Luckwell 2017), West Midlands (Neyroud and Slothower 2013; Neyroud et al. 2017), and Durham constabularies (Weir et al. 2021a, 2021b). A fourth scheme, trialled by Thames Valley Police (TVP) (Spyt et al. 2019), is novel in that it utilises current legal frameworks that are nationally endorsed, has lower administration costs than deferred prosecution schemes and current polices, constitutes a voluntary mechanism for attendance, and offers the potential for people found in possession of drugs to be subject to multiple referrals.

DOI: 10.4324/9781003154136-9

The authors of this chapter were, at the time of writing, both serving officers of TVP. They provided the impetus for the initial discussion at a strategic level within the organisation, then designed and were heavily involved in the implementation of two separate models of 'diversion' for drug possession. The initial drive for the realisation of a diversionary scheme originated from Detective Chief Inspector Jason Kew, whose personal experiences and over two decades of work in drug law enforcement led to a deep compassion for those individuals who use drugs and the impact that addiction has on their families and friends. Detective Sergeant Wojciech Spyt, working within a unit providing strategic guidance for the force, supported, developed, and co-designed the two separate models that were subsequently trialled. The latter's views on diversion were given formative shape through academia and embedded through 15 years of investigative experience. This is indicative of the view that police culture is diverse, dynamic, and evolving (Bacon 2022; Woods 2016).

The chapter begins by giving a brief overview of how drug policy came into being in the United Kingdom, how it has changed over time, and the drivers for this change. The chapter then brings into focus very recent changes in policy towards drug possession that are being implemented by local police forces in contrast to central governmental bodies. It considers three different schemes that have been introduced by three separate forces in England and Wales. The analysis of these programmes provides the rationale for the development of the TVP initiative in West Berkshire utilising existing criminal justice outcomes in the form of 'community resolutions' and subsequently the introduction of a second scheme in Windsor and Maidenhead.

A brief history of contemporary British drug policy

Drug policy in the United Kingdom is based upon the twin pillars of law enforcement and the simultaneous provision of treatment for addiction. This approach has persisted since the early 20th century (Pearson 1991; Seddon 2010).

The central aim of drugs prohibition is to prevent individuals from possessing and using drugs in order to protect their health, prevent harm to others, and preclude the spread of crime associated with drug use (Husak and De Marneffe 2005; Sher 2010). The Misuse of Drugs Act 1971 follows this premise of protecting drug users by classifying drugs that cause greater harm to individuals in higher categories and imposing harsher sentencing for those 'higher category' drugs (Police Foundation 2000; Ward 2013). The Act specifies three categories ranging from 'A' to 'C', the former being judged as more harmful and the latter as less. It acts to serve as a deterrent to possession, thereby minimising harm to individuals. It also criminalises the supply of drugs in a similar way.

The second strand of the 'British system' of providing treatment by medical practitioners, health care professionals, and intervention programmes is aimed firstly at preventing individuals from becoming involved in illicit drugs and secondly reducing users' dependency if they have an existing relationship with drugs (Pearson 1991; Seddon 2010). Public health approaches include behavioural programmes available through service providers in conjunction with pharmacological support.

In 2000, the Independent Inquiry into the Misuse of Drugs Act concluded that 'demand will only be significantly reduced by education and treatment, not by the deterrent effect of law' (Police Foundation 2000, p. 8). The inquiry also concluded that the law relating to cannabis was creating more harm than it was preventing, due to the criminalisation of large numbers of young people to the detriment of their futures and having a disproportionate effect on ethnic minorities (May et al. 2007; Police Foundation 2000), something since echoed by the Lammy Review (2017). The Lammy Review makes it clear that criminal justice processes, such as interviews and admissions of guilt, likely exclude certain ethnic minorities from more favourable outcomes due to a distrust of the criminal justice system. Diversionary schemes can be enacted without such requirements and thus have the potential to be less discriminatory.

Within just over six months of the inquiry being published, the Labour Party announced that it intended to reclassify cannabis from a Class B to a Class C drug (May et al. 2007; Mills 2008; Shiner 2015). This was one of several policy changes that were introduced. In reclassifying cannabis, the intention was not to decriminalise but to focus law enforcement resources on those drugs that were considered to be most harmful, with cannabis being seen as an outlier (Police Foundation 2000; Shiner 2015). On 23 October 2001, Home Secretary David Blunkett announced, 'it is time for an honest and common sense approach focussing effectively on drugs that cause most harm' (Shiner 2015, p. 3). Simultaneously, additional resources were made available to the police to tackle regional drug traffickers, research was commissioned on how best to tackle Class A drug use with a focus on heroin and crack cocaine, resources were made available for drug education for young people, and new legislation aimed at targeting drug-related crime was enacted (Home Office 2010; Reuter and Stevens 2008).

The legislative changes focused on the recovery of assets from organised crime through the Proceeds of Crime Act 2002, introducing drug abstinence orders through the Criminal Justice and Court Services Act 2000, and drug testing provisions for people charged with acquisitive crime and drugs offences through the 2005 Drugs Act (Home Office 2010; Reuter and Stevens 2008). Those testing positive for drugs were offered the opportunity to enter treatment and the test results could be provided to the court to assist with decision-making, with the presumption of bail being reversed if individuals tested positive for a Class A drug (Section 19, Criminal Justice Act 2003). This drug testing policy fell under the broad umbrella of the Drug Interventions Programme (DIP) (Reuter and Stevens 2008). Where persons have been arrested for certain 'trigger' offences and are present in custody, a power exists for police to carry out drug screening. Although a test can be refused, failing to provide a sample can carry up to a three-month prison sentence. These offences are centred on not only acquisitive crime but also include drug possession, fraud offences, and any other offences where police believe the crime has been driven by drug dependency (Home Office 2007, 2011). This had a 'net-widening' effect (Cohen 1985), increasing the number of people under correctional programmes as a consequence of changes in legislation rather than behaviour. However, the withdrawal of central government funding to a local funding model (Home Office 2011) for the DIP has meant that police forces across England and Wales have greatly reduced their use of it, preferring instead to use the funds for other purposes.

The reclassification of cannabis from a Class B to a Class C drug went hand in hand with the introduction of cannabis warnings (Lloyd 2008). These can be issued by officers 'on the street' and take up significantly less time than a caution or a charge to enact. The 'cannabis warning' forms a disposal that although recorded on police systems, does not constitute a criminal record (Monaghan and White 1998).

Within the criminal justice system in England and Wales, in addition to 'cannabis warnings', there are a number of out of court disposal (OOCD) options that can be employed by the police in lieu of charging people to appear at court. These include 'simple cautions', 'conditional cautions', 'fixed penalty notices', 'adult restorative disposals', 'youth restorative disposals', and 'youth cannabis warnings'. Nationally, approximately a third of all current recorded disposals are through these OOCDs (Neyroud 2018; Sosa 2012). Following the introduction of conditional cautions in 2003, the second important institutional development in OOCDs was the introduction of a 'community resolution' by the Home Office (2013). This is a non-statutory OOCD option for officers to utilise nationally and, similarly to the cannabis warning, does not constitute a disclosable criminal record. With this, there has been a movement across England and Wales to replace all other out of court disposals with the 'community resolution' and 'conditional caution' under the banner of a 'two-tier' system (NPCC 2017).

The cost of administering a cannabis warning is significantly cheaper than other disposal options. The rationale for the introduction of the 'cannabis warning' was to release police resources to deal with more harmful drugs (May et al. 2002). Perversely however, due to the introduction of 'sanctioned detections' as a key performance indicator for the police and the inclusion of 'cannabis warnings' under the banner of 'detections', while self-reported use of drugs was falling, the number of cannabis possession offences recorded by the police almost doubled between 2004/2005 and 2011/2012. As such, the attempt to refocus police efforts on more harmful drugs was an abject failure (Shiner 2015). While the creation of cannabis warnings had the aim of reducing the number of individuals gaining a criminal record and refocusing efforts to target Class A drugs, the effect, due to key performance indicators, was to bring more users of illicit drugs into contact with the criminal justice system. Once contact is made with the criminal justice system, and a cannabis warning has been issued, the impact is that for any subsequent possession offences, the sanction becomes ever more severe. The escalation involves a fixed penalty notice, followed by a caution and then a charge (ACPO 2009; College of Policing 2021). This added to the net widening associated with the DIP. While key performance indicators have been withdrawn and consequently the police focus on cannabis has decreased significantly, mechanisms for education and treatment for drug misuse have also been removed.

New directions in police-led diversion

The United Kingdom has the second highest levels of drug-related deaths per capita in Europe and higher drug dependency than seen in any country within the European Union (EMCDDA 2020). Illicit drug use in the United Kingdom has risen rapidly over the past four decades. In 1980, the total number of registered drug addicts with the Home Office numbered 2,846. In 1987, this figure had risen to over 10,000, and by 1996 there were over 43,000 registered users (Buchanan 2006; Buchanan and Young 2000; Reuter and Stevens 2008), with the total volume of heroin users estimated to number in the hundreds of thousands (Morgan 2014; ONS 2020). This rise in addiction is conjoined with a rise in deaths attributable to drug use. By 2015, there were 2,479 registered deaths related to drug misuse; almost commensurate to the entire registered cohort of drug addicts in 1980 (NHS 2017). This was accompanied by 8,621 hospital admissions (a rise of 6% on the previous year) and an estimate that during that year, 2.7 million people in the United Kingdom had taken drugs. By 2017, there were 3,756 recorded drug-related deaths, which was at a comparative level to the previous year (ONS 2018). It is against this backdrop that law enforcement policy in England and Wales has begun to shift.

How law enforcement policy is determined in England and Wales is subject to a range of forces that can be tiered as 'macro', 'meso', and 'micro' actors (Greene 2014; Serpa and Ferreira 2019). At the 'macro' level, central government can drive policy through legislation, Home Office circulars, and Ministry of Justice directives, and influence behaviour through key performance indicators and financial incentives. Separately, policymakers and drivers who are independent of the government exist at a national level. Historically, this would include the National Police Improvement Agency and the Association of Chief Police Officers, and currently the National Police Chief's Council and the College of Policing (Heaton and Tong 2016; Neyroud 2009). At the 'meso' level, actors comprised of individual police forces, chief constables, and police and crime commissioners can ascribe priorities to national policies, determine their uptake, and also drive their own strategic direction (Heaton and Tong 2016; Loader and Sparks 2002). Finally, at the 'micro' level, officers have a great deal of discretion as to whether and how to enforce directives and legislation as well as initiating new policies themselves (Health and Social Care Committee 2019; Spyt et al. 2019).

Over time, the drive for policy change for each of these three organisational levels has shifted to a greater emphasis on 'evidence-based policing' and 'what works' (Bullock and Tilley 2009; Heaton and Tong 2016; Neyroud and Weisburd 2014; Raynor 2002). In the case of diversion schemes, we can arguably see all levels in play. At the micro level, in the case of the DDP within TVP as discussed earlier, the inception of the scheme has been driven by individual officers, those being the authors of this chapter (Health and Social Care Committee 2019; Spyt et al. 2019). At the meso level, it has been exemplified by police forces employing their own policies on the basis of academic research and evidence gathered from trials (Dawson and Williams 2009; Neyroud et al. 2017; Weir et al. 2021a, 2021b). At the macro level, support for the trials has been provided by the Ministry of Justice, the Home Office, and parliamentary select committees (Health and Social Care Committee 2019).

Four such notable schemes in relation to drugs include the Drug Education Programme (DEP) instigated by Avon and Somerset Constabulary; two separate Drug Diversion Pilots (DDPs) run by Thames Valley Police (both of which have been aimed exclusively at individuals found in possession of drugs); Turning Point implemented by West Midlands Constabulary; and Checkpoint run by Durham Constabulary. The DEP, Checkpoint, Turning Point, and the Windsor and Maidenhead Drug DDP within TVP, are analogous in that they are 'deferred prosecution' schemes. The decision to implement all four schemes originated from the individual regional forces trialling them (Jamieson 2018; Luckwell 2017; Neyroud and Slothower 2013; Spyt et al. 2019; Weir et al. 2021a, 2021b).

The concept of a deferred prosecution scheme is for conditions to be set for an individual to abide by or complete. If the person complies with the conditions that have been set by the police, then the prosecution, in whatever form that may take, is not enacted. Furthermore, there is no recording of the offence against the individual's name. Thus, the stigmatisation involved in a person obtaining a criminal record is avoided. However, in the absence of fulfilling the conditions, the suspect is prosecuted. In the case of the DEP, Turning Point, and Checkpoint, the sanction for not meeting the conditions involves the individual being charged or summoned with an offence and being taken to court. Such schemes have been implemented and continue to be in use in the United States, and are under consideration more widely internationally (Eraga et al. 2018).

Turning Point was a randomised control study in implementing out of court disposal options conducted by West Midlands Police in conjunction with the University of Cambridge (Neyroud and Slothower 2013; Neyroud et al. 2017). It was applicable to offenders where the custody officer had decided that it was in the public interest to prosecute and the option of issuing an informal warning or caution was not appropriate. At that point, custody officers used a 'randomiser tool' which presented a series of triage questions that excluded offenders with multiple convictions, a high likelihood of prison, and having committed a serious offence. If the gateway passed offenders as eligible for the pilot, they were randomised to either being charged or sent for a TPP disposal. A contract was then made with the offender (in contrast to a conditional caution) that involved any of the following: community payback, a letter of apology, compensation, employment, mental health referral/treatment, housing, anger management counselling, drugs searches, exclusion zones, and/or non-contact with victim.

The programme showed the same reoffending rates for the sample of persons who went through the scheme as those who were charged with offences, with the exception of a 35% lower violent reoffending rate for the TPP. Furthermore, over a period of 12 months, from the control sample of persons charged with an offence there were 432 court cases as compared to 138 from the TPP. It is estimated this saved the police approximately £205,833 a year alone, not including the associated costs of taking cases through the criminal justice system (Neyroud 2018). While this scheme was not specific to drugs, it encompassed drugs possession and has been widely quoted in policy around drug diversionary schemes. The initial pilot programme has now finished; however, an extension of the scheme is being considered for drugs possession outside of custody (Jamieson 2018).

Durham's Checkpoint operates in the same vein as Turning Point and offers eligible offenders a four-month-long contract to engage as an alternative to prosecution. The contract offers interventions to address the underlying reasons for the commission of the offence in order to prevent them from repeating it. As with the West Midlands programme, while not tailored to drugs it has been widely cited in policy around drug diversionary schemes. Serious offences, driving offences, and cases of domestic abuse or hate crime are not eligible under the programme (Weir et al. 2021a, 2021b). The Checkpoint subject is supported through the process by a specialist 'navigator' who completes a detailed needs assessment with them and draws up the contract. This can include interventions around any of the issues the offender may have, including those that contributed to the subject committing the offence (Weir et al. 2021a, 2021b). There is a significant cost to the programme (in excess of £300,000 a year), through the use of navigators, tracking equipment, and administrative costs among others, although there is predicted to be a saving in the long term for the police due to reduced offending and lower associated court costs (Hogg 2017).

In relation to drug offences only, Avon and Somerset Police run a Drug Education Programme, which offers an alternative route for drug possession offences and allows a 'once only opportunity' for offenders to receive an intervention aimed at deterring them from further drug use and further involvement in the criminal justice system. The programme began on 1 April 2016. Since this time up until 17 July 2017, a total of 633 individuals were referred for drug possession offences (Luckwell 2017). The programme itself entails a four-hour intervention. The referral can be made either outside or within the custody process. Outside of the custody process, officers conduct an interview with the offender under caution. If the suspect is over ten years of age, an admission is made by them, and the officer dealing with the suspect believes that they would benefit from such an intervention, they can be offered a diversion into the programme in lieu of being charged or reported with the offence. Should there be non-compliance with attendance at the course, then a summons file will be completed by officers. If the suspect is under 18 years of age, the presence of an appropriate adult is required for the referral to be made. The programme constructed by Avon and Somerset Police was specifically designed to target possession of drugs and diversion as opposed to prosecution or traditional criminal justice resolutions.

Outside of these three pilots, deferred prosecution currently functions in England and Wales under the legislative framework of 'conditional cautions'. These were introduced in 2003 under the Criminal Justice Act 2003. The conditional caution allows officers to impose conditions on an offender which, if not fulfilled, result in the offender being prosecuted. In contrast to the above three schemes, the conditional caution nevertheless remains and constitutes a criminal record, even if the conditions are fulfilled. This criminal record, as mentioned earlier, is associated with damaging stigmatisation (Buchanan and Young 2000; Collison 1993; Ward 2013). For this reason, the application of conditional cautions as a type of deferred prosecution could be seen to be unsatisfactory.

A critique of deferred prosecution schemes

Compliance with conditions in the deferred prosecution schemes is high, reaching 90% for Checkpoint (Weir et al. 2021b) and 80% for the DEP. In other words, only between 10 and 20% of people failed to comply with the conditions that were set and were, as a result, subject to a charging decision. This means that the objective of putting a large proportion of individuals who come into police contact into an education programme – including drug diversion – was achieved. There are, nonetheless, caveats to the implementation of these schemes more widely.

The first objection to all three schemes is that they are the effective application of a sentence or punishment by the police without the involvement of a court. It is the police who are deciding on the resolution to an infringement of the law and what conditions or punishment the suspect must fulfil. This decision on a resolution has not been ratified in any way by a court or through government legislation as it has been in the case of conditional cautions or fixed penalty notices. The imposition of the sentence by a law enforcement agency is controversial, and especially so without the ratification of such a policy by the government for reasons of bias and corruption (Ashworth 2010). Furthermore, in all three schemes, non-adherence to the diversion results in the suspect being prosecuted. As with the imposition of a contract with the suspect without legal basis or ratification by government, the legality of this approach is not clear.

Second, deferred prosecution schemes require significant expenditure of police resources when compared to current disposals such as cannabis warnings, fixed penalty notices, and, in some cases, simple cautions. In a deferred prosecution scheme, if the conditions set are not met, a prosecution is required. This necessitates an investigation that will withstand scrutiny in court if challenged by a suspect. Failure to do so would result in the credibility of the scheme failing and any conditions set being potentially viewed as voluntary by suspects if they became aware that the penalty or prosecution is not credible (Neyroud and Slothower 2015).

Possession of a controlled drug, contrary to Section 5 of the Misuse of Drugs Act 1971, contains the following 'points to prove': (a) the drug must be in the custody or control of the defendant; (b) the defendant must know or suspect the existence of the drug in question; and (c) the drug must be a controlled drug within the meaning of the Act. For the purposes of the investigation of the offence of simple possession of a drug, fulfilling the 'points to prove' would require: (1) seizure of the drug for the potential of testing the substance and for forensic links between the packaging and the suspect; (2) a statement describing the seizure and circumstances in which the seizure came to pass, by the officer in the case; and (3) an interview of the suspect, to determine knowledge of the drug and potential defences that may be raised.

The interview is the most time-consuming aspect of the above-outlined investigation if it is to be conducted in line with our current policies. A contemporaneous note interview may be carried out in relation to cannabis and khat. However, possession of other Class B and Class A substances constitutes triable either-way offences; in other words, an offence that can be heard either in the Magistrates or the Crown Court. Any interview for a 'triable either-way' offence must comply with the requirements of the Police and Criminal Evidence Act 1984 (PACE) and be visually and audio recorded. Taking offenders to police stations in order to fulfil this requirement is costly in terms of officer time. There is provision under PACE that mobile devices such as body-worn video can be designated for fulfilling this purpose in relation to interviews; however, this must be endorsed by the chief constable of a force (Code E, Sections 1.6 and 2.3).

Third, the incentive to attend the diversion or education programme is provided as the result of the deferred prosecution. It cannot be seen to be voluntary, which is argued to be critical both from an ethical perspective and when judging the effectiveness of drug addiction treatment (Camerion et al. 2012; Klag et al. 2005). While mandated drug rehabilitation programmes imposed by the criminal justice system have shown significant and persistent reductions in drug use and offending that are comparable to voluntarily mechanisms (McSweeney et al. 2007; Stevens et al. 2005), their ethical justification for drug users has been questioned (Stevens 2012).

Fourth, in the case of the DEP, Turning Point, and Checkpoint, it is difficult to identify the efficacy of the diversionary schemes against traditional criminal justice disposals. In the case of both TPP and Checkpoint, a matrix was used to determine whether an individual is able to take part in the programme. If, through the application of the matrix, they were deemed too dangerous or liable to reoffend then this excluded them from taking part in the scheme. As such, people referred into the programme were more likely to be compliant and less likely to reoffend than those not eligible. There was evidence from the TPP to suggest that diversion was more successful at preventing violent reoffending, although it is not known whether this entailed or was related to possession of drug offences (Neyroud et al. 2017).

In a similar vein, the DEP requires the suspect to be interviewed on the street. The scheme also requires that suspects make admissions to offences. This means that the individuals referred to the diversionary scheme are more compliant than those who are not eligible for it in that they have firstly co-operated with the police in conducting an interview without a solicitor present and secondly made admissions to the offence. This again results in difficulty comparing the efficacy of the diversion scheme against traditional criminal justice resolutions if not subject to a randomised controlled trial (RCT). The requirement of an admission as well as the assent of the officer dealing with the offender in order to be referred into the scheme can also be questioned ethically. An offender or suspect not making an admission to an offence may derive the same benefit of diversion as someone who does make an admission. The decision not to make an admission while being interviewed on the street may be made for any number of reasons that may have no impact on the success of a diversionary scheme influencing the offender's behaviour. Additionally, the assent of the officer in whether an individual is referred into the scheme introduces personal bias into the decision.

Thames Valley Police West Berkshire Drug Diversion Pilot

The first DDP implemented in TVP in West Berkshire aimed to address the above concerns through the implementation of a voluntary referral scheme that functioned within the constraints of current nationally accepted legal frameworks.

The introduction of community resolutions in the two-tier format of conditional cautions and community resolutions (NPCC 2017) has allowed for a new policy approach to be trialled by the police in relation to drug possession offences. Community resolutions do not form part of a criminal record. In this regard, in relation to drug offences, they are equivalent to a cannabis warning, a fixed penalty notice disposal (FPND), and the deferred prosecution schemes described above. The advantage of the community resolution is threefold. The first is that any application of a community resolution does not result in a criminal record, thus avoiding the damaging stigmatisation of offenders. The second is in relation to the savings that can be made in resources used in contrast to cautions, charges, and deferred prosecution schemes. As no prosecution is threatened, there is no need to gather evidence of the offence for the purpose of presenting it in court. Moreover, community resolutions are not limited in their application to cannabis and can be applied to any drug type. Finally, community resolutions, in contrast to cannabis warnings, can involve voluntary conditions set by the officer in the case. Conditions can be far-reaching and can include a requirement to attend a drug service provider to address drug dependency issues. However, in contrast to the deferred prosecution schemes, the suspect's adherence to any conditions set by the officer is voluntary. This avoids the coercive element that has been argued to be both unethical and ineffective in the treatment of drug addiction.

The obvious question can be posed, that if there is no consequence to non-adherence to conditions, why would a suspect who has committed an offence observe them? It is useful at this juncture to compare the voluntary community resolution outcome with conditions to attend a drug diversion scheme to a cannabis warning. The practical application of a cannabis warning is just that: a warning that the next time the individual caught is found in possession of cannabis they will receive a more punitive outcome, whether that be a fixed penalty notice or a caution. This is, in practice, delivered either verbally or in writing by the officer dealing with the case. In this sense, a move to a two-tier OOCD outcome in relation to cannabis offers a greater disincentive to reoffend than a cannabis warning. In opposition to a cannabis warning where the next contact with the police would normally entail a fixed penalty notice, in a two-tier system the next contact would instead elicit a conditional caution. As such, the introduction of the community resolution offers the police much greater flexibility in dealing with drug possession offences than previously applicable outcomes.

Adjusting the community resolution mechanism

The voluntary mechanism of attendance is given gentle impetus by offering an incentive to attend the drug service provider. In contrast to the framework put forward by the NPCC (2017), providing the conditions are adhered to, the individual found in possession of drugs is informed that they will be eligible for another referral. If they do not adhere to the conditions of attendance at a drug service provider, they will not be eligible. This is both a 'carrot' and a 'stick': a stick because the threat hangs over them that if found with drugs again, they will be dealt with more severely if they don't attend; and a carrot because if they attend, they have the opportunity of the same resolution if caught another time. Once this adjustment is applied, the community resolution becomes a tool that offers incentive for an individual found in possession of a drug for voluntary submission to a drug service provider, that is not present in a cannabis warning.

From a practical perspective, this was deemed important for three reasons. The first is that an individual may be referred and not have had the opportunity to attend their appointment before they are caught again. The second is that even if an individual has attended and is in treatment, treatment is not an instantaneous process. For example, the issuing of a pharmacological therapy for heroin from first contact with an individual can take up to three weeks. A blood sample is needed, which then requires analysis, the results of which are subsequently sent to a general practitioner to inform them of a suitable treatment and dosage of drugs. While initial pharmacological treatment can be prescribed within three weeks, the tiering of the dosage to an appropriate level may take several more weeks. Third, the process of treatment of addiction is one that may take several attempts prior to being successful and may also involve relapses (Barnes 1988; See et al. 2003; Weddington 1991). If an individual abides by conditions and attends treatment, there does not appear to be any benefit from issuing them with a criminal record. As argued earlier, prohibition is a deterrent to possession. However, if someone is already in possession of a drug then this deterrent has failed. If they are engaging in an activity to reduce their use of drugs, then the deterrent of criminalisation or further criminalisation has no purpose.

Eligibility for referral

The starting point for referral in the West Berkshire DDP was that all people found in possession of a controlled drug, contrary to Section 5 of the Misuse of Drugs Act 1971, would be eligible. The drive to implement a diversion scheme came from personal experiences, compassion for those using illicit drugs and their families, and with the outlook that addiction should be treated as a public health issue. In this context, denying those persons using drugs, whatever the type, access to diversionary services did not seem ethical to its instigators. As described above, people could be referred numerous times provided they adhered to the conditions of each referral. If, however, a person was referred and they did not attend the drug service provider and complete the required number of sessions, then they would not be eligible for future diversions.

While seemingly a simple process to follow, it was emphasised in the pilot that officer discretion within it was crucial for several reasons. First, officer discretion would be required for the initial decision as to whether a suspect is in possession of drugs for their own personal use or suspected of supply. It was considered whether nominal limits could be used, such as are in place in Portugal where personal possession of drugs is deemed to be anything under ten days use (Greenwald 2009). However, it may be that a supplier of drugs is only carrying with them a small quantity of drugs that could be deemed to be for personal use, but through other evidence they are suspected by the officer to be supplying (e.g. through the possession of scales, mobile phones, and deal bags). Where supply of drugs was suspected, then the ethical reasons outlined above for the implementation of the pilot would not apply and thus diversion would not be appropriate.

Second, in whatever way an individual is to be dealt with, efforts to confirm their identity will need to be made. If a person is being considered for referral or summons to court, their identity will need to be ascertained to ensure that the correct suspect is recorded on police systems. If this were not completed and false details were provided by the offender, multiple issues would be caused for the administration of justice and for the functioning of the pilot study. Ascertaining the identity of a person outside of custody or a police station is executed on a regular basis and officers are adept at the process. Situations where this is the case include the issuing of fixed penalty notices for several different situations ranging from shoplifting and public disorder to driving-related offences.

Third, it is necessary for officers to be able to exercise discretion if their professional knowledge directs them to suspect that an individual would be better safeguarded through arrest rather than diversion. These three situations describe scenarios where the power of arrest can be exercised and where the 'necessity criteria' exist to do so under Code G of the Police and Criminal Evidence Act 1984.

Fourth, in circumstances where a person was found in possession of drugs but was not living in the locality where the DDP was being implemented, diversion becomes problematic. The remit of the drug service provider is to serve the inhabitants of the local community and not those in other areas of the country. Travel for people referred back to the locality where they were arrested also constitutes a barrier to attendance. A lack of information-sharing agreements and memorandums of understanding with drug service providers across the country meant that referral to their own areas was not possible.

Fifth, in the eventuality where a person presented a defence to possession of a drug, referral would not be appropriate. Under the Criminal Procedures Investigations Act 1996, police officers are bound to pursue reasonable lines of enquiry whether they point towards or away from a suspect. If a person raises a defence to an offence, then the police are duty bound to investigate this. Any investigation of this kind would displace the opportunity for a referral.

Finally, creating a process where officers were unable to exercise discretion within the constraints of the law, may have meant that the process set for them would be disregarded and discretion exercised in any case. In other words, they may have ignored the processes stipulated and enforced their own resolutions. This may have happened without the evaluators of the pilot being aware, which would, in turn, misrepresent any subsequent analysis.

Evaluating the DDP

The scheme was piloted with two primary aims. The first was to test the feasibility of out of custody referral to drug service providers for individuals found in possession of drugs; in other words whether it was practically feasible to do so. The second was to determine what the deterrent effect of traditional police disposals is, when compared to referral to drug service providers. These data are crucial, as the principle aim of prohibition and associated punishment is for there to be a deterrent effect which protects society from an uptake in drug use (Korf 2002; Van Dijk 1998). If referral removes this deterrent effect and the uptake of drug use increases, then ethically the implementation of a drug referral scheme would become questionable whether or not viewed through the lens of being a public health issue.

Initially, an RCT was proposed; however, this was rejected by the chief constable's management team (CCMT). By splitting the individuals who come into contact with the police into two randomised groups, one who are referred to drugs diversion and one who are dealt with through traditional measures and comparing the two, an indication could be sought as to the consequences of the two approaches and how they differ. While an indication would be given as to the effects of one approach over another, it would not be possible to conclusively attribute cause and effect due to the large amount of uncontrolled variables outside of the study parameters. However, this approach was rejected due to ethical concerns of providing different outcomes to people depending on a randomly generated output and the associated criticism that this might draw. Instead, a longitudinal comparison was approved as a methodology. Data as to the deterrent effect of those traditional disposals were taken from the year prior to the pilot in the same geographical policing area over the same calendar time period. In order to achieve this, the following information was sought and recorded:

1. The number of individuals referred to the drug service provider during the course of the pilot.
2. The number of individuals who attended the drug service provider for a diversionary scheme, in so doing providing a rate of compliance.
3. The number of persons not eligible for referral to a drugs diversionary scheme.
4. The number of persons and reasons for doing so who declined participation in a drugs diversionary scheme if offered the opportunity.
5. The number of individuals dealt with in line with traditional criminal justice outcomes from the previous period.
6. The disposal type for individuals dealt with in the previous period.

Data around the number of persons reoffending following being found in simple possession of drugs were subsequently taken from police systems. This allowed the testing of the secondary aim to determine what the deterrent effect of traditional police disposals is when compared to referral to drug service providers during the course of the study. In order to do this, reoffending rates – for drug possession and drug-related offences – for both those referred and those dealt with through traditional routes were examined. All offences were noted against linear temporal points: one month, two months, three months, and one-year post first offence recorded from the initiation of the pilot study and then from the same time period from the previous year.

The Drug Diversion Pilot has been running in the West Berkshire local policing area (LPA) since 10 December 2018, with funding secured up until the end of 2021. The cohort of people referred for diversion up until 10 March 2019 was, and will continue to be, subject to continued evaluation. The results shown in Table 8.1 provide figures in respect of the number of referrals made, overall attendance figures, and reoffending rates.

Engagement with the service provider

In total, 55 people were referred to the drug service provider in the first three months of the DDP in West Berkshire. Table 8.1 shows the take up of the diversion scheme following an encounter with the police.

Table 8.1 indicates that the greatest attrition from the diversion scheme occurs between referral by the police and initial contact with the drug service provider.

TABLE 8.1 Engagement with the drug service following referral by the police.

	Adults	*Children*	*Total*	*%*
Cases referred	46	9	55	100
Initial contact successfully made	46	9	55	100
Refused to engage	28	2	30	55
Number indicating they would engage with treatment	18	7	25	45
Number who attended initial assessment	18	7	25	45
Number who have completed entire programme	16	7	23	42

Thirty (55%) people declined to engage when contacted. It is encouraging that all of those who indicated they would engage with the treatment attended an initial assessment. Only two of those subsequently failed to go on to complete the treatment programme. Overall, 23 out of 55 individuals (42%) completed the initial assessment followed by three additional treatment sessions. Seven out of nine children and young people (78%) completed the full programme of treatment.

The attendance rate of children and young people is particularly positive. The local Youth Offending Service are keen for this approach to continue as a result of this success. Although there is no direct evidence that any of the children and young people referred through this scheme were either vulnerable or being exploited, it is clear that the diversion scheme allows for an intervention opportunity for children with these issues by offering specialist youth support. The approach also fits with the government's Serious Violence Strategy (2018), in which police were encouraged to review their approach to prosecution and diversion in relation to tackling drug-related exploitation and misuse of drugs.

Although the vast majority of referrals were for the possession of cannabis (79%), 13 individuals were referred for a range of other drug types, and some had more than one type of controlled substance. Interestingly, the drug service provider found that the referrals have led them to identify numerous underlying reasons for drug use which they have been able to address, including domestic violence, lack of employment, and housing. If the diversion scheme identifies those who have not developed problematic drug use, it seems likely that the treatment could represent early intervention and prevention of more harmful future drug use.

Cost and efficiency

While savings are not the key driver of this initiative (the ultimate aim is to reduce the harm caused by substance misuse), there has been a welcome reduction in costs, particularly in terms of officer time. Each case in the pilot cohort was reviewed to determine the outcome for the suspect had the diversion scheme not been available in order to accurately estimate the savings shown in Table 8.2.

TABLE 8.2 Estimated savings (non-cash) as a result of the introduction of a diversion scheme versus CJS options.

	Pilot: 10/12/2018–10/03/2019		*Projected: 12 months*	
	Hours	*£*	*Hours*	*£*
Sergeant	62	2,046	248	8,184
Constable	174	4,698	696	18,792
Total	236	6,744	944	26,976

Over the period of the pilot, non-cash savings totalled an estimated £6,744. If the results of the scheme are replicated over an entire year, it is estimated the non-cash savings will amount to £26,976. Given that this pilot took place in one of the smaller LPAs, it is likely that the non-cash savings would be considerable if implemented across the force.

One of the aims of the diversion scheme was to enable officers to deal with cases of possession more expeditiously, allowing them time to target those supplying drugs in the community. There was direct evidence of this working in practice during the pilot study. During a dedicated operation, diverting one individual allowed officers to resume patrol quickly. This led to the arrest of another individual suspected to be involved in the supply of drugs. The senior officer reported:

> The unit stopped some vehicles, two of which were carrying possession levels of drugs, one class B and one class A. The one carrying Class B was eligible for diversion, so was dealt with by the units at the roadside.... This took about ten minutes, with no long trip to custody. It meant they were then ready to deploy straight away. The other male [stopped after officers resumed], was arrested concerned in supply.

Recidivism

There are numerous reasons why an intervention may appear to have an impact on the dependent variable (in this case recidivism) but where this appearance does not actually hold true (Bayens and Roberson 2010). Many of these are relevant to the findings discussed here and they should be borne in mind when considering them. To begin with, the sample of individuals that we are able to examine with regard to the West Berkshire DDP is small. The reason for this is that the scheme is less than two years old and a limited number of individuals have been subject to the interventions. This means that the 'statistical power' confirming the effect of these interventions is low (Cook and Campbell 1979). Second, there are many variables that cannot be standardised, which in turn means that they may influence the rates of recidivism (King and Wincup 2008). These will include offending history, social, economic, and ethnic background, and other environmental factors. Third, the direct comparison of 'traditional criminal justice interventions' forms a heterogeneous group of mediations that could further be broken down into separate independent variables. There is, for example, a significant difference between a cannabis warning and a court appearance involving a drug rehabilitation order. Fourth, the type of drug for which the individual is referred may in itself affect reoffending. Finally, the study is not an RCT. Consequently, the environmental factors may be amplified due to changes that have taken place over time when comparing either the control cohort from the previous year or Home Office data on recidivism.

In this evaluation, 'reoffending' is taken to mean an individual committing an offence in a one-year period following a proven offence that leads to a court conviction, caution, reprimand, or warning. Offenders who commit multiple offences are counted only once. Only those offences that are recorded on the Police National Computer are included. This definition is one used in the government statistical database for recidivism. The latest figures from this database show reoffending rates for a drugs index offence for adults in the period October–December 2018 at 25.6% (Ministry of Justice 2020).

Out of the entire cohort of people who engaged in the programme, none reoffended in the 12-month period following the intervention. Out of those 18 individuals, 8 had offended previously, when compared to 5 who had not, from those who did not attend the diversion programme. This is important as those attending the course could be seen to be self-selecting. In other words, people may be more likely to adhere to a given direction who may not have reoffended in any case when subject to a traditional criminal justice outcome. The low numbers of people attending the intervention means that no meaningful statistical analysis can be completed on them alone. Moreover, they should not be taken in separation to the individuals who were referred but did not attend. The reason for this is that if 'traditional criminal justice outcomes' are more successful at deterring reoffending than those who are referred but do not attend, then the pilot, as a whole, may not offer lower rates of recidivism.

Considering this, of the 46 adults who were referred, a total of 4 reoffended: translating into an 8.7% reoffending rate. If our starting premise or null hypothesis is that the drug diversion intervention offers no difference to 'traditional criminal justice' interventions, then this, when compared to the reoffending rate of 25.6% for adults in the general population, translates into a p-value of less than 0.01. In other words, if our starting premise is true then we would expect to see these results less than 1% of the time. As time elapses, the number of individuals who have been diverted will allow for further analysis and to strengthen the statistical power of the data.

In the first three months of the pilot, a total of nine children were referred. Out of those, seven attended the intervention programme. The low number of those referred does not allow for a meaningful statistical analysis to be carried out.

The Windsor and Maidenhead pilot

The senior management team within TVP expressed concern at the relatively low levels of attendance to the drug service provider when compared to deferred prosecution schemes in place in Avon and Somerset, Durham, and the West Midlands. For this reason, a second pilot was put in place that constitutes a deferred prosecution scheme, similar in nature to Checkpoint and the DEP.

As discussed above, any deferred prosecution scheme must involve the credible threat of a penalty being imposed if the conditions set are not met. This necessitates that an investigation is completed that will withstand scrutiny in court if challenged by a suspect. Failure to do so would result in the credibility of the scheme failing and any conditions set being potentially viewed as voluntary by suspects if they became aware that the penalty or prosecution is not credible. It was accepted that this is resource intensive and thus the use of body-worn video for the purpose of interviewing was endorsed by the chief constable to reduce the investigative burden on officers. This was introduced first in the Windsor and Maidenhead LPA on 13 January 2021, and later across the whole of TVP.

The deferred penalty adopted was that used successfully by Avon and Somerset Constabulary: a summons to court in the absence of engagement with the intervention programme. The risk with this scheme is the premature criminalisation of offenders. It is plausible that an individual found with cannabis under this scheme would be referred to a drug service provider and with non-attendance, they would then be summoned to court for the offence of possession of cannabis. This could result in 'net-widening' (Cohen 1985) with a conviction for first time possession of cannabis, where current criminal justice outcomes would entail a non-recordable cannabis warning. It may, however, also result in the court either sending the case back to the police as unsuitable or not enforcing any penalty. Thus, in conjunction with this programme, engagement with the judiciary took place prior to its implementation.

The process of implementation of the Windsor and Maidenhead LPA pilot was akin to that of the West Berkshire model, aside from the evidence collection and construction of files required to summon an individual to court in the absence of engagement with the intervention programme. In line with the West Berkshire pilot, there is no requirement for an admission from an individual for them to be eligible for a referral and all drug-type possession offences can be considered. In contrast to West Berkshire, the individual is eligible for as many referrals as times they are found in possession of drugs irrespective of whether they have engaged with previous referrals. The rationale behind this is that if a person has been referred previously but not engaged, they have already been punished with a summons to court and potentially received a mandatory referral through the court. Thus, in contrast to the voluntary referral there is no further incentive required for an individual to attend. Furthermore, there is no reason to limit the intervention point to one chance. Preliminary findings show that out of a cohort of 40, over 80% have engaged in the diversion programme. However, the engagement is less onerous when compared to the West Berkshire pilot, as due to COVID-19 restrictions the interventions have taken place online rather than in person.

Conclusion

The last decade has seen policy shift in relation to those found in possession of drugs by the police, while remaining within the twin pillars of enforcement and treatment that have characterised the 'British system'. This has seen a greater emphasis being placed on the treatment of addiction. The most recent policy changes have seen the police themselves take a lead and five separate trials have taken place in different regions of England and Wales. The first three to be implemented are deferred prosecution schemes and were trialled by Avon and Somerset, Durham, and West Midlands constabularies. The fourth (one of two approaches trialled by TVP) was trialled in the West Berkshire LPA and, in contrast, utilises a nationally accepted criminal justice disposal, that of the community resolution. In so doing, it makes the process of referral voluntary with a view to increasing the efficacy of the intervention. Under the West Berkshire pilot, being found in possession of drugs for personal consumption and being subject to a referral does not constitute a criminal record, avoiding the damage of the stigmatisation associated with having a criminal record and the ethical reservations that are present with coercing individuals into drug rehabilitation. The model allows for officer discretion to be maintained, ensuring the ability to safeguard and to prosecute more serious offences. It also offers the potential of some non-cash savings in terms of officer time. Significantly, an admission to possession is not required by the suspect, potentially allowing increased participation by some ethnic minorities when compared to deferred prosecution models. Finally, in line with evidence around cycles of addiction, multiple referrals can take place.

The second pilot within TVP was introduced to address growing unease concerning a relatively low level of voluntary adherence to referral into the Drug Intervention Programme by the senior management team. It follows a path well trodden by the other deferred prosecution schemes allowing, however, for multiple referrals and not requiring an admission of guilt for a referral to take place.

The appetite for these diversionary programmes has been seen in, and driven forward independently by, four separate police forces. Furthermore, much interest has been expressed by other forces in England and Wales and farther afield in adopting versions of these diversion schemes. These changes and curiosity in an alternative approach have come amid record levels of illicit drug use, dependency, and drug-related deaths. As has been demonstrated above, each of the different approaches has strengths and weakness. Irrespective of which model(s) of diversion is preferred and continues in a long-term function, the direction of travel towards treating illicit drug use and addiction as a public health issue appears to be gathering momentum. This is evident across different organisational levels, with the instigation of the TVP pilots seen to be set in motion by individual officers, embraced by TVP as an organisation, and given acquiescence to do so by the Ministry of Justice and parliamentary bodies. All of this has taken place with a strong desire to identify policies that 'work' and with the pilots subject to evaluation. Given the strength of past and present research showing the effectiveness of treating drug misuse through behavioural strategies, this trend is likely to continue.

References

ACPO. (2009) *ACPO Guidance on Cannabis Possession for Personal Use*. London: Association of Chief Police Officers.

Ashworth, A. (2010) *Sentencing and Criminal Justice*. Cambridge: Cambridge University Press.

Bacon, M. (2022) 'Desistance from criminalisation: Police culture and new directions in drugs policing'. *Policing and Society*. 32(4): 522–539.

Barnes, D. (1988) 'Breaking the cycle of addiction'. *Science*. 241(4869): 1029–1031.

Bayens, G. and Roberson, C. (2010) *Criminal Justice Research Methods: Theory and Practice*. Boca Raton, FL: CRC Press.

Berridge, V. (2013) *Demons: Our Changing Attitudes to Alcohol, Tobacco and Drugs*. Oxford: Oxford University Press.

Braga, A., Weisburd, D. and Turchan, B. (2018) 'Focused deterrence strategies and crime control: An updated systematic review and meta-analysis of the empirical evidence'. *Criminology and Public Policy*. 17(1): 205–250.

Buchanan, J. (2006) 'Understanding problematic drug use: A medical matter or a social issue'. *British Journal of Community Justice*. 4(2): 387–397.

Buchanan, J. and Young, L. (2000) 'The war on drugs - A war on drug users'. *Drugs: Education, Prevention and Policy*. 7(4): 409–422.

Bullock, K. and Tilley, N. (2009) 'Evidence-based policing and crime reduction'. *Policing: A Journal of Policy and Practice*. 3(4): 381–387.

Camerion, T., Wolfe, J. and Hyshka, E. (2012) 'Consent and coercion in addiction treatment'. In Carter, A., Hall, W. and Illes, J. (eds.) *Addiction Neuroethics: The Ethics of Addiction Neuroscience Research and Treatment*. London: Academic Press: 153–174.

Cohen, S. (1985) *Visions of Social Control*. Cambridge: Polity Press.

College of Policing. (2021) *Possible Justice Outcomes Following Investigation*. https://www.app.college.police.uk/app-content/prosecution-and-case-management/justice-outcomes/?highlight=drugs?s=drugs.

Collison, M. (1993) 'Punishing drugs: Criminal justice and drug use'. *British Journal of Criminology*. 33(3): 382–399.

Cook, T. and Campbell, D. (1979) *Quasi-Experimentation: Design and Analysis Issues for Field Settings*. Chicago, IL: Rand McNally.

Dawson, P. and Williams, E. (2009) 'Reflections from a police research unit - An inside job'. *Policing: A Journal of Policy and Practice*. 3(4): 373–380.

EMCDDA. (2020) *European Drug Report: Trends and Developments*. Lisbon: European Monitoring Centre for Drugs and Drug Addiction.

Greene, J. (2014) 'New directions in policing: Balancing prediction and meaning in police research'. *Justice Quarterly*. 31(2): 193–228.

Greenwald, G. (2009) *Drug Decriminalisation in Portugal*. Washington, DC: Cato Institute.

Health and Social Care Committee. (2019) *Drugs Policy*. London: House of Commons.

Heather, N. (2006) *A Summary of the Review of the Effectiveness of Treatment for Alcohol Problems*. London: National Treatment Agency for Substance Misuse.

Heaton, R. and Tong, S. (2016) 'Evidence-based policing: From effectiveness to cost-effectiveness'. *Policing: A Journal of Policy and Practice*. 10(1): 60–70.

Herman, A. and Sofuoglu, M. (2010) 'Comparison of available treatments for tobacco addiction'. *Current Psychiatry Reports*. 12(5): 433–440.

HM Government. (2018) *Serious Violence Strategy*. London: Home Office.

Hogg, R. (2017) *Towards Safer Drug Policy*. Durham, NC: Office of the Durham Police, Crime and Victims' Commissioner.

Home Office. (2007) *DIP - Operational Process FAQs*. London: Home Office.

Home Office. (2010) *Operational Process Guidance for Implementation of Testing on Arrest, Required Assessment and Restriction on Bail*. London: Home Office.

Home Office. (2011) *Drug Interventions Programme (DIP): Introducing Locally Funded Drug Testing on Arrest (and Associated Interventions*. London: Home Office.

Husak, D. and De Marneffe, P. (2005) *The Legalization of Drugs*. Cambridge: Cambridge University Press.

Jamieson, D. (2018) *Reducing Crime and Preventing Harm: West Midlands Drug Policy Recommendations*. Birmingham: Office of the West Midlands Police and Crime Commissioner.

King, R. and Wincup, E. (2008) *Doing Research on Crime and Justice*. Oxford: Oxford University Press.

Klag, S., O'Callaghan, F. and Creed, P. (2005) 'The use of legal coercion in the treatment of substance abusers: An overview and critical analysis of thirty years of research'. *Substance Use and Misuse*. 40(12): 1777–1795.

Korf, D. (2002) 'Dutch coffee shops and trends in cannabis use'. *Addictive Behaviors*. 27(6): 851–866.

Lammy, D. (2017) *The Lammy Review: An Independent Review into the Treatment of, and Outcomes for, Black, Asian, and Minority Ethnic Individuals in the Criminal Justice System*. London: HM Government.

Lindquist-Grantz, R., Mallow, P., Dean, L., Lydenberg, M. and Chubinski, J. (2021) 'Diversion programs for individuals who use substances: A review of the literature'. *Journal of Drug Issues*. 51(3): 483–503.

Lloyd, C. (2008) *The Cannabis Classification Debate in the UK: Full of Sound and Fury, Signifying Nothing*. Paper presented to the second annual conference of the International Society for the Study of Drug Policy ISDDP.

Loader, I. and Sparks, R. (2002) 'Contemporary landscapes of crime, order, and control: Governance, risk, and globalization'. In Maguire, M., Morgan, R. and Reiner, R. (eds.) *Oxford Handbook of Criminology*. 3rd edn. Oxford: Oxford University Press: 83–111.

Luckwell, J. (2017) *Drug Education Programme Pilot: Evaluation Report*. Bristol: Avon and Somerset Constabulary.

May, T., Duffy, M., Turnbull, P. and Hough, M. (2002) *The Policing of Cannabis as a Class B Drug*. York: Joseph Rowntree Foundation.

May, T., Duffy, M., Warburton, H. and Hough, M. (2007) *Policing Cannabis as a Class C Drug: An Arresting Change*. York: Joseph Rowntree Foundation.

McSweeney, T., Stevens, A., Hunt, N. and Turnbull, P. (2007) 'Twisting arms or a helping hand? Assessing the impact of "coerced" and comparable "voluntary" drug treatment options'. *British Journal of Criminology*. 47(3): 470–490.

Mills, J. (2008) *Cannabis Nation: Control and Consumption in Britain, 1928–2008*. Oxford: Oxford University Press.

Ministry of Justice. (2020, October 29) *Proven Reoffending Statistics Quarterly Bulletin, October 2018 to December 2018*. London: Ministry of Justice.

Mold, A. (2018) 'Framing drugs and alcohol use as a public health problem in Britain: Past and present'. *Nordic Studies on Alcohol and Drugs*. 35(2): 93–99.

Monaghan, G. and White, A. (1998) *A Guide to Case Disposal Options for Drug Offenders*. London: ACPO.

Morgan, N. (2014) *The Heroin Epidemic of the 1980s and 1990s and Its Effect on Crime Trends - Then and Now* (Research Report 79). London: Home Office.

Neyroud, P. (2009) 'Squaring the circles: Research, evidence, policymaking, and police improvement in England and Wales'. *Police Practice and Research*. 10(5–6): 437–449.

Neyroud, P. (2018) *Out of Court Disposals Managed by the Police: A Review of the Evidence*. London: NPCC.

Neyroud, P. and Slothower, M. (2013) *Operation Turning Point: Interim Report*. Cambridge: Institute of Criminology.

Neyroud, P. and Slothower, M. (2015) 'Wielding the Sword of Damocles: The challenges and opportunities in reforming police out-of-court disposals in England and Wales'. In Wasik, M. and Santatzoglou, S. (eds.) *The Management of Change of Criminal Justice: Who Knows Best?* Basingstoke: Palgrave MacMillan: 275–293.

Neyroud, P., Slothower, M., Sherman, L., Ariel, B. and Neyroud, E. (2017) *Operation Turning Point*. Available from: https://whatworks.college.police.uk/Research/Research-Map/Pages/ResearchProject.aspx?projectid=307.

Neyroud, P. and Weisburd, D. (2014) *Transforming the Police Through Science: Some New Thoughts on the Controversy and Challenge of Translation*. Washington, DC: George Mason University.

NHS. (2017) *Statistics on Drug Misuse: England, 2017*. Retrieved from National Archives: https://webarchive.nationalarchives.gov.uk/20180328135520/http://digital.nhs.uk/catalogue/PUB23442.

NPCC. (2017) *Charging and out of Court Disposals: A National Strategy*. London: National Police Chiefs' Council.

ONS. (2018) *Deaths Related to Drug Poisoning in England and Wales: 2017 Registrations*. London: Office for National Statistics.

ONS. (2020) *Drug Misuse in England and Wales – Appendix Table*. London: Office for National Statistics.

Pearson, G. (1991) 'Drug-control polices in Britain'. *Crime and Justice*. 14: 167–228.

Police Foundation. (2000) *Drugs and the Law: Report of the Independent Inquiry into the Misuse of Drugs Act 1971*. London: The Police Foundation.

Raynor, P. (2002) 'Community penalties: Probation, punishments and "what works"'. In Maguire, M., Morgan, R. and Reiner, R. (eds.) *The Oxford Handbook of Criminology*. 3rd edn. Oxford: Oxford University Press: 1168–1206.

Reuter, P. and Stevens, A. (2008) 'Assessing UK drug policy from a crime control perspective'. *Criminology and Criminal Justice*. 8(4): 461–482.

Seddon, T. (2010) *A History of Drugs: Drugs and Freedom in the Liberal Age*. Abingdon: Routledge.

See, R., Fuchs, R., Ledford, C. and McLaughlin, J. (2003) 'Drug addiction, relapse, and the amygdala'. *Annals of the New York Academy of Sciences*. 985(1): 294–307.

Serpa, S. and Ferreira, C. (2019) 'Micro, meso and macro levels of social analysis'. *International Journal of Social Science Studies*. 7(3): 120–124.

Sher, G. (2010) 'On the decriminalization of drugs'. *Criminal Justice Ethics*. 22(1): 30–33.

Shiner, M. (2015) 'Drug policy reform and the reclassification of cannabis in England and Wales: A cautionary tale'. *International Journal of Drug Policy*. 26(7): 696–704.

Sosa, K. (2012) *Proceed with Caution: Use of Out-of-Court Disposals in England & Wales*. London: Policy Exchange.

Spyt, W., Barnham, L. and Kew, J. (2019) 'Diversion: Going soft on drugs?' *Thames Valley Police Journal*. 4: 44–58.

Stevens, A., Berto, D., Heckmann, W., Kerschl, V., Oeuvray, K. and Ooyen, M. (2005) 'Quasi-compulsory treatment of drug dependent offenders: An international literature review'. *Substance Use and Misuse*. 40(3): 269–283.

Stevens, A. (2012) 'The ethics and effectiveness of coerced treatment of people who use drugs'. *Human Rights and Drugs*. 2(1): 7–16.

Stevens, A., Hughes, C., Hulme, S. and Cassidy, R. (2022) 'Depenalization, diversion and decriminalization: A realist review and programme theory of alternatives to criminalization for simple drug possession'. *European Journal of Criminology*. 19(1): 29–54.

Van Dijk, J. (1998) 'The narrow margins of the Dutch drug policy: A cost-benefit analysis'. *European Journal on Criminal Policy and Research*. 6(3): 369–393.

Ward, J. (2013) 'Punishing drug possession in the magistrates' courts: Time for a rethink.' *European Journal on Criminal Policy and Research*. 19(4): 289–307.

Weddington, W. (1991) 'Towards a rehabilitation of methadone maintenance: Integration of relapse prevention and aftercare'. *International Journal of the Addictions*. 25(9): 1201–1224.

Weir, K., Kilili, S., Cooper, J., Crowe, A. and Routledge, G. (2021a) 'Checkpoint: An innovative programme to navigate people away from the cycle of reoffending – A randomised control trial evaluation. *The Police Journal: Theory, Practice and Principles*. https://doi.org/10.1177/0032258X211018774.

Weir, K., Routledge, G. and Kilili, S. (2021b) 'Checkpoint: An innovative programme to navigate people away from the cycle of reoffending: Implementation phase evaluation'. *Policing: A Journal of Policy and Practice*. 15(1): 508–527.

Woods, N. (2016) *Good Cop, Bad War*. London: Ebury Press.

9

'ANOTHER TOOL IN THE TOOLBOX'

An investigation of a drug diversion programme in a Danish police precinct

Tobias Kammersgaard, Esben Houborg, Thomas Friis Søgaard, and Sidsel Schrøder

Introduction

In most parts of the world today, the policy response to drug use is still based on prohibition, criminalisation, and punishment. However, in recent years some governments and authorities with jurisdiction in the field of drug control have started to question the effectiveness of this approach and are changing their policies in new directions. In this regard, commentators have argued that we are seeing an end to the 'war on drugs' era (Collins 2018). The most notable example of this is perhaps the nationwide decriminalisation of drug possession for personal consumption introduced in Portugal in 2001. However, in addition to such decriminalisation at the national level, governments and local authorities worldwide are increasingly operating with various forms of de facto decriminalisation, where drug possession is still prohibited on the national level, but without this prohibition being fully enforced locally. In accordance with this, Eastwood et al. (2016) found that more than 25 countries had introduced some form of loosening or removal of criminal penalties, encompassing what has been called a 'quiet revolution' in the field of drug policy (see also Bacon 2022).

An example of this is so-called 'diversion programmes'. These operate within a framework of prohibition but aim to divert drug users away from the criminal justice system and towards treatment and/or social services. Diversion programmes have been attempted in Australia, England, the Netherlands, and the United States (Spyt et al. 2019; Stevens et al. 2022). The specific aims and backgrounds of these programmes vary, but they are often motivated by a desire to reduce criminal justice expenditures and time connected to low-level drug offences, as well as a desire to reduce the harmful effects of criminal proceedings and criminal sanctions on individuals and provide opportunities to address problematic drug use and other criminal offending (Goetz and Mitchell 2006).

DOI: 10.4324/9781003154136-10

Furthermore, some of the programmes are explicitly guided by harm reduction principles, such as the Law Enforcement Assisted Diversion (LEAD) programmes in the United States (Beckett 2016), where the goal is to reduce the harms associated with drug use, without necessarily aiming to reduce drug use itself. According to Stevens et al. (2022), the culture and the priorities of the police are an important factor in the implementation of diversion programmes. In this regard, since 1999 all Australian states and territories have adopted various diversion schemes with broad support from police services (Hughes and Ritter 2008), while in the United States, the police have been more sceptical of this approach. In both Seattle and Albany, findings have pointed to how some officers were reluctant to use diversion instead of criminal sanctions, because they believed that this would enable addiction (Collins et al. 2015; Worden and McLean 2018).

While 'diversion' has usually been taken to refer to the act of diverting drug users *away* from the criminal justice system and towards treatment and social services, recently it has been noted that the term is also being used to refer to programmes that introduce various interventions, such as a referral to treatment at the point of contact with the police, but without this operating as an *alternative* to criminal sanctions. In their recent exploration of diversion policy and practice in Scotland, Price et al. (2021) found that, unlike the previously described programmes in other countries, Scottish diversions tended to embed treatment and social service referrals *within* the criminal justice system rather than these acting as alternatives. This broader understanding of 'diversion' encompasses 'any and all interventions that provide a route to "drug treatment" from within the criminal justice system […] the question of whether diversion moved people out of formal criminal sanctions (or not) was unimportant' (p. 121). According to Price et al., this was due to how the relationship between the police and the prosecution in Scotland requires police officers to report all offences to Scotland's Crown Office and Procurator Fiscal Service, who then have the jurisdiction to determine who will be prosecuted or not. Furthermore, Price et al. explain how this is different from the rest of the United Kingdom, and in particular from England and Wales, where officers can use discretionary police diversion schemes to divert people away from prosecution (Spyt et al. 2019; Spyt and Kew, this volume). Thus, while the term 'diversion' seems to suggest a *shift* away from criminal justice sanctions to treatment and social services, it is not always the case, as the Scottish example illustrates, and the term is also used to denote programmes where treatment interventions function more as an 'add-on' to criminal sanctions. Furthermore, the Scottish example illustrates that the overall legal framework of a country sets the parameters of how local diversion programmes can operate.

The national drug policy in Denmark, which is the focus of this chapter, is based on a zero-tolerance strategy, and the police are by law obligated to fine any person caught in possession of even small amounts of illicit drugs, except in cases where a person is identified to be both socially disadvantaged and dependent on drugs (Houborg et al. 2020). In most Danish police precincts, this has led to a situation where individuals let off with a warning are typically marginalised adults in possession of so-called 'hard' drugs, while young people in possession of cannabis are fined by default (Houborg and Pedersen 2013). In this chapter, we describe how this national policy and legal context shape the way police-led diversion aimed at young drug users unfolds in Denmark. More specifically, the chapter describes the first known diversion programme in Denmark, initiated by a local police precinct in the Copenhagen area. The police did not use the term 'diversion' to describe the project, perhaps because of language differences, as this word is not easily translated or understood in Danish. However, given the title of the project, we believe that it can be meaningfully understood as similar to 'diversion projects' in other countries, even though it did not aim to replace criminal sanctions with treatment, but rather saw treatment as an 'add-on'. The programme focused on young drug users encountered by the police in public spaces in possession of drugs and was officially named: 'From searching pockets to treatment'. At first glance, the title of the diversion programme could be interpreted to suggest a *replacement* of criminal justice measures with drug treatment. However, in this chapter we describe how police attempts to formulate a drug diversion programme, under the condition of a zero-tolerance policy framework, have led to the emergence of a hybrid governmental complex, where traditional criminal justice measures (stop and search and fines) are combined with treatment referrals, in the hope that the latter would lead young people to stop using drugs, which in turn would reduce the 'need' for future police 'pocket searches'.

The chapter is based on interviews with 20 police officers and a focus group of 9 officers. We use these interviews to explore the officers' attitudes towards the project, their diversion practices, as well as the conceptions of the 'problem' of youth drug use underpinning the police-led diversion project.

Continuity and change in responses to illicit drugs

Developments towards decriminalisation in international drug policy are indicative of how responses to the use of illicit drugs seem to be undergoing significant *changes* (Eastwood et al. 2016). However, critics have argued that even seemingly progressive decriminalisation reforms, such as the Portuguese one, are based on an understanding of drug use as a harmful and deviant activity, and thus also display *continuity* in the response and thinking about illicit drugs. In this regard, Walmsley (2019) has argued that decriminalisation responses do not necessarily break markedly with previous understandings and discourses associated with criminalisation and prohibition, as decriminalisation responses might still operate with a goal of reducing or preventing the use of drugs altogether, foreground the harms of illicit drugs, and neglect understandings of illicit drugs as potentially pleasurable and positive for those who use them (Duff 2008; O'Malley and Valverde 2004).

Similarly, while diversion programmes can be said to represent a move away from a criminal justice approach towards a treatment approach to drugs, various studies have also pointed to potential problems with the idea of drug treatment. One study that has critically assessed this is Bartoszko's (2019) exploration of the transfer of responsibility for treatment of opioid dependence from the social services to specialised health care in Norway. The aim of this was to afford drug users patient rights and facilitate a 'patient identity' in place of the former 'social client and/or criminal identity'. However, Bartoszko's findings indicate that some found the label 'patient' problematic, as they did not necessarily regard their drug use as an illness. Consequently, Bartoszko argues that while policy initiatives that call for a more humane drug policy and decriminalisation might 'promote human dignity and agency, they also encourage a particular approach to drug use and addiction' (p. 142). This is what she calls the 'medical approach' where drug users are regarded as sick and as 'patients' to be treated, rather than 'criminals' and 'social clients'.

This medical approach to drug use can be linked with the concept of 'treatmentality' introduced by Jöhncke (2009), to illustrate how drug use treatment is envisioned as one of the most essential parts of society's responses to drug use. Jöhncke argues that treatment is often positioned as the modern, enlightened, and humane alternative to criminal punishment in discourses around responses to illicit drug use. Thus, drug treatment is constituted as an indispensable institution in the political and cultural imagination of the welfare state and is envisioned as 'pure, rational and humane, based on scientific insights and clinical experience' (p. 14). Nevertheless, it can be problematic that treatment is often taken for granted as the 'obvious' answer to drug use, as Jöhncke argues, because this might result in negligence in understandings of drug use as potentially not warranting treatment at all. This has likewise been explored in now classic studies, which describe how people who use drugs may reject conventional morality and may not regard their use as problematic and warranting of treatment (see e.g. Becker 1963; Young 1971).

In order to assess and discuss the diversion project that we investigate in this chapter, we draw upon the above-mentioned studies in order to reflect on how and to what extent the project represents a reorientation in contemporary drug policing, both in terms of the project's conceptual logics and understandings of illicit drugs and in the practical interventions towards drug users. We illustrate how the project continued to operate with a 'use reduction' logic, where the ultimate goal was considered to be to dissuade young people from using drugs altogether, rather than to minimise drug-related harm. Furthermore, we illustrate how the overall project largely operated within a 'treatmentality' logic, where drug treatment was taken as the obvious and natural response to youth drug use, even though some officers contested whether all of the young people they encountered in possession of cannabis were in need of drug treatment.

Background and methods

In 2003, the Danish government presented a white paper called 'The Fight Against Drugs', which signalled a radical change in Danish drug control policy away from a policy that since 1969 had decriminalised the possession of illicit drugs for personal use to one where all possession of illicit drugs would be punished by at least a fine (Houborg et al. 2008). 'The Fight against Drugs' in Denmark clearly echoed the 'war on drugs' in the United States (Houborg and Pedersen 2013), and, couched in the rhetoric of 'zero tolerance', 'deterrence', and 'respect for the law', the new policy marked the beginning of a new tough on drugs approach (Frank 2008). A quintessential idea of the new drug policy was that increased punishment and policing would deter young people from using drugs (Houborg et al. 2020). In 2007, the new policy led to an increase in the minimum fine for the possession of illicit drugs from EUR67 to EUR269 (Houborg 2010), and from 2007 onwards it also led to a remarkable quantitative increase in police enforcement intensity of the Law on Euphoria-Inducing Substances (LES) used to sanction the possession of smaller amounts of drugs. Across the different police districts in Denmark, the average increase in reported LES offences rose by 42% from 2007 to 2017, with some police districts registering increases of 122% and 127% (Moeller 2020). Today, possession of smaller amounts of illicit drugs for personal consumption are usually settled with a fine, while cases of possession of larger amounts with intention to distribute usually result in a custodial sentence. Whether possession of illicit drugs can be characterised as for personal consumption depends on a concrete assessment by the police and the court, based on the amount possessed and/or possession of paraphernalia used for selling drugs (e.g. scales and small plastic bags). Cases of possession of illicit drugs can figure on the offenders' criminal record for up to five years.

While the national drug policy still rests on a punitive zero-tolerance approach, especially when it comes to young people's use of drugs (Houborg et al. 2020), some local police departments have recently started to question the effectiveness of traditional law enforcement methods. While not necessarily questioning the end goal of the zero-tolerance approach (youth abstinence from drug use), some street-level officers and local police managers have become increasingly frustrated by the fact that drug-using young people were sometimes repeatedly fined without this seemingly having any effect on their drug use habits. Against this background, in 2019 a police department operating in the western part of the Copenhagen metropolitan area initiated a pilot diversion project. The aim of the project was to refer young people (under 18) caught in possession of illicit drugs by the police to local drug treatment centres or other services that could assist the young people in ceasing or managing their drug use. The diversion project mostly focused on cannabis, as this was the drug most used by the young people encountered by the police. This goal was to be achieved through training local community police officers in issues around drug pharmacology, drug use and misuse, drug treatment, and motivational interviewing. Furthermore, the project aimed to familiarise police officers with the operations of relevant drug treatment services in their local area in order for them to inform and possibly refer young people to these services. To achieve this, 25 police employees participated in a three-day course organised by a local drug treatment centre and

14 police employees participated in an additional one-day course. Additionally, implementation workshops with local drug treatment centres were carried out in eight municipalities in order to introduce local treatment services and the police to each other and support cooperation between the two organisations.

Unlike some diversion programmes, the pilot project did not aim to make officers refrain from taking legal action by issuing a fine or confiscating illicit drugs if they found someone from the target group in possession. Nevertheless, while Danish police officers are formally required to react to all cases of drug possession, they might in practice decide not to act on their suspicion and refrain from searching someone, even though they might have reason to believe that person to be in possession of illicit drugs. Or they might decide not to charge someone they find in possession, and only give them an informal warning, even though this might constitute a breach of protocol (Holmberg 2000; Houborg et al. 2016). In that regard, the diversion project did seem to legitimise an approach where some officers used their discretion to refrain from charging for possession, as we show later in the chapter.

All the officers who participated in the pilot diversion project had a community-oriented policing role, meaning that they patrolled in a designated area in order to build relationships with the residents, engaged in various partnerships with community representatives, and generally engaged in broader policing functions than law enforcement (Cordner 2014). A central part of the officers' everyday activities was to engage with the local youth in the neighbourhood. In this regard, one of their main concerns was with young people hanging out in public places and causing distress and nuisance for other residents in the neighbourhood and sometimes also engaging in drug use and/or drug dealing. The diversion project was thus seen as a way to introduce the officers to new tools for working with this specific group.

Our research group was asked to evaluate this pilot project. The evaluation was intended to investigate to what extent the police referred the young people to drug treatment services, to what extent the young people started treatment, and how the police and the young people experienced the project, as well as the possible organisational and practical challenges connected to the project. Later in the process, it became apparent that the evaluation would not be able to address the question of the extent to which the officers referred the young people to treatment and the extent to which the young people started treatment, since there were very few registrations of this by the police and the treatment centres.

Consequently, the evaluation was primarily based on a survey (n = 37), qualitative interviews (n = 20), and a focus group with 9 police officers who were among the 20 with whom qualitative interviews were conducted. A short survey was completed by 23 officers participating in the three-day course and 14 officers participating in the one-day course. The survey involved questions about their knowledge, experiences, and attitudes towards young people and the use of illicit drugs. The interviews concerned the police background of the interviewees, their experiences with young people and illicit drugs, as well as their collaboration with drug treatment and other social services. Furthermore, the interviews concerned their thoughts on the course they had received about young people and drugs, as well as their assessment of the course, whether and how they had used the knowledge they had obtained, and whether they had recommendations about how to improve the training course. In addition, interviews were also conducted with the two organisers of the project. These interviews concerned the visions and ideas behind the project, the implementation of the project, organisational challenges, collaboration with the drug treatment and social services, and how best to support the officers in using the knowledge and methods from the training they had received. Interviews were transcribed and coded in regard to relevant themes.

In the following section, we first present the findings on how the officers perceived the diversion project, their attitudes towards drug law enforcement, and their reflections on the relevance of drug treatment for young people. Second, we discuss how the drug diversion project represents both change and continuity in the policing response to illicit drugs.

Findings

Motivation for the project and survey results

The diversion project was overseen by two coordinators from the crime prevention section of the police department, a police officer and a civilian, both of equal rank to the officers implementing the project. According to one of the two coordinators of the diversion project, reducing local youth's use and selling of drugs had for a long time been a key focus of the police. The hope was that the diversion project could provide new tools to help the police achieve this goal:

> The project has its origins in the general focus on fear-inducing drug dealing in the precinct [...] The local police typically identify the areas where there are problems with drug dealing and other forms of crime, such as noise and riding around on motor scooters. In this project we seek to address these problems with some alternative methods.
>
> *(Coordinator, female)*

As the coordinator suggests, the issue of drug using and selling was connected to wider issues of noisy, boisterous, and fear-inducing behaviour by young people. According to the coordinator, the officers had never received much training about illicit drugs and their use:

> They haven't been trained in this [...] like, what are drugs, why do people use them, how do they affect the brain, and what is drug treatment [...] all that was totally new to them. Even though one of their main tasks is to police drug dealing and they use much of their time on young people selling

> drugs. Also, a lot of the community work with young people concerns issues of illicit drugs. It is a great focus area, but without much knowledge.
> *(Coordinator, female)*

The fact that drugs play a significant role in encounters between officers and the local youth was confirmed by the survey conducted before the officers had received training in how to perform drug diversion.[1] A total of 37 officers answered the survey. The results show that the overwhelming majority of the officers encountered young people in possession of illicit drugs on a regular basis, with 94% of the officers indicating that they 'often' or 'sometimes' came into contact with young people in possession of cannabis. The survey also illustrates how drug law enforcement was something that the officers engaged in regularly. According to the survey, 78% of the officers reported that they, as part of their daily work, engaged in drug law enforcement to a 'great extent' or to 'some extent'.

Nevertheless, while young people's use of cannabis was an issue that took up much of the officers' time, many of the participating officers questioned or were uncertain about whether the police force was the right authority to handle this issue. In that regard, the survey results illustrate the number of officers who thought that the police only 'to some extent' (40%) or 'to a lesser extent' (30%) were the right authority to handle issues related to youth drug use. Furthermore, the survey also illustrates that the officers did not believe that they were able to markedly influence young people's use of or attitudes towards cannabis. The officers stated that they were only able to influence young people's use of and attitudes towards cannabis 'to a lesser extent' (40%) or 'not at all' (35%).

Overall, the survey results show not only that young people who use cannabis figure prominently in the everyday work of the officers, but also that a majority of the officers reported various difficulties related to working with this group. In that regard, the diversion project could be said to address two central problems with the policing of young drug users as experienced by the participating officers. Firstly, most of the officers experienced that they could not influence the young people and their drug use. The diversion project aimed to address this by training the officers and providing them with more knowledge about illicit drugs, their use, and the available drug use treatment. Secondly, most of the officers reported that they believed that they (i.e. the police) only to some extent or to a lesser extent were the right authority to handle the problem of youth drug use. The diversion project aimed to address this by furthering collaboration between the police and relevant drug treatment and social services, as this was believed to create better options for officers to refer drug-using youth to these services and ultimately dissuading young people from using drugs.

Officers' reactions and reflections on the project

In the following, we report on the results from the interviews with the officers that were conducted after they had received the training. The interviews generally pointed to how most of the officers found the course to be meaningful, appropriate, and useful. As one officer stated:

> I am extremely positively surprised by this. I think it was really good, because the most important thing when attending a course or a project is that you can use it in practice.
>
> *(Police officer, A, male)*

The practical relevance of the course was highlighted by several of the officers, which speaks to how the course addressed an issue that many of the officers wanted to learn more about. In addition, several officers also stressed how they found the overall aim and ambition of the project meaningful and how they were open to using other methods than just drug law enforcement in their interactions with young people in possession of drugs. Reflecting the overall logic of the diversion project, that getting young people into treatment could be a way to dissuade young people from using drugs and thus reduce the 'need' for future drug law enforcement by police, one officer argued that she found the project meaningful because it aimed to change the behaviour of young people by way of treatment referrals:

> I think it really makes sense. Instead of handing out fines to the same young people time after time, then we try to think a bit more about how we get the young people out of it [drug use]. So, I have been a big advocate for the project from the beginning.
>
> *(Police officer, B, female)*

Several of the officers reported that the course had aided them in their ability to converse with young people about drugs and their drug use and that it had given them a greater appreciation of how using drugs can serve various functions for those who use them. In this regard, several of the officers reported that the information they had received about youth drug use had given them a greater understanding of what (social) factors can lead to drug use. As one officer reflected:

> I have learned that it is better to focus on everything else rather than focus on the drugs. Because it [drug use] is a result of everything else [...] it is family, school, friends, self-esteem. (Police officer, B, female)

The officer here thus emphasises the importance of having a holistic approach that takes the general life situation of the young people into account when they talk with them about drug use, in order to help them to change or reflect on their behaviour. As another officer argued:

> Cannabis is a microscopic part of their overall problem. Usually it [drug use] has its origin in something.
>
> *(Police officer, E, female)*

On the other hand, several officers also highlighted how the information about the neurological properties of illicit drugs that they had received during the course was especially useful for warning young people about the dangers of illicit drugs:

> The information we have received about how drugs function and what they do to people is very useful when having conversations with the young people [...] I have talked a lot with some of the young people about cannabis, because that is a drug which is usually perceived as relatively harmless. But that is a misunderstanding that we can address now. By telling them how it affects their brain
>
> *(Police officer, D, male)*

According to the officers then, the knowledge that they had obtained about how cannabis affects the brain could be used to warn young people about the dangerous side effects of using this drug. In this regard, neurobiological knowledge could in some ways fortify beliefs about the dangers of illicit drugs. One of the officers even stated how the training had made him more 'conservative':

> The course has made me more conservative [...] regarding the use of drugs and especially cannabis. Previously people would say that they just smoked a little bit, but now I know what happens.
>
> *(Police officer, I, male)*

In that way, some forms of information that the officers received about illicit drugs might have reinforced understandings of these substances as dangerous and harmful, while other forms of information might have provided the officers with a greater and more nuanced understanding of the factors that can lead to problematic drug use.

Referring young people to drug treatment

Apart from gaining increased knowledge about illicit drugs and drug use, an important aspect of the diversion project was to refer young people to drug treatment. This referral was completely voluntary, and primarily consisted of informing young people of drug treatment options and where to find them. During the courses, the officers were introduced to drug treatment and the various services available in their local area. The officers found this to be very helpful when presenting these options to young people because young people might also be very sceptical about what drug treatment actually entails, as one officer explained:

> It is good to know a bit about it, because then you don't have to 'sell' an idea [to the young people] you don't really know anything about, other than that it is drug treatment [...] Now I can explain to the young people

that it isn't like in the American movies where they have to sit in a circle and then they have to stand up and say 'Hello, I am [a drug user]'. I think that is what a lot of them think it is.

(Police officer, G, female)

As this officer argues, having achieved detailed knowledge about what drug treatment actually entailed made it easier to 'sell' the idea of treatment to young people. This was highlighted by several of the officers as something especially helpful that they had gained from the course. One officer, for instance, explained how he had referred a young boy to the local treatment centre:

I charged four young people [with possession], one of them, a 17-year-old boy, has problematic drug use and his parents are divorced and he is having a really hard time. I took him to one side and had a conversation with him and referred him to the treatment centre [...] Afterwards I got a call from the treatment centre and they told me that he had started treatment. That was a really nice experience.

(Police officer, K, male)

The same officer explained that he had referred between 10 and 15 young people to the treatment centre and, according to him, about half of them had subsequently contacted the centre. However, most of the police officers reported having difficulties in referring the young people they met to the treatment centres. One main issue, according to several of the officers, was that the young people did not recognise themselves as misusing drugs and as being in need of treatment:

The challenge is that they will not admit that they are misusing drugs and because of this, they do not want anyone to interfere and they do not want any help.

(Police officer, A, male)

I haven't met anyone yet who felt that they needed help [with managing their drug use].

(Police officer, E, female)

Some officers also challenged the idea that the young people they met used drugs in a way that warranted drug treatment. As one argued:

I haven't met any young people where I thought: 'You have to go to a treatment centre'. Those I meet use drugs, but they do not really misuse them [...] Most of them attend school and have a normal everyday life. They just smoke a bit of cannabis [...] They are not really the target group for a drug treatment centre.

(Police officer, D, male)

Accordingly, the narrow aim of referring young people directly to treatment was reframed by some of the officers. Instead, these officers used the metaphor of 'planting a seed' to explain how their conversations with young people might prime them to reflect upon their drug use, which would perhaps lead them to seek treatment at some point. As two of the officers explained:

> I haven't succeeded in referring anyone to treatment. But perhaps at some point they will think 'Oh, what was it that the officer said that time?'. In that way, I hope that I can plant a seed.
>
> *(Police officer, G, female)*

> I tried telling one of the young people about the course we went to, and I gave him my number. I don't know if anything else will happen, but now he knows about it and then maybe at some point he will think that he want to do something about it […] So yeah, maybe planting a seed in that way.
>
> *(Police officer, C, male)*

As these officers saw it, it was a step forward if they were able to raise awareness about the availability of local treatment services. Even if the young people did not necessarily regard them as relevant at this point, if they changed their minds, they would then know where to go.

Criminal sanctions and drug law enforcement

As previously mentioned, the diversion project did not entail that the police officers should stop handing out fines for possession of drugs. Instead, the information they received about drugs, drug use, and drug treatment could be used by the officers to engage in conversation with young people and perhaps refer them to treatment, as they saw fit themselves. In accordance with the national zero-tolerance policy, some officers stressed they found it important to still fine young people for possession offences, as they still believed this to be a useful tool in making young people change their behaviour, as the following illustrates:

> Some of the good conversations happen when you have charged someone. Often when people are charged it is like a wakeup call. They maybe think 'What happened there? Now it is for real, because I have been busted by the police'.
>
> *(Group interview, participant 3)*

Aside from the fact that some officers continued to believe in the deterrent effects of fines, others also found that the use of fines served important functions in maintaining their authority:

> They [the young people] shouldn't think that you will never search them, because now you are just the 'nice cop'.
>
> *(Group interview, participant 2)*

This sentiment was also echoed by some of the officers during individual interviews. As two officers explained:

> It is another tool in the toolbox. It has not been presented like, now we can't hand out any fines and now we just have to pat them on the back.
>
> *(Police officer, H, male)*

> That's how we do it. You can hand them a fine, but you can also get them some help. It is a combination like that.
>
> *(Police officer, G, female)*

The interviews thus revealed how most officers saw the use of treatment referrals as an add-on to the continued use of traditional criminal justice measures such as stop and search and fines. However, some of the participants also mentioned how engaging in relationship building and dialogue, rather than strict drug law enforcement, was a central part of their work as community officers. In this regard, some officers stressed how they operated within a framework where a broader policing function was prioritised over strict law enforcement. As one officer explained:

> I usually don't charge them for simple possession. Not the ones always hanging out in the centre of the city. Because if I start charging them and searching them every time I see them, then they wouldn't talk to me anymore [...] So the ones I know and the ones I am trying to help to change their behaviour, those I don't charge that often.
>
> *(Police officer, E, female)*

As this officer explains, she was reluctant to search and charge the young people with whom she was attempting to establish a good relationship. This was because establishing a good relationship with the young people was seen as a more effective means for making them change their behaviour, rather than searching and charging them. Similarly, another officer highlighted how he found that the diversion project had legitimised a more lenient approach to drug possession, where he could use warnings rather than fining young people:

> It is really great that it now is okay that we can give a warning instead [...] Now that is an acceptable way to do it. To say: 'I will take your joint now' and then ask if they need help with their use. I think it makes a lot of sense for the officers that have attended this course. Because they know that giving out fines doesn't work at all. It just makes it all worse. In some cases, anyway.
>
> *(Police officer, H, male)*

It is important to note that the national legislation does not officially allow for the use of warnings in cases of young people caught in possession of cannabis. What the officer explains here is that, in his interpretation, the project had signalled that his local management tolerated that he used discretionary leniency in his dealings with young people in possession of drugs and perhaps used a warning rather than a criminal sanction in some cases (Holmberg 2000). His practice could also be characterised as reminiscent of the time before the introduction of zero tolerance in 2004, when the police would confiscate drugs from people in possession of small amounts, but not press charges against them (Houborg 2010).

Taken together, these different statements reflect different attitudes regarding whether searching and charging young people could have a negative effect on some of the relationship-building and dialogue-oriented policing that the community officers attempted to engage in. Or, whether it sometimes could be a viable tool that could signal to young people that they were doing something wrong. In this regard, several officers seemed to appreciate that the diversion project did not entail a reorientation of drug policing away from the use of criminal sanctions, but that it provided 'another tool in the toolbox'. In the same way, some also welcomed what they perceived as an opportunity to give young people a warning instead of a fine when they saw this as appropriate, and perceived the project as legitimising such a course of action as well. The statements by the police officers reflect that, in the day-to-day business of police work, even under zero-tolerance drug legislation, they use their discretion to decide whether to search young people for possession of illicit drugs.

Discussion and conclusion

Rather than representing a complete reorientation away from the criminal justice system, this diversion project is indicative of a new dual-police approach to youth drug use, entailing a combination of traditional punitive deterrence as well as treatment strategies. Under Danish legislation and without a formal exemption from the zero-tolerance policy this was the only possible way to test a diversion programme by the police precinct. Therefore, unlike some other diversion programmes internationally, this project did not aim to make the involved officers stop using criminal sanctions and use referrals instead, when they encountered someone in possession of small amounts of illicit drugs. In this regard, referral to treatment services was presented as 'another tool in the toolbox', rather than as a replacement for criminal sanctions. This is in some ways similar to how diversion is practiced and understood in Scotland, where Price et al. (2021) have argued that instead of entailing 'a binary shift from criminal justice to health [...] diversion could best be understood as a coming together of the two' (p. 123). However, as we have seen, under the overall framework of the project, police officers would still use their discretion. For some officers, the project seems to have legitimised a practice of using warnings instead of criminal sanctions. But the project as such did not represent a general reorientation away from the use of criminal sanctions and several of the officers argued for the continued relevance of criminal sanctions in countering youth drug use.

Instead, the main content of the project was to provide community police officers with new knowledge about young people, drugs, and drug treatment and create new or stronger relations between the police and the drug treatment system. The training might have given the officers a better understanding of drugs and youth drug culture, which they could use in their work with this target group. The ambition of the project was to use treatment as a means of dissuading young people from using drugs, which in effect would create a situation where it was no longer necessary for the police to search pockets and hand out fines. Consequently, the project could be said to largely operate within a 'treatmentality' logic, since treatment was taken for granted as the obvious and natural answer to youth drug use (Jöhncke 2009). This can be problematic because it might result in neglecting understanding of drug use as recreational and potentially not warranting treatment at all. Some of the officers point to this themselves in the interviews, where they question whether the young people they meet in their daily work actually use drugs to an extent and in a way that warrant them being referred to drug treatment. However, other interviewed officers argued that the biggest obstacle for the success of the project was that the young people would not *admit* that they had a problematic use of drugs.

Furthermore, some of the neurobiological information that the officers received about drugs and the brain seemed to reinforce and enhance a view of illicit drugs as harmful, dangerous, and problematic. While this knowledge about the effects of illicit drugs on the brain may be entirely accurate, it could still be argued that it disregards other understandings of illicit drugs. The potential harms of using drugs seem to have been foregrounded without leaving any room for an understanding of illicit drugs as potentially pleasurable and positive for those who use them, with the understanding of recreational drug use as a 'normal' part of youth culture being neglected. In other words, drug use was still largely pathologised and constructed as a fundamentally deviant and problematic activity (Walmsley 2019).

In addition to this, the operating principle of the diversion project could be said to remain 'use reduction', meaning that the ultimate goal of policing was referred to as getting young people *into* treatment and *out of* drugs. A commitment to 'harm reduction' rather than 'use reduction' could possibly reorient this and similar programmes in productive ways. The term 'harm reduction' has been used to designate policies aimed at reducing the harms associated with drug use, without necessarily eliminating drug use itself. The concept has traditionally been most closely associated with measures aimed at reducing health risks for drug users, such as through the establishment of safe injection sites, drug/pill testing at music festivals, and education on safer drug use practices. However, it has been argued that the principles of harm reduction could also be applied to the field of drug policing (Beckett 2016; Caulkins and Reuter 2009; Kammersgaard 2019). An ambition to reduce overall 'harm' rather than 'drug use' would also include a consideration of the substantial harms that stop and search and drug law enforcement can cause. In this regard, Harkin (2015) has pointed to how '[s]tigma, trauma, intimidation, as well as generalised feelings of insecurity can all be a consequence of police intervention on individuals' (p. 46). Following this, Flacks (2018) has argued that under-18s should be entitled to more protection from stop and search practices than adults, but also points to how questions about child protection have been overruled by crime control rationalities, and one could add, in this case also 'treatmentality' rationalities.

Regarding this diversion project, a more harm reduction-oriented strategy could more fully turn the focus away from the drugs themselves. As community police officers, a central aspect of the interviewed officers' operations was to make sure that the neighbourhoods that they patrolled were regarded as safe and pleasant by the residents and visitors. In this respect, smaller or larger groups of young people, sometimes being loud and boisterous, were the main concern of many of the officers. Consequently, the fact that these young people sometimes used cannabis did not seem like the main concern of the officers, whose main occupation could be said to be 'keeping the peace' (Bittner 1967). Thus, it may be more important to establish a good connection with young people than to stop and search them for illicit drugs and, possibly, refer them to treatment for use of drugs that they do not themselves find warrants treatment. This was also highlighted by some of the officers, who argued that they prioritised a good relationship with young people, rather than enforcing the law against drug possession, as they found this to be a more promising way of trying to manage young peoples' presence in the neighbourhood.

It is encouraging that a police precinct in Denmark has initiated a diversion project that provides 'another tool in the toolbox' and which is born out of a realisation that criminal sanctions in themselves do not work if the ambition is to reduce drug consumption among young people. However, in its current form the project does not represent a significant reorientation of Danish drug policing, as the use of criminal sanctions could not be eliminated as part of the project and thus the project did not so much offer an alternative to criminalisation, as it offered a supplement to it. Nevertheless, programmes such as this one can be seen as an implicit critique of the zero-tolerance policy and could perhaps be taken as a signal of coming changes in how the 'problem' of illicit drug use will be addressed in the future.

Note

1 The survey was conducted in connection with the training course, which might have influenced how the respondents answered the questions.

References

Bacon, M. (2022) 'Desistance from criminalisation: Police culture and new directions in drugs policing'. *Policing and Society*. 32(4): 522–539.

Bartoszko, A. (2019) 'Patient is the new black'. *Journal of Extreme Anthropology*. 3(2): 141–149.

Becker, H. (1963) *Outsiders: Studies in the Sociology of Deviance*. New York: The Free Press.

Beckett, K. (2016) 'The uses and abuses of police discretion: Toward harm reduction policing'. *Harvard Law and Policy Review*. 10: 77–100.

Bittner, E. (1967) 'The police on Skid-Row: A study of peace keeping'. *American Sociological Review*. 32(5): 699–715.

Caulkins, J. and Reuter, P. (2009) 'Towards a harm-reduction approach to enforcement'. *Safer Communities*. 8(1): 9–23.

Collins, J. (2018) 'Beyond UNGASS 2016: Drug control multilateralism and the end to the "war on drugs"'. In Reitano, T., Jesperson, S. and Bird Ruiz-Benitez de Lugo, L. (eds.) *Militarised Responses to Transnational Organised Crime*. London: Palgrave Macmillan: 279–297.

Collins, S., Lonczak, H. and Clifasefi, S. (2015) *LEAD Program Evaluation: Criminal Justice and Legal System Utilization and Associated Costs*. Washington, DC: University of Washington.

Cordner, G. (2014) 'Community policing'. In Reisig, M. and Kane, R. (eds.) *The Oxford Handbook of Police and Policing*. Oxford: Oxford University Press: 148–171.

Duff, C. (2008) 'The pleasure in context'. *International Journal of Drug Policy*. 19(5): 384–392.

Eastwood, N., Fox, E. and Rosmarin, A. (2016) *A Quiet Revolution: Drug Decriminalisation Across the Globe*. London: Release.

Flacks, S. (2018) 'The stop and search of minors: A "vital police tool"?' *Criminology and Criminal Justice*. 18(3): 364–384.

Frank, V. (2008) 'Danish drug policy – Shifting from liberalism to repression'. *Drugs and Alcohol Today*. 8(2): 26–33.

Goetz, B. and Mitchell, R. (2006) 'Pre-arrest/booking drug control strategies: Diversion to treatment, harm reduction and police involvement'. *Contemporary Drug Problems*. 33(3): 473–520.

Harkin, D. (2015) 'The police and punishment: Understanding the pains of policing'. *Theoretical Criminology*. 19(1): 43–58.

Holmberg, L. (2000) 'Discretionary leniency and typological guilt: Results from a Danish study of police discretion'. *Journal of Scandinavian Studies in Criminology and Crime Prevention*. 1(2): 179–194.

Houborg, E., Bjerge, B. and Frank, V. (2008) 'Introduction: Danish drug policy – History, theory and the international framework'. In Frank, V., Bjerge, B. and Houborg, E. (eds.) *Drug Policy. History, Theory and Consequences*. Aarhus: Aarhus University Press: 9–32.

Houborg, E. (2010) 'Control and welfare in Danish drug policy'. *Journal of Drug Issues*. 40(4): 783–804.

Houborg, E. and Pedersen, M. (2013) *Håndhævelse af narkotikalovgivningen vedr. besiddelse af illegale stoffer til eget forbrug efter 2004*.Copenhagen: Justitsministriets Forskningskontor.

Houborg, E., Kammersgaard, T. and Pedersen, M. (2016) 'Drug policing in four Danish police districts'. *Police Practice and Research*. 17(4): 329–340.

Houborg, E., Søgaard, T. and Mogensen, S. (2020) 'Making up a new drug user from depenalization to repenalisation of drug users in Denmark'. *International Journal on Drug Policy*. 80: 1–9.

Hughes, C. and Ritter, A. (2008) *A Summary of Diversion Programs for Drug and Drug-Related Offenders in Australia*. Sydney: National Drug and Alcohol Research Centre.

Jöhncke, S. (2009) 'Treatmentality and the governing of drug use'. *Drugs and Alcohol Today*. 9(4): 14–17.

Kammersgaard, T. (2019) 'Harm reduction policing: From drug law enforcement to protection'. *Contemporary Drug Problems*. 46(4): 345–362.

Moeller, K. (2020) 'Enforcement intensity in Danish drug control, 1996–2017'. *European Journal on Criminal Policy and Research*. https://doi.org/10.1007/s10610-020-09437-4.

O'Malley, P. and Valverde, M. (2004) 'Pleasure, freedom and drugs: The uses of "pleasure" in liberal governance of drug and alcohol consumption'. *Sociology*. 38(1): 25–42.

Price, T., Parkes, T. and Malloch, M. (2021) '"Discursive struggles" between criminal justice sanctions and health interventions for people who use drugs: A qualitative exploration of diversion policy and practice in Scotland'. *Drugs: Education, Prevention and Policy*. 28(2): 118–126.

Spyt, W., Barnham, L. and Kew, J. (2019) 'Diversion: Going soft on drugs?' *Thames Valley Police Journal*. 4(1): 44–68.

Stevens, A., Hughes, C., Hulme, S. and Cassidy, R. (2022) 'Depenalization, diversion and decriminalization: A realist review and programme theory of alternatives to criminalization for simple drug possession'. *European Journal of Criminology*. 19(1): 29–54.

Walmsley, I. (2019) 'Drugs decriminalization: The art of governing drug using populations'. In Wilson, S. (ed.) *Prohibitions and Psychoactive Substances in History, Culture and Theory*. London: Routledge: 190–208.

Worden, R. and McLean, S. (2018) 'Discretion and diversion in Albany's lead program'. *Criminal Justice Policy Review*. 29(6–7): 584–610.

Young, J. (1971) *The Drugtakers: The Social Meaning of Drug Use*. London: MacGibbon and Kee.

10

BEYOND HARM REDUCTION POLICING

Katherine Beckett, Monica Bell, and Forrest Stuart[1]

Introduction

The US drug war has been vigorously fought and has produced many casualties. The number of drug arrests taking place in the United States nearly quadrupled from 1981 to 2006, from a half a million to a peak of nearly 1.9 million. The human costs associated with the US anti-drug campaign have been massive: many of those who are arrested on drug charges are also convicted, fined, incarcerated, and even deported. As of 2019, more than a million people were under criminal justice supervision, and roughly 400,000 were behind bars, as a result of a drug conviction (Kaeble 2018, appendix Table 4; Sawyer and Wagner 2019). These misguided interventions have unfolded in a wildly disproportionate manner. As a result, the war on drugs has had a uniquely damaging impact on Black and brown communities (Alexander 2010; Duster 1997; Lynch 2016; Provine 2007).

The war on drugs represents one of the least effective ways of responding to substance misuse that humans might ever have devised. Punishing people who use drugs does not improve health or address the circumstances that fuelled the use of drugs in the first place.[2] In fact, punishment merely adds to the trauma with which many people who use drugs in harmful ways contend, while incarceration puts them at grave risk of overdose upon release (Ranapurwala et al. 2018). Nor has the drug war achieved its stated objectives, namely, reducing the demand for drugs by shrinking supply and increasing prices. In fact, illicit drugs remain more ubiquitous and affordable than ever (Drug Enforcement Administration 2019; Keck and Correa-Cabera 2015). Efforts to disrupt local drug markets through law enforcement have also been ineffective; these interventions often trigger competition and violence but have not reduced the supply of drugs (Reuter 2009, 2016).

DOI: 10.4324/9781003154136-11

At the same time that billions have been spent to reduce supply and interrupt drug distribution, drug treatment remains underfunded. Over seven million Americans struggle with a substance use disorder involving one or more illicit drugs; only about one in five of them receives treatment (SAMHSA 2018).[3] The most efficacious approach to chemical dependency – medication-assisted treatment – remains especially difficult to access (Ghandnoosh 2017). The US overdose death rate has reached record levels and is 3.5 times higher than the average rate of 17 other high-income countries (Ho 2019).

It is clear, then, that the US drug war has failed and must end. The question is how – and what should replace it? Ideally, the alternative policy approach would not just reduce the harm caused by the criminal legal system but also reduce the suffering associated with unmanaged addiction and unregulated drug markets. These harms are also substantial and widespread. For example, overdose deaths stem to a significant degree from the unregulated nature of the illicit drug market, which ensures that the contents and potency of illegal substances are highly variant and therefore unpredictable. The spread of fentanyl and other potent synthetic opioids that are inexpensive to manufacture and relatively compact has led to a surge in the overdose death rate (Center for Disease Control n.d.). Illicit drug markets are also characterised by high price mark-ups and profit margins, as well as unregulated competition among traffickers and dealers, both of which fuel systemic, drug-related violence (Engel 2014; Goldstein 1985; Reuter 2009, 2016).

Unmanaged addiction and illicit markets affect people who use and sell drugs as well as those who do not. For example, many drug users commit property crimes in order to generate monies that can be used to obtain drugs (Bennett and Holloway 2009). In fact, more than one in five (21 percent) people who are sentenced to prison or jail were convicted of crimes aimed at obtaining drugs or money for drugs (Bronson et al. 2017). These findings suggest that nearly half a million people are behind bars for engaging in illegal conduct aimed at enabling the acquisition of illicit drugs, while an estimated 400,000 are serving time for a drug law violation (Kaeble 2018, appendix Table 4).

In short, drug policy reform advocates are right to emphasise the harm caused by criminal legal system involvement. Unmanaged substance misuse and illicit drug markets also cause significant harm. Most recent drug policy reforms do next to nothing to address these harms, and even comparatively bold decriminalisation plans fail to address many of these issues. While full-blown drug legalisation and regulation, accompanied by massive investments in low-income housing, public health, education, communities, and treatment, would arguably be the most efficacious way to reduce drug-related harm, political realities make this option unlikely for drugs other than cannabis, at least for the foreseeable future. The remainder of this chapter describes the development of a harm reduction approach in Seattle, Washington, and suggests that this framework – which increasingly operates independently of the police and the criminal legal system – offers a compelling vision of what the path towards legalisation, regulation, and meaningful investment in health-focused approaches to substance abuse might look like.

Below, we describe a shift towards – and beyond – harm reduction policing that has taken place in Seattle, Washington. Specifically, we describe the emergence and evolution of Law Enforcement Assisted Diversion (LEAD) 1.0 – a harm reduction–oriented, pre-booking diversion framework in which the police serve as gatekeepers – to LEAD 2.0, in which the police no longer serve as controlling gatekeepers, housing and service provision are dramatically enhanced, and medical providers work to expand access to medication-assisted treatment and health care more generally. If brought to scale, the approach embodied by LEAD 2.0 would facilitate a shift in which extreme poverty, chemical dependency, and other behavioural health issues are rendered 'unpoliceable'. 'Policeability' refers to the now-dominant cultural frame that designates the police as the most appropriate and effective first response to behaviours such as drug use (Gascón and Roussell 2019; Roussell 2015; Stuart 2016). It would also notably reduce drug-related suffering, the harm associated with the illicit drug market, and the misery caused by the criminal legal system for people who use illicit substances. Before developing this argument, however, we first describe the current state of the US drug war and explain why it has attenuated only modestly.

The state of the US drug war

The nation's most recent drug war has many drivers, but the centrality of race may be its most notable feature (Alexander 2010). Numerous studies show that the discourse through which the drug issue was framed in the 1980s and 1990s was, as in previous decades, highly racialised (Duster 1997; Provine 2007; Reeves and Campbell 1994; Reinarman and Levine 1997). Policy developments mirrored this unforgiving and racist rhetoric, as lawmakers at the federal level and in many states ratcheted up criminal sanctions for those who possessed or sold drugs, especially crack (Alexander 2010; Lynch 2016). At the same time, the police and prosecutorial focus on people alleged to have possessed or distributed crack cocaine amplified racial disparity in drug arrests and convictions (Beckett et al. 2005, 2006; Lynch 2011, 2016; Lynch and Omori 2018).

In this context, the number of drug arrests taking place in the United States increased by nearly fourfold between 1981 and 2006. Black, Native, and Latinx people bore the brunt of law enforcement's intensified campaign to punish those who used and/or sold controlled substances (Alexander 2010). Between 1980 and 2006, for example, the national Black drug arrest rate increased from roughly 5 to 15.9, while the White drug arrest rate increased more modestly, from approximately 2.2 to 5 per 1,000 persons (Snyder, Cooper and Mulako-Wangota 2020).[4]

Commitment to the war on drugs remained strong through the early 2000s. Over the past two decades, however, awareness of the shortcomings of the war on drugs has grown, and the politics around it have shifted. For example, whereas some Black leaders and the Congressional Black Caucus initially supported the expansion of the drug war (Forman 2017), most have since recognised the devastation it causes to Black families and communities. Now, the racial disparities and the injustices of the drug war are a top priority for advocates of racial justice, from the National Association for the Advancement of Colored People (NAACP) to Black Lives Matter (ibid). At the same time, a well-funded international drug policy reform movement involving high-profile advocates has emerged. While many on the left have long been critical of the failures and inequities of the drug war, a growing number of conservatives have also become concerned about the fiscal and social costs of the drug war and mass incarceration more generally (Dagan and Teles 2014, 2016).

Recently, the focus of concern has shifted to the increased use and abuse of opiates – a trend that has disproportionately impacted White people and led to an unprecedented number of drug overdose deaths (Katz and Goodnough 2017). In this context, opiate users tend to be portrayed through a lens that emphasises the possibility of recovery and humanises those struggling with addiction (Netherland and Hansen 2016; Stone 2018). The contrast between this rhetoric and the way in which those entangled with crack cocaine were portrayed in the 1980s and 1990s is especially sharp. Some researchers argue that the Whiteness of the current drug crisis has precipitated a change not just in media representations, but also in drug policy (Netherland and Hansen 2016; Stone 2018). And yet the drug war trundles on. Drug arrests did decline after 2006, falling from roughly 1.9 to 1.45 million in 2015, but have been rising again since 2015, reaching nearly 1.6 million in 2019 (see Figure 10.1). Judging by historical standards, it appears that the drug war is alive and well (see also Stellin 2019).

Similarly, although the number of people serving time in prison for a drug offence has dropped, this decline has been fairly modest. The total number of

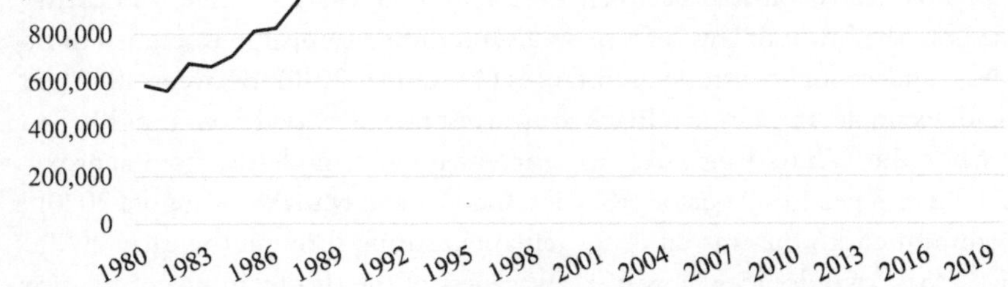

FIGURE 10.1 Number of drug arrests in the United States, 1980–2019. Source: Federal Bureau of Investigations, Uniform Crime Reports.

people in state or federal prison as a result of a drug conviction fell by 32.3 percent from 2007 to 2017.[5] Although this is a non-trivial reduction, the incarceration of drug law violators in the mid-2000s had reached historically unprecedented levels. Recent reductions in the imprisonment of people who were convicted of drug charges therefore do not signal a clear and unequivocal rejection of the drug war, but rather a more minor modification of its intensity. As of 2016, approximately 400,000 people were behind bars,[6] and another 1 million were under correctional supervision, as a result of a drug conviction (Kaeble 2018, appendix Table 4; Sawyer and Wagner 2019).

The modest nature of the impact of recent drug policy reforms is surprising for several reasons. First, as noted previously, representations of (mainly White) people struggling with (mainly opioid) addiction have become more sympathetic. In addition, elected officials on both sides of the aisle now question the wisdom of the drug war and virtually all states have enacted one or more drug policy reforms intended to reduce drug penalties (Beckett 2021; Beckett et al. 2016; Subramanian and Moreno 2014). Moreover, many states have legalised some or most of the cannabis market.

Given widespread efforts to de-escalate the war on drugs, the persistence of historically high levels of drug arrest, incarceration, and supervision requires explanation. The fact that state lawmakers have focused overwhelmingly on reducing penalties for drug possession (as opposed to distribution) is clearly a factor (Beckett 2021; Beckett et al. 2016), as people who were convicted of drug possession comprise just 3.5 percent of the prison population (Bronson and Carson 2018, table 12). Reforms that target drug possession alone will thus have a very small impact on the size of state prison populations, though they may have a slightly larger impact on jail and probation populations.

Second, although reducing the use of confinement for drug distribution could have a more meaningful impact on the scale of incarceration, the policy zeitgeist is moving in the opposite direction. In fact, recently enacted state sentencing reforms are more likely to have shifted penalties for drug distribution in a punitive direction than to have reduced those sentences (Beckett and Brydolf-Horwitz 2020). Moreover, the argument that drug distribution is, and should be treated as, a violent crime is increasingly widely accepted. In this context, more states are enacting drug homicide laws and more prosecutors are charging people who provide or share drugs with overdose victims with homicide (Beletsy 2019; Boecker 2015; Goldensohn 2018; La Salle 2017). Thus, although many states have reduced penalties for drug possession, penalties for drug distribution are moving in the opposite direction in many cases.

Third, the ongoing commitment to drug war practices in rural and suburban areas is sustaining high drug arrests rates and incarceration. People arrested for all kinds of felony offences are more likely to receive a prison sentence if they are arrested in a suburban or rural county versus a large urban county (Beckett 2021; Beckett and Beach 2021). This geographic difference in penal intensity is especially pronounced in drug cases (ibid; see also Keller and Pearce 2016). The drug war thus continues to be fought with vigour by prosecutors and judges in many non-urban areas across the United States.

Fourth, one of the most pervasive kinds of drug policy reforms – drug courts – augment rather than reduce criminal legal system involvement. Research shows that drug courts increase drug arrests, presumably because their existence encourages the police to make arrests and prosecutors to file charges as a way of getting people into treatment (Lilley 2017; Lilley et al. 2019b). Moreover, drug court participants may end up serving more time spent behind bars than would have occurred absent diversion (Rossman et al. 2011; Sevigny et al. 2013). This is because people who are unable to 'graduate' from drug court often face even more severe penalties than they would have if they had not participated in drug court at all (ibid; Gallagher et al. 2019). Moreover, drug courts enhance racial disparities in case outcomes (Howard 2016; Lilly et al. 2019a; Marlowe 2013; Walsh 2011). And even when drug cases are diverted, drug court participants are subjected to extended periods of court supervision as well as compulsory treatment programmes that entail many hardships and offer limited treatment options (Kaye 2012, 2020; Tiger 2013, 2017).

In short, current drug policy reforms do not meaningfully reduce the scale of punishment or the harm the criminal legal system inflicts on people who struggle with addiction. While drug legalisation/regulation, accompanied by massive investments in housing, education, health care, drug treatment, education, and communities, may represent the most humane and efficacious way to reduce the harm associated with addiction and illicit drug markets, these shifts appear to be unlikely to occur in the near future. In the meantime, interventions that focus on the most vulnerable drug users (and distributors) and provide long-term care based on harm reduction principles represent a compassionate and effective way of responding to harmful drug use. In fact, if done carefully, such approaches may well sow the seeds for even broader changes in the future.

Towards, and beyond, harm reduction policing

Towards harm reduction policing: LEAD 1.0

One of the first known pre-booking diversion processes for people arrested on drug and prostitution charges in the United States was launched in October 2011, in Seattle, Washington. This innovation was dubbed LEAD which stood, at the time, for Law Enforcement Assisted Diversion. The adoption of LEAD in 2011 marked a dramatic shift in Seattle's approach to drug markets and associated problems. Like many urban police departments, the Seattle Police Department (SPD) was actively engaged in the drug war through the late 2000s. In fact, the city's drug arrest rate was comparatively high, and levels of racial disproportionality in drug law enforcement outcomes were extraordinarily pronounced (Beckett et al. 2005, 2006).

In response to the severity and persistence of racial disparity in Seattle's drug arrests, attorneys at the Racial Disparity Project mounted a selective enforcement challenge on behalf of a consolidated group of 19 criminal defendants in 2003. All of the defendants involved in this 'criminal class action' case were Black and/or Latinx and all had been arrested for delivering drugs downtown. As a group, these defendants were alleged to have delivered an amount of crack cocaine weighing the equivalent of six plain M&Ms. Collectively, they faced the prospect of well over 100 years in prison. Perhaps unsurprisingly, the litigation that ensued proved to be lengthy, complex, and time-consuming. At the same time, the persistence of visible drug market activity continued to generate significant community pressure to 'do something' about drugs. By the late 2000s, all of the main actors were dissatisfied with the status quo, including the SPD itself (Beckett 2016).

Eventually, litigation fatigue and the persistence of significant public concern about Seattle's still-active drug markets inspired SPD personnel, the King County prosecutor, the American Civil Liberties Union (ACLU), and Racial Disparity Project staff to work together to identify an alternative approach that not only avoided reliance upon jail and prison but also took the harm associated with untreated addiction and outdoor drug market activity seriously. The result, eventually, was the implementation of LEAD in Seattle. LEAD sought to reduce the neighbourhood- and individual-level harm associated with drug and sex markets – as well as the criminal justice costs and human suffering associated with conventional enforcement practices – by diverting people who would otherwise be arrested on low-level drug (or other misdemeanour) charges into an intensive, community-based, case management approach that is guided by harm reduction principles.

The harm reduction philosophy is also central to LEAD, and rests on the assumption that some people will always engage in risky behaviours such as drug use.[7] From a harm reduction point of view, the active intervention of the criminal legal system is often counterproductive. A person who is convicted, incarcerated, and loses their ability to secure work and housing as a result of a drug conviction is more likely to relapse. Absent an immediate threat to public safety, arrest and punishment are, from the harm reduction point of view, inappropriate responses to drug use. Instead, priority should be placed on the provision of health care and social services guided by harm reduction principles to help reduce overall levels of suffering. Harm reduction practitioners also emphasise that the path towards abstinence is often long, and sometimes non-existent. Nonetheless, meaningful reductions in human suffering can be achieved via harm reduction measures, even in the absence of abstinence. For this reason, LEAD does not require abstinence: as the Seattle LEAD referral and diversion protocol states, participants 'will not be penalized or denied services if they do not achieve abstinence'.[8]

Early in the process, Seattle LEAD stakeholders expanded the potential participant pool from people who had been arrested (or, as discussed below, were arrestable) on low-level drug charges to also include sex workers in order to ensure significant participation by women who suffer from addiction and/or extreme poverty. In the intervening years, the pool of people who may be diverted to LEAD has further expanded to include people who are (or are likely to be) arrested for misdemeanour theft, misdemeanour property destruction, criminal trespass, unlawful bus conduct, and obstruction of a police officer.[9] Other jurisdictions have identified yet more 'LEAD-eligible' offences (Malm et al. 2020).

Referrals to the original LEAD occurred in two different ways. First, in 'arrest referrals', LEAD-trained police officers and sergeants diverted people suspected of one of the aforementioned offences upon arrest. In such cases, the potential LEAD participant is arrested but is not booked into jail (hence the description of LEAD 1.0 as a 'pre-booking diversion' framework). Instead, in an arrest referral, the officer contacts a LEAD case manager, who then meets with and assesses the needs of the person who is being referred to LEAD. The officer relinquishes custody of the referred person as soon as a caseworker arrives (Beckett 2016).

Potential participants may also be referred to LEAD through a 'social contact' process that enables law enforcement officers to refer people who struggle with addiction, homelessness, and/or extreme poverty even in the absence of an arrest. Until recently, all referrals were reviewed by LEAD-trained law enforcement officers, who were tasked with confirming that the referred person was justice-involved and that the behaviour of concern stemmed from behavioural health issues, involvement with drugs, trauma, and/or extreme poverty.

Shortly after a referred person agrees to participate in LEAD, they meet with a LEAD case manager. In their first meeting, LEAD case managers conduct an intake assessment and connect their client with services that address their most acute needs. At this point, they are a LEAD participant. In the following weeks, case managers work with participants to create an individual intervention plan that is tailored to people's particular needs and goals, and may include assistance with housing, treatment, education, job training, job placement, licensing assistance, transportation, small business counselling, childcare, or other services.

Several core-operating principles guide LEAD's provision of social services. First, consistent with the harm reduction philosophy, LEAD case managers focus on individual and community wellness rather than exclusively on sobriety. That is, case managers accept that not all participants will pursue sobriety, and expect setbacks when they occur, but emphasise that meaningful improvements may occur even in the absence of abstinence. Furthermore, case managers assist participants in identifying their own goals and supporting them as they work to meet those goals. The hope is that as a result of engaging and developing meaningful relationships with people participating in LEAD, helping them to identify and articulate their own goals, and providing emotional, practical, and financial support as they work towards those goals, LEAD participants will be in a position to stabilise their lives, address their physical and mental health issues, reduce their use of drugs, and cause less harm to themselves and to others than they would absent LEAD's intervention.

Case managers hired by LEAD are accustomed to working in an intensive and 'hands-on' manner with their clients, which stakeholders refer to as the 'guerilla approach' to social work. In this approach, case managers do not simply supply their clients with a to-do list, but rather spend most of their time outside of the office, actively seeking out clients, visiting newly housed clients, accompanying people as they complete paperwork, keep appointments, and apply for services and housing, and engaging in a myriad of other behaviours aimed at helping their clients achieve their stated goals.[10] In one recent (but pre-pandemic) case, for example, a LEAD caseworker accompanied her client to medical appointments, located and paid for a motel room, delivered snacks and toiletries, and drove the LEAD participant to visit her grandmother on the other side of the state – long before the participant expressed any interest in getting sober.[11]

LEAD participants' eligibility for services and benefits are not time delimited, and the LEAD protocol does not authorise any sanctions for 'non-compliance'.[12] Although the King County prosecuting attorney and the Seattle City attorney retain their authority to file charges against LEAD participants for crimes committed in the past or while participating in LEAD, they are not charged with the underlying drug violation, if an arrest occurs, and prosecutors have committed to working in cooperation with LEAD, which means *not* bringing charges against LEAD participants where filing would undermine LEAD clients' therapeutic progress.

Early on, some stakeholders expressed concern that officers might be more inclined to refer White people to LEAD, an understandable concern given the history of drug law enforcement in Seattle (and elsewhere). To ensure that this is not the case, data regarding the racial and ethnic composition of LEAD clients have been periodically collected and monitored. The most recent data show that the majority (56.1 percent) of LEAD participants are people of colour (compared to 36 percent of the Seattle population). Similarly, in San Francisco and Los Angeles, half to three-fourths of those participating in LEAD are people of colour (Malm et al. 2020). In all three sites, roughly four of five participants are homeless; most others are unstably housed. LEAD sites are encouraged to monitor LEAD referrals to ensure that people of colour and other groups that often experience bias (such as the homeless) are afforded the opportunity to participate in LEAD and to identify any obstacles that may prevent this from occurring. In this way, LEAD endeavours to reduce the role of the law in the lives of the most socially marginalised (more generally, see Stuart et al. 2015). In other jurisdictions, however, there is evidence that police have been more likely to refer people of colour to LEAD, and the fact that police control access to LEAD services in LEAD 1.0 means that this is an ongoing concern.

The benefits of LEAD 1.0

LEAD 1.0 has been found to be quite effective in reducing the harm associated with illicit drug use. A recent outcome evaluation compared the system utilisation of approximately 200 LEAD clients with 115 others with similar criminal records who, by virtue of the time or place of arrest, did not participate in LEAD. The results reveal statistically significant reductions for the LEAD group in average yearly criminal legal system utilisation and associated costs (Clifasefi et al. 2017). For example, LEAD clients spent 39 fewer days in jail than similarly situated people who did not enter LEAD. Similarly, the odds that a LEAD participant was sentenced to prison in the first year after their enrolment in LEAD were 87 percent lower than for people who were not referred to LEAD. As a result, criminal legal system costs associated with LEAD clients decreased by roughly 30 percent relative to the year prior to enrolment in LEAD, while those costs for non-LEAD participants more than doubled in the same time period. Similarly, in San Francisco, felony and misdemeanour arrests were two and half and six times higher, respectively, among the non-LEAD comparison group than among LEAD participants after 12 months (Malm et al. 2020). This difference translates to cost savings of $3,651 per person in LEAD.

Studies suggest that LEAD has had a number of other positive effects as well. LEAD participants report dramatic improvements in their health and well-being (Collins et al. 2019). For example, participants were twice as likely to have been sheltered, and were 89 percent more likely to have obtained permanent housing, after their referral to LEAD. Participants were also 33 percent more likely to receive income and/or benefits subsequent to their LEAD involvement.

Challenges associated with LEAD 1.0

Although it is clear that LEAD 1.0 produced many benefits, the paucity of needed services and resources for LEAD participants pose a significant challenge. For example, case managers often struggled to find housing for their clients, mainly because affordable housing is quite limited, especially for people who are using drugs and/or have extensive criminal records. Access to other needed services, including mental health and chemical dependency treatment, is also constrained for a variety of reasons. These limitations not only impair case managers' capacity to assist LEAD participants but also create certain practical and moral quandaries with which LEAD stakeholders continue to wrestle.

In addition, the SPD notably reduced the number of people it referred to LEAD via the arrest referral process over time. And during the pandemic, the SPD also began to slow down the speed with which it 'cleared' people referred via a social contract referral process. These developments underscored the risk associated with relying on the police to serve as gatekeepers to services. In 2020, frustration regarding the SPD's failure to clear many referred persons, combined with the recognition that police referral was extremely unlikely to occur in the context of the pandemic, fuelled the birth of LEAD 2.0 in Seattle.

Beyond harm reduction policing: LEAD 2.0 and the JustCARE coalition

The emergence of uprisings around police violence and systemic racism in the summer of 2020 had a pronounced impact on LEAD. In this context, LEAD made the decision to terminate the arrangement in which the police function as gatekeepers to LEAD services (Kroman 2020). Today, potential participants may be referred to LEAD by neighbours, treatment and social service providers, the Department of Corrections, the Mobile Crisis Team, the Crisis Diversion Center, public defenders, family members, and others through a new community-referral process. These referrals may be verified by *either* law enforcement or the LEAD project management team. As a result, law enforcement can no longer block access to LEAD.

The pandemic also had a pronounced effect on LEAD operations. While the paucity of housing options and other needed services has long posed challenges for LEAD case managers and participants (Beckett 2016), this problem became even more acute in the context of the pandemic.[13] Courts effectively closed for an extended period of time. The King County Executive, recognising that correctional facilities were at particular risk for the spread of COVID-19, declared an intent to reduce the jail population during the emergency period. Yet, many people who were candidates for jail release lacked housing.

In this context, stakeholders developed a new version of LEAD that was adapted to meet the needs of the people it serves under emergency, pandemic conditions. Like LEAD, this adaptation – called Co-LEAD (for COVID and Co-Responder) – is a harm reduction intervention aimed at improving public safety and the well-being of people contending with extreme poverty, behavioural health issues, and criminal legal system involvement. Yet, Co-LEAD differs from LEAD in several important ways. First, Co-LEAD draws on newly available funds to use hotels and motels (available as a result of the pandemic) to provide interim supportive housing for participants. Second, some Co-LEAD clients came directly from jail. Third, Co-LEAD uses continual staffing and the assertive case management model to ensure that support staff are always available to Co-LEAD participants. Finally, Co-LEAD staff include a dedicated medical provider who provides on-site care and health care coordination. While Co-LEAD was originally conceived as a temporary response to the pandemic, it underscored the importance of housing to any successful effort to reduce the harm associated with substance abuse. It has also suggested the viability of a revised version of the model that does not depend on the police as gatekeepers, as well as the potential need to move to a 24/7 staffing model and to ensure greater access to health care and medication-assisted treatment.

Although pleased with the design and operations of Co-LEAD, its leadership recognised fairly quickly that it would be difficult to document Co-LEAD's impact because its operations spanned King County, Washington, which spans over 2,000 square miles and is home to over 2 million residents. In order to show impact at scale, a more geographically focused approach was required.[14] At the same time, the number of people living outside in the downtown area appeared to be growing, sweeps of homeless encampments continued (despite their purported suspension), and people living and working in impacted areas continued to express a high level of concern about public safety and quality-of-life issues associated with large and growing encampments throughout the spring and summer of 2020.

Fortuitously, newly available Coronavirus Aid, Relief, and Economic Security (CARES) Act monies became available to support emergency initiatives aimed at reducing the spread of COVID-19. The availability of these monies made the possibility of conducting an intensive operation in a particular locale conceivable. JustCARE, a novel and multifaceted collective impact model emerged in this context. At one level, JustCARE is a Housing First, harm reduction intervention that provides interim housing and trauma-informed care to people who are often described as service and housing resistant. Yet, it is also a public and behavioural health initiative aimed at reducing the transmission of COVID-19 and addressing the myriad health needs of participants. At the same time, JustCARE is a neighbourhood-focused public safety and quality-of-life initiative – one that avoids reliance on the police, the criminal legal system, and disruptive and counterproductive sweeps.[15]

In short, LEAD has evolved considerably in recent years. LEAD 2.0 is characterised by the end of the police gatekeeping role, intensified and expanded service provision, and, optimally, the implementation of a Housing First approach. LEAD now works independently and in collaboration with other community-based organisations to improve public safety, decrease criminal legal system involvement, and expand access to housing and services guided by the harm reduction philosophy. Today, and to reflect the shift away from relying on the police as gatekeepers, the LEAD acronym stands for Let Everyone Advance with Dignity.

LEAD and its critics

LEAD was developed in Seattle but is now in place or in development in more than 80 jurisdictions around the United States.[16] While the previously cited outcome evaluations of LEAD are quite positive, LEAD remains controversial in some circles. From the perspective of therapeutic court advocates, LEAD likely seems far too radical. One of the main differences between drug courts and LEAD is that advocates of the former assume that both carrots and sticks are required to compel people with chemical dependency issues to avail themselves of treatment and to succeed in it (National Association of Drug Court Professionals 2004). As one state Supreme Court Justice put it:

> drug courts are effective only when they combine the 'carrot' of treatment and support with the 'stick' of judicial accountability, including incarceration when needed. It is this carrot-and-stick approach that enables judges and drug court teams to use a variety of tools to help people overcome addiction.
> *(O'Conner 2018)*

By contrast, LEAD operates on the theory that substance abuse has many complex causes and is often rooted in trauma as well as extreme poverty. Healing occurs when traumatised and marginalised people form trusting relationships with people who help them clarify their own goals and priorities and support them in their efforts to pursue those goals. From this perspective, 'sticks', threats, and sanctions reinforce the isolation, stigma, and hardship with which addicts already contend and are therefore unhelpful. It is only by helping people to feel less alone, and more supported, that meaningful, long-term change is likely to occur.

As Table 10.1 shows, LEAD/JustCARE and drugs courts differ in a number of other important ways as well. While LEAD 1.0 sometimes involves arrest referral, LEAD participants are not booked into jail, unlike drug court participants. Participation in LEAD 1.0 or 2.0 does not hinge on being charged or pleading guilty; in fact, charges stemming from the arrest (if it occurred) are not filed. While LEAD participants may be subject to arrest and incarceration for committing more serious offences while participating in LEAD, they are not incarcerated for the triggering drug law violation or for non-compliance or lack of sobriety. Whereas LEAD notably reduces system involvement among participants, many studies find that drug courts increase arrests and incarceration, as noted previously. Further, LEAD intentionally seeks to include the most marginalised people – those with the longest rap sheets, unmet behavioural health needs, the unhoused, and the extremely poor. By contrast, studies suggest that at least some drug courts 'cherry pick' participants in order to achieve evidence of 'success' (DeMatteo et al. 2009; Shah et al. 2015). And finally, because people of colour are, on average, less likely to 'graduate' from drug court, and because people who fail to 'graduate' often serve even more time in jail or prison than they would have otherwise, drug courts appear to enhance racial inequality in drug case outcomes (Howard 2016; Marlowe 2013; Walsh 2011). By contrast, because LEAD does not send people to jail or prison for failure to achieve sobriety or comply with programme requirements, LEAD ameliorates rather than exacerbates racial inequality in drug enforcement. Moreover, Co-LEAD and JustCARE intentionally targets encampments whose inhabitants are primarily people of colour as part of its commitment to racial justice.

TABLE 10.1 Comparison of drug courts, LEAD 1.0, and LEAD 2.0.

	Drug courts	*LEAD 1.0*	*LEAD 2.0/ JustCARE*
Participation depends on arrest	Yes	Sometimes	No
Police as gatekeepers	Yes	Yes	No
Participants are booked into jail	Yes	No	No
Participation depends on guilty plea	Yes	No	No
Incarceration as sanction	Yes	No	No
Reduces justice involvement	No	Yes	Not yet assessed
Systematic inclusion of most marginalised	No	Yes	Yes
Exacerbates racial inequity in criminal legal involvement	Yes	No	Not yet assessed

Source: Federal Bureau of Investigations, Uniform Crime Reports

In short, while some maintain that the use of 'sticks' by therapeutic courts is essential, the available evidence suggests that LEAD notably reduces criminal legal system involvement and drug-related harm among the most marginalised groups *without* the threat of incarceration or other sanctions for 'non-compliance'.

LEAD is also controversial among some people on the political left, especially police and prison abolitionists. The main concern is that LEAD 1.0 requires cooperation with the police and thus remains 'firmly within the contours of the contemporary carceral state' (Fedders 2019, p. 439). It is true that LEAD 1.0 necessitates cooperation with the criminal legal system officials, with whom it collaborates in order to address outstanding warrants and criminal charges among LEAD participants, and that it seeks to transform policing rather than to abolish it altogether. It is also true that LEAD 1.0 referrals sometimes involve arrest. At the same time, one of LEAD 1.0's most distinguishing characteristics is that it gives the police an alternative way to respond to people involved in illicit drug markets, one that diverts people from jail and reduces rather than compounds harm. Moreover, the police do not play a gatekeeping role in LEAD 2.0. And in Seattle and in other jurisdictions, LEAD has kept a group of people that is overwhelmingly homeless and, in most jurisdictions, predominantly of colour out of the criminal legal system, and endeavours to secure services, benefits, and housing wherever possible. The relationship of LEAD to the criminal legal system is thus complex.

Conclusion

Inspired by Seattle's example, more than 80 jurisdictions have established, or are in the process of establishing, LEAD 1.0, 2.0, or something in between. As research on the human costs of homelessness, extreme poverty, untreated addiction, unmanaged mental illness, and mass incarceration makes abundantly clear, cities, towns, and tribal communities across the United States desperately need such alternatives. Over time, the expansion of LEAD – especially LEAD 2.0 alone and in partnerships such as JustCARE – may help to reverse the complex social processes through which extreme poverty, homelessness, and behavioural health issues came to be defined as eminently 'policeable'. Through the development and implementation of frameworks for care provision that are rooted in harm reduction principles and employ trauma-informed practices, municipalities may be able to transform the response to drug use, low-level crime, and what is perceived as disorder from one that exponentially increases harm to one that notably reduces individual and community suffering. The examples of LEAD 2.0 and JustCARE show that this can be done without reliance on the police as gatekeepers to services or the threat of criminal legal sanctions. While drug legalisation, regulation, and investment in the social safety net are appropriate long-term goals, recent initiatives in Seattle illuminate what a transition towards these ambitious long-term objectives might look like.

Notes

1 Our research on JustCARE was conducted pursuant to an agreement with the Public Defender Association to conduct independent research assessing, contextualising, and proposing adjustments to LEAD and models it has generated to provide community-based care for people exposed to the criminal legal system. Those funds were provided to PDA by Blue Meridian Partners. Other funders include the University of Washington's West Coast Poverty Center, the S. Frank Miyamoto Endowed Professorship, and a generous gift from Laurie Black and Stafford Mays. We are deeply grateful for the support.
2 Nearly two-thirds of all people who are imprisoned meet the medical criteria for an alcohol or drug disorder. Of these, only one in ten receives any kind of professional treatment while behind bars (National Center on Addiction and Substance Abuse at Columbia University 2010).
3 An additional 12 million people struggle with alcohol dependence (SAMHSA 2018).
4 Because the majority of Latinx people are classified as White in the Uniform Crime Report arrest data, this is likely a conservative estimate of the degree to which the Black drug arrest rate outstrips the White arrest rate.
5 This figure is based on analysis of data from the Bureau of Justice's Prisoner's Series.
6 This estimate uses detailed jail data from 2002 to estimate the share of jail inmates who are behind bars as a result of a drug arrest.
7 For a useful overview of harm reduction, see Marlatt and Witkiewitz (2010).
8 *Law Enforcement Assisted Diversion (LEAD) Referral and Diversion Protocol*, November 2018.
9 *Law Enforcement Assisted Diversion (LEAD) Referral and Diversion Protocol*, November 2018. Qualifying drug arrests are those that involve seven or fewer grams of illicit drugs. If the person is arrested for drug delivery or drug possession with intent to deliver, the person arrested is LEAD eligible as long as they are not dealing for profit above a subsistence income.
10 Interview with Lisa Daugaard, director of the Public Defender Association, 21 June 2013.
11 Evans, 'Lessons from Seattle'.
12 *Law Enforcement Assisted Diversion (LEAD) Referral and Diversion Protocol*, November 2018.
13 Interview with Tara Moss, Seattle-King County LEAD project director, 27 January 2021.
14 Interview with Jesse Benet, director of Co-LEAD, and Lisa Daugaard, executive director of the Public Defender Association, 18 February 2021.
15 Wheeler Davis Conglomerate provides safety teams and services in the hotels in which JustCARE participants reside in order to facilitate de-escalation and reduce reliance on 911.
16 See the LEAD National Bureau website at www.leadbureau.org/.

References

Alexander, M. (2010) *The New Jim Crow: Mass Incarceration in the Age of Colorblindness*. New York: The New Press.

Beckett, K., Nyrop, K., Pfingst, L. and Bowen, M. (2005) 'Drug use, drug possession arrests, and the question of race: Lessons from Seattle'. *Social Problems*. 52(3): 419–441.

Beckett, K., Nyrop, K. and Pfingst, L. (2006) 'Race, drugs and policing: Understanding disparities in drug delivery arrests'. *Criminology*. 44(1): 105–138.

Beckett, K. (2016) 'The uses and abuses of police discretion: Toward harm reduction policing'. *Harvard Law & Policy Review*. 10(1): 77–100.

Beckett, K., Reosti, A. and Knaphus, E. (2016) 'The end of an era: Understanding the contradictions of criminal justice reform'. *Annals of the American Academy of Political & Social Science*. 664(1): 238–259.

Beckett, K. (2021) *Ending Mass Incarceration*. New York: Oxford University Press.

Beckett, K. and Beach, L. (2021) 'The place of punishment in 21st century America: Understanding the persistence of mass incarceration'. *Law & Social Inquiry*. 46(1): 1–31.

Beckett, K. and Brydolf-Horwitz, M. (2020). 'A kinder, gentler drug war? Race, drugs, and punishment in 21st century America'. *Punishment and Society*. 22(4): 509–533.

Beletsky, L. (2019) 'America's favorite antidote: Drug-induced homicide in the age of the overdose crisis'. *Utah Law Review*. 4: 833–890.

Bennett, T. and Holloway, K. (2009) 'The causal connection between drug misuse and crime'. *British Journal of Criminology*. 49(4): 513–531.

Boecker, K. (2015) *Charging Drug Sellers with Murder If Someone Dies from Overdose Will Ruin Lives, Save None*. Washington, DC: Drug Policy Alliance.

Bronson, J., Stroop, J., Zimmer, S. and Berzofsky, M. (2017) *Drug Use, Dependence and Abuse among State Prisoners and Jail Inmates, 2007–2009*. Washington, DC: Bureau of Justice Statistics.

Bronson, J. and Carson, A. (2018) *Prisoners in 2017*. Washington, DC: Bureau of Justice Statistics.

Center for Disease Control. *Opioid Overdose: Fentanyl*. Available from: https://www.cdc.gov/drugoverdose/opioids/fentanyl.html [Accessed 27 January 2021].

Clifasefi, S., Lonczak, H. and Collins, S. (2017) 'Seattle's Law Enforcement Assisted Diversion (LEAD) program: Within-subjects changes on housing, employment and income/benefits outcomes and associations with recidivism'. *Crime & Delinquency*. 63(4): 429–445.

Collins, S., Lonczak, H. and Clifasefi, S. (2019) 'Seattle's Law Enforcement Assisted Diversion (LEAD): Program effects on recidivism outcomes'. *Evaluation & Program Planning*. 64(2017): 49–56.

Dagan, D. and Telles, S. (2014) 'Locked in? Conservative reform and the future of mass incarceration'. *The Annals of the American Academy of Political & Social Science*. 651(1): 266–276.

Dagan, D. and Telles, S. (2016) *Prison Break: Why Conservatives Turned Against Mass Incarceration*. New York: Oxford University Press.

DeMatteo, D., Marlowe, D., Festinger, D. and Arabia, P. (2009) 'Outcome trajectories in drug court: Do all participants have serious drug problems?' *Criminal Justice & Behavior*. 36(4): 354–368.

Drug Enforcement Administration (DEA). (2019) *National Drug Threat Assessment*. Washington, DC: Department of Justice.

Duster, T. (1997) 'Pattern, purpose and race in the drug war: The crisis of credibility in criminal justice'. In Reinarman, C. and Levine, H. (eds.) *Crack in America: Demon Drugs and Social Justice*. Berkeley, CA: University of California Press: 260–287.

Engel, P. (2014) 'This chart shows incredibly high markups on illegal drugs'. *Business Insider*. Available from: https://www.businessinsider.com.au/london-school-of-economics-chart-on-illegal-drug-markups-2014-5 [Accessed 2 March 2021].

Fedders, B. (2019) 'Opioid policing'. *Indiana Law Journal*. 389(2): 94. Available from: https://www.repository.law.indiana.edu/ilj/vol94/iss2/2 [Accessed 3 November 2020].

Forman, J. Jr. (2017) *Locking Up Our Own*. New York: Farrar, Straus and Giroux.

Gallagher, J., Wahler, E. and Lefebvre, E. (2019) 'Further evidence of racial disparities in drug court outcomes: Enhancing service-delivery to reduce criminal recidivism rates for non-white participants'. *Journal of Social Service Research*. 46(30): 1–10.

Gascón, L. and Roussell, A. (2019) *The Limits of Community Policing: Civilian Power and Police Accountability in Black and Brown Los Angeles*. New York: New York University Press.

Ghandnoosh, N. and Anderson, C. (2017) *Opioids: Treating an Illness, Ending a War*. Washington, DC: The Sentencing Project.

Goldensohn, R. (2018) 'They shared drugs. Someone died. Does that make them killers?' *New York Times*. Available from: https://www.nytimes.com/2018/05/25/us/drug-overdose-prosecution-crime.html [Accessed 7 January 2020].

Goldstein, P. (1985) 'The drugs/violence nexus: A tripartite conceptual framework'. *Journal of Drug Issues*. 15(4): 493–506.

Ho, J. (2019) 'The contemporary American drug overdose epidemic in international perspective'. *Population & Development Review*. 45(1): 7–40.

Howard, D. (2016) 'Race, neighborhood, and drug court graduation'. *Justice Quarterly*. 33(1): 159–184.

Kaeble, D. (2018) *Probation and Parole in the United States, 2016*. Washington, DC: Bureau of Justice Statistics.

Katz, J. and Goodnough, A. (2017) 'The opioid crisis is getting worse, particularly for Black Americans'. *New York Times*. Available from: https://www.nytimes.com/interactive/2017/12/22/upshot/opioid-deaths-are-spreading-rapidly-into-black-america.html [Accessed 17 March 2020].

Kaye, K. (2012) 'Rehabilitating the "drugs lifestyle": Criminal justice, social control, and the cultivation of agency'. *Ethnography* 14(2): 207–232.

Kaye, K. (2020) *Enforcing Freedom: Drug Courts, Therapeutic Communities, and the Intimacies of the State*. New York: Columbia University Press.

Keck, M. and Correa-Cabera, G. (2015) 'U.S. drug policy and supply-side strategies: Assessing effectiveness and results'. *Norteamérica*. 10(2): 47–67>47–67.

Keller, J. and Pearce, A. (2016) 'This small Indiana county sends more people to prison than Durham, North Carolina and San Francisco combined Why?' *New York Times*. Available from: https://www.nytimes.com/2016/09/02/upshot/new-geography-of-prisons.html. [Accessed 2 May 2020].

Kroman, D. (2020) 'Seattle's arrest alternative, lead, moves beyond police'. *Crosscut*. Available from: https://crosscut.com/2020/07/seattles-arrest-alternative-lead-moves-beyond-police [Accessed 17 February 2021].

LaSalle, L. (2017) *An Overdose Death Is Not Murder: Why Drug-Induced Homicide Laws Are Counter-Productive and Inhumane*. New York: The Drug Policy Alliance.

Lilley, D. (2017) 'Did drug courts lead to increased punishment of minor drug offenses?' *Justice Quarterly*. 34(4): 674–698.

Lilley, D., DeVall, K. and Tucker-Gail, K. (2019a) 'Drug courts and arrest for substance possession: Was the African American community differentially impacted?' *Crime & Delinquency*. 65(3): 352–374.

Lilley, D., Stewart, M. and Tucker-Gail, K. (2019b) 'Drug courts and net-widening in U.S. cities: A reanalysis using propensity score matching'. *Criminal Justice Policy Review*. 31(2): 287–308.

Lynch, M. (2011) 'Crack pipes and policing: A case study of institutional racism and remedial action in Cleveland'. *Law & Policy*. 33(2): 179–214.

Lynch, M. (2016) *Hard Bargains: The Coercive Power of Drug Laws in Federal Court*. New York: Russell Sage Foundation.

Lynch, M. and Omori, M. (2018) 'Crack as proxy: Aggressive federal drug prosecutions and the production of black-white racial inequality'. *Law & Society Review*. 52(3): 773–809.

Malm, A., Perrone, D. and Magaña, E. (2020) *Law Enforcement Assisted Diversion (LEAD) External Evaluation*. Long Beach, CA: California State University Long Beach.

Marlatt, G. and Witkiewitz, K. (2010) 'Update on harm-reduction policy and intervention research'. *Annual Review of Clinical Psychology*. 6: 591–606.

Marlowe, D. (2013) 'Achieving racial and ethnic fairness in drug courts'. *Court Review*. 436. Available from: https://digitalcommons.unl.edu/cgi/viewcontent.cgi?article=1416&context=ajacourtreview. [Accessed 1 March 2020].

National Association of Drug Court Professionals (Drug Court Standards Committee). (2004) *Defining Drug Courts: The Key Components*. Washington, DC: Bureau of Justice Assistance.

National Center on Addiction and Substance Abuse at Columbia University. (2010) *Behind Bars II: Substance Abuse and America's Prison Population*. New York: Columbia University.

Netherland, J. and Hansen, H. (2016) 'The drug war that wasn't: Wasted whiteness, dirty doctors and race in media coverage of prescription opioid misuse'. *Culture, Medicine & Psychiatry*. 40(4): 664–686.

O'Connor, M. (2018) *The Hidden Disaster of State, Issue 1*. Available from: http://ohiopa.org/oconnor1.pdf [Accessed 21 April 2020].

Provine, D. (2007) *Unequal Under the Law: Race in the War on Drugs*. Chicago, IL: University of Chicago Press.

Ranapurwala, S., Shanahan, M., Alexandridis, A., Proescholdbell, S., Naumann, R., Edwards D. Jr. and Marshall, S. (2018) 'Opioid overdose mortality among former North Carolina inmates: 2000–2015'. *American Journal of Public Health*. 108(9): 1207–1213.

Reeves, J. and Campbell, R. (1994) *Cracked Coverage: Television News, the Anti-cocaine Crusade and the Reagan Legacy*. Durham, NC: Duke University Press.

Reinarman, C. and Levine, H. (1997) 'Crack in context: America's latest demon drug'. In Reinarman, C. and Levine, H. (eds.) *Crack in America: Demon Drugs and Social Justice*. Berkeley, CA: University of California Press: 1–17.

Reuter, P. (2009) 'Systemic violence in drug markets'. *Crime, Law & Social Change*. 52(3): 275–284.

Reuter, P. (2016) 'On the multiple sources of violence in drug markets'. *Criminology & Public Policy*. 15(3): 877–883.

Rossman, S., Rempel, M., Roman, J., Zweig, J., Lindquist, C., Green, M., Mitchell Downey, P., Yahner, J., Bhati, A. and Farole, D. (2011) *The Multi-site Adult Drug Court Evaluation: The Impact of Drug Courts, Volume 4*. Washington, DC: The Urban Institute.

Roussell, A. (2015) 'Policing the anticommunity: Race, deterritorialization, and labor market reorganization in south Los Angeles'. *Law & Society Review*. 49(4): 813–845.

Sawyer, W. and Wagner, P. (2019) *Mass Incarceration: The Whole Pie, 2019*. Northampton, MA: Prison Policy Initiative.

Sevigny, E., Fuleihan, B. and Ferdik, F. (2013) 'Do drug courts reduce the use of incarceration?: A meta-analysis'. *Journal of Criminal Justice*. 41(6): 416–425.

Shah, S., DeMatteo, D., Keesler, M., Davis, J., Heilbrun, K. and Festinger, D. (2015) 'Addiction Severity Index scores and urine drug screens at baseline as predictors of graduation from drug court'. *Crime & Delinquency*. 61(9): 1257–1277.

Snyder, H., Cooper, A. and Mulako-Wangota, J. (2020) *Arrests in the United States, 1980 to 2014*. Generated Using the Arrest Data Analysis Tool. Available from: www.bjs.gov [Accessed 15 July 2020].

Stellin, S. (2019) 'Is the drug war over? Arrest statistics say no'. *New York Times*. Available from: https://www.nytimes.com/2019/11/05/upshot/is-the-war-on-drugs-over-arrest-statistics-say-no.html [Accessed 4 April 2020].

Stone, E. (2018) 'Is there "hope for every addicted American"? The new U.S. war on drugs'. *Social Sciences*. 7(1). Available from: https://doi.org/10.3390/socsci7010003 [Accessed 21 August 2020].

Stuart, F. (2016) *Down, Out, and Under Arrest: Policing in Everyday Life in Skid Row*. Chicago, IL: University of Chicago Press.

Stuart, F., Armenta, A. and Osborne, M. (2015) 'Legal control of marginal groups'. *Annual Review of Law & Social Science*. 11(1): 235–254.

Subramanian, R. and Moreno, R. (2014) *Drug War Détente: A Review of State-Level Drug Law Reform*, 2009–2013. New York: Vera Institute of Justice and Center on Sentencing and Corrections.

Substance Abuse and Mental Health Services Administration (SAMHSA). (2018) *Key Substance Use and Mental Health Indicators in the United States: Results from the 2017 National Survey on Drug Use and Health*. Washington, DC: US Department of Health and Human Services.

Tiger, R. (2013) 'Race, class and the framing of drug epidemics'. *Contexts*. 16(4): 46–56.

Tiger, R. (2017) *Judging Addicts: Drug Courts and Coercion in the Justice System*. New York: New York University Press.

Walsh, N. (2011) *Addicted to Courts: How a Growing Dependence on Drug Courts Impacts People and Communities*. Washington, DC: Justice Policy Institute.

11

LAW ENFORCEMENT AND PUBLIC HEALTH PARTNERSHIPS

Opportunities and perils

Evan Anderson and Ruth Shefner

Introduction

The enforcement of drug control laws is a source of enormous harm. Drug policing in the United States has been a main driver of fatal drug overdose (Beletsky and Davis 2017), which is five times more common in the United States than in the median Organisation for Economic Co-operation and Development (OECD) country (OECD 2019), as well as HIV transmission (Burris et al. 2009) and other harms. Arrests and incarcerations are traumatic (De Veaux 2013; Geller et al. 2014) and erect persistent barriers to employment and housing (National Research Council 2014), both of which impose intergenerational stress and suffering on families and communities (Comfort et al. 2011; Muñiz and Turney 2020). At the same time, there is little evidence that aggressive enforcement of prohibitionary drug laws has reduced substance use and associated harms (Grossman et al. 2002).

Despite the clear and long-standing need to repeal punitive drug control laws and to reform policing practices, change has been painfully slow (Burris et al. 2020). The United States continues to arrest over a million people every year for mere drug possession (FBI 2020), and while decriminalisation efforts have emerged in some spaces (Fuller 2020), policymakers are doubling down on harsh practices in others (Beletsky 2019; Comer et al. 2021). Given this unflinching commitment to criminalisation, and the enormous racial disparities in arrest and incarceration for drug-related offences it produces, drugs policing is often described as a system designed for racial oppression (Alexander 2020). There is certainly truth to that account: law enforcement is a key structural driver of avoidable harm, and people of colour have borne a much greater burden of the resulting inequities (Simckes et al. 2021). But it is difficult to explain the growth and persistence of drugs policing in the United States entirely in terms of racial

DOI: 10.4324/9781003154136-12

social control; some of the harshest drugs policing happens in politically liberal cities, led by people of colour (Forman Jr. 2017).

Drugs policing is best understood within a broader pattern of chronic disinvestment in poor communities and alongside deeply pathological systems for delivering social and health services. Since the abolition of slavery, discriminatory laws have severely limited access to housing, education, and employment (Rothstein 2017). The resulting racial disparity in wealth is astonishing: median net worth is $170,000 for White non-Hispanic households in the United States today, but less than $21,000 for Black and White-Hispanic households (Oliver and Shapiro 2019). Over half of all families experiencing homelessness in the United States are Black, despite the fact that Black people represent less than 15% of the US population (HUD 2020). The harmful effects of poverty for Black and White-Hispanic people in the United States accumulate over the life course (Osypuk 2013), intensify across generations (Pais 2017), and concentrate in neighbourhoods (Sharkey 2019).

The effects of this upstream deprivation are compounded by strikingly inadequate access to downstream health and social services. While the United States leads the world in per capita health care spending, huge portions are diverted to private health insurers and wealthy hospitals (Sage 2017). The administrative spending by these entities is about $2,500 per capita annually, which is five times higher than in Canada (Himmelstein et al. 2020). The resources left over for patient care are disproportionately directed towards expensive tertiary medicine, crowding out investments in key preventative services and in basic resources for those with the greatest unmet needs (Bradley and Taylor 2013; Reinhardt et al. 2019). There are, for example, four times more magnetic resonance imaging (MRI) tests conducted per capita in the United States, at five times the unit cost, compared to the median OECD country (OECD 2021), yet millions of people in the United States lack health insurance (Robin 2021) and hundreds of thousands are unstably housed (Henry et al. 2015). Most US states spend less than $100 per capita on public health activities (Weber et al. 2020). Total public health budgets at the federal, state, and local level account for less than 3% of total annual US health care spending (Himmelstein and Woolhandler 2016).

Drugs policing in the United States targets people victimised by these processes (Cooper 2015). Black people are four times more likely to be arrested for marijuana possession than their white counterparts despite reporting the same amount of marijuana use (ACLU 2020), a pattern observed with other substances too (Hart and Hart 2019). These disparities reflect both racially disparate treatment by the police and racial disparities in accessing wealth, both of which influence whether and how drugs policing is experienced. Laws criminalising drug paraphernalia, for example, only practically affect people who have to carry syringes because they lack a private space to store or use drugs, or who are likely to experience a police search because of where they live and how they look (Huq 2016). Drugs policing rarely if ever involves knocking down doors in affluent suburbs or searching the cars travelling through them; in fact, police often shield the wealthy youth they encounter from the effects of drugs policing with informal 'warnings' (Clair 2020). Deeper in the criminal justice system, prosecutorial processes often display a perverse system of reverse triage: people with the most acute needs are often the least likely to receive scarce 'therapeutic' court programming because of eligibility criteria based on previous criminal history (Shefner et al. 2020).

A policy trap

The persistence of these drugs policing practices reflects not only enduring racism but also a cruel policy trap. The result of long-standing structural immiseration in many communities is chronic and overlapping crises of violence, housing instability, and drug-related harms such as overdose. These crises produce government responses, which tend to look like emergency health care in their inherent risks and harms (Anderson and Burris 2017). Investments in housing, education, and other resources and services are widely recognised as better approaches over the long term. But these take time to implement and to meaningfully effect change. Instead, the crisis interventional response to acute community distress overwhelmingly relies on policing-centred models, because police, like emergency clinicians, are always available and are designed for rapid response. Communities in crisis in the United States often ask for infusions of resources and social services as well as more and better policing; they typically just get more policing (Forman Jr. 2017). Repeated failure to reverse chronic disinvestment may explain why many Black Americans are sceptical about shifting financial support from policing to other services (Saad 2020), which can look, in historical perspective, like even deeper neglect masked in naïve hope. It is not that these communities trust the police; it is that they seem to trust other government sectors, including those delivering public health and social services, even less to meet their needs (Pew Research Center 2019).

Drugs policing is one of the few tools the police have when responding to people and communities in crisis (Helfgott et al. 2019). That it is poorly suited to that task and enormously harmful is obvious, but acute needs often elicit harmful interventions when problems are poorly understood and when other strategies are unavailable (Anderson and Burris 2017). With growing appreciation that the incidence and risks of substance use are largely social and medical in origin, there has been increasing willingness to develop policing strategies that avoid forcing people into a harmful criminal justice system for minor drug-related activity (Warner and Kramer 2009). One is the creation of programmes that enable police to divert people to supportive services at the time of arrest rather than directing them through the conventional prosecution process (Palmer 1975; Lattimore et al. 2020). As described in Beckett et al. (this volume), the Law Enforcement Assisted Diversion (LEAD) programme in Seattle exemplifies this model, and was the first to demonstrate documented improvements in outcomes for programme enrolees, including increases in stable housing and employment (Clifasefi et al. 2017) and reductions in arrests and incarceration (Collins et al. 2017, 2019).

LEAD emerged as a strategy to minimise incarceration and to reduce behaviour viewed as public disorder. Local police had been sued repeatedly for racially disparate arrest patterns, and local communities had complained about petty theft, homelessness, and public injection drug use (Beckett 2014). LEAD is a diversionary approach in the sense that it redirects people away from prosecution to services aimed at behaviour change. LEAD uses law enforcement interactions as an entry point to services. This requires ongoing collaboration between police and service providers. In Seattle, that is accomplished through frequent operational meetings, which build and maintain trust and a sense of shared purpose (Beckett 2014). It also means, given the overlapping vulnerabilities of many clients, that backend services must be immediate, low threshold, and appropriately intensive. Unstably housed clients with ongoing substance use need more than a referral to housing services, for example; they need immediate access to housing that is not contingent on sobriety (Larimer et al. 2009). Early experiences with LEAD demonstrated how diversion to such services can disrupt increasing criminalisation by convincing community members that arrest is not the only or the best tool for reducing some types of community disorder (Morrissey et al. 2019).

Other cities, however, have struggled to replicate the LEAD model, in programmes variously described as pre-booking, pre-arrest, or police-led diversion. An evaluation of a programme in Albany found only 43 diversions out of 543 eligible encounters, and that most people who were diverted had few if any arrests despite the programme being aimed at assisting individuals whose substance use and other vulnerabilities produce frequent contact with the criminal justice system. Half of surveyed officers in Albany held negative views towards diversion generally, and two-thirds had serious concerns about the programme specifically (Worden and McLean 2018). A programme in New Haven was only able to make two referrals over eight months before it disbanded (Breen 2020) due to implementation challenges including insufficient officer training, poor communication with service providers, stigma, and polarised views regarding the purpose of the programme (Joudrey et al. 2020). A pilot programme in San Francisco came to a similar end in 2020 (Magaña et al. 2022). In its first year of operation, an Atlanta programme only completed 100 referrals among 7,000 eligible arrests (Jefferson and Jamision 2019).

These difficulties are hardly surprising. Programmes such as LEAD require transformations in institutions, which are large and slow to change. These include not only law enforcement but also office-based health and social service organisations not structured or oriented towards providing immediate and direct care in the community (Schuchman et al. 2018). Decades of norms, practices, financing arrangements, and workforce characteristics are not easily or quickly reshaped (Cornwell 2019; Lapidos et al. 2019). Inertia is intensified by impoverished and rigid budgets. Community-based service providers operate on shoestrings, and programming is often dictated by the terms of grants and funders. Police budgets are significantly larger, but around 98% of them are devoted to salary and benefits (Urban Institute 2017), leaving little money for new training and capital investments supporting innovation. Meanwhile, the deep-pocketed hospitals that control the primary share of health spending in most US cities profit from highly reimbursable health care technology rather than primary care, which explains why it is easy to find palatial oncology pavilions in urban areas, but impossible to locate robust hospital-sponsored programmes serving people out in the community.

Diversion programmes also require trust between community members, law enforcement, and social services providers. Recently, these fragile and traditionally adversarial relationships have grown even more strained. A welcome reckoning with racial injustice and police brutality has surged through the United States in the last few years (Chang and Martin 2020), transforming the possibility horizon for policing reform and challenging arguments for incrementalism. Municipal investments in police diversion programming, which would have been celebrated as progressive only a few years ago, are increasingly viewed as conciliatory at best, if not problematic in supporting existing carceral systems. Some now question the underlying assumption that police should ever play a role in incidents involving substance use even when they coincide with other prohibited activity, arguing instead for only social service or community-based responses (American Public Health Association 2018; Gormley 2021). There is also considerable distrust between communities and social and health services providers, the latter of which are often criticised for imposing needless and dehumanising requirements on people seeking care (Feldman 2019).

That programmes such as LEAD continue to emerge despite these challenges is a testament to the flaws in conventional drugs policing and to the difficulty of implementing alternate reforms. In the remainder of this chapter, we explore the development of a pre-booking programme in Philadelphia, a city that exemplifies how concentrated and intergenerational disinvestment creates and sustains drugs policing long after its harms have been widely documented as outweighing any benefits. The pre-booking programme is an attempt to reduce both the negative effects of drug policing and the harm from decades of inadequate access to basic resources and supportive services. The model is healthier by design than conventional drugs policing. But it is still a police-centred interventional model, which raises legitimate concerns about medicalisation and iatrogenesis, notwithstanding sincere attempts to embrace public health practices and principles. We explore these concerns and offer some other insights into the complicated role of such programmes during the current campaign to reimagine the boundaries and purposes of policing.

Philadelphia

Philadelphia is a city of stark contrasts. As the birthplace of American independence, colonial and revolutionary landmarks are common in its quaint downtown streets. It is also a major hub of research and education, with the fifth largest population of college students in the United States attending more than 100 area colleges and universities. The local economy relies on these 'eds and meds', which include some of the country's best medical facilities. Although technically not-for-profit entities that do not pay income or real estate taxes, some of Philadelphia's hospitals are among the most profitable in the United States, with hundreds of millions of dollars in annual net income (George 2021). To qualify for not-for-profit status in the United States, hospitals must provide measurable community benefits. This mostly takes the form of uncompensated 'charity care' within the hospital; less than 10% of community benefit spending happens out in the community (Rosenbaum et al. 2015). The local economy's reliance on educational and public sector entities poses a significant challenge for the city's revenue stream; in 2020, 8 of the top 15 employers in Philadelphia were universities or university-affiliated medical centres and 5 of the others were public sector entities (The Pew Charitable Trusts 2021b), meaning that only two contributed to the city's budgetary resources through income or real estate taxes.

Not far from towering dorms and shining medical complexes, hundreds of thousands of Philadelphians are trapped by legacies of de-industrialisation, racist housing policies, and racially exclusive union membership. A quarter of Philadelphia residents live in poverty, the highest rate of any large US city; 14% live in deep poverty, which is defined as living with income less than half the poverty threshold (The Pew Charitable Trusts 2019). Poverty is especially concentrated in majority-minority neighbourhoods in West and North Philadelphia, where the percentage of the population living below the poverty line reaches as high as 45%. Across the city, 10% of housing units sit vacant, while wait times for public housing average ten years on wait lists that have been closed since 2013 (Philadelphia Housing Authority, no date). Access to quality substance use and mental health services, especially for inpatient or long-term treatment, is often difficult and limited, as are opportunities for paid job or vocational training (Ao 2021; Read 2020).

The intergenerational transmission of poverty and its associated harms is unmistakable in Philadelphia. More than 20% of children in the city are food insecure. Less than half of local students finish high school on time, the lowest among all large cities, and only a quarter enter college (Mcraff 2013). Childhood adversity is especially common in Philadelphia. Compared with nationally representative populations, three times more Philadelphians (37%) report experiencing four or more types of adversity during childhood (Bloom 2015), a level of childhood adversity that is associated with more than 4 times higher risk of depression and more than 12 times greater likelihood of suicidality (Burke et al. 2011). One third and one quarter of Philadelphia adults report experiencing emotional and physical abuse during childhood, respectively; another 12% report having lived with someone who was sentenced to prison (Findings from the Philadelphia Urban ACE Survey 2013).

These early life experiences and their long-term harms cluster. Depending on race and social position, a Philadelphian experiences either the financial and cultural offerings of a World Heritage City, or constant, concentrated, and overlapping crises. In 2020, Philadelphia had 1,214 fatal drug overdoses, the highest per capita rate among large US cities (The Pew Charitable Trust 2021b), and about the same number as in all of Germany. For much of the recent era, Philadelphia has also been the nation's most incarcerated city, as well as one of the most highly supervised (Schiraldi 2018). The local court system has sentenced more juveniles to life sentences than any other city in the world and leads the country in its ratio of people serving sentences of life without parole (Golden 2021). Black people in Philadelphia are arrested at two times the rate of White people, are incarcerated in jails and prisons at five times the rate of White people, and are supervised on probation and parole at almost three times the rate of White people (Melamed and Purcell 2019). Aggressive prosecution has not translated into public safety. Philadelphia has had one of the highest homicide rates in large cities for decades and, like many other cities, saw its rates surge in the last year. The 499 fatal shootings in Philadelphia in 2020 represented the highest gun homicide rate among all large US cities (The Philadelphia Center for Gun Violence Reporting 2021). These shootings are overwhelmingly concentrated in neighbourhoods subject to racist housing laws in the early 20th century (Jacoby et al. 2018).

The views of Philadelphia residents on policing are accordingly polarised and context dependent. There was widespread criticism of the police response to political protests in June 2020 following the murder of George Floyd in Minneapolis (Taylor 2021). According to local polling, trust in the ability of the police to treat White and Black residents with equal fairness fell to 50% during the fall of 2020, down from 75% in 2016. In some areas of the city, like West Philadelphia, that percentage fell to well under 30%. Despite reduced trust in and respect for police, however, more than 40% of all residents, and more than 50% of all Black residents indicated a preference for more police on city streets. About a quarter of White respondents suggested that there were too many police compared to only 6% of Black respondents. In the same survey, public safety was identified as the most important challenge, with less than half of the participants responding that they feel 'completely' or 'pretty safe' around their home at night, the lowest percentage since 2009 (The Pew Charitable Trust 2020).

Police-Assisted Diversion

In response to the fatal overdose and over-incarceration crises, the city launched a pre-booking diversion programme in 2017 called Police-Assisted Diversion, or (PAD). PAD was created through a collaborative process involving police, prosecutors, public defenders, and health services providers. Community members (described hereafter as 'clients') enter the programme in one of two ways. A stop referral occurs when a client enrols in PAD in lieu of being arrested for minor criminal activity. A social referral occurs when a client enters the programme through officer outreach or by actively requesting to enrol. Upon entry into the programme, all clients are connected with community-based organisations that provide services directly or make referrals as part of ongoing case management. PAD personnel attempt to address unmet needs at the time of arrest, aspiring towards a 'warm handoff' model deployed in other settings (Ahmed et al. 2019; Campbell Britton et al. 2019), with access to services, including substance use treatment, provided at the moment someone is ready to engage. Case management by service providers follows a harm reduction approach of 'meeting people where they are' and does not require sobriety as a precondition for receiving social and health services.

The PAD programme started as a pilot in late 2017 in an area with about 90,000 residents who are overwhelmingly Black and who experience some of the highest and most concentrated rates of deep poverty in the country. This neighbourhood has high rates of serious violent crime, distinguishing PAD from some other pre-booking programmes that emerged in more commercial areas where law enforcement was more focused on public disorder offences. In 2018, PAD expanded to a second pilot zone encompassing a much larger area with about 240,000 residents, who are more racially and socio-economically diverse. This zone includes a sizeable area of open-air injection drug use. People who inject drugs are drawn to this corridor given the city's reputation for having especially cheap and potent heroin (Mars et al. 2014).

When PAD began, only arrests relating to illegal purchasing and possession of drugs were eligible for stop referrals. However, eligibility quickly expanded to include retail thefts involving less than $500 in value, in response to feedback from police officers that such offences tend to involve people with chaotic substance use. The citywide police assignment enforcing prostitution prohibitions started making referrals the next year, and there has been expansion into other geographic areas and assignments since. There have been constant efforts to reduce and remove eligibility restrictions. Altogether, the programme has completed about 2,000 referrals since it began, with enrolment increasing consistently before the COVID-19 pandemic (Anderson et al. 2022).

Navigating choppy and dangerous downstream waters

The continuing expansion of PAD, both in terms of increasing geographic reach as well as widening eligibility, is encouraging. It is the type of evidence celebrated by those who believe that incremental policing reform is the best way to achieve substantial and durable change. Proceeding along its current path, PAD could soon offer immediate linkages to services in place of arrests for a growing number of offences across the city, creating a more direct mechanism for filling unmet needs while reducing harmful interactions with the criminal justice system. The process of creating and reforming PAD may also lubricate reform efforts in other areas of persistent policy dysfunction. The collaborative process of developing the LEAD programme in Seattle transformed local relationships between disparate agencies, unlocking other opportunities for positive change, such as the attempted creation of supervised injection facilities (Beckett 2014).

But there is also plenty of reason to worry about whether PAD and similar programmes are sufficient bridges away from harmful drugs policing and towards a truly healthy response to substance use and its associated harms. This includes practical concerns about whether such programmes are capable of making immediate linkages to the resources and services clients need. Some basic necessities, such as housing, remain incredibly limited. Others, such as substance use treatment and case management exist, but not always in forms that are readily available, which is important because readiness to engage with services is often fleeting for people experiencing the overlapping stresses common among programme clients (Cicero and Ellis 2017; Garland et al. 2019). Providing rapid community-based care is difficult in the United States generally, as noted above, and specifically in urban areas like Philadelphia, where community needs vary greatly between neighbourhoods. The first PAD pilot zone differs dramatically from the second on multiple dimensions, including types and patterns of substance use, residential and commercial characteristics, resident ties to the community, and relations between law enforcement and community groups. The service providers aligned with PAD in each pilot zone reflect these differences. The main provider in one pilot zone embodies a case management model oriented around vigorous outreach and community building; while the main provider in the second pilot zone is a long-standing harm reduction clinic that provides essential health services to a largely transient population (Anderson et al. 2022).

Further expansion of PAD requires protocolised collaborations with these and many more community-based providers. This is administratively challenging due to limited and rigid budgets. Differences in treatment modalities and engagement philosophies between and among service organisations are also confusing and alienating for law enforcement partners, explaining, in part, why some police officers question the ability of service providers to meet the needs of clients. This scepticism is not unfounded and is rooted in the difficult reality of the US social service ecosystem. In the United States, social and health care services are financed principally on a fee-for-service model. As a result, services are usually only available when there is a sizeable, predictable, and manageable volume of reimbursable appointments. One reason why there is such a shortage of mental health care in the United States, for example, is because only 55% of psychiatrists accept any insurance, and only 40% accept Medicaid, which is public insurance for people who are poor (Bishop et al. 2014). This behaviour is partly explained by low reimbursement rates for mental health care (Olfson 2016). But it also reflects the administrative burden of providing care outside of hospitals and the difficulty of sustaining mental health care practices when appointments are often missed because of sporadic referral pathways and the unaddressed challenges patients face in making it to appointments (Specht et al. 2004; Thomas et al. 2018).

Building up referral pathways for programmes such as PAD is complicated by simultaneous efforts to reduce the role of the police in the response to public disorder and distress. The obvious contradiction this poses, in Philadelphia and elsewhere (Joudrey et al. 2020), reflects the lack of alternate responses, and the considerable immediate needs of people and communities in the city. It also complicates the idea that programmes such as PAD actually embody a public health approach to substance use. PAD and similar programmes are well-intentioned attempts to reverse harmful criminalisation of substance use and other behaviours, staffed by hard-working stakeholders bridging considerable disciplinary gaps. And the goals of this multidisciplinary collaboration – reducing punitive policies and providing linkages to services – are surely consistent with public health principles. In practice, however, these programmes represent more of a medicalised approach to identifying people in distress or at high risk, and then trying to reshape their behaviour with curative services and health care. These are logical aims because many clients engage in high-risk behaviour, often with serious co-occurring health conditions. But experience with health care in the United States illustrates the incidental and moral hazards of medicalised models operating so far downstream.

Medicalisation is problematic for three reasons. The first is the tendency to rely on interventions with risks that outweigh likely benefits. Risk of incidental harm, also described as iatrogenesis, grows with the intensity of the intervention and the precarity of the person receiving it. Huge portions of common medical practices in the United States have demonstrated problematic balances of risks and benefits under the scrutiny of rigorously designed research. For decades, for example, cardiologists inserted stents into the hearts of patients who experienced chest pain upon exertion and who had signs of narrowing in their major heart vessels. These patients were experiencing serious conditions and the popular intervention was intuitive: to keep blood circulating, prop narrowing vessels open. Cardiologists performed the procedure hundreds of thousands of times each year in the United States and Europe even as research questioned the therapeutic payoff. In 2017, the issue was definitively settled when a randomised trial showed no benefits compared to medication therapy (Al-Lamee et al. 2018). The incidental risk of the surgical procedure, on the other hand, was considerable: out of every 100 people receiving it, 2 suffered a serious complication or died from the surgery (Stergiopoulos and Brown 2012). Similar examples are found throughout medicine (Epstein and ProPublica 2017).

Programmes such as PAD are less harmful than conventional drugs policing. But they still rely on the use of arrests when making stop referrals, and arrests are like heart stents: intensive, inherently risky, and best avoided wherever possible. Police stops are often traumatising (Geller et al. 2014) and frequently trigger detention even when the precipitating circumstances are not, upon deeper investigation, themselves grounds for arrest. A 2019 analysis of state data revealed that 45% of admissions to state prison result from technical violations of probation or parole, less than half of which involve a new crime (Council of State Governments 2019). Trauma, technical violations, and other risks, like police-involved shootings, are inherent to arrest, and like stent placement for many patients with chest pain, they cannot be eradicated through the training and good intentions of the person initiating them. Stents do have a role to play in cardiovascular health care. They are life saving for patients whose chest pain is caused by sudden blockages. The key with stents – and arrests – is reducing their use to only those instances when they are absolutely unavoidable (Anderson and Burris 2017).

The second problem with medicalisation is that it engenders a distorted view of the most effective way to reduce common harms. Our culture celebrates the use of technology in curative care. Lives are saved every day by wondrously sophisticated techniques performed in the medical complexes that dominate most urban skylines in the United States. Those same places conduct research illuminating the intricate biological processes at play in addiction and depression and other conditions. Yet, heroic interventions and mechanistic biological research have produced few scalable cures. Most causes of harm and poor health today are chronic diseases and social conditions, which can be managed through ongoing care but not reversed through intensive treatment. Lack of investment in simple preventative resources with established benefits, such as supportive housing, is especially frustrating given the billions of dollars flowing into interesting research with, as yet, marginal population-level benefits. As the former director of the National Institute of Mental Health recently lamented:

> The scientific progress in our field was stunning, but while we studied the risk factors for suicide, the death rate had climbed 33 percent. While we identified the neuroanatomy of addiction, overdose deaths had increased by threefold. While we mapped the genes for schizophrenia, people with this disease were still chronically unemployed and dying 20 years early.
>
> *(Carey 2021)*

None of these are intractable when viewed within the appropriate social context. Strategies that reshape the social environment of injection drug use, for example, are very effective at reducing overdose and other harms (Potier et al. 2014). It is the medicalised approach of treating substance use as a problematic and curable behaviour, which has and continues to fail (Burris et al. 2020). Pre-booking programmes such as PAD often explicitly embrace a harm reduction approach that recognises that treatment modalities are supportive but not determinative in reducing harms associated with substance use. But the emergence of these programmes also frequently relies on a tacit political consensus that providing more health care will result in less substance use, which will in turn minimise public disorder. This presents not only a problem of iatrogenesis but also one of cynicism for the communities experiencing the effects of chaotic substance use and for police officers who understandably expect, given prevailing notions and programme marketing, that access to health care and social services will produce immediate and durable change in behaviour.

A third problem with medicalisation is that it crowds out more effective approaches for reducing harm. The analogy between stents and arrest is illuminating here as well. Purchasing and placing a stent easily costs $100,000 in the United States, meaning that the 500,000 stents placed in recent years resulted in as much as $50 billion dollars in spending on hospital services. It is estimated that it would cost $30 billion to provide every unstably housed person in the United States with a housing voucher (Congressional Budget Office 2015). Unstable housing is widely acknowledged as a fundamental cause of worsening health, but the cost to address unstable housing is perceived as too expensive. Yet, we spend orders of magnitude more on health care practices in the United States, much of which remains overpriced (Reinhardt et al. 2019) and unnecessary (Fisher et al. 2003).

In response to these observations, hospitals have slowly developed programmes aimed at addressing the social determinants of health for people at high risk of repeated hospital admissions and other harms. One of the better-known programmes, which operates across the Delaware River from Philadelphia in Camden, New Jersey, sends nurses and social workers to patient homes to arrange services addressing their ongoing social and health needs. Notwithstanding great intentions, high face validity, and glowing publicity, a recent randomised trial found that the model failed to demonstrate anticipated benefits (Finkelstein et al. 2020), exhibiting yet again the often surprisingly limited reach of downstream approaches. But even if it and other such programmes succeed in helping individual people, they offer little to the broader community. In celebrating these hospital efforts as 'a strong scaffolding… [to] support search and rescue efforts for individuals as they struggle in unhealthy currents', Paula Lantz reminds us that although

> these efforts are indeed necessary and generally positive, they are also woefully insufficient if the overarching goal is improved health outcomes and health equity at the societal level. There is a difference between upstream efforts aimed at increasing affordable housing within gentrifying urban neighborhoods and downstream efforts that provide supportive housing to chronically homeless individuals. There is a difference between broad public education system reform and patient-centered interventions focused on health literacy. And there is a difference between advocating for public policies aimed at poverty prevention/income security and screening patients for trouble paying for their prescriptions or utility bills.
>
> *(Lantz 2019)*

The hospitals and the health care system, in this account, could easily be replaced by police departments and the criminal justice system. Intervening so far downstream is inherently risky, limited in effectiveness, and creates a moral hazard for neglecting other upstream work.

Some realism about using public health partnerships to replace drugs policing

Describing pre-booking programmes such as PAD as problematically medicalised models does not imply that they should be suspended any more than noting an overreliance on emergency medical care suggests the closure of emergency departments. This chapter offers three observations, which are no less valuable, hopefully, for being fairly obvious. First, police diversion models operate very far downstream, which limits their capacity to reverse harms caused by decades of persistent structural discrimination. Second, public health architecture in the United States is fragmented and underfunded, which is a challenge for programmes predicated on rapid community-based social and health services. Third, overlapping crises and growing urgency for transformative change complicate efforts to replace conventional drugs policing practices with diversionary models.

Downstream programming – that is, trying to support people who are already in distress – is essential. In Philadelphia, ambitious and multifaceted criminal justice reforms over the last decade have changed the downstream experience of people caught in the 'revolving door' of the criminal justice system. For years, the city's judicial system has operated more than a dozen problem-solving courts and pre-trial diversion programmes. In 2017, the city elected one of the nation's most progressive district attorneys, who has taken on bail and probation systems while reducing prosecution of many low-level drug offenses (Gonnerman 2018). A vibrant collection of over 115 community-based organisations now provide re-entry support services under the umbrella of a citywide re-entry coalition. Along with the development of PAD, the police department has deployed a co-responder model utilising behavioural health partnerships, and the city is undertaking a comprehensive overhaul of systems for processing and responding to emergency calls for people in distress (Orso 2021). In just the last few years, these and other reforms have halved the number of people in local jails, reducing overcrowding and closing a number of county jail facilities (Philadelphia's participation in the Safety and Justice Challenge 2021).

More transformative change, however, has proven elusive. One recent commentary suggests that the city is 'caught between a recognition that racism is rooted in unfair and unequal conditions, created within public and private sectors, and reproduced over time and place, and a reluctance to take drastic action to cure it' (Taylor 2021). That seems a bit tough on city leaders, given the fiscal constraints of being a large poor city in a state and country that do not support large poor cities (Peck 2012). But with an inability to address systemic disadvantage, some hard-fought gains over recent years appear worryingly fragile. The county jail census ticked up in the last year, partly as a result of pandemic-related distress, and partly due to disturbing increases in violent crime and homicides. The crisis of fatal drug overdose continues to escalate. The overall rate of fatal overdose in 2020 increased 10% overall, with an especially troubling 29% increase among Black Philadelphians (Whelan 2021). The city also still struggles profoundly with housing insecurity. There are a number of recent efforts – notably, the city is piloting a small tiny house village (Lubrano 2020), and also has a housing repair (City of Philadelphia, no date) and rapid rehousing programme (City of Philadelphia: Rapid Rehousing, no date). While intensive, these efforts require considerable commitments of time and resources for only a small number of service recipients (File 2021). There are no large-scale efforts underway to address the proximal causes of housing instability – lack of affordable housing, lack of supportive housing for people with mental illness, lack of housing for people with ongoing substance use – or their distal risk factors tied to poverty, low wages, education, and other disadvantages.

Lack of robust upstream programming reflects the marginalised status of public health locally and nationally. Public health encompasses a broad range of downstream activities such as surveillance and education. But given its preventative orientation, its strength in any setting can be measured by its ability to reshape unhealthy environments before they produce injury and disease. Since the 1970s there has been far less investment in the public health system in the United States compared to industrialised peers (Bradley and Taylor 2013). The COVID-19 pandemic made this clear on a national level. In addition to terrible transmission and death rates in the first year of the pandemic, the country still lacks adequate testing capacity. An ocean of ink has lamented how disinvestment in public health infrastructure prevented a coherent response. Few places exhibited the impossible choices facing a depleted public health workforce more than Philadelphia. The municipal department of health accounts for 4% of the local budget, and when the pandemic struck, the department lacked the resources to provide testing and vaccination. As a result, it had to partner with non-governmental entities, which resulted in a dismal failure when it became clear that one organisation run by recent college graduates was misappropriating vaccines and negotiating political favours (Murrell 2021). While the incident was infuriating in its specifics, the broader and more relevant story is one of an impoverished public health workforce, with far too little funding to meet the public health needs of its community members. That these deficiencies in national and local public health spending track racial disparities in COVID-19 transmission and death rates is just another tragic reminder of the failure to address structural disadvantage.

There is an urgent need to reverse the disinvestment in public health services and to invest large amounts appropriately in areas that have suffered from generational neglect. The political strategy for achieving this remains unclear in the United States, despite growing rhetorical support for the importance of the social determinants of health. The point we make here is bitter: notwithstanding incredibly hard-working practitioners and good intentions, the public health system in the United States has limited capacity to deliver community-based care in many places with the most unmet social and health needs. The private health care system has the capacity to create high-quality programmes, but lacks the financial incentives, and therefore motivation to do so.

These limitations are especially frustrating at a time when the possibilities and expectations have never been greater for substantive reform of law enforcement practices including reduction if not elimination of drugs policing. This window of opportunity might not exist for long. In one of the PAD pilot zones, some residents are starting to call for a return to harsher drugs policing. A recent community meeting with city leadership there captured the frustrations of repeated failures of downstream programmes to reverse or even slow harms resulting from decades of discrimination and disinvestment. As one resident and the executive director of a community group noted:

> After 20 years of interventions, racial disparities in areas ranging from housing to health outcomes have increased. While every effort has claimed success at some point – none have had any form of measurable, sustainable success for residents, only for those leading the efforts.

As a harbinger of the fragility of the current moment, another community member ominously but understandably stated that her 'neighborhood is unsafe', and that she wants it 'back, and I want there to be no more violence, no more drugs. I need my community to be safe and clean for the kids' (Savage 2021). Although PAD and similar programmes might have benefitted from the support of progressive advocates and public health champions a few years ago, today they are often viewed as tentative and conciliatory, if not problematically supportive of carceral systems, which further undermines their political support.

The PAD programme, and similar efforts in other cities, raise a number of important and difficult questions for activists, policymakers, and service practitioners. These relate to uncertainty about the right pace of change, not in terms of preference, but in terms of capacity to replace harmful drugs policing in ways that are sustainable. It is likewise critical to understand whether programmes like PAD are necessary incremental reforms on the way to durable transformations or if they frustrate deeper changes. Most importantly, PAD raises the fundamental and perpetual question of how government and service providers can be responsive to the scale, acuity, and immediacy of community distress, without leaning on old and ineffective methods of control and punishment. The answers to some of these questions will be intensely local. While policymakers debate and consider these questions and tensions theoretically, frontline workers and communities will continue to live and experience them in practice.

Conclusion

Programmes such as PAD are better than conventional drugs policing. No one should be arrested for drug possession or purchasing, and everyone who needs social and health services should have ready access, especially in times of crisis. PAD is an important step towards actualising those ideals. Yet, programmes such as PAD operate too far downstream, limiting their effectiveness and increasing the chances of incidental harm. Whether the balance of benefits and harms justifies investments in these programmes, versus investments in other approaches, is likely context dependent. Ultimately, most if not all policing practices should converge on models like PAD and LEAD, which emphasise health and address problems with supportive services. But transforming upstream conditions is essential to reversing historical discrimination, decentring the police from the response to harms related to substance use, and promoting healthier communities long term.

References

ACLU. (2020) *A Tale of Two Countries: Racially Targeted Arrests in the Era of Marijuana Reform*. ACLU. Available from: https://www.aclu.org/report/tale-two-countries-racially-targeted-arrests-era-marijuana-reform.

Ahmed, O., Mao, J., Holt, S., Hawk, K., D'Onofrio, G., Martel, S. and Melnick, E. (2019) 'A scalable, automated warm handoff from the emergency department to community sites offering continued medication for opioid use disorder: Lessons learned from the EMBED trial stakeholders'. *Journal of Substance Abuse Treatment*. 102: 47–52.

Alexander, M. (2020) *The New Jim Crow: Mass Incarceration in the Age of Colorblindness*. New York, NY: The New Press.

Al-Lamee, R., Thompson, D., Dehbi, H., Sen, S., Tang, K. Davies, J., Keeble, T., Mielewczik, M., Kaprielian, R., Malik, I. and Nijjer, S. (2018) 'Percutaneous coronary intervention in stable angina (ORBITA): A double-blind, randomised controlled trial'. *The Lancet*. 391(10115): 31–40.

American Public Health Association. (2018) *Addressing Law Enforcement Violence as a Public Health Issue*. APHA. Available from: https://www.apha.org/policies-and-advocacy/public-health-policy-statements/policy-database/2019/01/29/law-enforcement-violence.

Anderson, E. and Burris, S. (2017) 'Policing and public health: Not quite the right analogy'. *Policing & Society*. 27(3): 300–313.

Anderson, E., Shefner, R., Koppel, R., Megerian, C. and Frasso, R. (2022) 'Experiences with the Philadelphia police-assisted diversion program: A qualitative study'. *International Journal of Drug Policy*. 100: 103521.

Ao, B. (2021) 'Philadelphia-area mental health crisis centers and hospitals grapple with shortage of inpatient beds'. *The Philadelphia Inquirer*. Available from: https://www.inquirer.com/health/coronavirus/philadelphia-area-mental-health-crisis-centers-hospitals-grapple-with-shortage-inpatient-beds-20210315.html.

Beckett, K. (2014) *Seattle's Law Enforcement Assisted Diversion Program: Lessons Learned from the First Two Years*. Seattle, WA: University of Washington: Law, Societies & Justice Program and Department of Sociology.

Beletsky, L. and Davis, C. (2017) 'Today's fentanyl crisis: Prohibition's iron law, revisited'. *International Journal of Drug Policy*. 46: 156–159.

Beletsky, L. (2019) 'America's favorite antidote: Drug-induced homicide in the age of the overdose crisis'. *Utah Law Review*. 4: 833–890.

Bishop, T., Press, M., Keyhani, S. and Pincus, H. (2014) 'Acceptance of insurance by psychiatrists and the implications for access to mental health care'. *JAMA Psychiatry*. 71(2): 176–181.

Bloom, S. (2015) *Why Should Philadelphia Become a Trauma-Informed City?* Philadelphia, PA: School of Public Health, Drexel University.

Bradley, E. and Taylor, L. (2013) The American Health Care Paradox: Why Spending More is Getting Us Less. New York, NY: Public Affairs.

Breen, T. (2020) 'Pilot effort fails: Who's to blame?' *New Haven Independent*. Available from: https://www.newhavenindependent.org/index.php/archives/entry/lead_report/.

Burke, N., Hellman, J., Scott, B., Weems, C. and Carrion, V. (2011) 'The impact of adverse childhood experiences on an urban pediatric population'. *Child Abuse & Neglect*. 35(6): 408–413.

Burris, S., Anderson, E., Craigg, A. and Davis, C. (2009) 'Racial disparities in injection-related HIV: A case study of toxic law'. *Temple Law Review*. 82(5): 1263–1307.

Burris, S., Anderson, E., Davis, C. and Beletsky, L. (2020) 'Toward healthy drug policy in the United States – The case of safehouse'. *New England Journal of Medicine*. 382(1): 4–5.

Campbell Britton, M., Hodshon, B. and Chaudhry, S. (2019) 'Implementing a warm handoff between hospital and skilled nursing facility clinicians'. *Journal of Patient Safety*. 15(3): 198–204.

Carey, B. (2021) 'Science plays the long game: But people have mental health issues now'. *The New York Times*. Available from: https://www.nytimes.com/2021/04/01/health/mental-health-treatments.html.

Chang, A. and Martin, R. (2020) 'Summer of racial reckoning'. *NPR*. Available from: https://www.npr.org/2020/08/16/902179773/summer-of-racial-reckoning-the-match-lit.

Cicero, T. and Ellis, M. (2017) 'The prescription opioid epidemic: A review of qualitative studies on the progression from initial use to abuse'. *Dialogues in Clinical Neuroscience*. 19(3): 259–269.

City of Philadelphia. (n.d.) *Get Housing Repair Help*. Available from: https://www.phila.gov/departments/division-of-housing-and-community-development/get-help/get-home-improvement-help/ [Accessed 15 June 2021].

City of Philadelphia. (n.d.) *Office of Homeless Services – Rapid Rehousing*. Available from: http://philadelphiaofficeofhomelessservices.org/services/rapid-re-housing/ [Accessed 15 June 2021].

Clair, M. (2020) *Privilege and Punishment: How Race and Class Matter in Criminal Court*. Princeton, NJ: Princeton University Press.

Clifasefi, S., Lonczak, H. and Collins, S. (2017) 'Seattle's Law Enforcement Assisted Diversion (LEAD) program'. *Crime & Delinquency*. 63(4): 429–445.

Cohen, R. et al. (2021) Health Insurance Coverage: Early Release of Estimates From the National Health Interview Survey, January–June 2020. National Center for Health Statistics. U.S. Department of Health and Human Services, Centers for Disease Control and Prevention, Atlanta, GA

Collins, S., Lonczak, H. and Clifasefi, S. (2017) 'Seattle's Law Enforcement Assisted Diversion (LEAD): Program effects on recidivism outcomes'. *Evaluation & Program Planning*. 64: 49–56.

Collins, S., Lonczak, H. and Clifasefi, S. (2019) 'Seattle's Law Enforcement Assisted Diversion (LEAD): Program effects on criminal justice and legal system utilization and costs'. *Journal of Experimental Criminology*. 15(2): 201–211.

Comer, S., Pravetoni, M., Coop, A., Baumann, M. and Cunningham, C. (2021) 'Potential unintended consequences of class-wide drug scheduling based on chemical structure: A cautionary tale for fentanyl-related compounds'. *Drug & Alcohol Dependence*. 221: 108530.

Comfort, M., Nurse, A., McKay, T. and Kramer, K. (2011) 'Taking children into account: Addressing the intergenerational effects of parental incarceration'. *Criminology & Public Policy*. 10(3): 839–850.

Congressional Budget Office. (2015) *CBO, Increase the Number of Housing Choice Vouchers*. Available from: https://www.cbo.gov/budget-options/other/51473 [Accessed 1 June 2020].

Cooper, H. (2015) 'War on drugs policing and police brutality'. *Substance Use & Misuse*. 50(8–9): 1188–1194.

Cornwell, T. (2019) 'House calls are reaching the tipping point — Now we need the workforce'. *Journal of Patient-Centered Research & Reviews*. 6(3): 188–191.

Council of State Governments Justice Center. (2019) *Confined and Costly: How Supervision Violations Are Filling Prisons and Burdening Budgets*. Available from: https://csgjusticecenter.org/publications/confined-costly/.

De Veaux, M. (2013) 'The trauma of the incarceration experience'. *Harvard Civil Rights-Civil Liberties Law Review*. 48(1): 257–278.

Epstein, D. and ProPublica. (2017) 'When the evidence says no, but doctors say yes'. *The Atlantic*. Available from: https://www.theatlantic.com/health/archive/2017/02/when-evidence-says-no-but-doctors-say-yes/517368/.

FBI. (2020) *FBI Uniform Crime Report*. Crime in the United States 2019 - Arrests and Arrest Table: Arrests for Drug Abuse Violations. Washington, DC: Department of Justice.

Feldman, N. (2019) *Philly Health Officials, Advocates Split on Impact of Smoking Ban at Inpatient Rehabs*. Philadelphia, PA: WHYY. Available from: https://whyy.org/articles/philly-health-officials-advocates-split-on-impact-of-smoking-ban-at-inpatient-rehabs/.

File, N. (2021) 'Philly's housing encampments of 2020 led to a nationally celebrated deal. Then it all began to unravel'. *Philadelphia Magazine*. Available from: https://www.phillymag.com/news/2021/10/09/parkway-encampments-housing-agreement/.

Findings from the Philadelphia Urban ACE Survey. (2013) 'Institute for safe families'. Available at: https://www.rwjf.org/en/library/research/2013/09/findings-from-the-philadelphia-urban-ace-survey.html.

Finkelstein, A., Taubman, S. and Doyle, J. (2020) 'Health care hotspotting - A randomized, controlled trial'. *New England Journal of Medicine*. 382(22): 2173–2174.

Fisher, E., Wennberg, D., Stukel, T., Gottlieb, D., Lucas, F. and Pinder, E. (2003) 'The implications of regional variations in medicare spending. Part 1: The content, quality, and accessibility of care'. *Annals of Internal Medicine*. 138(4): 273–287.

Forman, J. (2017) *Locking Up Our Own: Crime and Punishment in Black America*. Farrar, New York, NY: Straus and Giroux.

Fuller, T. (2020) 'Oregon decriminalizes small amounts of heroin and cocaine; four states legalize marijuana'. *The New York Times*. Available from: https://www.nytimes.com/2020/11/04/us/ballot-measures-propositions-2020.html.

Garland, E., Hanley, A., Kline, A. and Cooperman, N. (2019) 'Mindfulness-oriented recovery enhancement reduces opioid craving among individuals with opioid use disorder and chronic pain in medication assisted treatment: Ecological momentary assessments from a stage 1 randomized controlled trial'. *Drug & Alcohol Dependence*. 203: 61–65.

Geller, A., Fagan, J., Tyler, T. and Link, B. (2014) 'Aggressive policing and the mental health of young urban men'. *American Journal of Public Health.* 104(12): 2321–2327.

George, J. (2021) 'These Philadelphia-area hospitals made, and lost, the most money in fiscal 2020'. *Philadelphia Business Journal.* Available from: https://www.bizjournals.com/philadelphia/news/2021/06/11/philadelphia-hospitals-profit-loss-2020-covid-19.html?mc_cid=880f6e783d&mc_eid=3fdb9a74dc.

Golden, P. (2021) 'The other death penalty: How Philadelphia leads America in life without parole sentences'. *Penn Political Review.* Available from: http://pennpoliticalreview.org/2021/03/the-other-death-penalty-how-philadelphia-leads-america-in-life-without-parole-sentences/ [Accessed 1 July 2021].

Gonnerman, J. (2018) 'Larry Krasner's campaign to end mass incarceration'. *The New Yorker.* Available from: https://www.newyorker.com/magazine/2018/10/29/larry-krasners-campaign-to-end-mass-incarceration.

Gormley, E. (2021) 'Social workers can't help people in crisis by partnering with police'. *Jacobin.* Available from: https://www.jacobinmag.com/2021/04/social-workers-police-chicago-co-responder-model.

Grossman, M., Chaloupka, F. and Shim, K. (2002) 'Illegal drug use and public policy'. *Health Affairs.* 21(2): 134–145.

Hart, C. and Hart, M. (2019) 'Opioid crisis: Another mechanism used to perpetuate American racism'. *Cultural Diversity & Ethnic Minority Psychology.* 25(1): 6–11.

Helfgott, J., Parkin, W. and Fisher, C. (2019) 'Crisis-flagged misdemeanors in Seattle: Arrests, referrals, charges, and case dispositions'. *Criminology, Criminal Justice, Law & Society.* 20(2): 59–85.

Henry, M., Shivji, A., de Sousa, T. and Cohen, R. (2015) *The 2015 Annual Homeless Assessment Report (AHAR) to Congress Part 1: Point-in-time Estimates of Homelessness.* US Department of Housing and Urban Development: Office of Community Planning and Development.

Himmelstein, D., Campbell, T. and Woolhandler, S. (2020) 'Health care administrative costs in the United States and Canada, 2017'. *Annals of Internal Medicine.* 172(2): 134–142.

Himmelstein, D. and Woolhandler, S. (2016) 'Public health's falling share of US health spending'. *American Journal of Public Health.* 106(1): 56–57.

Housing and Urban Development (HUD). (2020) *2019. AHAR: Part 1 - PIT Estimates of Homelessness in the U.S.* Available from: https://www.hudexchange.info/resource/5948/2019-ahar-part-1-pit-estimates-of-homelessness-in-the-us/ [Accessed 1 June 2021].

Huq, A. (2016) 'The consequences of disparate policing: Evaluating stop and frisk as a modality of urban policing'. *Minnesota Law Review.* 101(6): 2397–2480.

Jacoby, S., Dong, B., Beard, J., Wiebe, D. and Morrison, C. (2018) 'The enduring impact of historical and structural racism on urban violence in Philadelphia'. *Social Science & Medicine.* 199: 87–95.

Jefferson, K. and Jamision, C. (2019) *Year One Police Process Evaluation for Atlanta's Pre-arrest Diversion Program.* Atlanta, GA.

Joudrey, P., Nelson, C., Lawson, K., Morford, K., Muley, D., Watson, C., Wang, E. and Crusto, C. (2020) *Formative Evaluation of the City of New Haven Law Enforcement Assisted Diversion (LEAD) Pilot Program.* New Haven, CT.

Lantz, P. (2019) 'The medicalization of population health: Who will stay upstream?' *The Milbank Quarterly.* 97(1): 36–39.

Lapidos, A., Lapedis, J. and Heisler, M. (2019) 'Realizing the value of community health workers — New opportunities for sustainable financing'. *New England Journal of Medicine.* 380(21): 1990–1992.

Larimer, M., Malone, D., Garner, M., Atkins, D., Burlingham, B., Lonczak, H., Tanzer, K., Ginzler, J., Clifasefi, S., Hobson, W. and Marlatt, G. (2009) 'Health care and public service use and costs before and after provision of housing for chronically homeless persons with severe alcohol problems'. *JAMA*. 301(13): 1349–1357.

Lattimore, P., Tueller, S., Levin-Rector, A. and Witwer, A. (2020) 'The prevalence of local criminal justice practices'. *Federal Probation*. 83(1): 28–37.

Lubrano, A. (2020) 'Tiny-house villages coming to NE and West Philly, part of deal that closed Parkway homeless encampment'. *Philadelphia Inquirer*. Available from: https://www.inquirer.com/news/homeless-tiny-house-parkway-encampment-philadelphia-20201212.html#loaded.

Magaña, E., Perrone, D. and Malm, A. (2022) 'A process evaluation of San Francisco's Law Enforcement Assisted Diversion program'. *Criminal Justice Policy Review*. 33(2): 148–176.

Mars, S., Bourgois, P., Karandinos, G., Montero, F. and Ciccarone, D. (2014) '"Every "never" I ever said came true": Transitions from opioid pills to heroin injecting'. *International Journal of Drug Policy*. 25(2): 257–266.

Melamed, S. and Purcell, D. (2019) 'The probation trap'. *The Philadelphia Inquirer*. Available from: https://www.inquirer.com/news/inq/probation-parole-pennsylvania-philadelphia-criminal-justice-system-20191024.html.

Moraff, C. (2013) '"Opportunity index" ranks Philly 'burbs for social mobility'. *Philadelphia Magazine*. Available from: https://www.phillymag.com/news/2013/10/31/opportunity-index-philadelphia-suburbs-social-mobility/.

Morrissey, S., Nyrop, K. and Lee, T. (2019) 'Landscapes of loss and recovery: The anthropology of police-community relations and harm reduction'. *Human Organization*. 78(1): 28–42.

Muñiz, J. and Turney, K. (2020) 'Collateral consequences of incarceration on community'. In Gould, L. and Brent, J. (eds.) *Routledge Handbook on American Prisons*. Abingdon: Routledge: 280–293.

Murrell, D. (2021) 'The bizarre, infuriating story of Philly fighting COVID's meteoric rise and swift fall'. *Philadelphia Magazine*. Available from: https://www.phillymag.com/news/2021/05/01/philly-fighting-covid-andrei-doroshin/.

National Research Council. (2014) *The Growth of Incarceration in the United States: Exploring Causes and Consequences*. Washington, DC: National Academies Press.

OECD. (2019) *Addressing Problematic Opioid Use in OECD Countries*. Paris: OECD.

OECD. (2021) *Magnetic Resonance Imaging (MRI) Units (Indicator)*.Paris: OECD.

Olfson, M. (2016) 'Building the mental health workforce capacity needed to treat adults with serious mental illnesses'. *Health Affairs*. 35(6): 983–990.

Oliver, M. and Shapiro, T. (2019) 'Disrupting the racial wealth gap'. *Contexts*. 18(1): 16–21.

Orso, A. (2021) 'Following other cities, Philly will soon send specialists alongside cops to some mental health calls'. *The Philadelphia Inquirer*. Available from: https://www.inquirer.com/news/philadelphia-police-mental-health-specialists-co-responder-unit-20210504.html.

Osypuk, T. (2013) 'Invited commentary: Integrating a life-course perspective and social theory to advance research on residential segregation and health'. *American Journal of Epidemiology*. 177(4): 310–315.

Pais, J. (2017) 'Intergenerational neighborhood attainment and the legacy of racial residential segregation: A causal mediation analysis'. *Demography*. 54(4): 1221–1250.

Palmer, J. (1975) 'Pre-arrest diversion'. *Crime & Delinquency*. 21(2): 100–108.

Peck, J. (2012) 'Austerity urbanism: American cities under extreme economy'. *City*. 16(6): 626–655.

Philadelphia Housing Authority. (n.d.) Available from: http://www.pha.phila.gov/housing/admissions.aspx [Accessed 1 May 2021].

Philadelphia's Participation in the Safety and Justice Challenge. (2021) 'City of Philadelphia'. Available at: https://www.phila.gov/programs/philadelphia-safety-and-justice-challenge/ [Accessed 15 June 2021].

Potier, C., Laprévote, V., Dubois-Arber, F., Cottencin, O. and Rolland, B. (2014) 'Supervised injection services: What has been demonstrated? A systematic literature review'. *Drug & Alcohol Dependence*. 145: 48–68.

Read, Z. (2020) 'Stigma, cost and lack of access mean fewer mental health resources for Black men'. *The Philadelphia Tribune*. Available from: https://www.phillytrib.com/news/health/stigma-cost-and-lack-of-access-mean-fewer-mental-health-resources-for-black-men/article_c48ebc83-dc98-5f1d-bc30-639696a5c271.html.

Reinhardt, U. (2019) *Priced Out*. Princeton, NJ: Princeton University Press.

Rosenbaum, S., Kindig, D., Bao, J., Byrnes, M. and O'Laughlin, C. (2015) 'The value of the nonprofit hospital tax exemption was $24.6 billion in 2011'. *Health Affairs*. 34(7): 1225–1233.

Rothstein, R. (2017) *The Color of Law: A Forgotten History of How Our Government Segregated America*. New York, NY: Liveright Publishing.

Saad, L. (2020) 'Black Americans want police to retain local presence'. *Gallup: Politics*. Available from: https://news.gallup.com/poll/316571/black-americans-police-retain-local-presence.aspx?utm_source=tagrss&utm_medium=rss&utm_campaign=syndication.

Sage, W. (2017) 'Fracking health care: How to safely de-medicalize America and recover trapped value for its people'. *New York University Journal of Law and Liberty*. 11(2): 635–671.

Savage, H. (2021) 'Kensington to Mayor Kenney: "You're the captain of this ship, and you either have to sail the ship or step on down"'. *The Kensington Voice*. Available from: https://kensingtonvoice.com/en/kensington-philadelphia-city-council/.

Schiraldi, V. (2018) *The Pennsylvania Community Corrections Story*. Columbia University Justice Lab. Available from: https://justicelab.columbia.edu/sites/default/files/content/PACommunityCorrections4.19.18finalv3.pdf.

Schuchman, M., Fain, M. and Cornwell, T. (2018) 'The resurgence of home-based primary care models in the United States'. *Geriatrics*. 3(3): 41.

Sharkey, P. (2019) *Neighborhoods and the Black White Mobility Gap*. Pew Charitable Trusts. Available from: https://www.pewtrusts.org/~/media/legacy/uploadedfiles/wwwpewtrustsorg/reports/economic_mobility/pewsharkeyv12pdf.pdf.

Shefner, R., Sloan, J., Sandler, K. and Anderson, E. (2020) 'Missed opportunities: Arrest and court touchpoints for individuals who fatally overdosed in Philadelphia in 2016'. *International Journal of Drug Policy*. 78: 102724.

Simckes, M., Willits, D., McFarland, M., McFarland, C., Rowhani-Rahbar, A. and Hajat, A. (2021) 'The adverse effects of policing on population health: A conceptual model'. *Social Science & Medicine*. 281: 114103.

Specht, E., Powell, K. and Dormo, C. (2004) 'Factors affecting missed appointment rates for pediatric patients insured by medicaid in a traditional hospital-based resident clinic and hospital-owned practice settings'. *Clinical Pediatrics*. 43(8): 749–752.

Stergiopoulos, K. and Brown, D. (2012) 'Initial coronary stent implantation with medical therapy vs medical therapy alone for stable coronary artery disease: Meta-analysis of randomized controlled trials'. *Archives of Internal Medicine*. 172(4): 312–319.

Taylor, K.-Y. (2021) 'Did last summer's Black Lives Matter protests change anything? Public officials favored symbolic gestures over policy reforms, but the country is still dramatically different than it was a year ago'. *The New Yorker*. Available from: https://www.newyorker.com/news/our-columnists/did-last-summers-protests-change-anything.

The Pew Charitable Trust. (2020) *How COVID-19 has Undercut Philadelphians' Physical and Financial Well-being*. Available from: https://www.pewtrusts.org/en/research-and-analysis/issue-briefs/2020/10/how-covid-19-has-undercut-philadelphians-physical-and-financial-well-being.

The Pew Charitable Trust. (2019) *Philadelphia 2019 the State of the City*. Available from: https://www.pewtrusts.org/-/media/assets/2019/10/sotc_2019.pdf.

The Pew Charitable Trust. (2021a) *8 Trends that Defined the Past Year in Philadelphia*. Available from: https://www.pewtrusts.org/en/research-and-analysis/articles/2021/04/13/8-trends-that-defined-the-past-year-in-philadelphia.

The Pew Charitable Trust. (2021b) *Philadelphia 2021: State of the City*. Available from: https://www.pewtrusts.org/en/research-and-analysis/reports/2021/04/philadelphia-2021-state-of-the-city.

The Pew Research Center. (2019) *Why Americans Don't Fully Trust Many Who Hold Positions of Power and Responsibility*. Available from: https://www.pewresearch.org/politics/2019/09/19/why-americans-dont-fully-trust-many-who-hold-positions-of-power-and-responsibility/.

The Philadelphia Center for Gun Violence Reporting. (2021) *Tracking Gun Violence in Philadelphia*. Available from: https://www.pcgvr.org/2021/01/06/tracking-gun-violence-in-philadelphia-january-6-2021/ [Accessed 1 June 2021].

Thomas, L., Wedel, K. and Christopher, J. (2018) 'Access to transportation and health care visits for medicaid enrollees with diabetes'. *The Journal of Rural Health*. 34(2): 162–172.

Urban Institute. (2017) *Criminal Justice Expenditures: Police, Corrections, and Courts*. Urban Institute. Available from: https://www.urban.org/policy-centers/cross-center-initiatives/state-and-local-finance-initiative/state-and-local-backgrounders/criminal-justice-police-corrections-courts-expenditures.

Warner, T. and Kramer, J. (2009) 'Closing the revolving door?' *Criminal Justice & Behavior*. 36(1): 89–109.

Weber, L., Ungar, L. and Smith, M. (2020) 'Hollowed-out public health system faces more cuts amid virus'. *KFN News*. Available from: https://khn.org/news/us-public-health-system-underfunded-under-threat-faces-more-cuts-amid-covid-pandemic/.

Whelan, A. (2021) 'Philadelphia drug deaths soared again in 2020, hitting Black residents hardest: "It's a racial justice issue"'. *The Philadelphia Inquirer*. Available from: https://www.inquirer.com/health/opioid-addiction/drug-overdoses-fatalities-philadelphia-fentanyl-20210603.html.

Worden, R. and McLean, S. (2018) 'Discretion and diversion in Albany's lead program'. *Criminal Justice Policy Review*. 29(6–7): 584–610.

12

FROM OPPONENTS TO 'INTERESTED' PARTNERS?

A case study of police and harm reduction service collaboration[1]

Esben Houborg, Tobias Kammersgaard, and Thomas Friis Søgaard

Introduction: harm reduction and drug control

This chapter presents a case study of how police and low-threshold social and harm reduction services went from being opponents to becoming partners in a joint effort to reduce drug-related harm and nuisance in relation to an open drug scene in Copenhagen. Central to this is the development of new police practices that aim to support harm reduction services and create a safer environment for drug users. The case study shows that there does not have to be a contradiction between policing and harm reduction, which has often been the case in the area of drug policy. Many studies have thus described the contradictions between drug control and harm reduction, with particular focus on how policing can undermine harm reduction or even increase the risks and harms that drug users are exposed to (Burris et al. 2004; Cooper et al. 2005; Maher and Dixon 1999). Reflecting a more general trend where collaboration between police and social and health services is increasingly set up in relation to vulnerable groups (Wood et al. 2015), in many countries, there has been an increased focus on how new forms of collaboration between police and harm reduction services can minimise risks and harms to drug users (Bacon 2016a; Burris et al. 2004). Thus, in drug research, some researchers speak of 'harm reduction policing' (Caulkins 2017; Caulkins and Reuter 2009; Dorn and South 1990; Greenfield and Paoli 2012; Kammersgaard 2019; Shiner 2016; Spooner et al. 2004). One of the places where there is a particular focus on cooperation between the police and harm reduction is in connection with the establishment of drug consumption rooms. Watson et al. (2018) have, for instance, shown that collaboration between police and social and health authorities is important for the successful establishment of drug consumption rooms. Such collaboration can make policy on drug consumption rooms suit local needs and provide a strong basis for a public health approach to local drug problems.

DOI: 10.4324/9781003154136-13

While cross-institutional collaboration has often been highlighted as a key element in harm reduction policing, there remains a need for empirical explorations of the diverse networking processes giving shape to particular harm reduction approaches, as well as a conceptual framework for understanding such processes. In this chapter, we propose that the concepts of 'policy network' (Carlsson 2000) and actor-network theory (ANT) (Latour 1993) can productively be used to analyse the various networking processes involved in the construction of harm reduction policing. More specifically, the chapter explores the work that went into 'interesting' and 'enrolling' (Callon 1984) the police as well as local harm reduction and low-threshold services in a network of collective action in the largest open drug scene in Scandinavia, located in the neighbourhood of Vesterbro in Copenhagen, Denmark. Aside from providing insights into the networking processes involved in the construction of a harm reduction policing scheme at the Vesterbro scene, we also show how the scheme has created new ways of working for the various actors involved and made new types of collective action possible in relation to the local drug environment.

Local drug policy network

In Denmark, the development of close cooperation between the police and social and health authorities in relation to marginalised drug users is a relatively new phenomenon. At the drug scene in Vesterbro, Copenhagen, the development of a local drug policy based on cross-institutional collaboration is, however, part of a longer process involving dialogue between different public and private stakeholders such as the local police, the municipality, and local non-governmental organisations (NGOs). One way to understand the current policy towards the drug scene and its development is to see it as a 'policy network' (Carlsson 2000). The concept of policy networks provides a horizontal perspective on policy that focuses on how public and private stakeholders including third-sector actors, connect in ways that enable them to act collectively. Policy networks often develop around specific problems or situations that particular actors (stakeholders) find it necessary to handle in one way or another (Marres 2005). Network arrangements between public and private actors have, for instance, played a particularly important role not only in the making of local drug policies, including the implementation of drug consumption rooms (Houborg and Frank 2014; Kübler and Wälti 2001; Percival 2009; Wälti and Kübler 2003), but sometimes also in the making of national drug policies (Common and Acedvedo 2006). Policy networks thus involve the organisation and coordination of action, but the scope and nature of this organisation may vary.

In our analysis of the composition of the policy network at Vesterbro, we draw on elements from actor-network theory. While this theoretical framework has been applied in social drug research (e.g. Demant and Dilkes-Frayne 2015; Duff 2011; Nielsen and Houborg 2015), it has less often been used in drug policy analysis (Dányi 2017; Houborg 2012). In the first part of the analysis, we examine how the policy network was created and subsequently achieved a degree of institutionalisation. We use ANT to show how stakeholders were 'interested' in being part of a network and how they became 'enrolled' in the network. Researchers such as Latour (1993), Callon (1984), and Law (1986) have studied how different kinds of (human and non-human[2]) actors come to act collectively – become part of an actor-network – through various methods, techniques, tactics, and strategies. The premise is that different actors have different interests and that these interests need to be 'translated' into a form of alignment where they contribute to collective action. If successful, the actors will take on certain roles and functions within the network. A key point in ANT is that it can require a great deal of work both to make actors interested and to enrol them (give them a role) in a network and that it may require just as much work to maintain the network, that is to keep the actors 'interested' and make them fulfil specific 'roles'.

In the second part of the analysis, we examine how participation in the policy network evokes certain characteristics and capacities in the participating stakeholders. We focus particularly on how local police participation in the policy network enabled them to work in new ways towards the drug scene. Here, we are inspired by the idea expressed in assemblage theory that a network or an assemblage is not just the sum of the parts, but that networks have emergent properties because participation in a network mobilises or activates particular characteristics and capacities of the involved actors (Delanda 2006). This perspective rests on the assumption that actors, at any given time, realise only certain distinctive characteristics and capabilities, which is why it becomes an empirical question to explore how the composition of certain network relations shapes what specific actors (can) do. In other words, to understand the governance of the drug scene in Vesterbro, it is necessary to examine both the relationships between the actors involved in the local policy network and how participation in the network shapes the capabilities and doings of the different actors.

Methods and data

The analysis is based on data collected between 2014 and 2017 when the first author (EH) started to document the policy changes towards the open drug scene in Vesterbro, Copenhagen. During this period, we conducted 33 interviews with drug users, 33 interviews with local residents, and 22 interviews with local social workers and police officers. In addition to the interviews, 249 hours of field observations were conducted in the drug scene in Vesterbro in 2017. Furthermore, we collected official status reports produced by police officers about their work in the Vesterbro drug scene. These status reports cover two months in 2017.

A historical perspective on collaboration in Vesterbro

In Vesterbro, the relationship between the police and social and health service organisations (both governmental and non-governmental) has undergone significant historical changes and can be divided into three periods. The first period was from 1990 to the mid-2000s. This period was characterised by little or no collaboration and even occasional hostility between the police and the other actors. The second period was from the mid-2000s until 2012, when collaboration gradually started to develop. Lastly, from 2012 to the present day, collaboration between the police and social and health service organisations has expanded and become institutionalised. Below, we review the development from opposition to collaboration by looking at how the initial (and conflicting) interests of the different actors were gradually aligned and how actors were enrolled in a policy network focusing on harm reduction in the local drug scene.

Contradictions and lack of collective action

From 1990 to the mid-2000s, little collaboration existed between the police and the various governmental and non-governmental low-threshold organisations at Vesterbro. The reason for this lack of collaboration was that the police in 1990, after receiving complaints from residents and business owners, decided to launch a new strategy aimed at 'stressing' the local drug users, in the hope that this would lead drug users to disperse or to relocate to other areas. The new 'stress strategy' was based on a zero-tolerance approach towards disorder, crime, and behaviour believed to constitute a nuisance or inconvenience to other citizens, and included the use of zonal banning orders. The police divided the Vesterbro area into separate zones. If a person acted inappropriately, they could be fined and banned from a particular or several zones (for a more detailed description, see Frantzsen 2003; Houborg et al. 2014). Drug users were thus constituted as a criminal and public order problem that should be dealt with through the criminal justice system. The stress strategy was supported by some citizens, who saw drug users as a nuisance and a source of insecurity. Other residents and NGOs, however, believed that drug users had a right to stay in Vesterbro, and worked towards the establishment of low-threshold and harm reduction services in the area. The municipality similarly wanted to address the social and health problems of the drug users but also recognised the nuisances experienced by some residents, such as drug use in public space and discarded needles (see Houborg and Frank 2014). As this illustrates, the drug scene and the drug users at Vesterbro were problematised and made into an object of government in very different and contradictory ways.

Establishment of dialogue and incipient cooperation

During the mid-2000s, things started to change, laying the basis for the present collaboration between police and low-threshold and harm reduction services, to which various factors contributed. While studies of partnership policing have described how police often take a steering role in facilitating and shaping multi-agency collaboration (Cherney et al. 2006; Crawford 2006; Lister 2006; Søgaard et al. 2017), at the Vesterbro scene, civil society actors took on the facilitating role. At Vesterbro,

NGOs, working to develop harm reduction services such as drug consumption rooms, took the initiative of trying to establish a dialogue between different drug scene stakeholders: the police, residents, businesses, and the municipality. In doing so, they attempted to *interest* the different stakeholders in collaborating to find new common solutions to the drug scene issues. A key element in this was to try and convince the various stakeholders that it was to their benefit if the conditions for the local drug users were improved. A central slogan was: 'What's good for the drug users is good for the residents'. Since the police were concerned with drug-related disorder and other nuisances, as these were likely to generate complaints from residents and business owners, it was particularly important to make the police realise that an improvement in the conditions for the drug users was likely to result in a reduction in complaints. In other words, making the police believe in the abovementioned slogan was central to the 'interestment' of the police. The police did get interested, partly because they realised that despite their efforts to 'stress' drug users, the drug scene and the level of complaints from residents remained. There was, therefore, a gradual realisation among police leaders that the zero-tolerance strategy was not sustainable. Another contributing factor was that the NGOs used a double tactic of initiating dialogue with the police, on the one hand, while on the other, continuously filing complaints about the unlawful treatment of drug users by the police. At Vesterbro, this came to involve more foot patrols tasked with getting 'closer' to the citizens and drug users (Vesterbro Bladet 2007). In the early and mid-2000s, there was thus a coincidence of stakeholders from civil society who initiated a dialogue with the police as well as interest among the police to engage in a dialogue in the hope of developing a new policy towards the local drug scene.

Crucial for the development of a functioning policy network is the step from dialogue to actual cooperation in solving specific issues and problems. While the initial dialogue *interested* the police in engaging in collaboration, concrete collaborations had the effect of *enrolling* the police in a collaborative setup where they took on a new role both in relation to the drug users and in relation to the other stakeholders working in the area (Callon 1984). The establishment of a new drop-in centre and a low-threshold health service played a central role in this process. While these two services were established through collaboration between public and private stakeholders (see Houborg and Frank 2014), the local police were part of the monitoring group following the projects. This meant that the police got involved in discussing many of the practical details in the establishment of the new services. One central issue was to make drug users move from their old 'hang out' places to the new services. Here, the police contributed by suspending the prohibition zones around the new services and by engaging in dialogue with drug users to convince them to relocate to the new services. As an officer explained:

> You can say that we tried to work on the attitudes [of the drug users]. [We said]: 'Now an initiative has been set up for you, so now you can have a place where you can be without being bothered. But if you keep hanging

> out here on the street, then it has no effect, then people cannot see the positive in it, if you still hang out at their doorstep. So now, try to help, make sure the project gets a good start, and go over there [to the drop-in centre]'. I think they have been very responsive to that. Just by saying, 'It's your place, and you must use it. And you don't have to hang out here because then there is no need for it [the drop-in-centre]'.
>
> *(Police Officer, 2014)*

Within a short period of time, the drug scene relocated, something the police had attempted to achieve through many years of zero-tolerance policing. This demonstrated that through collaboration and by improving the conditions for drug users, it was possible also to improve the conditions for (some) residents, who were now less bothered by the drug users. The relocation did give rise to some new complaints about gatherings of drug users, public drug use, and discarded needles. Particularly concerned was a local high school located close to the drop-in centre. However, the complaints were not on the same scale as previously (Bancroft and Houborg 2020).

The monitoring group became a forum for discussions about the drug scene between the municipality, police, and civil society. It came to function as a place where the different stakeholders could discuss their perspectives and as a place where they learned to cooperate in solving specific problems linked to drug users in Vesterbro. In an interview, one central civil society actor expressed surprise about how easy it was to collaborate with the police:

> In general, I think they [the police] have been very responsive. And what has been important with the monitoring group is that everyone (...) is represented and listens to each other's situation. (...) it is really important if you are to make some proper decisions that you (...) listen to each other and understand one another's everyday life and situation.
>
> *(NGO activist, 2015)*

With the collaboration around the establishment of the drop-in centre and the health service, the policy network started to take form. Crucial to this was that the police went from being an opponent to becoming a collaborator. They went from chasing drug users (and in turn potentially increasing the risks and harms to drug users) to becoming an actor that would support harm reduction efforts.

Institutionalisation and formalisation of the policy network

In 2012, the Danish Parliament passed an amendment to the Narcotic Drugs Act, which allowed municipalities to establish drug consumption rooms (Act No. 606, 18 June 2012). In Copenhagen, the municipality had for many years pushed for permission to establish drug consumption rooms and thus immediately set out to establish one. As legally required, the municipality made an agreement with the local police that defined an area 'in the immediate vicinity of' the drug consumption room where the police would refrain from prosecuting users for possession of small amounts of illegal drugs if they were in the target group of the drug consumption rooms, that is, people over 18 years who had a 'strong addiction as a consequence of a long and persistent abuse of drugs' (Law on Euphoriant Substances §3b). The leader of the local police precinct decided to define the whole area of inner Vesterbro as an area excepted from conventional drug law enforcement. According to the leader, it was important to include all of the different services that drug users would make use of in the area as part of this 'buffer zone', as he called it (Police manager, 2015). This meant that the last of the remaining prohibition zones from the era of zero-tolerance disappeared.

Furthermore, the police leader also appointed two seasoned police officers to conduct foot patrols in the area. These were to engage in dialogue with drug users, residents, and low-threshold services in an effort to maintain public order and to support the services. At the same time, other patrols were ordered to refrain from prosecuting drug users in the area (though not including the drug squad, who investigated organised drug crime in the city, which was not under this authority). As a result, police officers at Vesterbro were now to use dialogue to regulate the drug scene and mediate between the drug scene and the local community. The establishment of the drug consumption rooms and the agreement between the police and the municipality can be seen as a formalisation of the cooperation that already existed. This was also illustrated in an interview with a manager of one of the drug consumption rooms, who emphasised the importance of 'seeing each other as partners':

> It's about trying to see each other as partners all the time and get rid of the bumps on the road. Because, after all, it has changed completely. It is a remarkable change that has taken place. But it is clear that we have different functions, and we all have different roles, and we also have different cultures and different professional backgrounds (...). So it's obvious there are some clashes, of course there are. But they are nothing compared to what they have been.
>
> *(Head of drug consumption room, 2017)*

Aside from facilitating cross-institutional collaboration, the establishment of drug consumption rooms also meant a marked qualitative change in the practical cooperation between police and social workers, which we now turn to.

New roles and forms of collaboration

Previous ethnographic studies of the street-level work of police officers have highlighted two important things. Firstly, the special role of the beat officer is to take care of emergency situations that require a solution here and now. In Bittner's (1974/2005) words, the police must take care of everything that falls under the category: 'something that should not happen and that someone should do something about now!' (p. 161). Secondly, according to Bittner (1974/1990), the police comprise a distinctive social institution because of their authority to use coercive force in these situations, as he argued: 'The role of the police is best understood as a mechanism for the distribution of non-negotiable coercive force employed in accordance with the dictates of an intuitive grasp of situational exigencies' (p. 131). However, most situations are still resolved without the use of coercion, and the use of force is often only a last resort. There are various studies of how police officers handle situations with mentally ill people, homeless people, and other vulnerable people without the use of force (Bittner 1967; Morabito 2007; Punch 1979; Teplin and Pruett 1992; Wood et al. 2014, 2015). These studies show how police officers can act as 'secret social workers' (Punch 1979) or 'street-level psychiatrists' (Teplin and Pruett 1992). The possibility for officers to work in this way is dependent on the availability of health and social services and on the legislative and organisational framework that officers work under (Morabito 2007). However, according to Wood et al. (2017), much police work with vulnerable people often takes place in a 'grey zone' (see also Hartmann 2014), where local and often informal resources and actors are involved in resolving problematic situations.

When we look at the local police at Vesterbro, much of the work can be characterised as 'grey zone work', where knowledge of local people and 'grey zone resources' play an important role, alongside the use of more formal resources. At Vesterbro, for example, the local police often participate in psychiatric admissions of persons considered to be a danger to themselves or others. Local knowledge and close collaboration are also important in relation to both formal and more informal action. At Vesterbro, the local police do regular one-person foot patrols, where the officers come into contact with staff and users both inside and outside the various social and health services. In an interview, an officer emphasises the importance of being present even 'when nothing is happening' (see also Rowe and Rowe 2021):

> It is also important to be there when nothing has happened, because that's when you get the informal chat. When they have seen you many times, they find out that 'he is all right'. But it can take a really long time, sometimes a half to a whole year. It is also important to be able to be recommended, that is, that someone else 'in the street'[3] says; 'That guy, you can talk to him, he is just your local officer'.
>
> *(Local officer, 2016)*

Using observations and conversations with users and other professionals, the officer gets detailed knowledge about local people, relationships, and events, which in turn expands their ability to use alternatives to the use of force when interacting with drug users. By collaborating closely with other professionals and institutions in the area, it becomes much easier for officers to use so-called 'social' interventions. For example, if an officer finds a person asleep in the street, the officer will escort this person to a shelter or a drop-in centre, where they know people who can help.

It is, however, not only police officers who draw on grey zone resources to handle situations at the Vesterbro drug scene. Professionals from social and health care facilities also use police officers as a resource. Due to their extensive knowledge about the local drug scene and the individuals who populate it, police officers can function as a resource for social and health care professionals. Based on their local knowledge, police officers can, for instance, assist in finding a missing person, monitor a vulnerable person, and contribute to the de-escalation of potentially violent situations. In a conversation, a police officer emphasised the particular interpretation of the police role that this involves. When the police enter a situation, they often find that they themselves and others expect that they 'take charge', which is why the situation in one way or another becomes 'a police matter'. This, however, is not necessarily the case for the foot patrol officers at Vesterbro. They see it as one of their most important functions to support the work of the social and health workers, even if it may sometimes be at odds with conventional law enforcement goals and logics. One police officer explained that his collaboration with social and health workers is not one where they are supposed to help him do his job as a police officer, for example, by finding a person who is wanted by the police or provide information about a criminal offence. If he takes on the role of law enforcer, it might undermine the collaboration and trust between him and the other professionals and users. He says:

> If I violate their boundaries, I jeopardise their relations with the group of people they are supposed to help. I am very conscious about that. (…) I do not want them to do things for me. They are not supposed to investigate things for me.
>
> *(Police officer, 2016)*

For the officers, redefining their role in the drug scene also involves being willing to help out in different situations, for example, by escorting a user to the emergency room or by helping users not to get expelled from opioid-substitution drug treatment. Such a situation is described in the following excerpt from one of the police status reports:

> It is important to work together on [name]'s medication, which is why we must be helpful in finding her in order to get her to go to the medication delivery.
>
> *(Excerpt from status report)*

It can also be about helping a user return to their home or to get away from the drug scene for a period of time:

> [Name] was about to collapse at [low-threshold institution], and it was necessary to get him away from the area. Previously, we have had a good dialogue with him and offered to drive him home to [other part of Copenhagen] when it no longer worked out for him at Vesterbro. Despite [him] being angry and frustrated, we succeeded in getting him away Monday night, and he was not back at Vesterbro before Thursday.
>
> *(Excerpt from status report)*

The grey zone work where police and social workers draw on each other as resources has created new ways for both parties to act in relation to the drug scene, which importantly often combines and merges police and social worker resources and approaches. On the one hand, the unique authority of the police to use coercive force is sometimes brought into play in the regulation of unruly drug users in various social and health services. On the other hand, social and health workers' perspectives are also brought into play when police officers try to resolve situations on the streets. The latter is especially important in situations and places where there is no outreach social work.

Policing the drug consumption rooms

The drug consumption rooms at Vesterbro have become an integral part of the drug scene. From 6 August 2013 to 1 June 2018, 866,476 drug intakes were made in one drug consumption facility (The Cloud) and from 2 August 2016 to 24 May 2018, 391,475 drug intakes were made in the other drug consumption facility (H17), making this a total of 1,257,951 drug intakes. This means that many drug intakes, which previously would have taken place on the streets, are now conducted inside a public institution. Along with the drug intakes, other aspects of the drug scene have also moved inside these facilities, including the often complex and conflict-ridden interactions associated with buying, selling, sharing, and using drugs (see Houborg and Holt 2018). The boundaries between the 'street' and the institution are thus, at times, fluid and something that constantly has to be regulated. In the following interview excerpt, the manager of a drug consumption room explains that while small-scale drug dealing and sharing cannot be avoided, because some of the users of the drug consumption room are 'user-dealers' (Moyle and Coomber 2015) or are entrenched in a so-called 'moral economy of drugs' (Bourgois and Schonberg 2009), the staff try to prevent organised drug dealing inside the drug consumption room:

> Drug dealing is, of course, not legal, nor here nor anywhere else in the world or in society. But what we say is that you should not enrich yourself at the expense of someone else's misery. That means that sharing small balls of drugs and sharing and things like that, we know that is going on, and

> we do not crack down on it. We crack down when we see more organised drug dealing.
>
> *(Head of consumption room, 2017)*

The manager continues to explain how they try to regulate the drug dealing inside through dialogue but that it may also be necessary to threaten users with expulsion or the threat of being reported to the police:

> What we do is that we have a chat with the persons we believe are dealing drugs and tell them to stop. And that does not always have much effect. But then we go on, and on and on and, in the end, we say that if they don't stop, they cannot use the facility (...) And to some of them, we also say that we are obliged to tell the police if we suspect that more serious dealing is taking place. Most of them respect that, and then they go outside to deal drugs, and that's what we want.
>
> *(Head of drug consumption room, 2017)*

Bacon and Seddon (2020) found a similar form of behavioural regulation in drug treatment services in the UK. While the regulation of the drug scene inside the drug consumption room is done primarily through dialogue, as the above shows, it can also be backed up by the threat of coercion and police involvement. Social and health workers do not possess any coercive powers, but they can mobilise such resources by calling the police if necessary. In other words, the authority to use coercive force by the police is in this way mobilised in the actor-network towards the collective goal of supporting harm reduction activities. It is not just in relation to drug dealing that social workers may need police powers. Sometimes, such powers are also necessary to deal with unrest, threats, and violence inside drug consumption rooms. Some of the users may have withdrawal symptoms, be intoxicated, psychotic, show symptoms of mental illnesses, or be generally stressed by their precarious living conditions. This poses a challenge to creating and maintaining a safe, secure, and calm environment where users can consume drugs and the staff can do their work. The weekly reports by the local police indicate that the police quite often expel one or more unwanted persons from drug consumption rooms. The most frequent reason for this is that some users make other users and the staff feel insecure. Sometimes it is sufficient to expel one or a few persons, but other times the police have to assist in closing the facilities down for some time for order to be restored:

> Saturday night at eight o'clock we closed [drug consumption room] in agreement with the staff, due to a very bad atmosphere. The users (...) did exactly as they pleased and insulted the staff. (...) It took approx. 45 minutes to get everybody out. Shortly afterwards, the same thing happened at the [homeless shelter] and at [another drug consumption room].
>
> *(Excerpt from status report)*

The authority of the police to use coercive force thus plays a very important role in regulating the drug consumption facilities and in the policing of the boundaries between the drug scene on the street and the drug scene inside the drug consumption rooms. However, rather than resorting to force, the local police try to handle conflicts by using dialogue in most cases. The local police, and in particular the local street officers, have good relations with several of the drug users, which means that they typically do not have to make use of their authority to use coercive force to handle the situations. As one officer explained:

> The staff at the low-threshold services and the drug consumption rooms can call us when there is a bad atmosphere and say: 'Do you have time to come by because we are afraid that this will escalate'. Then we do that. Many times, it is just a matter of turning up and saying: 'Hey, how are you'... they may need an arm around the shoulder: 'Tell me what's wrong'... [it can] sometimes bring heated minds to rest.
>
> *(Patrol officer)*

Sometimes, the patrol officers will also participate in conflict mediation between staff and users in different areas. Several of the services have a policy where a user who has been expelled for being violent or threatening towards the staff needs to participate in mediation before they can return.

Making a safe environment

People who participate in a drug scene like the one at Vesterbro often live in something akin to a stateless society regarding their security and possibilities of achieving justice; this holds true for both drug users and drug sellers (see also Jacques and Allen 2015). Often, such people are seen as creating insecurity for other people, but what is sometimes forgotten is that the people who are part of the drug scene live much more dangerous and insecure lives than the residents and 'decent' citizens who sometimes fear them. The role of the local patrol officers at Vesterbro is not just to support the low-threshold and harm reduction services. As the officers see it, their role is to include drug users into what one officer called: 'The state's guarantee of safety to its citizens'. They know that many of the local drug users are very sceptical towards the police and for this reason it is important that the officers spend time on the streets, talk with people, and refrain from treating them as criminals. In an article in a Danish magazine for practitioners working with drug-related issues, one of the police officers explained his role in the following way:

> It is my experience as a street officer at Vesterbro that it is possible to help marginalised citizens, but it requires that they know their cop. The relationship and the trust are crucial if you are to be able to have conversations

> where the marginalised person can explain their situation without fearing the consequences.
>
> *(Ellegaard 2018, p. 20)*

In the article, the officer emphasised the importance of signalling to drug users that 'I am not here to control you'. The police officers' effort to make the lives of drug users safer can at times involve criminal justice interventions; however, more often, it involves mediation and other ways of handling conflicts than criminal proceedings. One officer, for instance, explained:

> These people have nowhere else to go. They have to live with each other even though they are enemies and one abuses the other. So, the good solution is not always a formal criminal case because that may just make things worse. The thing we usually say [to other people] is that if you get violated in some way, you should report it to the police. This is not always the best solution in this environment. We often have to try to solve things in some other way, because otherwise it will often worsen the situation for them.
>
> *(Patrol officer)*

However, mediation and other informal methods are not always sufficient to create a more secure environment for drug users. Through police knowledge of the drug scene, they also get tips about persons who are particularly violent and make other people afraid. This enables officers not only to identify and keep a watch on aggressive, threatening, and violent drug dealers and their accomplices, but also to pay special attention to a specific group of drug users or a mentally ill person. In such cases, street officers sometimes try to use dialogue or the assistance of low-threshold services or the drug squad to remove specific individuals who create insecurity at the drug scene. The following is an illustration of how the local police try to keep watch on individuals who are believed to be a risk to the drug users at the Vesterbro drug scene:

> New focus person [name]. Known user. In the past week, he has drawn more and more attention to himself at [low-threshold facility], where he has been fighting with other users. He is mentally unstable and a big person. He is verbally confrontational to the staff and the other users. He is a person whose movements and behaviour must be monitored.
>
> *(Excerpt from status report)*

The above is notable because it represents an extension of what researchers have called 'harm-reducing policing' (Dorn and South 1990; Shiner 2016). Harm reduction policing is typically described as a type of policing that is mainly focused on users' health or their access to social services (social rights). At the Vesterbro drug scene, it also focuses on drug users' civil rights, their right as citizens to be protected from abuse and to live in safety and security (see also Kammersgaard 2019).

Persistent conflicts between the various sectors

At Vesterbro, the construction of a policy network has not removed all differences of interest and disagreements between the police and social and health services. This is particularly the case in relation to the drug squad that operates at Vesterbro with the purpose of investigating organised drug dealing. The drug squad still works according to a repressive strategy that includes stopping and searching drug users to make cases against drug dealers. This is seen as counterproductive in relation to reducing drug-related harm and creating a safer environment for drug users, as the leader of a social service explained:

> We are not very happy about the drug squad; they treat neither our employees nor our guests with respect. (…) They come down here to find someone. Usually, some dealers, and they come forcefully, and it is bloody annoying for us because it creates a bad atmosphere. (…) Fortunately, they do not come so often. And it's a shame because we actually have a pretty good relationship with the local police, even though it's an extremely chaotic environment we operate in.
>
> *(Leader of social service)*

It is not only the drug squads' methods and behaviour that is criticised; it is also the fact that the drug squad lacks the knowledge about the users and the drug scene that is known to the local police. The drug squad is part of a coordinating group at Vesterbro. In an interview, the leader of a social service explained that he has an ongoing dialogue with the leader of the drug squad:

> I have an ongoing dialogue with their boss about what happens when they come down here. And he passes this on to them, and sometimes it also goes the other way, when they think that our staff is not very cooperative. (…) It's actually some interesting discussions we have about that, and also a realisation on the part of their leader, and on my part, that his people and my people may never completely agree on how to do it, but then we take the discussion on a regular basis when something happens.
>
> *(Interview with head of social services)*

As this illustrates, members of the drug squad and the social workers have fundamentally different ideas and goals regarding the drug scene, which makes it difficult to reach agreement and cooperation. Accordingly, conflicts can still be observed between parts of the police and the low-threshold organisations. Thus, there are still certain limits to the cooperation between the various stakeholders around the drug scene at Vesterbro. The antagonistic relationship between parts of the police and the social organisations cannot be said to have been completely resolved. In other words, the policy network has not fully succeeded in interesting nor enrolling the drug squad in collective action towards the goal of harm reduction. This might have to do with this particular section of the police having drug law enforcement as their main activity, and thus it might be more difficult to reorient and reframe their activities as harm reduction (but see e.g. Spicer 2021).

Conclusion

At Vesterbro in Copenhagen, a large number of stakeholders have, over a long period, developed a coherent harm reduction policy that involves both police and social and health services. It is a policy that seeks to balance the health and well-being of drug users with an aim to minimise the nuisance that the drug scene and drug users may create for their surroundings. What is new about this policy as opposed to the previous incoherent and contradictory situation is that the efforts of the local police to create security, peace, and order in the local community now take place in a way that supports harm reduction efforts rather than working against these. However, the drug squad's efforts to combat organised drug dealing remain outside the policy network and have not been integrated in a way that supports the harm reduction policy (see also Bacon 2016b).

We have chosen to understand the new policy towards the drug scene at Vesterbro as a product of a policy network in which various local stakeholders have come to cooperate and take on particular roles and functions. The analytical tools from actor-network theory proved to be useful for understanding how this policy network was developed and worked. We have found that both the idea about 'interestment', that is, the translation and aligning of interests, and the idea about enrolment where different actors take on particular roles in a collaborative network to be useful for the analysis. The development of the Vesterbro policy network bears resemblance to what is sometimes described as plural or partnership policing (Crawford 2006). Importantly this line of research has described how police tend to take on a steering role in the facilitation and shaping of multi-agency collaboration. As an example of this, Cherney et al. (2006) describe how 'third-party policing' involves police efforts to persuade or coerce civil or private partners to take actions that support crime control goals, such as the reduction of illicit drug production, supply, or usage (see also Søgaard et al. 2017; Webster et al. 2018). Complementing this line of research, our study showed how the Vesterbro policy network was developed particularly through the initiative of committed citizens and NGOs, and how they invested considerable efforts into interesting and enrolling (part of) the local police into a common effort aimed at engaging with the drug scene in a new way. Thus, the development of the policy network is largely a product of translating different local interests into a collective project. However, national policy has also played an important role in establishing drug consumption rooms and creating a zone where possession of illicit drugs for personal use by users of the drug consumption room could be decriminalised. Local police officers affected and were affected by being part of the network in significant ways. It realised officers' capacity to act as harm reduction agents and to act as a police force *for* and not *against* participants in the drug scene. Similar to the finding of O'Neill and McCarthy (2012), our study thus showed how involvement in multi-agency partnerships can change the culture and workings of police units. Importantly, however, police officers also affected the harm reduction network by providing it with the capacity to enforce the law, which would sometimes be required to keep the drug consumption rooms and other services functioning.

Drug consumption rooms have created a new physical and social space for drug users at Vesterbro and, in some ways, reconstituted the drug scene as less risky. The establishment of this space has been conditional on the establishment of new cooperative relations between the local police and the social authorities. And particularly with the low-threshold approach chosen for the drug consumption rooms at Vesterbro, they needed close collaboration with the police to enforce borders between the drug scene inside and the drug scene outside the drug consumption rooms. In this way, the police and their coercive powers were mobilised in the policy network towards the collective goal of supporting harm reduction efforts. Through this collaboration, it has become possible for the local police and their partners to develop new properties and action capacities, which together make new ways of acting collectively in relation to the drug environment possible.

Notes

1 This chapter is based on work that has previously been published in Danish (Houborg, Søgaard and Kammersgaard 2019).
2 In this analysis, we do not consider the role of 'non-human' actors but instead mainly focus on processes and practices of 'interestment' and 'enrolment' whereby actors are connected.
3 'The street' is slang for the drug scene at Vesterbro.

References

Bacon, M. (2016a) *Taking Care of Business: Police Detectives, Drug Law Enforcement and Proactive Investigation*. Oxford: Oxford University Press.

Bacon, M. (2016b) 'Maintaining order in the drug game: Applying harm reduction principles to drug detective work'. *Police Practice and Research*. 17(4): 306–316.

Bacon, M. and Seddon, T. (2020) 'Controlling drug users: Forms of power and behavioural regulation in drug treatment services'. *British Journal of Criminology*. 60(2): 403–421.

Bancroft, M. and Houborg, E. (2020) 'Managing coexistence: Resident experiences of the open drug scene and drug consumption rooms in inner Vesterbro, Copenhagen'. *Contemporary Drug Problems*. 47(3): 210–230.

Bittner, E. (1967) 'Police discretion in emergency apprehension of mentally ill persons'. *Social Problems*. 14(3): 278–292.

Bittner, E. (2005) 'Florence Nightingale in pursuit of Willie Sutton: A theory of the police'. In Newburn, T. (ed.) *Policing: Key Readings*. London: Routledge: 150–172.

Bittner, E. (1990) *Aspects of Police Work*. Boston, MA: Northeastern University Press.

Bourgois, P. and Schonberg, J. (2009) *Righteous Dopefiend*. Berkeley, CA: University of California Press.

Burris, S., Blankenship, K., Donoghoe, M., Sherman, S., Vernick, J., Case, P., Lazzarini, Z. and Koester, S. (2004) 'Addressing the "risk environment" for injection drug users: The mysterious case of the missing cop'. *Milbank Quarterly*. 82(1): 125–156.

Callon, M. (1984) 'Some elements of a sociology of translation: Domestication of the scallops and the fishermen of St Brieuc Bay'. *The Sociological Review*. 32(1): 196–233.

Carlsson, L. (2000) 'Policy networks as collective action'. *Policy Studies Journal*. 28(3): 502–520.

Caulkins, J. (2017) 'Improving research on drug law enforcement'. *International Journal of Drug Policy*. 41: 158–159.

Caulkins, J. and Reuter, P. (2009) 'Towards a harm-reduction approach to enforcement'. *Safer Communities*. 8(1): 9–23.

Cherney, A., O'Reill, J. and Grabosky, P. (2006) 'Networks and meta-regulation: Strategies aimed at governing illicit synthetic drugs'. *Policing and Society*. 16(4): 370–385.

Crawford, A. (2006) 'Networked governance and the post-regulatory state? Steering, rowing and anchoring the provision of policing and security'. *Theoretical Criminology*. 10(4): 449–479.

Common, R. and Acevedo, B. (2006) 'Governance and the management of networks in the public sector: Drugs policy in the United Kingdom and the case of cannabis reclassification'. *Public Management Review*. 8(3): 395–414.

Cooper, H., Moore, L., Gruskin, S. and Krieger, N. (2005) 'The impact of a police drug crackdown on drug injectors' ability to practice harm reduction: A qualitative study'. *Social Science and Medicine*. 61(3): 673–684.

Demant, J. and Dilkes-Frayne, E. (2015) 'Situational crime prevention in nightlife spaces: An ANT examination of PAD dogs and doorwork'. In Robert, D. and Dufresne, M. (eds.) *Actor-Network Theory and Crime Studies: Explorations in Science and Technology*. London: Routledge: 5–19.

Dányi, E. (2017) 'Good treason: Following actor-network theory to the realm of drug policy'. In Berger, T. and Esguerra, A. (eds.) *World Politics in Translation*. London: Routledge: 25–38.

De Landa, M. (2006) *A New Philosophy of Society*. London: Bloomsbury.

Dorn, N. and South, N. (1990) 'Drug markets and law enforcement'. *British Journal of Criminology*. 30(2): 171–188.

Duff, C. (2011) 'Networks, resources and agencies: On the character and production of enabling places'. *Health and Place*. 17(1): 149–156.

Ellegaard, R. (2018) 'Gadebetjenten – Et lavtærskeltilbud for udsatte borgere'. *Stof, Nr. 30: 19–20.*

Frantzsen, E. (2003) 'Drug enforcement in Copenhagen: Negotiating space'. In Houborg, E. (ed.) *Regulating Drugs - Between Users, the Police and Social Workers*. Helsinki: Nordic Council for Alcohol and Drug Research: 75–84.

Greenfield, V. and Paoli, L. (2012) 'If supply-oriented drug policy is broken, can harm reduction help fix it? Melding disciplines and methods to advance international drug-control policy'. *International Journal of Drug Policy*. 23(1): 6–15.

Hartmann, M. (2014) *In the Gray Zone: With Police in Making Space for Creativity*. Copenhagen: Copenhagen Business School.

Houborg, E. (2012) 'The political pharmacology of methadone and heroin in Danish drug policy'. *Contemporary Drug Problems*. 39(1): 155–192.

Houborg, E. and Frank, V. (2014) 'Drug consumption rooms and the role of governance and politics in policy processes'. *International Journal of Drug Policy*. 25(5): 972–979.

Houborg, E., Frank, V. and Bjerge, B. (2014) 'From zero-tolerance to non-enforcement: Creating a new space for drug policing in Copenhagen, Denmark'. *Contemporary Drug Problems*. 41(2): 261–291.

Houborg, E. and Holt, J. (2018) *Substance Environment and Everyday Life in Indre Vesterbro*. Copenhagen: Ministry of Justice Research Office.

Jacques, S. and Allen, A. (2015) 'Drug market violence: Virtual anarchy, police pressure, predation, and retaliation'. *Criminal Justice Review*. 40(1): 87–99.

Kammersgaard, T. (2019) 'Harm reduction policing: From drug law enforcement to protection'. *Contemporary Drug Problems*. 46(4): 345–362.

Kübler, D. and Wälti, S. (2001) 'Drug policy-making in metropolitan areas: Urban conflicts and governance'. *International Journal of Urban and Regional Research*. 25(1): 35–54.

Latour, B. (1993) *The Pasteurisation of France*. Cambridge, MA: Harvard University Press.

Law, J. (1986) 'Technology and heterogenous engineering: The case of Portuguese expansion'. In Bijker, W., Hughes, T. and Pinch, T. (eds.) *The Social Construction of Technological Systems: New Directions in the Sociology and History of Technology*. Cambridge, MA: MIT Press: 111–134.

Lister, S. (2006) 'Painting the town blue: The pluralisation of policing'. *Criminal Justice Matters*. 63(2): 22–23.

Maher, L. and Dixon, D. (1999) 'Policing and public health: Law enforcement and harm minimisation in a street-level drug market'. *British Journal of Criminology*. 39(4): 488–512.

Marres, N. (2005) 'Issues spark a public into being'. In Latour, B. and Weibel, P. (eds.) *Making Things Public*. Cambridge, MA: MIT Press: 208–217.

Morabito, M. (2007) 'Horizons of context: Understanding the police discretion to arrest people with mental illness'. *Psychiatric Services*. 58(12): 1582–1587.

Moyle, L. and Coomber, R. (2015) 'Earning a score: An exploration of the nature and roles of heroin and crack cocaine "user-dealers"'. *British Journal of Criminology*. 55(3): 534–555.

Nielsen, B. and Houborg, E. (2015) 'Addiction, drugs, and experimentation: Methadone maintenance treatment between "in here" and "out there"'. *Contemporary Drug Problems*. 42(4): 274–288.

O'Neill, M. and McCarthy, D. (2012) '(Re)negotiating police culture through partnership working: Trust, compromise and the "new" pragmatism'. *Criminology and Criminal Justice*. 14(2): 143–159.

Percival, G. (2009) 'Exploring the influence of local policy networks on the implementation of drug policy reform: The case of California's substance abuse and crime prevention act'. *Journal of Public Administration Research and Theory*. 19(4): 795–815.

Punch, M. (1979) 'The secret social service'. In Holdaway, S. (ed.) *The British Police*. London: Arnold: 102–117.

Rowe, M. and Rowe, M. (2021) 'Understanding the quiet times: The role of periods of "nothing much happening" in police work'. *Journal of Contemporary Ethnography*. 50(6): 751–774.

Shiner, M. (2016) 'Drug policing: What is it good for?' In Collins, J. (ed.) *After the War on Drugs*. London: London School of Economics: 59–66.

Søgaard, T., Houborg, E. and Pedersen, M. (2017) 'Drug policing assemblages: Repressive drug policies and the zonal banning of drug users in Denmark's club land'. *International Journal of Drug Policy*. 41: 118–125.

Spicer, J. (2021) *Policing County Lines: Responses to Evolving Provisional Drug Markets*. London: Palgrave.

Spooner, C., McPherson, M. and Hall, W. (2004) *The Role of Police in Preventing and Minimising Illicit Drug Use and Its Harms*. Australia: Australasian Center for Policing Research.

Teplin, L. and Pruett, N. (1992) 'Police as a streetcorner psychiatrist: Managing the mentally ill'. *International Journal of Law and Psychiatry*. 15(2): 139–156.

Vesterbrobladet 11. April 2007, Mere politi på gaden: 4.

Watson, T., Bayoumi, A., Hopkins, S., Wright, A., Naraine, R., Khorasheh, T., Challacombe, L. and Strike, C. (2018) 'Creating and sustaining cooperative relationships between supervised injection services and police: A qualitative interview study of international stakeholders'. *International Journal of Drug Policy*. 61: 1–6.

Webster, J., Mazerolle, P., Ransley, J. and Mazerolle, J. (2018) 'Disrupting domestic "ice" production: Deterring drug runners with a third-party policing intervention'. *Policing and Society*. 28(9): 1025–1037.

Wood, J., Sorg, E., Groff, E., Ratcliffe, J. and Taylor, C. (2014) 'Cops as treatment providers: Realities and ironies of police work in a foot patrol experiment'. *Policing and Society*. 24(3): 362–379.

Wood, J., Taylor, C., Groff, E. and Ratcliffe, J. (2015) 'Aligning policing and public health promotion: Insights from the world of foot patrol'. *Police Practice and Research*. 16(3): 211–223.

Wood, J., Watson, A. and Fulambarker, A. (2017) 'The "gray zone" of police work during mental health encounters: Findings from an observational study in Chicago'. *Police Quarterly*. 20(1): 81–105.

Wälti, S. and Kübler, D. (2003) '"New governance" and associative pluralism: The case of drug policy in Swiss cities'. *Policy Studies Journal*. 31(4): 499–525.

13

LEADING LOCAL CHANGE

Police and crime commissioners and drug policy

Meg Jones and Ben Twomey

Introduction

The introduction of directly elected police and crime commissioners (PCCs) in 2012 represented a significant shift in policing governance and a new model of political leadership in the United Kingdom (Lister 2013; Loveday 2013). The statutory functions of a PCC include holding their police force to account on behalf of the public, setting the policing priorities for their force in a police and crime plan, and appointing a chief constable. In just a decade, PCCs have transformed policing governance, unlocking new opportunities to introduce harm reduction approaches to local drug policy across England and Wales. Following Bacon and Spicer (this volume), we define harm reduction policing as 'policing measures that aim to reduce the adverse health, social and economic consequences of drug use, drug markets and efforts to control them through the criminal justice system'. Since their introduction, some PCCs, most notably in Durham, North Wales, Avon and Somerset, and the West Midlands, have become key drug policy actors, shifting the framing of drug-related issues from being a criminal problem to a health issue. By 'drug policy actors', we are drawing on Seddon (2011) who uses this term to define those who can highlight to others, such as policy professionals, where the 'levers for change may lie' (p. 419). Their unique role as a directly elected leader, responsible to the public and working for their benefit, has allowed greater innovation and creativity when identifying solutions to complex problems. For example, the development of a police and crime plan means that PCCs can focus on priorities that are specific to the needs of their local population. They can focus on a small area of policy, such as the impact of high-harm drugs including heroin and crack cocaine.

We, the authors of this chapter, have between us developed and delivered policy for seven different PCCs. In this chapter, we focus on the West Midlands,

DOI: 10.4324/9781003154136-14

where we have both been responsible for drug policy, as a case study to demonstrate the new opportunities for harm reduction. We co-authored the original West Midlands Drug Policy Recommendations (West Midlands Police and Crime Commissioner 2018a) and have both had responsibility for the delivery of those recommendations with partners. A PCC is supported in their functions by a team who have responsibility for helping them to hold the force to account, to engage and consult with the public, and to deliver on their priorities set out within a police and crime plan. Policy officers and advisers have an opportunity to present evidence and innovative ideas and approaches directly to their PCCs. This is exactly how we managed to effect change in the West Midlands, by supporting a PCC to develop and deliver a harm reduction approach to drugs.

We begin by demonstrating how the PCC role fundamentally changed and localised police governance, before setting out the wider drug policy context into which the new role was established. Through our own experience working for PCCs, we also give an insight into the individuals who support PCCs in their offices and support them to become drug policy actors. We then outline the harm reduction journey of the West Midlands – from assessing the scale of the problem, to the publication and implementation of the PCC's eight drug policy recommendations. We outline the advantages of a PCC-led approach, before discussing what the future might hold for the relationship between PCCs and harm reduction, with particular focus on the interconnectivity between local, regional, and national approaches to drug policy.

We conclude with our 'top tips', which are rooted in the pragmatic, practically orientated, and humanistic philosophy of harm reduction and from our own experience of developing, delivering, and driving forward change for PCCs. Our top tips are for policymakers on achieving change, followed by our top tips for the public, based on our experience of delivering harm reduction policies in the West Midlands and elsewhere. This chapter not only explores change, but is also intended to empower readers to make change. We invite you to take the next steps towards reducing harm in your local area, your work, or your day-to-day life.

What are police and crime commissioners?

The introduction of PCCs under the Police Reform and Social Responsibility Act 2011 was one of the most radical changes to governance structures in England and Wales (Lister 2013; Loveday 2013). The local police authority committee structure was replaced by the PCC, one directly elected individual with a singular focus on policing and crime. The PCC role is innovative in its relatively unchallenged position in the related hierarchies, as well as in its composition as a 'corporation sole' (Home Office 2011), or individual human holder of executive office. Within this new structure, the chief constable is accountable to the PCC, while the PCC is scrutinised by a police and crime panel made up mostly of local councillors (Figure 13.1).

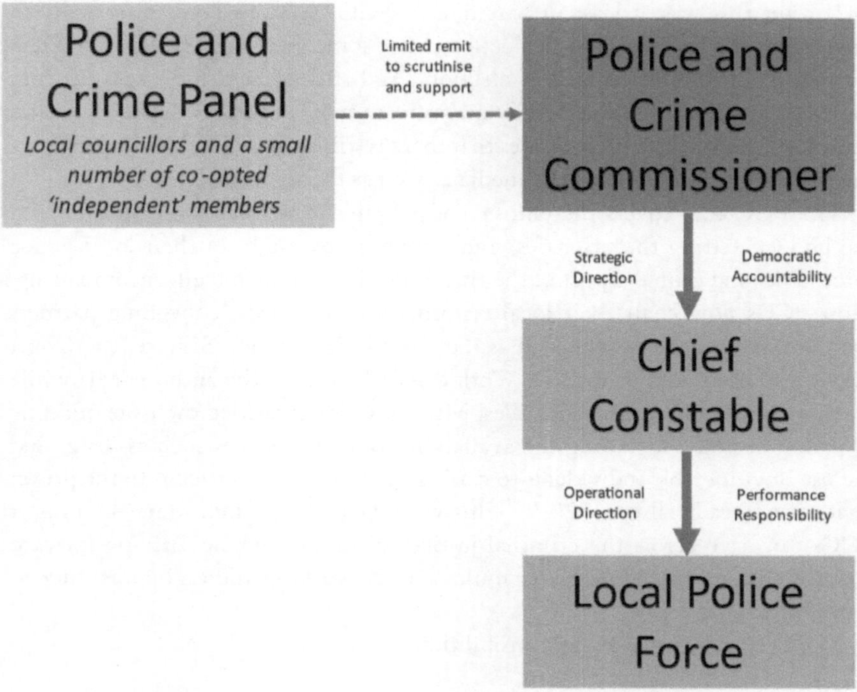

FIGURE 13.1 The local PCC governance structure.

The reasons behind the reform have been explored within academic literature and featured in the media, both in the lead up to the change and post-2012. The development of the localism agenda (Jones and Lister 2019) and democratic accountability have been key drivers. Police authorities were also seen to be ineffective and not visible to the public. Both the Conservative Party and the Liberal Democrats called for reform or replacement of police authorities in their 2010 manifestos (Conservatives 2010; Liberal Democrats 2010). In an independent inspection of police authorities in 2009, the average scoring was 'performs adequately' but many fell into the inadequate category (HMIC 2010). Police authorities were generally criticised for their lack of visibility and accountability to the public and the communities they served. The emergence of stronger and more visible leadership also aligned with the devolution agenda of the coalition government (Lowndes and Pratchett 2012).

The PCC model was introduced to resolve the accountability and visibility criticisms, with the introduction of one individual who is elected and thus directly accountable to the public. However, polling commissioned by the Electoral Reform Society in 2016 suggested that nine out of ten people could not name their PCC (Guardian 2016). In addition, the 2012 election had the lowest turnout for any national election in UK history, at just 15% (Guardian 2016).

Average turnout more than doubled to an estimated 33.2% in 2021 (Danechi 2021), but this was at least in part due to PCC elections coinciding with an unprecedented number of local elections since some were postponed from 2020, as well as the Welsh Parliament election. And still, around a decade on from their introduction, the coverage by mainstream media of the PCC elections and results was minimal. This indicates that there is still a general lack of understanding of the PCC role, within the media as well as the wider public.

The PCC role covers the entirety of policing. They have responsibility for the budget, setting the priorities, and providing oversight of their local police force. The 'and crime' aspect of the title is also important and all-encompassing. Most PCCs now chair their local criminal justice boards, convening partners that work across the system such as the Crown Prosecution Service, the Court Service, Prisons, and Probation. Work driven by one of the authors (MJ) while working for PCCs in the wider West Midlands region tackled the issue of crime in prison custody, including the availability of commodities such as drugs and the use of vulnerable individuals to carry such commodities back into the prison estate (see Treadwell et al. 2019). This work helped to demonstrate the impact PCCs can have across the criminal justice system as a whole, driving forward positive change, including better multi-agency working and an opportunity to prevent reoffending.

The PCC has three key responsibilities:

1. Setting the budget for the local police force, including deciding the rate of policing precept (local council tax for policing).
2. Establishing the strategic policing priorities of the area through a local police and crime plan.
3. Holding the chief constable to account on behalf of the public, including the power to hire or fire the chief constable.

As a consequence of these responsibilities, PCCs will often be involved in drug policy. Since the 1990s, drug policy has had a specific crime reduction focus and has been set by the Home Office at the national level. This focus has been on 'problem drug users', the links between drug use and serious acquisitive crime, and the criminalisation of drug policy (Seddon et al. 2008). By 'criminalisation', Seddon et al. (2008) are referring to policies that develop and enhance the pathways between the criminal justice system and drug treatment services. For PCCs, there is an overlap with reducing reoffending, demand on policing, serious acquisitive crime, open drug use including needle litter, and commissioning some elements of drug support such as 'test on arrest' schemes (drug intervention programmes[1]) (WMPCC 2018b).

For PCCs, setting priorities for policing provides a lot of freedom to focus on specific issues, which will shape the work of the police force and their own office over their four-year term. Drug policy is a key feature in many police and crime plans, but the extent to which that has led to practical harm reduction initiatives has varied across England and Wales (Revolving Doors 2017). The Revolving Doors report does acknowledge some PCCs who are delivering or considering 'innovative measures and responses' (p. 3), and that not all of this work will necessarily be captured in a review of police and crime plans which are produced very early in the PCC's term of office. However, during the May 2016 PCC elections, it is notable that only 2 out of 40 newly elected or re-elected PCCs mentioned drugs or drug policy explicitly in their manifestos (Choose my PCC 2016).

West Midlands: scale of the problem

Every PCC is required to develop a police and crime plan for their policing area, which outlines the priorities for the police force. The public should be consulted in its development. In the West Midlands police and crime plan, drugs, and the issues associated with addiction, intersect a number of thematic topics including reducing reoffending and preventing harm (West Midlands Police and Crime Commissioner, 2016).

It was important to begin this work in the West Midlands by establishing the impact of the current approach to drug policy. We set out the costs and impact, both human and financial, on wider society that exist under the status quo. This was important in establishing the narrative in our public communications. We were keen to demonstrate how the current approach to drugs was costly, created further harm, and caused or enabled significant levels of serious criminality. It was considered essential that if a new approach to drug policy was to be created, the public must first be able to compare its intended outcomes with the harm that was already happening under the current approach.

To this end, the West Midlands's PCC's Cost of Drugs report was published in September 2017 (West Midlands Police and Crime Commissioner 2017a). The paper was designed to set out the scale and breadth of the problem of drugs in the West Midlands and seek public support from the chief constable. The paper asked the PCC's Strategic Policing and Crime Board to support work for a new approach to drug policy and agree to a wide-ranging summit on the topic. To produce this report, we largely drew on data from public bodies such as the Home Office, Ministry of Justice, Office for National Statistics, National Crime Agency, and Public Health England. We also negotiated publishable information from West Midlands Police's organised crime tracker and mapped needle litter in each of the region's local authorities.

The report highlighted that approximately 22,500 people use heroin and crack cocaine in the West Midlands. These people were estimated to be costing the region approximately £1.4 billion per year. This figure was calculated using just four indicators – drug-related crime, health service use, drug-related deaths, and social care – meaning the true cost is likely to be higher. The statistic that appeared to shock people most in our work came from the Ministry of Justice: of all prisoners who report using heroin, one in five of them tried it for the first time while in prison. The report also found that around half of all serious acquisitive crime is committed by people who use heroin, crack, or powder cocaine regularly, representing one in five crimes reported to West Midlands Police and tens of thousands of victims. In new analysis, it found that the majority of organised crime groups in the West Midlands were heavily involved in the drugs trade. Those organised criminals involved in drugs were more likely to be operating internationally, and more likely to have links to firearms. Linking back to cost, the report highlighted that organised criminals in the West Midlands were profiting from a drug market worth approximately £188 million. In terms of harm, it found that somebody dies of drug poisoning every three days in the West Midlands. A total of 701 discarded needles were recorded by local councils in the West Midlands in just one year, likely a fraction of the total number on the streets. An estimated 22,500 children in the West Midlands have a parent or parents with serious drug problems.

West Midlands: public journey

Following the Cost of Drugs report, there was a public call for evidence. Academics, third-sector organisations, health professionals, and other members of the public were invited to respond. It was important that there was an open and transparent process to develop ideas. The Cost of Drugs report demonstrated an open and transparent governance process in the development of policymaking, an example of 'good governance' (European Commission 2001). As part of the PCC role as the public's representative, it was considered important that members of the public could influence the development of policy in their local area. Equally, there are a wide range of experts in the drug policy field, such as academics and third-sector organisations, who had already completed their own research that could inform this work. In the context of evidence-based policymaking (Sherman 1998; Stoker and Evans 2016), this allowed a range of evidence to be gathered that included academic reports and lived experience, as well as findings from evaluations of previous pilots and policies.

The call for evidence and the resulting report in December 2017 (West Midlands Police and Crime Commissioner 2017b) collated 65 submissions from a host of stakeholders, including public sector agencies, charities, people who use drugs, concerned parents, and serving professionals within the police and health sector. The submissions were collated by theme, with the key themes set out within the report itself, including offering diversion, early intervention and prevention, and addressing multiple complex needs (Figure 13.2).

In December 2017, the West Midlands PCC convened a summit on the issue of drugs. The findings from the call for evidence helped to shape the agenda for the day, the attendees, and the discussions. We worked to develop cross-party buy-in, invited key experts to speak, ensured that individuals with lived experience were empowered to speak about their own experiences, and worked with the media on coverage for the day. We deliberately invited speakers to the

Submissions, themes and full responses are detailed below:

<table>
<tr><th colspan="3">PCC's Drug Policy Call for Evidence</th></tr>
<tr><td>65 submissions</td><td>Open for 2 months</td><td>15th September – 17th November 2017</td></tr>
<tr><th colspan="3">Two Questions Asked:</th></tr>
<tr><td colspan="2">1) What are the costs of drugs and/or drug policy (human and/or economic) as you see it in relation to the capacity in which your respond?</td><td>2) What practical new initiatives or changes to drug policy could be introduced to prevent harm and/or reduce crime?</td></tr>
<tr><th colspan="3">Including submissions from:</th></tr>
<tr><td colspan="2">• three Police and Crime Commissioners
• the National Probation Service
• Council Chief Executives
• a Council Leader
• Public Health England
• NHS Foundation Trusts
• local medical and pharmaceutical committees
• drug and alcohol treatment providers
• a drug testing charity
• mutual aid groups
• a coalition of homelessness and mental health charities
• substance misuse commissioners</td><td>• doctors
• serving police officers
• drug treatment workers
• a patients' alliance
• a medical director
• a youth offending team
• a homeless outreach nurse
• a behavioural therapist
• a community organisation
• a large number of people in recovery for addiction
• current drug users
• concerned parents
• people bereaved with loved ones lost to drugs</td></tr>
</table>

FIGURE 13.2 Types of respondents to the PCC's Drug Policy Call for Evidence. (West Midlands Drug Policy Call for Evidence – Report, 2017).

summit who, given the politically sensitive nature of drug policy discussions in the United Kingdom, added legitimacy to our proposed course of action. This included opening remarks from the Labour PCC David Jamieson, followed by Conservative Mayor Andy Street and Crossbench peer Baroness Molly Meacher, chair of the All-Party Parliamentary Group for Drug Policy Reform. Cross-party involvement reduced the risk of party-political criticism of the summit or later recommendations. This was supplemented by multi-agency buy-in, as other speakers included representatives of West Midlands Police, Public Health England, the Advisory Council on the Misuse of Drugs, local prisons, councils, and the regional organised crime unit. Personal experiences helped build the case for change to the summit attendees, including Rose Humphries from Anyone's Child who tragically lost two sons to heroin, and Neil Woods from Law Enforcement Action Partnership, a former undercover police officer. Ultimately, the summit was an opportunity for people to shape future action in the West Midlands, foster partner buy-in to help deliver whatever the future action and recommendations from the summit would be, and to facilitate a transparent and multi-agency approach to the development of the subsequent eight recommendations.

West Midlands: the eight recommendations

The West Midlands PCC decided on eight drug policy recommendations which were embedded in the principle of harm reduction and predicated in existing law. These are

1. *Diverting people away from the criminal justice system*: a formal scheme to divert those suffering from drug addiction away from the criminal justice system into proper treatment, building on the success of West Midlands Police's Turning Point pilot. Those suffering from addiction should be treated as having a health problem, not just as criminals.
2. *Regional Drug Interventions Programme*: current funding for drug interventions is dispersed between community safety partnerships, West Midlands Police, and Public Health teams in local councils. Funding should be joined up to increase efficiency and ensure all funding is supporting the same goals.
3. *Heroin-assisted treatment* (HAT): prescribe heroin in a medical setting to people suffering from addiction who have not responded to other forms of treatment. This will take the market away from organised criminals and reduce crime to fund people's addiction.
4. *Drugs Early Warning Programme*: to reduce harm, a comprehensive regional warning programme should be established to make the public, outreach workers, and medical professionals aware of the danger of emerging drugs and reduce the number of deaths.
5. *Safety testing of drugs in night-time districts or festivals*: to reduce the number of deaths at night-time economy venues, city-centre testing of drugs should be introduced. This can reduce harm, by making people aware of the dangers they face and increasing intelligence on the nature and identity of drugs in circulation.
6. *End the postcode lottery of naloxone provision*: train and equip first responders in the application of naloxone and make naloxone consistently available in places where overdose risks are higher, such as bail hostels. Naloxone is a medication used to block or reverse opioid overdoses. It has little effect if opioids are not present, so is safe to be administered by first responders such as police officers.
7. *Drug consumption rooms* (DCRs): consider the benefits of drug consumption rooms to see if they would add value to current services in the West Midlands. Drug consumption rooms are clinical spaces in which people suffering from addiction can access clean equipment, medical support, and drug treatment services. This support is typically targeted at hard-to-reach homeless people, improving their access to treatment while taking their injecting and needle litter off the streets.
8. *Taking money from organised criminals to improve drug services*: those profiting from the misery of drug addiction should pay for treatment. All the organised crime groups of the greatest concern to local police are involved with drugs and firearms. West Midlands Police is seeking to maximise the money

it seizes from large-scale drug dealers. The extra money seized relating to drugs should be reinvested into helping those suffering from addiction.

Three years of harm reduction progress in the West Midlands

As of 2021, all of the eight recommendations have been implemented in the West Midlands. The impact has been substantial. The author, Ben Twomey, led the PCC's efforts on the recommendations from February 2018 to January 2019. After this the other author, Meg Jones, led the delivery of the recommendations until July 2021. This section outlines how these recommendations have been implemented.

Diversion has been developed in the West Midlands for drugs possession through the DIVERT programme. DIVERT is a pre-arrest drug diversion scheme that is available for any individuals in possession of any drug. The individual is offered a referral rather than a criminal justice outcome and police officers can refer the individual using an app on their mobile device. Cranstoun – a charity offering a wide range of services across England, including substance use services – engage through an initial assessment, book the individual onto a group session if deemed appropriate, and educate and provide harm reduction advice to the individual through an online session. In most cases, the education session has been engaging with individuals who have never discussed their drug taking, many being between 18 and 30 years old. In cases where the individual has additional vulnerabilities, Cranstoun work with the individuals to support them into local support such as drug treatment, housing, or mental health support. In a press release about the DIVERT programme in June 2021, it was noted that over 400 individuals had completed the DIVERT course (West Midlands PCC 2021). As of 2022, over 4,000 people have been through DIVERT instead of receiving a criminal sanction and the impact has also shown reduced disproportionality in the criminal justice system. The programme has since begun to support schools and colleges to offer DIVERT to students instead of an exclusion for drug possession.

The Cranstoun Arrest Referral Service (CARS) was commissioned and went live in January 2020. The service works consistently across all police custody blocks in the West Midlands and in partnership with the probation service in courts. Individuals in custody are assessed and engage with workers to discuss their drug and alcohol use. This could be individuals who have been referred via the test on arrest process, but the majority are actually voluntary assessments. Individuals are also assessed for their suitability for a drug rehabilitation requirement (DRR) or alcohol treatment requirement (ATR). These are orders that can be issued at court as an alternative to a custodial sentence or other criminal justice sanction. This means that the root cause of the criminality can be addressed. In 2020, over 2,400 people were assessed in custody, despite the COVID-19 pandemic. Over 1,000 of those individuals were not engaged in local treatment and were supported by the CARS team to engage, resulting in a cost saving to the public purse of over £8 million. The number of DRRs and ATRs has also risen dramatically in the West Midlands, particularly in comparison to other areas of the country. The cost avoidance figure is now estimated to be at least £15 million per year.

Heroin-assisted treatment or diamorphine assisted treatment (DAT) operates in Middlesbrough, led by Danny Ahmed and Foundations Tees. Cranstoun have developed a full model to be delivered in the West Midlands. The programme works to identify the most chaotic individuals who have struggled to maintain engagement with treatment. The top 10% of this group can make up nearly 60% of the illegal market due to their high rates of consumption (Transform 2019). HAT/DAT, despite the small numbers of people involved, has the potential to save millions of pounds by reducing crime and therefore cost to policing. It also has significant health benefits, such as reductions in A&E admissions, ambulance callouts, and treatment of complex health problems such as injecting-related infections.

Drugs early warning systems are a vital way of using intelligence to reduce harm. Information shared quickly about current drugs trends can assist professionals in delivering harm reduction advice. In 2018, the PCC's recommendation helped encourage every local authority in the West Midlands to introduce a local drugs early warning system, which was supplemented by a new regional system run by Public Health England. While progress was being made on the PCC's recommendation in early 2018, a further catalyst occurred in May of that year when tragically five people died from drug poisoning (in seemingly unrelated incidents) during four days in Birmingham. The PCC's office supported Public Health England to run a structured debrief of the multi-agency response to these events, which identified a clear need for a formalised local warning system in Birmingham and for a review of the regional alert system. This strengthened both the local and regional systems, with Birmingham's approach becoming a blueprint for other local authorities in the West Midlands who were yet to create their own systems.

The safety testing of drugs was delivered for the first time in the West Midlands region during MADE festival in Birmingham on 28 July 2018. This recommendation was delivered through collaboration of the PCC's office, West Midlands Police, Birmingham City Council's licensing team, the commissioned drug treatment service (CGL), the festival organisers, and the drug safety testing agency (The Loop). On the day, 39 brief interventions were delivered by The Loop's staff to a total of 70 service users. An overwhelming 36 interventions (92%) were to people who had never discussed their drug or alcohol use with a health care professional prior to using the testing service. Five (14%) service users disposed of their drugs after receiving a harm reduction intervention, either through The Loop or by themselves. Another eight (22%) service users said that they intended to take a lower dose of that substance having received forensic information on strength combined with harm reduction advice on dosage. Five

(14%) asked for signposting to access further support from local drugs services. The strongest pill tested contained 240 mg methyl enedioxy methamphetamine (MDMA), which is two to three times an average adult dose. Crucially, The Loop, in conjunction with West Midlands Police, issued a drug alert which warned people about this particularly dangerous substance in circulation at the event and may have saved lives.

Naloxone is a drug that rapidly reverses an opioid overdose. It is an opioid antagonist, attaching to opioid receptors, reversing and blocking the effects of other opioids. This means that naloxone can restore normal breathing which has either slowed or stopped because of an opioid overdose. Naloxone has no effect on a person who does not have opioids in their system. In the West Midlands, through the PCC's recommendations, West Midlands Police were the first in the country to offer training and equip officers with Nyxoid, a spray version of Naloxone. There have been positive uses of naloxone which have reversed an overdose and significantly, the work developed to equip officers in the West Midlands with naloxone has been shared with partners across the United Kingdom, with Police Scotland, North Wales Police, and other areas following suit.

The recommendation for drug consumption rooms called for the PCC to consider the benefits of a DCR in the West Midlands. The Out of Harm's Way report was completed by Strategic Policing and Crime Board member, Ernie Hendricks, in March 2020 with the support of experts from the third sector, treatment providers, and academics. The global evidence collated in the report is overwhelming. DCRs, or overdose prevention sites, would add huge value to the response to drugs policy. The recommendations included working with partners and government to develop a DCR pilot site in the West Midlands, which will be the next stage in the West Midlands approach.

The final recommendation from the report on developing a financial investigation team was coined Operation Pound. The Proceeds of Crime Act (POCA) targets individuals who profit from their illegal business, with some of the proceeds returning to the police force area, but at least 50% retained by the Home Office. Working with officers in West Midlands Police, a business case was developed and approved to set up a small team of three financial investigators and one analyst. This team is funded by the POCA to target individuals who are making significant profit from the drugs market, not the vulnerable individuals they exploit. Proceeds returned back to the force area are then used to fund the team itself in the hope of sustainability, while any money brought in over and above the cost of the team is available to reinvest in the PCC's other drug policy recommendations that loosen the grip of organised crime, such as HAT/DAT or diversion.

West Midlands: benefits of a PCC-led approach

A PCC is in a unique position to effect change and progress drug policy reform at a local level. As previously outlined, Seddon (2011) identifies the role of 'drug policy actors' as those who can highlight to others, such as policy professionals, where the 'levers for change may lie' (p. 419). Austen (2016) suggests that PCCs have emerged as drug policy actors and that, alongside chief constables, can be a more effective vehicle for change, rather than national-level debates and campaigns. In our experience, we have found that action can be taken very quickly by a PCC and their team as they have a public mandate and little bureaucracy to work through in comparison to big government departments and the way ministers work with the rest of cabinet and treasury.

The balance between operational policing and the PCC's oversight and strategic function could lead to criticism of PCCs trying to become lawmakers. However, in our experience, a PCC has key convening power, with the ability to bring partners together, commission services, and work across sectors such as policing, health, and with local authorities. PCCs are not lawmakers, but can utilise existing tools within the current legal framework to create far-reaching policies. PCCs in the West Midlands, North Wales, Durham, and Avon and Somerset have driven forward an approach to drug policy that is evidence based, harm reductionist, and a key tool to help reduce reoffending and shift the focus of drugs from a crime-led approach to a health one. The development of violence reduction units, funded by government and led by PCCs in areas with higher violent crime rates in England and Wales, has further enhanced the unique role for PCCs in bringing together partners locally to effect systems change (Binns 2021). The focus and financial support from government on a public health approach to violence through the creation of VRUs also supports a harm reduction approach to drugs, due to the prohibition of drugs being one of the main drivers of violence across the United Kingdom.

In academic work by one of the authors (Jones 2019), interviews were conducted with PCCs, key players in a harm reduction approach, and their staff. The literature review, primary qualitative research, and findings led to the development of the below model, proposing that three key drivers are optimum for delivery of a PCC-led, harm reduction approach. The findings identified that the levers available to a PCC such as the statutory role, convening power, and prioritisation and management of a force budget mean that a PCC is well placed to make a change at a local level. Therefore, PCCs can be a leader and driver of change, but they can also be a blocker. These drivers are presented in Figure 13.3, which indicates that an optimum combination of evidence, deliverability, and morals/ideology is needed for a PCC to deliver change.

The case study of the West Midlands has provided a narrow focus on a PCC who has championed a harm reduction approach to drug policy and practice through evidence, deliverability, and morals/ideology. Other PCCs, who either do not vocally support a harm reduction approach or completely oppose it, can hinder future progress. Frustratingly, this can also lead to a postcode lottery in the experience of members of the public. The police diversion schemes for drug possession in areas such as the West Midlands, Thames Valley, and Avon and Somerset mean that many individuals can now avoid a criminal justice sanction

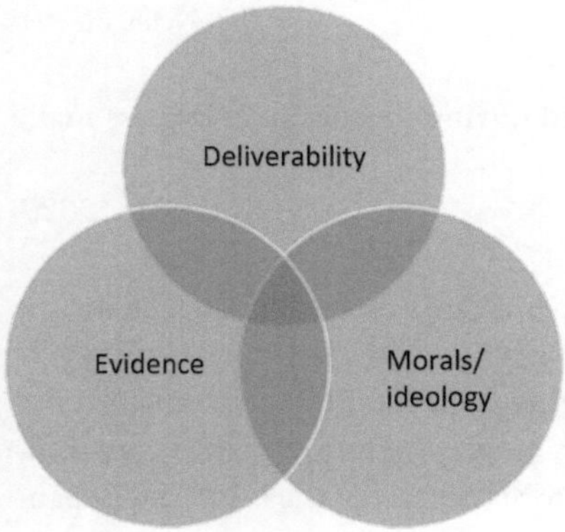

FIGURE 13.3 Drivers for a PCC-led approach.

when found in possession of a drug for personal use. However, individuals in areas where PCCs have not prioritised the same approach will continue to be criminalised for drug possession offences.

What next? Police and crime commissioner elections, expanding powers, and the shifting sands of national policy

After reaching a low point of over 22,000 fewer police officers being employed compared to ten years ago, we are now promised a similar number of police being recruited in the next five years (HM Government 2019). The Dame Carol Black Review (2021) was clear that the treatment sector is underfunded, with a recommendation that an additional £552 million be invested over the next five years. Yet, despite the recommendations within the report, there is no guarantee that the government will deliver on them in their entirety. The impact on other services such as youth services, and an increase in poverty and deprivation, have to be tackled in tandem with increasing support for drug and alcohol treatment. Stevens (2019) highlights that government inaction on drug policy is driven by conservative values of conformity and purity. He argues that the government defends inaction and ignores evidence for harm reduction approaches through a 'moral sidestep', defending existing policy due to its adherence with set principles, not the effectiveness of alternative approaches.

The COVID-19 lockdowns gave national and local enforcement agencies a unique opportunity to try to 'win' the war on drugs. Examples of news headlines on this topic included:

> 'Police exploit lockdown to mount raids on wanted criminals'
>
> *(Stephens and Evans 2020)*

> 'Hundreds arrested as crime chat network cracked'
>
> *(Shaw 2020)*

'County lines raids: 1,000 arrests and £1.2m drugs seized'

(BBC News 2020a)

'Recorded drug offences rise by a third during lockdown as dealers make 'risky' home deliveries'

(Mee 2020)

Whether these raids and arrests had any meaningful or lasting impact on the market must surely be weighed against the case for new policies. A survey of 2,621 adults who buy drugs in the United Kingdom found that the majority of respondents did not report finding a supplier, or a desired drug, to be more difficult when comparing their experiences to before the start of the COVID-19 pandemic (Aldridge et al. 2021). The government has made no assessment of their impact during the pandemic, and does not appear to have plans to make such an assessment (Nicholls 2020). This may mean that an opportunity to consistently move away from enforcement-led approaches has been missed, which emphasises again the importance of PCCs as potential local champions of harm reduction.

Preceding the pandemic, the UK government began investing in a public health approach to violence, with the emergence of violence reduction units in many areas of the country. The public health approach involves understanding the root causes of the problem and testing, evaluating, and upscaling interventions (Christmas and Srivastava 2019). Many violence reduction units are focused on tackling organised crime, knife crime, and 'county lines', which are intrinsically associated with drugs policy. As such, this public health approach to violence could be replicated in drugs policy. The ambition of treating drugs first and foremost as a public health issue, which is a founding principle of the West Midlands PCC's approach, could therefore become more widely embedded in policies across the United Kingdom.

So, does the future of harm reduction rely on the latest set of 40 PCCs, or the next lot after that? Thus far, the actions of a few pioneering PCCs have led to more progressive drug policies in some local police force areas, but the continuation of this depends on the 40 personalities elected in May 2021. The three most public PCC voices who have arguably become 'drug policy actors' will no longer be making the case. County Durham's Commissioner Ron Hogg sadly passed away in December 2019, while the West Midlands' David Jamieson and North Wales' Arfon Jones retired at the May 2021 election. Local drug policy reform by its nature is precarious and potentially temporary, yet while national reform varies between slow and static, it remains the clearest way to demonstrate the effectiveness of harm reduction. PCCs, with their democratic mandate, convening power, and access to budget, are clearly in a position to be drug policy actors (Seddon 2011). Given this convening power, despite the change in PCCs, the development of other drug policy actors in the local area through existing work is likely to help continue to develop this approach. Where PCCs have been investors through using their budget to transform approaches to drug policy, a change in PCC may be detrimental to future investment. In Cleveland, for example, the new PCC removed funding from HAT (ITV News 2021). He argued that the evidence was not strong enough to support funding the project and that he expected other partners, such as health agencies, to bear the costs of the project instead.

Meanwhile, there is an expectation that metro mayors will begin to incorporate the PCC role into their offices by appointment, rather than election. Appointed deputy mayors for policing and crime already exist in London and Greater Manchester, while plans for the West Midlands mayor to incorporate the PCC role stalled in 2017. Considering that many PCCs have managed to leave drug policy relatively unchanged in their areas, it may be even easier for a mayor to ignore the problem in the hope it goes away. Then again, wider responsibilities such as housing, health, fire, and transport all have some links to drug policy, so it is possible that mayors could see the bigger picture and adopt a wider harm reduction strategy. For now, however, this is just speculation and depends wholly on the decisions and whims of the local politicians

If the trend of reducing police enforcement through diversion schemes continues, it will be worth exploring whether the police stepping back means that health bodies or harm reduction professionals step forward. Harm reduction cannot be delivered by the police alone. If treatment services continue to be overstretched and underfunded, where can the police divert people with addictions to? If police officers save someone's life by using naloxone medication, are there people on hand to take advantage of that teachable moment where the person using drugs is more open to receiving support? If a drug alert is put out through an early warning system, which agencies act quickly to ensure appropriate harm reduction advice reaches those who need it? Local areas will need coherent multi-agency strategies and proper resourcing for all sectors, to adequately support people who use drugs. The Dame Carol Black (2021) recommendations highlight that too many people with addictions are revolving in and out of prison and that there should be greater use of police diversion and community sentences with treatment as an alternative to custody.

Moving forward, this could mean that national government will become less important. Debates around devolution are taking place at national, regional, and local levels across the United Kingdom. The role of PCCs and other local devolved offices such as the mayoralty are currently being strengthened. Most PCCs now chair their local criminal justice boards, with an ability to influence across the whole system. The introduction of violence reduction units throughout the country also means that the role of the PCC is widening to include broader system change and greater interaction with education and health.

As long as the law allows harm reduction approaches, PCCs and chief constables are able to tailor local policies at their own discretion. The big tests may be where harm reduction could conflict with the legal framework. One of these tests has already been overcome, with examples of onsite safety testing of drugs at music festivals. In the case of the West Midlands in 2018, this was approved with the backing of professional legal advice, and a memorandum of understanding was drawn up between the testing company, the event promoter, the licence holder, and West Midlands Police. However, at the time of planning, no clear view was expressed either way by the government or the courts. Three weeks before the festival, Policing Minister Nick Hurd MP confirmed that 'these are local operating decisions that we are not standing in the way of' (Hurd 2018). Just over six months later, the Home Office brought safety testing under a national licensing regime (Weston Mercury 2019). The Loop provided the testing when we introduced it for the first time in the West Midlands, and their director has been at the forefront of the evidence base in England since the first testing began in 2016 (Measham 2019).

The next big challenge could be DCRs/overdose prevention sites, which have support from some PCCs across England and Wales (Learmonth 2018), as well as the devolved Scottish government (Sturgeon 2021). In the Scottish context, where drug-related deaths and HIV rates are the highest in the United Kingdom, the UK government has been characterised as blocking harm reduction by refusing to offer 'legal cover' for any DCR. In 2020, a mobile DCR (or 'safer injection facility') began operating in Glasgow through Peter Krykant, without any explicit consent from the relevant authorities, and the UK government has maintained that anyone running such a facility would be committing criminal offences (BBC News 2020b). Will the government silently watch the domino effect and then publicly endorse DCRs a few years later, as with safety testing? Or will they more actively try to prevent such facilities, pitting their lawyers against harm reduction?

Where next? Top ten tips for policymakers on achieving change

Whether you are a PCC or director of public health, police officer or doctor, member of Parliament or civil servant, local councillor or community leader, clinical prescriber or outreach worker, you have the power to shape drug policy. Here are ten tips, developed from our extensive experience of achieving change, to help you do so:

Break the silence. The days of appearing to be 'tough on drugs' for political capital are slowly disappearing. Instead, the war on drugs continues amid a deafening silence from politicians and policymakers. The first step on the way to harm reduction is to break that silence and begin to talk about effective policies. Some of the most ambitious harm reduction approaches we have implemented have grown from the seed of an end-of-the-day conversation in the office with a decision-maker. Do not involve obstructive agencies or individuals in your new approach if you do not have to. For example, if local reform can be achieved without government support, then the government's choice of silence should be fine by you.

Frame your purpose. Be clear on the principles for reform as well as the tangible outcomes you are trying to achieve. We framed our argument around cost, crime, and harm. When developing the policy, we made sure to have powerful statistics accompanying it, such as the fact that someone dies from an overdose in England every four hours (harm), and that half of all burglary, shoplifting, and theft is committed by people who use heroin or crack cocaine (crime), which costs the region £1.4 billion every year (cost). Whenever possible, we developed our policy in layman's terms, talking about reducing harm rather than 'harm reduction', as well as saving the taxpayer money or protecting people's homes from burglars. Communication is important because we are unpicking a 'just say no to drugs' narrative that has been ingrained over many years.

Flip the argument. Just as we set out our purpose to reduce cost, crime, and harm, it was essential to link this to the drug policies that existed before our new approach. If those drug policies had been working then the cost, crime, and harm simply would not be as high as it was. We repeated this often. If it is argued then that a harm reduction approach is too risky or too expensive, we would flip this challenge to highlight the enormous levels of risk and expense present in previous policies. It is too risky and too costly not to change course.

Plan the journey. In the West Midlands, we carefully set out phases of demonstrating the failures of the status quo for drug policy, then building consensus and bringing partners together, before finally announcing a full programme of recommendations and delivering change. The journey was established before we set out on phase one, giving a sense of certainty as we reached each milestone and a focus to overcome any bumps in the road. Transparency and openness are important within the public sector but also to demonstrate the practicality of a harm reduction approach to drug policy.

Keep moving forward. Throughout our efforts, it has been vital to always have a next step in mind. This applied to the planned journey, but equally to the most intricate details of delivering each policy recommendation. If you find yourself blocked or frustrated in your next step, then try to be aware of it as soon as possible. That way, you can find means to overcome that obstacle, circumvent the frustrater, or settle on a new next step that keeps you moving forward.

Plug into the network. Throughout our efforts to introduce harm reduction policies, we have benefited from being part of a network of professionals with a shared goal. Many of our co-authors of this book are part of that network. We support each other, learn from each other, inspire each other, and offload our frustrations on one another. When things are particularly tough, we are sure to remind each other why it matters that we do what we do. Harm reduction saves lives. Surround yourself with these people, embrace their energy, and build on their expertise.

Learn from lived experience. Involve those with a stake in your policies. People for whom harm reduction is more than just a term in a report, but could have been the difference between life and death. This includes people who have lost loved ones to drug poisoning, or those trapped in a cycle of trauma, addiction, and prison. The best policy is co-created with the people most likely to be impacted by it. To quote harm reduction champion George Charlton (2020), who has lived with addiction, 'Drug users should know their place, and that place is firmly front and centre and at the heart of every treatment system and service across the UK'.

Use the space within the law. For a policymaker, this is about picking the right battles. Significant change can happen through the right policies, even if you disagree with the legal framework. In almost all cases, the law does not prevent police discretion, local partnership agreements, and more effective problem-solving. Where necessary, if pushing new boundaries legal opinions can be very reassuring. We made sure we had one when introducing drug safety testing to a music festival in the West Midlands for the first time. If life-saving and crime-reducing policies are blocked by the law, then of course the law should change. But the case for that change is made more credible if a policymaker has a track record of successes with harm reduction.

Stay practical. The most important part of any policy is making it a reality. No single policy or project will be a silver bullet for drug harms, so consider developing a programme that maximises the tools at your disposal. Our programme initially focused on heroin and crack cocaine because people addicted to those substances disproportionately cause the most harm and crime, cost the most to society, and put the most money into the pockets of organised criminals. While the programme is ambitious and far-reaching, it has included cannabis or other elements tangentially rather than as the focus, in order to avoid overstretching. Delivering practical results shows that the policies are working, and let the symbolic messages write themselves. West Midlands Police became the first force in the country where officers carry naloxone. This means officers are saving the lives of people with addictions. It builds confidence in policing. It may make it more likely for people to call 999 for an overdose, assured by the message that the preservation of life will always be the priority. The practical and the symbolic approach to harm reduction is therefore saving lives on both fronts.

Evidence the impact. The pursuit of a better drugs policy must be the same as the pursuit for evidence-based policy. It must evidence lives saved, harm prevented, crime reduced, and costs saved. In the history of harm reduction this has sometimes involved expensive randomised clinical trials, and yet these have not always convinced policymakers to change course. So, evidencing impact is about not only being robust, but also being clear. It is about framing your purpose and flipping the argument. The right policies can be temporary and change according to political whim, particularly where elections are concerned. That is why it is absolutely vital that any contribution to harm reduction adds to the evidence base. We acknowledge that this is holding our policies to a higher standard than those of national government and international enforcement agencies. The power of reason and evidence, communicated in the right way and over time, will prevail.

You next? Top three tips for the public on achieving change

Write to your police and crime commissioner. This chapter has focused on how one role, the PCC, can transform local drug policy to reduce harm. So our first tip to the people of England and Wales is to write to that person. If you do not have a PCC then it is likely that policing governance is the responsibility of your local metro mayor. Tell them why harm reduction matters to you. Tell them they do not have to continue with the status quo. Recommend this book and this chapter to them.

To make the most impact, try to frame your letter in the context of the PCC's priorities, which can be found on their website usually under the 'police and crime plan'. For example, if they want to tackle organised crime, crack down on burglary, protect mental health, and so on, let them know why drugs and harm reduction must be a key part of those ambitions.

Be a harm reduction champion. There are so many ways to contribute to reducing harm – this book is packed full of them. If there is even a small risk you could encounter someone overdosing on heroin, then contact your local drug treatment service and ask for a naloxone kit. Love music and harm reduction? Volunteer with a drug safety testing service at a music festival. Help break the cycle for people who have been trapped in addiction by offering to mentor or support people in your local drug rehabilitation house. Champion harm reduction in any way you can, the possibilities are endless. You could save lives.

Reassure politicians and decision-makers. There is a phenomenon called 'post-retirement drug policy enlightenment syndrome' (Macgregor 2013). You can help to end it. More politicians, including PCCs, are coming out in favour of harm reduction while they still have the powers and authority to implement policy. These are pioneers, and they need your help to do the right thing.

A small number of PCCs have already become 'innovators'. The 2021 cohort could become 'early adopters' of drug policy change, before the tipping point is reached and change reaches the majority (Rogers 2003). Reassurance and encouragement from the public could lead us to the next phase. Experience has taught us this. In the words of a PCC with whom one of us worked, who has not received as much attention in this chapter, when presented with the evidence and the opportunity to pursue effective harm reduction policies, he asked 'do I really want to stick my head above the parapet?' Once he had framed the debate in such a way, he concluded that he would be better off keeping below the imagined parapet. The public can do more to convince local politicians that becoming drug policy actors is not inherently politically risky.

Conclusion

Very few policymakers defend the war on drugs anymore, yet in their silence, it continues to destroy communities and wreck lives. A key problem with the UK approach to drug policy is that an orthodoxy of thought has been embedded, enforced, and communicated to the public over decades. The 'just say no' campaign of President Reagan and the decades of US-imposed foreign policy that preceded and succeeded it have cemented the idea that society must wage a 'war on drugs' (Woods and Rafaeli 2018). It takes time and, more importantly, leadership to begin to change that narrative.

Many politicians have avoided engaging in the debate about the war on drugs or the approach to drug policy in the United Kingdom, seeing it as a significant political risk. The West Midlands PCC was paraphrased (Jones 2019) as saying that a politician's role should not fall behind public opinion, but nor should they be ten steps ahead and risk losing support. Instead, in order to lead, they should be two paces ahead of the public, bringing them on the journey towards a better world. The role of brave leadership and communications has been vital to starting to shift public opinion. The West Midlands' focus on reducing cost, crime, and harm is important because it does not rely solely on moral arguments for change, but highlights the unsustainably high financial cost to the taxpayer and demands on an overstretched police force.

Some PCCs, including the West Midlands PCC, have become drug policy actors and are using their unique civic leadership role to shift both the policies and narrative relating to drugs at a local level. The PCC role itself provides the ideal opportunity to test innovation and new approaches. PCCs have commissioning power and funding, they can work with their police force to pilot approaches or projects and then share the findings with other PCCs, local leaders, and national government. We have set out the key drivers and tools at a PCC's disposal to lead a harm reduction approach to drug policy. The combination of evidence, deliverability, and morals or ideology is the optimum combination for a PCC to deliver a changing approach. The findings identified that the levers available to a PCC such as the statutory role, convening power, and prioritisation and management of a force budget mean that a PCC is well placed to make a change at a local level. PCCs can be a leader and driver of change.

Some PCCs have already made significant changes to drugs policy. The role of PCC is still new and some are pushing the boundaries and changing the local governance landscape with new, innovative approaches. However, there are inconsistencies across the country which could create a postcode lottery for the public. As devolution continues to evolve in the United Kingdom, a major factor that this chapter has not explored in depth is the relationship between local and national approaches to harm reduction, and the extent to which one is an enabler or catalyst for the other. PCCs are largely independent drug policy actors, which has contributed to the successes outlined in this chapter, but does that allow the national government to evade responsibility and ignore calls for change at that level?

An overwhelming tide of evidence demonstrates the effectiveness of a harm reduction approach to drugs, and slowly but surely it is sweeping down the walls of decades of poorly evidenced and counterproductive policy. But evidence alone will not create change. Change requires people. It requires people like you. Stand up and demand better.

Note

1 Launched in England in 2003, the Drug Interventions Programme (DIP) aimed to get adults who misuse drugs out of crime and into treatment. The DIP focused on heroin and crack/cocaine and on 'trigger offences' known to be associated with drug misuse. Trigger offences include theft, robbery, burglary, aggravated burglary, taking motor vehicle or other conveyance without authority, aggravated vehicle-taking, obtaining property by deception, going equipped for stealing, restriction on the production and supply of controlled drugs, possession of controlled drugs, and possession of controlled drug with intent to supply (see Seddon et al. 2012).

References

Aldridge, J., Garius, L., Spicer, J., Harris, M., Moore, K. and Eastwood, N. (2021) *Drugs in the Time of COVID: The UK Drug Market Response to Lockdown Restrictions.* London: Release.

Austen, L. (2016) 'Police and crime commissioners – Emerging "drug policy actors"?' *Safer Communities.* 15(1): 4–10.

BBC News. (2020a) 'County lines raids: 1,000 arrests and £1.2m drugs seized'. *BBC News.* Available from: https://www.bbc.co.uk/news/uk-england-54282448 [Accessed 24 November 2021].

BBC News. (2020b) 'Mobile "fix room" begins operating in Glasgow'. *BBC News.* Available from: https://www.bbc.co.uk/news/uk-scotland-53991090 [Accessed 24 November 2021].

Binns, C. (2021) 'Violence reduction units: 'Systems change' or more of the same?' *Talk Social Justice.* Available from: https://talksocialjustice.com/violence-reduction-units-systems-change-or-more-of-the-same/.

Black, C. (2021) *Review of Drugs: Phase Two Report.* London: HM Government.

Charlton, G. (2020) 'Developing peer to peer naloxone training and supply programs'. *Talk Social Justice.* Available from: https://talksocialjustice.com/peertopeernaloxone/.

Choose My PCC. (2016) *Choose My PCC* (online). choosemypcc.org. Available at: https://www.choosemypcc.org.uk/ [Accessed 25 August 2016].

Christmas, H. and Srivastava, J. (2019) *Public Health Approaches to Policing.* London: College of Policing and Public Health England.

Conservative Party. (2010) *The Conservative Manifesto 2010.* Available from: https://issuu.com/conservatives/docs/cpmanifesto2010_hires.

Danechi, S. (2021) *PCC Elections 2021.* House of Commons Library. Available from: https://commonslibrary.parliament.uk/research-briefings/cbp-9244/.

European Commission. (2001) *European Governance: A White Paper.* Brussels: European Union.

Guardian. (2016) 'Nine in 10 say they cannot name local police and crime commissioner'. Available from: https://www.theguardian.com/uk-news/2016/apr/30/nine-in-10-cannot-name-local-police-and-commissioner-pcc [Accessed 24 November 2021].

HM Government. (2019) 'National campaign to recruit 20,000 police officers launches today'. Available from: https://www.gov.uk/government/news/national-campaign-to-recruit-20000-police-officers-launches-today.

HMIC. (2010) *A Report on the Work of HMIC in the Year from 01 April 2009 to 31 March 2010.* London: Her Majesty's Inspectorate of Constabulary.

ITV News. (2021) 'Cleveland's new police and crime commissioner says he won't continue funding Middlesbrough's heroin assisted treatment'. Available from: https://

www.itv.com/news/tyne-tees/2021-05-18/clevelands-new-police-and-crime-commissioner-says-he-wont-continue-funding-middlesbroughs-heroin-assisted-treatment [Accessed 24 November 2021].

Jones, M. (2019) *The Impact of Police and Crime Commissioner Governance in Drug Policy: Utilising the West Midlands as a Case Study*. MSc Dissertation. University of Birmingham.

Jones, T. and Lister, S. (2019) 'Localism and police governance in England & Wales: Exploring continuity and change'. *European Journal of Criminology*. 16(5): 552–572.

Home Office. (2011) *Police Reform and Social Responsibility Act 2011*. London: The Stationery Office Limited.

Hurd, N. (2018) 'Music festivals: Drug safety testing (debate)'. *Hansard*. Available from: https://hansard.parliament.uk/commons/2018-07-06/debates/E0DEEB30-1E43-44C7-AFF6-108381E254F4/MusicFestivalsDrugSafetyTesting.

Learmonth, A. (2018) 'Campaign for legal drug consumption rooms backed by police'. *The National*. Available from: https://www.thenational.scot/news/16227731.campaign-legal-drug-consumption-rooms-backed-police/ [Accessed 24 November 2021].

Liberal Democrats. (2010) *Liberal Democrat Manifesto (2010)*. Available from: https://www.markpack.org.uk/files/2015/01/Liberal-Democrat-manifesto-2010.pdf.

Lister, S. (2013) 'The new politics of the police: Police and crime commissioners and the "operational independence" of the police'. *Policing*. 7(3): 239–247.

Lowndes, V. and Pratchett, L. (2012) 'Local governance under the coalition government: Austerity, localism and the "big society"'. *Local Government Studies*. 38(1): 21–40.

Loveday, B. (2013) 'Police and crime commissioners: The changing landscape of police governance in England and Wales'. *International Journal of Police Science and Management*. 15(1): 22–29.

MacGregor, S. (2013) 'Barriers to the influence of evidence on policy: Are politicians the problem?' *Drugs: Education, Prevention and Policy*. 20(3): 225–233.

Measham, F. (2019) 'Drug safety testing, disposals and dealing in an English field: Exploring the operational and behavioural outcomes of the UK's first onsite "drug checking" service'. *International Journal of Drug Policy*. 67: 102–107.

Mee, E. (2020) 'Recorded drug offences rise by a third during lockdown as dealers make "risky" home deliveries'. *Sky News*. Available from: https://news.sky.com/story/recorded-drug-offences-rise-by-a-third-during-lockdown-as-dealers-make-risky-home-deliveries-12008438 [Accessed 24 November 2021].

Nicholls, J. (2020) 'Will the government assess the impact of drug seizures?' *Transform Drug Policy Foundation*. Available from: https://transformdrugs.org/blog/why-is-the-government-not-assessing-the-impact-of-drug-seizures.

Revolving Doors. (2017) *Under the Spotlight: Reviewing Police and Crime Plans for Multiple and Complex Needs, and Transition to Adulthood*. London: Revolving Doors Agency.

Rogers, E. (2003) *Diffusion of Innovations*. 5th edn. New York: Free Press.

Shaw, D. (2020) 'Hundreds arrested as crime chat network cracked'. *BBC News*. Available from: https://www.bbc.co.uk/news/uk-53263310 [Accessed 24 November 2021].

Sherman, L. (1998) *Evidence Based Policing*. Washington, DC: Police Foundation.

Seddon, T., Ralphs, R. and Williams, L. (2008) 'Risk, security and the "criminalization" of British drug policy'. *British Journal of Criminology*. 48(6): 818–834.

Seddon, T. (2011) 'Explaining drug policy: Towards an historical sociology of policy change'. *International Journal of Drug Policy*. 22(6): 415–419.

Seddon, T., Williams, L. and Ralphs, R. (2012) *Tough Choices: Risk, Security, and the Criminalization of Drug Policy*. Oxford: Oxford University Press.

Stephens, M. and Evans, M. (2020) 'Police exploit lockdown to mount raids on wanted criminals'. *The Telegraph*. Available from: https://www.telegraph.co.uk/news/2020/04/25/police-exploit-lockdown-mount-raids-wanted-criminals/ [Accessed 24 November 2021].

Stevens, A. (2019) '"Being human" and the "moral sidestep" in drug policy: Explaining government inaction on opioid-related deaths in the UK'. *Addictive Behaviours*. 90: 444–450.

Stoker, G. and Evans, M. (2016) *Evidence-Based Policy Making in the Social Sciences*. Bristol: Policy Press.

Sturgeon, N. (2021) 'Drugs policy – Update: Statement by the first minister –20 January 2021'. Scottish Government. Available from: https://www.gov.scot/publications/update-drugs-policy/.

Transform Drug Policy Foundation. (2019) *Hitting Heroin and Crack Markets: Funding Heroin Assisted Treatment through Increased Proceeds of Crime Act Money*. Bristol: Transform.

Treadwell, J., Gooch, K. and Barkham, G. (2019) *Crime in Prisons: Where Now and Where Next?* Available from: https://staffordshire-pfcc.gov.uk/cms/wp-content/uploads/plan-to-government-to-tackle-organised-crime-in-prisons.pdf.

West Midlands Police and Crime Commissioner. (2016) *The West Midlands Police and Crime Plan, 2016 – 2020*. Available from: https://www.westmidlands-pcc.gov.uk/wp-content/uploads/2019/04/2016-2020-Police-and-Crime-Plan-digital.pdf.

West Midlands Police and Crime Commissioner. (2017a) *Substance Misuse Report*. Available from: https://www.westmidlands-pcc.gov.uk/wp-content/uploads/2019/04/Key-facts-and-full-report-Substance-Misuse-SPCB-05.09.17.pdf.

West Midlands Police and Crime Commissioner. (2017b) *West Midlands Drug Policy Call for Evidence – Report*. Available from: https://www.westmidlands-pcc.gov.uk/wp-content/uploads/2019/04/West-Midlands-Drug-Policy-Call-for-Evidence-Report-12.12.17.pdf.

West Midlands Police and Crime Commissioner. (2018a) *Reducing Crime and Preventing Harm: Drug Policy Recommendations*. Available from: https://www.westmidlands-pcc.gov.uk/wp-content/uploads/2019/04/West-Midlands-Drug-Policy-Recommendations.pdf.

West Midlands Police and Crime Commissioner. (2018b) *A Review of the Legacy of the Drug Interventions Programme*. Available from: https://www.westmidlands-pcc.gov.uk/wp-content/uploads/2021/06/A-Review-of-the-Legacy-of-the-Drug-Interventions-Programme.pdf.

West Midlands Police and Crime Commissioner. (2021) *Hundreds Offered the Chance to Turn Their Back on Drugs*. Available from: https://www.westmidlands-pcc.gov.uk/hundreds-offered-the-chance-to-turn-their-back-on-drugs/.

Weston Mercury. (2019) 'Home office grants addaction first licensed drug checking service'. Available from: https://www.thewestonmercury.co.uk/news/home-office-grants-addaction-in-weston-super-mare-first-licenced-4539068 [Accessed 24 November 2021].

Woods, N. and Rafaeli, J.S. (2018) *Drug Wars: The Terrifying Inside Story of Britain's Drug Trade*. London: Ebury Press.

CONCLUSION

From stalemate to progress

Matthew Bacon and Jack Spicer

The motivation for writing this book was to produce something of lasting value to the fields of policing and drug policy. From the initial conversations that sparked the idea to the completion of the final manuscript, we have been driven by our shared research interests, desire to advance scholarship, and have a transformative impact on how drugs policing is theoretically conceived and practically undertaken. We wanted the book to capture some of the changes currently observable in this area and highlight the need for further developments. Change is needed because attempts to tackle drug problems have tended to 'allow avoidable harm by their ineffectiveness and create needless suffering by their excesses' (Kleiman et al. 2011, p. xxi). The pages that precede us have critically examined the ramifications of forms of policing that have followed this path in pursuit of fighting crime through punitive interventions. They have also demonstrated that harm reduction policing offers a workable alternative that can reduce the adverse health, social, and economic consequences associated with drug use, drug markets, and efforts to control them through the criminal justice system. This common purpose is what brought the authors together and binds their contributions into a cohesive endeavour. We are grateful to them for turning our idea into a reality.

To conclude, we want to pick up where we left off in the introduction and recommend some directions for future research on drugs policing. Our aim is to encourage research that builds on the contributions of this book and addresses its limitations. While a wide range of issues, contexts, and countries are covered, the picture remains inevitably incomplete. More research is needed so that we have a better understanding of the full gamut of activities related to the policing

DOI: 10.4324/9781003154136-15

of drugs. In particular, empirically grounded case studies undertaken across the world provide an excellent way of documenting the nuanced and complex nature of drugs policing. Case studies also allow for comparative research on the manner in which different nations, regions, and localities deal with similar problems across diverse cultural contexts. Many of the chapters in this collection have demonstrated the value of such theoretically informed studies and the insights they can provide. There needs to be more of these, especially from the Global South, to continue to develop our understanding of how drugs policing operates, the outcomes associated with it, and how things can be done differently.

Conceptually, there is significant scope to develop many of the ideas, arguments, and explanations put forward in this book. A logical starting point would be to test the definition of harm reduction policing that we put forward in the opening chapter. This could include a deeper consideration of how the principles and goals of harm reduction – which are rooted in public health – might be applied to policing. Given its clear analytic utility and practical focus, it would be beneficial to see research continuing to engage with Rhodes' (2002) 'risk environment' framework to map out how policing can be reoriented around harm reduction principles to create enabling environments that reduce harm. We would also suggest looking at harm reduction policing through the lens of regulation to further enhance our analytical tools and build upon the work of researchers who have applied regulatory theory to drug policy (Ritter 2010; Seddon 2010, 2020). With the exception of cryptomarkets and drug trafficking in the Caribbean, the chapters in this book are largely concerned with policing people who use drugs and local distribution at the retail level of the market. Future research could explore harm reduction approaches to suppressing supply further up the chain and disrupting organised crime groups, perhaps attempting to revisit and update some earlier influential contributions in this area (e.g. Dorn et al. 1992).

Empirically, as changes in the strategic direction of drugs policing continue and the contexts in which it operates shift, the need to gather and analyse rich data will be vital in continuing to improve the state of knowledge. There is a compelling case for more ethnographic research. Within the sociology of policing, ethnography has proved to be a crucial methodology for documenting and making sense of the everyday realities of policing (Bacon et al. 2020; Manning 2014). Participant observation in particular is unparalleled for accessing the 'back stage' – where 'illusions and impressions are openly constructed' (Goffman 1959, p. 114) – and examining the working rules, tacit understandings, and underlying assumptions that invariably operate beneath the presentational canopy of police organisations. Police culture most readily reveals itself as officers engage in spontaneous talk and handle the demands of police work. Long-term presence and familiarisation allows for 'the unveiling of discrepancies between what is said and what is done, what is presumed to be and what really is' (Fassin 2017, p. 5). Writing about the importance of narratives, van Hulst (2020, p. 106) argues that ethnography enables researchers 'to get behind or beyond interview stories or canteen stories that officers tell and through which they legitimate, obscure, misrepresent or ignore events that actually took place'. By immersing themselves within the police milieu, ethnographers are in an ideal position to unearth valuable information about many different aspects of (drugs) policing, including police perceptions of their role, how they exercise discretion, and processes of organisational change. Observing enforcement interventions and police interactions with drug law offenders and partner agencies at the coalface of policing is crucial for explaining differences between laws and policies 'in the books' and 'in action' on the ground. It is here where police (mis)use their powers and grapple with the tensions, dilemmas, and contradictions of drug policy and practice.

A perennial problem faced by police ethnographers is gaining and maintaining access to organisations that are sceptical of the value of ethnographic research and wary of exposing themselves to outsiders. It is worth noting Fassin's (2013, p. 21) assertion that what police organisations have difficulty with 'is research being carried out on the police, and, more specifically, this research being ethnographic in nature'. Based on our own ethnographies (Bacon 2016; Spicer 2021), we are well aware that backstage access is not easy to come by. The promises and expectations of the 'research bargain' (Becker 1970) have to be negotiated. In addition, while in the field, openness from the police is hard earned through acceptance, trust, and mutual respect, which are gained as relationships develop over time through conversations, shared experiences, and reciprocity. Despite these challenges, as well as the time commitments and emotional energy involved, ethnographic projects must continue to be pursued if the body of knowledge on drugs policing is to continue to progress.

Evaluation research on the impacts of different types of drugs policing is widely acknowledged to be lacking. In the United Kingdom, for example, the government (2017, p. 107) concluded that there was insufficient evidence 'to robustly measure the overall impact of enforcement or enforcement-related activity on levels of drug use and harm, or value for money'. As a result, strategies and interventions to suppress supply and demand are built on a 'distressingly weak' (Babor et al. 2018, p. 190) evidence base. That said, although there are significant gaps in the impact evaluation literature, a number of key findings are worth summarising here because of their implications for harm reduction policing. We focus on reviews of evaluations that employ a randomised or quasi-experimental design, not because they are the only ways to evaluate drugs policing, or for that matter necessarily the most valuable, but because they produce the forms of evidence that are most commonly used by policymakers and practitioners (Ritter 2022; Stevens 2011).

In relation to drug supply, key aims of enforcement interventions are to disrupt distribution networks and bring those involved to justice. Eggins et al.'s (2020) systematic review suggests that there is limited research examining the impact of supplier arrest and seizures on a range of drug-related outcomes. These outcomes include drug crime, use, price, purity, and harms. The findings from the reviewed studies on the effectiveness of these approaches are mixed. In relation to drug harms, two studies suggest that increased seizures are associated with decreased mortality, decreased ambulance callouts, and increased seeking help for drug use. However, the other four studies suggest that supplier arrests or seizures tend to increase drug-related harms, including police expenditure, drug-related deaths, presentation to emergency departments for drug-related health issues, and drug-related violence. At the street level, Mazerolle et al.'s (2007) systematic review of drug law enforcement evaluations found that crackdown operations were largely ineffective in dealing with supply but appeared to have more success addressing associated crime problems. Some studies suggest that crackdowns can be effective under certain circumstances. The literature, however, 'is silent about the finer details that would inform police and policy makers as to what makes a crackdown successful and what makes it fail' (p. 125). Proactive policing approaches that combine problem-oriented, geographical targeting with efforts to create and maintain partnerships have the most potential to sustain reductions in drug markets and related harms. The review also reveals that diversionary interventions that target people who use drugs offer some promise. These findings are consistent with the partial update conducted by Mazerolle et al. (2020).

The subject of diversion is discussed in various chapters of this book and appears to be something that will continue to have a presence on the policy landscape. Recent international reviews of the literature, which include studies of police diversion measures in Australia, the United Kingdom, and the United States, suggest that diversion away from criminal justice processes can reduce harm (Blais et al. 2022; Stevens et al. 2022). Diverting people into effective treatment or social services can reduce health and crime harms, as well as the harms associated with criminalisation. It also has strong potential to reduce public expenditure, for criminal justice, health, and other budget holders, which is perhaps one of the reasons why it has become a relatively popular development among those who are not always so amenable to progressive drug policy reform. However, more research is needed to draw conclusions about the effects of police diversion on drug use, socio-economic conditions, and inequalities. Researchers should also pay close attention to the risk of diversion increasing the scale and intensity of coercive control of people who use drugs. This might occur through processes of 'net widening' or 'mesh thinning' (Cohen 1985). Diversion can widen the net when it brings people into the criminal justice system who would otherwise have been dealt with informally or by a less intrusive intervention. Mesh thinning occurs when controls are tighter or more severe than they would have been previously under a different intervention. For diversion to fulfil its potential, these outcomes must be avoided.

Critical research on policing and the police is a vital scholarly enterprise. It provides penetrating insights into the role of the police in society and policing as a mode of control and governance. It wrestles with complex questions, contested views, and uncomfortable truths about power, justice, accountability, and democracy, contributing to public debate and the political agenda of policing reform. Drugs policing, with its particular moral dimensions and myriad controversies, must remain as a focus point for such critical work. Shining a light on the direct and indirect harms that drugs policing causes is necessary to develop understanding, raise awareness, and mobilise support for change. These harms, many of which are rooted in broader issues of inequality, structural racism, and social welfare, are precisely the reason why researchers, policymakers, and practitioners should seriously engage with recent calls to rethink the nature, role, and limits of policing (Fleetwood and Lea 2022; Vitale 2017).

But, at the same time, to advance knowledge on harm reduction policing – especially regarding research that has a pragmatic focus, aiming to directly inform and improve police policies, strategies, and tactics – there is a need for academics and the police to work together. In other words, the research agenda for drugs policing should be diverse and include both research *on* and *with* the police. It can take inspiration from the ambitions set out in the tradition of left realism by not being afraid to be 'radical' in its analysis where necessary, yet simultaneously not shying away from being practical in its engagement with policy suggestions (Lea and Young 1984). Literature on the challenges and opportunities of 'applied police research' or 'evidence-based policing' indicates that it 'necessitates strong partnerships and increased communication and collaboration among researchers, analysts, and law enforcement officers' (Lum and Koper 2017, p. 5). For Cockbain and Knutsson (2015, p. 4), evidence-based policing requires academics to be 'active collaborators in finding practical, workable solutions, rather than distant critics or elite scientists imposing top-down prescriptions with little regard for varied temporal, spatial, organisational and social contingencies'. Such an approach to research could involve the co-production of a harm reduction policing framework for informing and evaluating police interventions. This could also lead to the modification of police performance indicators so that they incorporate a wide range of drug-related harms and measures of success. Future research and knowledge exchange activities could seek to enhance understandings of 'harm' and 'harm reduction' and have a practical impact in a conceptual sense by encouraging the police to critically reflect on the purpose and consequences of drugs policing in various contexts.

The path towards harm reduction policing so far has been fragile and often difficult to navigate. This is likely to continue and resistance will no doubt be experienced. But as we and many of this book's contributors have found, there is an increasing appetite in some quarters for rethinking, sometimes in fundamental ways, what matters in drugs policing and what forms it could or should take. There is a willingness among some involved in drugs policing to take a seat and listen to what is being discussed at the drug policy reform table or even help drive the conversation. This can lead to real and positive change, with a 'desistance' from criminalisation when it comes to responding to drugs possibly showing signs of moving closer to the centre ground of police culture (Bacon 2022). It is important that this momentum continues. With this in mind, we hope readers find the individual chapters and this collection as a whole thought provoking and useful in their work, whatever that might be. More generally, we hope that this book will help to end the stalemate that has often come to dominate drugs policing and act as a source of inspiration for where it could go in the future.

References

Babor, T., Caulkins, J., Fischer, B., Foxcroft, D., Humphreys, K., Medina-Mora, M., Obot, I., Rehm, J., Reuter, P., Room, R., Rossow, I. and Strang, J. (2018) *Drug Policy and the Public Good*. 2nd edn. Oxford: Oxford University Press.

Bacon, M. (2016) *Taking Care of Business: Police Detectives, Drug Law Enforcement and Proactive Investigation*. Oxford: Oxford University Press.

Bacon, M., Loftus, B. and Rowe, M. (2020) 'Ethnography and the evocative world of policing (Part I)'. *Policing and Society*. 30(1): 1–10.

Bacon, M. (2022) 'Desistance from criminalisation: Police culture and new directions in drugs policing'. *Policing and Society*. 32(4): 522–539.

Becker, H. (1970) *Sociological Work: Method and Substance*. Chicago, IL: Aldine.

Blais, E., Brisson, J., Gagnon, F. and Lemay, S. (2022) 'Diverting people who use drugs from the criminal justice system: A systematic review of police-based diversion measures'. *International Journal of Drug Policy*. 105: 103697.

Cockbain, E. and Knutsson, J. (2015) 'Introduction'. In Cockbain, E. and Knutsson, J. (eds.) *Applied Police Research: Challenges and Opportunities*. London: Routledge: 1–8.

Cohen, S. (1985) *Visions of Social Control*. Cambridge: Polity Press.

Dorn, N., Murji, K. and South, N. (1992) *Traffickers: Drug Markets and Law Enforcement*. London: Routledge.

Eggins, E., Hine, L., Higginson, A. and Mazerolle, L. (2020) 'The impact of arrest and seizure on drug crime and harms: A systematic review'. In *Trends & Issues in Crime and Criminal Justice* (No. 602). Canberra: Australian Institute of Criminology.

Fassin, D. (2013) *Enforcing Order: An Ethnography of Urban Policing*. London: Polity Press.

Fassin, D. (2017) 'Introduction: Ethnographying the police'. In Fassin, D. (ed.) *Writing the World of Policing: The Difference Ethnography Makes*. Chicago, IL: University of Chicago Press: 1–20.

Fleetwood, J. and Lea, J. (2022) 'Defunding the police in the UK: Critical questions and practical suggestions'. *Howard Journal of Crime and Justice*. https://doi.org/10.1111/hojo.12468.

Goffman, E. (1959) *The Presentation of Self in Everyday Life*. London: Penguin Books.

HM Government. (2017) *An Evaluation of the Government's Drug Strategy 2010*. London: HM Government.

Kleiman, M., Caulkins, J. and Hawken, A. (2011) *Drugs and Drug Policy: What Everyone Needs to Know*. Oxford: Oxford University Press.

Lea, J. and Young, J. (1984) *What Is to Be Done about Law and Order?* Harmondsworth: Penguin.

Lum, C. and Koper, C. (2017) *Evidence-Based Policing: Translating Research into Practice*. Oxford: Oxford University Press.

Manning, P. (2014) 'Ethnographies of the police'. In Reisig, M. and Kane, R. (eds.) *The Oxford Handbook of Police and Policing*. New York: Oxford University Press: 518–547.

Mazerolle, L., Soole, D. and Rombouts, S. (2007) 'Drug law enforcement: A review of the evaluation literature'. *Policing Quarterly*. 10(2): 115–153.

Mazerolle, L., Eggins, E. and Higginson, A. (2020) 'Street-level drug law enforcement: An updated systematic review'. In *Trends & Issues in Crime and Criminal Justice* (No.599). Canberra: Australian Institute of Criminology.

Rhodes, T. (2002) 'The "risk environment": A framework for understanding and reducing drug-related harm'. *International Journal of Drug Policy*. 13(2): 85–94.
Ritter, A. (2010) 'Illicit drug policy through the lens of regulation'. *International Journal of Drug Policy*. 21(4): 265–270.
Ritter, A. (2022) *Drug Policy*. Abingdon: Routledge.
Seddon, T. (2010) *A History of Drugs: Drugs and Freedom in the Liberal Age*. London: Routledge.
Seddon, T. (2020) 'Markets, regulation and drug law reform: Towards a constitutive approach'. *Social and Legal Studies*. 29(3): 313–333.
Spicer, J. (2021) *Policing County Lines: Responses to Evolving Provisional Drug Markets*. London: Palgrave.
Stevens, A. (2011) Telling policy stories: An ethnographic study of the use of evidence in policy-making in the UK. *Journal of Social Policy*. 40(2): 237–255.
Stevens, A., Hughes, C., Hulme, S. and Cassidy, R. (2022) 'Depenalization, diversion and decriminalization: A realist review and programme theory of alternatives to criminalization for simple drug possession'. *European Journal of Criminology*. 19(1): 29–54.
van Hulst, M. (2020) 'Ethnography and narrative'. *Policing and Society*. 30(1): 98–115.
Vitale, A. (2017) *The End of Policing*. London: Verso.

INDEX

Page numbers in **bold reference tables.
**Page numbers in *italics* reference figures.